CATHOLIC SCHOOLS
AND THE
COMMON GOOD

Catholic Schools and the Common Good

Anthony S. Bryk
Valerie E. Lee
Peter B. Holland

Harvard University Press
Cambridge, Massachusetts
London, England

Library of Congress Cataloging-in-Publication Data
Bryk, Anthony S.
Catholic schools and the common good /
Anthony S. Bryk, Valerie E. Lee, Peter B. Holland.
p.   cm.
Includes bibliographical references (p.   ) and index.
ISBN 0-674-10310-6 (alk. paper) (cloth)
ISBN 0-674-10311-4 (pbk.)
1. Catholic high schools—United States—History.
2. Catholic high schools—United States—Administration.
I. Lee, Valerie E. II. Holland, Peter Blakely. III. Title.
LC501.B624   1993
377'.82'73—dc20
92-32312
CIP

In memory of Stanley

Contents

Preface

THIS BOOK BRINGS together findings from a set of investigations that span almost ten years: an in-depth study of a small number of Catholic high schools, statistical analyses of large national data bases, and an exploration of the philosophical and historical roots of Catholic schools. One of our purposes in *Catholic Schools and the Common Good* is descriptive—to offer a portrait of Catholic high schools, a book of record at this point in their history. A second and more important aim is to examine the distinctive features of Catholic high schools and the ways in which these features combine to form supportive social environments that promote academic achievement for a broad cross section of students. For anyone who is concerned about the renewal of America's educational institutions, the organization and operation of Catholic schools offer important lessons to ponder.

This project began in the fall of 1981. Peter Holland, who had entered the doctoral program in administration at the Harvard Graduate School of Education (HGSE) the year before, brought to Tony Bryk's attention a request from the National Catholic Educational Association for proposals to study effective Catholic high schools. Prior to enrolling at HGSE, Peter had been a Xaverian brother and the headmaster at St. Joseph's, a private Catholic boys' secondary school in Baltimore. Drawing on related work on effective public schools, Holland and Bryk eventually crafted a proposal to undertake a parallel investigation in the Catholic sector. The centerpiece of the study was to be an intensive examination of a small number of carefully chosen U.S. Catholic high schools. Holland and Bryk collaborated on developing the field research plan, and Ruben Carriedo joined a bit later to participate in the conduct of the fieldwork. Carriedo, like Holland, was also a doctoral student in administration at HGSE and had previously been a principal in the San Diego public school system. The members of the research team thus brought diverse views to the field study. Holland had the perspective of a close insider, Carriedo added a comparative public school orientation, and Bryk acted as the critical outside researcher.

The school visits helped us frame our overall research activities. They also provided the major source of data for our analysis in Part II of the common features that characterize Catholic schools.

In tandem with this field research activity, we began statistical analyses of *High School and Beyond* data and other related information. Valerie Lee, who was also a doctoral student at HGSE at that time, joined in this effort. Lee and Bryk collaborated on an evolving set of analyses that are interwoven throughout the book. In Part II, these analyses help generalize our field observations about the special organizational features of Catholic high schools. In Part III, they document the diversity among Catholic high schools in terms of students' background, operational characteristics of the schools, the kinds of experiences students have, and the academic, affective, and social consequences that accrue. Similarly, these analyses provide the core empirical evidence in Part IV, where we link the distinctive academic and social organization of Catholic high schools, described in Part II, to high levels of teacher commitment, student engagement, and a more effective and equitable distribution of student achievement.

Lee's participation in the project further broadened the perspective of the research team. Prior to enrolling at HGSE, she had over a decade of experience as a teacher in a variety of schools, including nonsectarian private schools, U.S. public schools, and a four-year stint at the Marymount (Catholic) school in Paris. As the only member of the research team who had not been raised as a Catholic, Lee was particularly uneasy about the "Catholic dimension" of the schools we were studying. She regularly questioned whether any of their "Catholicness" really mattered much in accounting for their special effectiveness in educating disadvantaged children. Her perspective was a major influence in critiquing our first efforts on this topic and in the final development of the argument presented here.

By 1986, most of the main themes of this book were identified. Both Holland and Carriedo had moved on to careers in public school administration. Holland is currently Superintendent of Schools in Belmont, Massachusetts, and Carriedo is Assistant Superintendent for Research and Planning in the San Diego public schools. Lee, who had joined the faculty of the School of Education at the University of Michigan, and Bryk, who had

moved to the University of Chicago, continued to pursue additional lines
of inquiry that would eventually come together in this book. The importance of the academic organization of Catholic high schools and its contribution to educational excellence and equality of achievement had been established. Our field studies had also identified a distinctive social environment
in Catholic schools that was highly regarded by both students and adults. It
was at this point that Mary Driscoll, then a doctoral student in the sociology
of education at the University of Chicago and now on the faculty of the
School of Education at New York University, became intrigued by the
idea of a "school as a community" that we had identified in our field study.
She and Bryk collaborated to develop a more specific conceptualization of
this idea and to devise an empirical test of its effects on students and staff.
This work helped to reframe Chapter 5 and provided the related empirical
evidence in Chapter 11.

In 1988, we turned to the question of why Catholic schools were
organized as they were and, in particular, why the schools we had visited
were radically different from Catholic schools of just two or three decades
earlier. Understanding the forces shaping this transformation became the
last major topic for pursuit. An earlier paper by Carriedo on the social
history of Catholic schools encouraged a closer look at the tradition on
which these schools were formed. As Lee and Bryk turned their attention
to reworking the initial materials generated by Holland, Carriedo, and
Driscoll and drafting Chapter 12, Helen Marks joined the project to assist
Bryk in the exploration of the social and intellectual roots of contemporary
Catholic schools. A graduate student in Educational Foundations at the
University of Michigan, Marks brought to the project a valuable background
as a former Dominican sister, a director of religious education, and an
adjunct seminary faculty member. The results of this inquiry, reported in
Chapter 1, provide perspective for the implications of our research discussed
in Chapter 12.

What began as a modest exploration of the characteristics of effective
Catholic high schools thus eventually led to four doctoral theses (of Carriedo, Driscoll, Holland, and Lee), an early descriptive report on the characteristics of effective Catholic high schools (Bryk et al., 1984), and several
journal articles, including reports on the academic organization of U.S. high
schools (Lee and Bryk, 1988, 1989), a comparison of single-sex versus
coeducational schooling (Lee and Bryk, 1986; Lee and Marks, 1990), and
an exploration of the moral life of schools (Bryk, 1988). This book represents
the synthesis of these strands of inquiry. Together they tell the story of a
remarkable set of institutions that brings new vitality to an old idea: that

full development of all students, both their minds and their hearts, is education for democracy and advances the common good.

Just as intellectually the research had an evolving character, so did its sources of support. We are indebted to the National Catholic Educational Association for the initial grant for the project. Early support also came from a junior faculty grant to Bryk from the Spencer Foundation through Harvard University. Ted Sizer's project, *A Study of High Schools,* also assisted by making available their data on St. Cornelius High School. The Murray Research Institute at Radcliffe College provided funding for the investigation of the relative effectiveness of single-sex and coeducational schools. We are especially grateful to Fred Newmann, who, as director of the Effective Secondary School Center at the University of Wisconsin–Madison in 1987, was willing to gamble that we could take a very soft idea—that good schools have a sense of community—and subject it to rigorous specification and empirical scrutiny. A second grant from the Spencer Foundation, to investigate the moral life of schools, also helped to support the evolving work on the Catholic school tradition. More generally, we wish to acknowledge the institutional contributions afforded by the Educational Testing Service, which supported Valerie Lee for two years as a pre- and post-doctoral fellow in 1984–1986, and the Benton Center for Curriculum and Instruction at the University of Chicago, which, along with the School of Education at the University of Michigan, provided supplemental funds to sustain this project.

We also want to thank the principals, teachers, and students in the seven field-site schools who gave so generously of their time during our visits. In order to protect the anonymity of the institutions and individuals involved in the field study, the names of the seven schools and key participants have been changed and some potentially identifying details have been altered slightly. In all other respects, however, the field reports are accurate accounts.

Along the way, many friends and colleagues offered advice and support—far too many to thank individually. We do, however, wish to acknowledge numerous conversations with Patricia Bauch. Although a proposed collaborative paper between Bryk and Bauch never came to fruition, their preliminary discussions influenced the context provided in Part I.

Lee and Bryk spent much of 1990 and 1991 writing and rewriting the chapters of this book. We wish to acknowledge several other co-authors on selected chapters of the book. Helen Marks contributed to the Prologue, Chapter 1, and the Epilogue. Mary Driscoll's work is reflected in Chapters 5 and 11, and Ruben Carriedo contributed material to Chapter 3. We are also especially indebted to those who read early versions and offered advice about revisions. Our appreciation is extended to Charles Bidwell, David Cohen, Paul Dean, Kim Hermanson, David Jacobsen, Richard Laine, William Lichten, William McKersie, and Joseph O'Keefe. In addition, we thank Carmen Valverde, Ann Webster, and Jennifer Cox, who supported manuscript production here in Chicago, and Julie Smith, who assisted with graphics in Ann Arbor. They worked cheerfully while often under a deadline of "I need it yesterday." We are also grateful to Elizabeth Gretz for her tactful advice and skillful editing.

Finally, Tony Bryk offers a special acknowledgment to Sharon, Jake, and Mia for their support and for their patience with the many sustained absences required to bring this book to completion. Similarly, Peter Holland extends special thanks to Bea, Bekki, and Jane for their understanding, and to his parents, Linnie and Blake, for instilling in him a love of learning.

August 1992

Prologue

FOUNDED IN 1889, St. Madeline's Academy in Los Angeles was the first secondary school west of St. Louis established by the Sisters of St. Joseph of Carondolet, a French community of religious women dedicated to education and hospital work. Since its establishment as an academy to provide for the classical education of young women, the school has been owned, administered, and, until recent years, largely staffed by the Sisters of St. Joseph. But as it moves into its second century, St. Madeline's has evolved in ways impossible for earlier generations of sisters to have foreseen.

From its first class of seven students, St. Madeline's experienced slow but steady growth until it enrolled nearly a thousand students in 1955. Girls from white, mostly upper middle-class families filled the school's classrooms and constituted the focus of the sister's ministry—to prepare young women for their roles as Catholic wives, mothers, and dutiful daughters of the Church. Although many graduates went on to some form of postsecondary education, most often to Catholic colleges or universities, St. Madeline's functioned as a somewhat elite finishing school for Catholic girls.

But in the mid-1960s, caught up in newly emerging social norms and rapidly changing urban demographics, the student population shifted dramatically. Enrollment tumbled to under five hundred, and the proportion of black students grew substantially. By 1975 the decline had stabilized, and enrollment gradually began to increase. The St. Madeline's that emerged in the 1980s, however, was a very different institution, and one with a renewed sense of mission. Now the Sisters of St. Joseph would educate young black women from the inner city. Education would mean preparation for full participation in American society.

We offer two sketches of St. Madeline's, first in the mid-1950s and then in the mid-1980s. The first is a composite, drawing on oral histories, historical documents, and more general Catholic school lore. The second description is based on extensive visits we made to the school. Formally, these are stories about a particular place, but they also signify much about contemporary Catholic schools—where they have come from, and what they are like now.

The years 1955 and 1985 are deliberately chosen. Much of the daily life of St. Madeline's in 1955 perpetuated traditions and mores that had originated in medieval institutions. The school we visited in the 1980s, however, was definitely postmodern. Although it maintained connections to its earlier traditions, St. Madeline's had become vitally engaged with contemporary culture. Similar transformations occurred for many Catholic schools during the late 1960s and the 1970s, driven in large part by the social and cultural change sweeping the United States. Equally important was the process of change initiated in 1962 within the Catholic Church itself, through the second Vatican Council, or Vatican II. The decisions it made eventually reshaped Catholicism across the world. The American Catholic school would never be the same.

Just as these changes were becoming institutionalized, moreover, research studies focused broad public attention on Catholic schooling. The 1980s were marked by several major publications that claimed a special effectiveness for Catholic high schools, particularly in educating disadvantaged youth. Yet relatively little is known about these schools—how they are organized, why they work the way they do, and how this is linked to the effects that appear to accrue. Examining these questions is what this book is about.

St. Madeline's Academy in 1955

A large four-story wooden structure, located on a grassy expanse only a few blocks from downtown Los Angeles, housed St. Madeline's Academy in 1955, just as it had at the turn of the century. The building's first two floors held the high school classes. Above, on the third and fourth floors, lived the Sisters of St. Joseph of Carondolet. The academy occupied a corner of an enclosed fifteen-acre site, known as the provincialate of the community. The provincial superior and her staff lived on the property, as did sisters retired from active ministry.

In 1955 St. Madeline's recalled an earlier era. Serenity pervaded the sequestered campus. From time to time the chapel bell would ring, signaling the beginning of a service or marking a moment for prayer. Alone or in groups, sisters moved about in long black habits, their heads covered with veils and white wimples that left just a portion of their faces visible. With brass crucifixes suspended from their necks and long strands of black rosary beads hanging from their cinctures, the sisters shared a common, hallowed appearance. In reality, however, they were colorfully individual—scholarly, jovial, cantankerous, young, old, pretty, strict, pious, worldly—as the students quickly learned. These religious women found daily expression for their life's commitment as teachers at St. Madeline's, and from them the school took much of its character.

All white, mostly of Irish descent, the student population appeared to be as homogeneous as the sisters. With their hair cut short above the shoulders and curled at the ends, the girls wore school uniforms consisting of a navy-blue serge skirt and matching woolen sweater, a crisply starched white cotton blouse, and black-and-white saddle shoes with white socks. Following a tradition that dated back to the early years of the school, the girls wore thin, colored cloth ties—red, blue, green, and yellow—designating their graduating class.

Almost monastic in its austerity, the school building stood as a monument to socialization in the Catholic faith. Upon entering St. Madeline's each morning through heavy oak doors as the first bell rang, most girls dipped their fingertips into the marble fountain of holy water and crossed themselves as they stepped into the dustless, walnut-paneled foyer. An assigned sister, monitoring both deportment and uniform, kept a careful eye on the arriving students. Filing through the halls, the girls were usually oblivious to the signs of Catholicism all about them, for this was the world they took for granted. They were sure to pass bulletin boards featuring monthly religious themes—among them, the holy rosary, foreign missions, souls in purgatory, and especially vocations to the religious life. During the liturgical seasons of Advent and Lent and during May, the month of Mary, the school took on an atmosphere of heightened spirituality, reflected in such observances as visits to the school chapel for devotional services or praying the rosary together daily.

In each classroom the statue of the Blessed Virgin Mary was likely to occupy a place of honor in one corner. The girls frequently brought in flowers to place in vases before the statue. All the girls were enrolled in the Sodality of the Blessed Virgin and were exhorted to be "Marylike" in their demeanor and way of life, practicing the Christian virtues, especially modesty. A crucifix hung on the wall at the front of every room, a reminder of Jesus who suffered for their sins. Blackboards frequently carried a stenciled border with a prayerful motto, such as "To Jesus through Mary" or "Ad Maiorem Dei Gloriam" (for the greater glory of God). The girls often put such phrases in abbreviated form at the very top of their homework or test papers.

During homeroom period, when all students assembled for morning prayers, attendance check, and announcements, they would undergo a further inspection of their uniform attire, this time by their homeroom teacher, almost always a sister. Closely supervised by her, the students read quietly at their desks for ten or fifteen minutes after the conclusion of homeroom business. Occasionally the sister would give two students permission to work together on an assignment during this time, but the norm was individual effort. Homeroom period would frequently be spent collecting lunch fees, donations for the propagation of the faith, payments for school newspaper or yearbook ads, as well as tallying up the proceeds from such fund-raising projects as raffles, magazine drives, or candy sales— activities in which all students were expected to participate, because these efforts resulted in lower school costs. The class goal for a particular project was usually chalked on a section of the blackboard, with the total tallied each day after the students had turned in their money. Rewards for high sellers, among both individuals and classes, often inspired heated competition.

The 1955 core curriculum at St. Madeline's included religion, English, mathematics, history and civics, Latin and foreign languages, and science. Based on their performance on an entrance test, the students were grouped by ability, with freshman-year placement often determining their math, English, and other sections for all four years. A few year-long elective courses were available to juniors and seniors; they had some choice in foreign language (Latin, French, or Spanish), science (physics, chemistry, or physical science), business courses (bookkeeping, accounting, stenography, or typing II), and home economics (clothing or foods). Because of the emphasis placed on Catholic values, the school's textbooks in English and history as well as in religion came from Catholic publishers.

After homeroom, each day at St. Madeline's began with religion class. Traditional Catholic doctrine constituted the class's curriculum, which incorporated dogma, morals, and Church history but very little Bible. During their senior year girls studied apologetics to help them defend the faith through systematic argumentation demonstrating the truth of such beliefs as the existence of God, the divinity of Jesus, the Catholic Church as the one true church, and the infallibility of the Pope. Uncompromising in its claims on truth, the language was didactic and triumphal—focusing on the unchanging nature and eternal destiny of the Catholic Church. Authors and teachers viewed Catholic doctrine as received truth, the unchanging "deposit of faith" that must be handed down through successive generations.

The sisters dominated the teaching staff of forty-five women. Because qualified religious were lacking for home economics and business, two lay teachers taught the courses in those areas. The sisters ranged in age from their early twenties to their mid-seventies, the median age falling in the mid- to late thirties. A younger sister typically taught at the school for only three or four years before being reassigned to another school, which caused considerable turnover in the teaching staff. Even the principal, who also served as the mother superior of the community, was limited by canon law to two three-year terms. This system was deliberately designed to encourage a spirit of detachment from worldly roles and acquired status.

In large classes of from thirty-five to fifty students, the girls took each of their courses with the same classmates. Except to travel to the cafeteria for lunch and to makeshift labs for science, the students remained in the same room all day, with the subject-area teachers moving from class to class. Teaching strategies varied only slightly among the faculty. Recitation, homework review, and oral or written quizzes were part of a typical class. When teachers lectured, students took notes. Rarely did the instructor vary the class with a film or filmstrip. Group discussions or group projects were infrequent. Most teachers also administered weekly tests on regular test days. For their English classes, students typically read two books, memorized and recited a poem, gave a speech, and wrote weekly compositions during each marking period.

Extracurricular activities were often religious in nature. All students belonged to the Catholic Students Mission Crusade, for example, which raised money for Catholic missionaries in foreign countries. The Legion of Mary, whose weekly meetings focused on the personal piety and "good works" of the members, also involved many girls. Nonreligious activities included speech and debate clubs, newspaper and yearbook, and sports teams in field hockey, softball, and basketball. A social committee sponsored mother and daughter teas, father and daughter communion breakfasts, mixer dances, and winter and spring formals. Mixers, frequently held in conjunction with nearby Catholic boys' schools, were intended to enable the girls to meet the "right type of young man." Dating non-Catholics was frowned upon by the Church.

School rules, made clear to all students, received rigorous enforcement. Students accumulated demerits and spent time in detention for such infractions as being out of uniform, tardiness, failing to bring in an excuse when absent, and incomplete or undone homework. Expulsions, averaging about thirty a year, were usually due to academic failure, excessive tardiness or absences, repeated uniform infractions, or more generally any actions "unbecoming a St. Madeline's girl."

St. Madeline's of the 1950s was a total institution with a consistent philosophy of education in which religion played the preeminent role. To the entire school community, this role was simple, clear, and definite. St. Madeline's saw itself as intimately bound to the Catholic Church. Loyalty and obedience to this institution were the fundamental organizing principles for school life.

St. Madeline's Academy in 1985

In 1966, with a pressing need for more space and a newer facility, St. Madeline's moved to its present site in south central Los Angeles. Located on an attractively landscaped campus with well-kept lawns and shrubbery and an ample parking area for faculty and students, the current school building is a contemporary two-story structure of glass and brick. Functionally designed with wide hallways and indirect lighting in the classrooms, the interior affords spacious and bright quarters. Clean and uncluttered, the halls are alive with student artwork and striking graphic displays.

Although half of the faculty of thirty-eight are sisters, it is now hard to distinguish them from the other teachers. Except for a small silver crucifix worn on their blouse or lapel, the attire of the sisters is much like that of their well-dressed lay colleagues. Some sisters still live in an adjacent convent, but others reside in apartments a few minutes' drive from the school. As the sisters arrive at school, they are likely to meet up with their lay colleagues for coffee in the large faculty lounge. Furnished comfortably and decorated with contemporary artwork, the room is a popular gathering place. Sharing stories and light banter, exchanging ideas or concerns about students, the faculty are a warm and congenial community. The personal distance that typified relationships between the sisters and lay teachers in an earlier era has disappeared.

A visitor walking through the school building is unlikely to identify St. Madeline's immediately as a Catholic school. Plants, carpeted floors, and a wide range of colors are more evident than in 1955. The crucifix in each classroom is the only obvious religious symbol. A sense of order and purpose, though still pervasive, is tempered now by a general ambience of warmth and personal kindness. A shared sense of ownership among teachers and students proudly proclaims, "This is *our* school." In the hallways and lobbies, groups of girls stand or sit in small circles on the highly polished floors, talking excitedly to one another or a passing teacher about the events of the day or an upcoming drama production. The tone of their voices, the smiles on their faces, their easy postures—all suggest an affectionate rapport. Hugs are common as students greet classmates and teachers. These interactions suggest a great deal of human caring. Students and faculty speak warmly of the environment and culture of the school. They say, "Our school feels like home."

Unlike the students of 1955, almost all of the girls at St. Madeline's today are black, reflecting the new population of the neighborhoods left behind by whites as they began to migrate to the suburbs many years back. The girls of 1985, though wearing the traditional white blouses, blue skirts and sweaters, white socks and saddle oxfords, and colored class ties, also differ from the girls of 1955 in another fundamental way: almost half of the student body is non-Catholic.

The St. Madeline's curriculum still has a strong academic core, required of all students, which includes four years of English and religion, two years of mathematics and foreign language, five semesters of social studies, and three semesters of science. Over 70 percent of a student's courses are specifically required for graduation. Although the number of electives that the school offers has increased since 1955, the number available to any individual student is still limited. Ninth graders have no electives, sophomores only one, juniors two, and seniors three. In addition to advanced academic courses, which include calculus, human physiology, fourth-year French and Spanish, and advanced placement English, there is a selection of offerings in fine arts, business, and home economics. Despite the increased number of courses offered, the curriculum remains heavily structured toward college preparation.

Though somewhat more student-centered than thirty years ago, classroom teaching is only marginally more varied, with lecturing still the dominant mode. In subject areas more disposed to discussion, such as English, religion, and social studies, the girls display skill in articulating their points of view. Some classes use the resources of the local community in visits to art galleries, museums, and sites for service programs. It is much harder to characterize a typical day for students at St. Madeline's than in 1955, because the schedule varies daily for each student, but academic courses still make up the major part of each day. Classes are smaller than in the 1950s, and typically have about nineteen students. As both students and teachers move between classes, the hallways teem with animated but respectful activity.

Having moved away from an emphasis on received truth, the current religion program focuses on the personal engagement of students with the content of scripture and the sacraments and with moral issues such as peace, justice, and corporate responsibility. Gone is the didacticism of the past; religion teachers now encourage personal interpretation and discussions in which students share their religious views. All the girls also participate each year in a class retreat, spending three days together at a woodland campsite. During this time away, students reflect on their relationships with friends, parents, and God and share their concerns with others in a relaxed atmosphere. Talks by students and faculty express their struggles to lead personally and socially meaningful lives. Student-led prayers and creative liturgies center on friendship, belonging, and reaching out to others.

Vital to the school's religion program, though a relatively new presence in Catholic schools, is the emphasis on a personal response to social justice issues. Under the sponsorship of a faculty member, students have the opportunity to participate in community service projects that include homes for battered women, soup kitchens, retirement homes, and voter registration drives. Although optional, the social action course at St. Madeline's attracts nearly 80 percent of the student body.

The faculty of St. Madeline's spans a wide range of ages and backgrounds. There are three lay teachers and one sister in their mid-twenties; at the other end of the spectrum are four sisters and one lay teacher (a veteran who has spent thirty years teaching at the school) in their early sixties. Although the faculty remains largely white, there are four blacks, two Hispanics, and two Asians. Four faculty members are male, including the school chaplain, a priest who devotes a portion of his ministry to the school.

More distinctive than the faculty composition are the kinds of people who choose to teach at the school and the roles they come to play there. Sister Jeannette, for example, left the teaching ministry of her order after spending several years in their elementary and secondary schools for what she described as more "socially relevant" work. For five years she organized peace groups and worked at shelters for mothers and children. Having heard about the changes at St. Madeline's, she decided to work once again in a school community with her sisters. Sister Jeannette teaches two courses—American Literature and Contemporary Problems—the latter treating issues such as peace, hunger, disarmament, pollution, and family values. Her knowledge of and personal involvement in social justice issues provide important leadership for the school in this area. In coaching the tennis team, Sister Jeannette expresses another side of herself, letting the students see her competitive and playful nature. In the eyes of her students, she is informed, energetic, and interested in their development. They regard her as a mature, competent, loving woman.

Because many St. Madeline's students come from single-parent families, they frequently have domestic responsibilities, perhaps supervising younger siblings or preparing dinner for the family. Although teachers indicate that students should spend two to three hours on homework every evening, a survey by the assistant principal found that they actually spend much less time on home study. Tensions between students and teachers revolve around these conflicting expectations. Teachers constantly push students to face up to the demands that fulfilling their dreams will require. Many of the girls look upon St. Madeline's as a ticket to a prestigious college and a high-paying career, a vision shaped by parental hopes and media images. Some aspire to glamorous careers making more money at an entry-level position than their parents do after twenty-five years of work. Focusing more on the joys and successes than on the struggles, such students tend to romanticize notions of love and marriage. Against this backdrop, the St. Madeline's faculty emphasizes a need for diligence and hard work. Similarly, the school's focus on values leads the girls to confront unrealistic visions and encourages them to recast naive aspirations, a painful and sometimes unsuccessful process.

Student rules are fewer and are enforced more compassionately than they were in 1955. A board composed of teachers and administrators now handles most disciplinary matters. When offenses against the school community are particularly serious, students must appear before the board with their parents. Although the principal has the authority to expel students, this action occurs infrequently and only after all other attempts to change the student's behavior have failed. Reflecting the philosophy that "no one fails who works hard," St. Madeline's is committed to helping all students it enrolls progress to graduation, and the school provides significant personal support and guidance along the way.

Because St. Madeline's is a caring community of learning, teachers and students alike actively support the school and its environment. They want to be there to share in its mission and spirit. Although barely half of the students are Catholic, the religion program remains vital, at the center of the school's purpose. With the greater emphasis on personal and social responsibility, the teaching of Catholic doctrine is no longer all-encompassing. The school's statement of philosophy is clear and the faculty espouse its values. As one teacher told us, the purpose of the school is "to educate the young black woman to take her place in society. We try to *empower* young women through education while inculcating moral and ethical values, including a strong social conscience."

THE STORY OF ST. MADELINE'S reflects the evolutionary transformation within Catholic schools over three decades. Some of the changes are obvious: an increasing number of minority and non-Catholic students, increased representation and responsibility for lay faculty, a more contemporary style of dress and way of life among the religious faculty, an improved physical space, smaller classes, and a more flexible school schedule. Other changes, particularly those in the culture of the school, are more subtle. While preserving the order of an earlier era, Catholic schools are less rigid and austere. Their environment is warm and welcoming, modeling a family atmosphere. The curriculum, while maintaining an emphasis on a traditional core of academic subjects, now includes more choices. The religion program remains a central element in the school, but the focus has shifted. No longer a syllogism to commit to memory, religion has become a way of interpreting daily life and one's role in the world. The transformation of Catholic secondary education, reflecting larger changes within the Church, involves a blend of tradition and change.

Not all Catholic high schools are like the contemporary St. Madeline's, of course, and individual schools resembling the St. Madeline's of 1955 may still be found. Nonetheless, the St. Madeline's of today is more the norm than the exception. It exemplifies three major characteristics that are widely shared by Catholic secondary schools: an unwavering commitment to an academic program for all students, regardless of background or life expectations, and an academic organization designed to promote this aim; a pervasive sense, shared by both teachers and students, of the school as a caring environment and a social organization deliberately structured to advance this; and an inspirational ideology that directs institutional action toward social justice in an ecumenical and multicultural world.

These characteristics vitalize an educational philosophy that aims not only to influence what students know and can do but also the kind of people they will become. Central to this philosophy are certain shared aims for all students: to develop the necessary skills and knowledge to function in a world economy; to foster an appreciation for their social connectedness and individual responsibility to advance social justice; and to stimulate those critical dispositions of mind and heart essential to the sustenance of a convivial democratic society.

This book argues that a constrained academic structure, a communal school organization, and an inspirational ideology are the major forces that shape the operations of individual Catholic schools and contribute to their overall effectiveness. We also argue that these schools expose a broad, diverse cross section of students to a distinctive vision of active participation in a humane society. This vision of the Catholic school contrasts sharply with the contemporary rhetoric of public schooling that is increasingly dominated by market metaphors, radical individualism, and a sense of purpose organized around competition and the pursuit of individual economic rewards. Although the common school ideal inspired the formation of American public education for over one hundred years, it is now the Catholic school that focuses our attention on fostering human cooperation in the pursuit of the common good. While the Catholic school, like the Catholic Church itself, has become increasingly public, the public schools have become increasingly private, turning away from the basic social and political purposes that once lent them the title of "common school." It is in the spirit of renewing public interest in these concerns that we offer this book.

❖ I ❖
CONTEXT

❖ 1 ❖

The Tradition of
Catholic Schools

CATHOLIC SCHOOLS are among the oldest educational institutions in the United States. Built up from colonial times, the American Catholic school system has had no parallel in Europe or, for that matter, anywhere in the world. Its story is a distinctly American one that involves both active engagement with the world and, at times, strong reaction against it. This social and intellectual tradition, in modern form, undergirds the educational experience of millions of Americans.

Nevertheless, Catholic schools have received relatively little public attention until very recently. Histories of education record that Catholic schools played an important role in the assimilation of diverse European ethnic groups into mainstream American life,[1] but the processes by which this was accomplished remain largely unknown. In the last several decades Catholic schools have gone through another remarkable but largely unexamined process of social change, as suggested by the portraits of St. Madeline's in 1955 and 1985 in the Prologue. In the 1950s, Catholic schools might appropriately have been described as culturally isolated, doctrinaire, and racially segregated. In the 1960s, critics argued about whether these schools should even continue to exist. In the 1990s, schools such as St. Madeline's educate a broad cross section of students, including large numbers of minorities and non-Catholics, and in the process contribute to educational opportunity nationwide.

Understanding contemporary Catholic high schools is the aim of this book. We have approached this task through three interrelated streams of inquiry. Our work began with extensive field visits to seven high schools around the country that represent the diversity of Catholic secondary education. These visits were particularly important in helping us to see and understand the operation of each institution through the eyes, voices, and actions of its participants—teachers, principals, students, and parents. These field observations constitute the major data source for the descriptive portion of our research, presented in Part II.

The second major strand of our research involved extensive analyses of a large national data base on high schools of the early and mid-1980s, *High School and Beyond*.[2] These analyses form the core for Parts III and IV, which examine the processes and effects of Catholic schools. Together with information gathered by the National Catholic Educational Association, these data also help us to generalize our field observations to the Catholic school sector as a whole.[3]

Through these two empirical efforts, we identified a group of distinctive organizational characteristics common in Catholic high schools: a delimited academic curriculum with a proactive view about what students can and should learn; a broad role for staff that embodies a transformative view of teaching; a conception of the school as a community where daily life educates in profound ways; small school size; and decentralized governance. Each of these features contributes in important ways to school functioning. Nevertheless, we gradually came to believe that these organizational features did not fully explain why Catholic schools work the way they do. We remained unsettled about the answers to certain key questions: What motivates the human behavior that we observed in these places? What grounds the forms of collective action undertaken? What gives rise to the distinctive meanings of their social lives expressed by participants?

In search for a more complete explanation, we found it necessary to initiate a third stream of inquiry—to explore the social and intellectual history of these schools. Making up this history is a rich set of experiences, ideas, and symbols, which together constitute a tradition that both explains much about the dramatic changes at St. Madeline's and continues to shape school life today. This tradition is a source of inspiration for St. Madeline's vision of itself as a community. It inspires personal effort by both teachers and students and is ultimately the foundation of the school's effectiveness.

The majority of this book is devoted to an organizational analysis of the structure and functioning of Catholic schools. But in this chapter we examine the institutional roots of Catholic schools and explore the main themes that combine to form their tradition.[4] This history provides essential background for understanding the lessons of the Catholic school for educational reform. As we argue in Part V, schools exist within a larger culture that has important implications for the work of teachers and the education of young people. If we fail to consider the distinctive culture and traditions of Catholic schools, we may misread their policy lessons. That is, we believe that the structural features of Catholic schools, divorced from their traditions, would likely produce a set of school consequences quite different from those described in this book.

Similarly, we argue that contemporary Catholic schools are not the narrow sectarian institutions of an earlier age. This chapter surveys the history and philosophy of Catholic schooling in order to enable a fuller understanding and appreciation of the current Catholic school system. We also examine the link between contemporary Catholic social ethics and the common school ideal—a now much neglected consideration in the public sector. We suspect that the ideas introduced here, combined with the reflections offered in Part V, may induce a bit of unease. The seemingly straightforward separation of the religious and secular realms in education may no longer appear as clear as it once did.

In broad strokes, the development of Catholic schools can be divided into three periods.[5] The first, spanning the period from colonial times until approximately 1830, represents the birth of a new Church in a new nation. The second period, from 1830 through 1960, sees Catholic schools expanding rapidly in response to immigration and confronting many divisive issues that shaped the formal system and gave it a distinctly American character. The third period, from 1960 to the present, has been described as the "Catholic moment," during which Catholics have become part of the mainstream of American political, social, and economic life, and Catholic social ethics have become a vibrant voice on the national scene.[6] Our discussion begins with a brief review of the major events and conflicts within each of these periods that have combined to form the current Catholic school system. We then backtrack a bit, to consider the intellectual movements that undergird this history of institution-building and also provide much of the rationale for the recent transformation of Catholic education in America. Here we consider the institutional retrenchment affirmed by the first Vatican Council, the revival of Neoscholasticism as the Church's intellectual armament for its encounter with modernity, the emergence of social Catholicism as both an intellectual and activist enterprise, and finally the remarkable reinterpretation of tradition set out at Vatican II.

From Colonial Times to 1830

Catholic schools took root in colonial America. The development of schools in Catholic communities during this period closely paralleled activities occurring in Protestant communities. Education was viewed as a fundamentally moral enterprise, and Protestants and Catholics alike sought to ground the education of their children in their particular beliefs. Until about 1830, the provision of education was an informal local matter.[7]

The Catholic college-seminary, like early Protestant schools such as Harvard and Princeton, emerged during the colonial period. The college-seminary gave rise to three modern institutions: the seminary to prepare men for the priesthood, the liberal arts college, and the secondary school for boys. Also appearing during the colonial period was the girls' academy. These institutions were sponsored by individual female religious orders, initially from Europe and then in the nineteenth century increasingly from America. The tuition the academies charged allowed religious women to sponsor free primary schools for poor children who otherwise would have gone uneducated. Eventually these free schools were replaced by parochial schools that could more broadly address this goal. Organized by individual communities around their parish church, parochial schools became the base for the current Catholic elementary school system.

The Development of Secondary Schools for Boys

As far as the bishops were concerned, the most important schools were the college-seminaries.[8] Priests were in short supply in the colonies, and the colleges became a major recruiting ground. The college and seminary had a symbiotic relationship, whereby part of the tuition generated by the college was directed to support the costs of seminarian preparation, and the young seminarians acted as unpaid teachers for the college.[9] As early as 1640, English Jesuits in Maryland operated a few such schools, and there had been even earlier efforts by Spanish missionaries in Florida and the Southwest in the sixteenth century. Most of these early schools survived for only a short period. The first Catholic school to take root and endure within the original English colonies was Bohemia Manor in Maryland, founded by the English Jesuits in the 1740s. This school became the institutional foundation for Georgetown Preparatory School (a boys' secondary school) and Georgetown University (originally a college-seminary for men). Bohemia Manor educated sons of the Catholic colonial aristocracy, such as Charles Carroll, a signer of the Declaration of Independence, and his cousin, John Carroll, the first bishop of the United States.[10] The formal separation of the boys' secondary school from the men's college did not occur until late in the nineteenth century.

Both intellectually and institutionally, the Jesuits are seen as responsible for the formation of Catholic secondary and postsecondary education in America.[11] This order, which had emphasized work in higher education from its inception in 1534, had already made major contributions in Europe to the development of curriculum and teaching methods, the preparation of teachers, and actual experimentation with teaching.[12] The Jesuits' practical expertise was formalized into a plan of study, the *Ratio Studiorum*. First printed in 1586, the document had widespread influence in western Europe and, eventually, in the colonies. The *Ratio Studiorum* specified a curriculum and teaching method, organized by classes and grade levels. Patterned after Renaissance humanism, the program of classical studies spanned approximately seven years of instruction, roughly equivalent to secondary and college education.[13] The *studia inferiora* (secondary) curriculum emphasized the study of the classics (Latin and Greek), grammar, and rhetoric. The *studia superiora* (college) curriculum emphasized philosophy, mathematics, and science.

Drawing on the Scholasticism of St. Thomas Aquinas, the *Ratio* affirmed the value of classical study, the transmission of the accumulated wisdom of Western culture, and individual contemplation. It emphasized a mental training in logical argument: thesis, evidence, objections, discussion, and final proof. In modern terms, such a curriculum might be described as focusing on cultural transmission with a heavy emphasis on higher-order thinking skills. Much of this was quite literally "higher order," emphasizing rather arcane supernatural concerns such as logical proofs of the existence of God. Absent this otherworldly focus, the *Ratio Studiorum* has much in common with modern educational reform initiatives such as that suggested by Mortimer J. Adler in his *Paideia Proposal*.[14]

The Emergence of Parochial Primary Schools

A century after the initial publication of the *Ratio Studiorum,* the first curriculum and method for elementary schools were published by Jean Baptiste de la Salle, the founder of the Christian Brothers teaching order. First printed in 1720, the *Conduct of Schools* specified a curriculum of the 4R's: reading, 'riting, 'rithmetic, and religion, with whole-class recitation as a favored method. As was generally true in colonial schools, Catholic elementary schools stressed the importance of religious education. Instruction in secular subjects, however, had a great deal in common with Protestant schools. For curricular basics, such "secular" instructional materials as Webster's *American Spelling Book,* Murray's *English Reader,* and Colburn's *First Lessons in Arithmetic on the Plan of Pestalozzi* were commonly used.[15]

The first parochial primary schools appeared in Pennsylvania in the mid-1700s, although we know little about them. The first parish school of record was established in 1782 by St. Mary's Church in Philadelphia, which had the largest Catholic population at the time (400 Catholics out of a total population of 18,000). In general, the American elementary school was just emerging as a distinct social institution at the end of the eighteenth century. The new nation was a preindustrial society, with the home still the central workplace and education the task of women in the home. The separate elementary school awaited the industrialization that would sweep across the nation in the next century.

The Catholic Church in the United States of 1800 had a very simple organizational structure. Bishops were little more than parish pastors, priests were in short supply, and laypersons took major roles in building parishes and schools.[16] The American Church had few human, social, or fiscal resources to organize parishes and their accompanying elementary schools. As late as 1815, Catholics had very few churches, let alone schools, relative to their numbers.[17]

With the beginning of mass immigration early in the nineteenth century, however, parishes multiplied, and parochial elementary schools developed. These early parish schools were small neighborhood institutions enrolling both boys and girls. They varied considerably, some existing only briefly. The idea of a parochial school was nevertheless well established by 1830 in such places as New York, where most parishes operated a school in some form.[18] In no sense, however, were these schools a separate system. Prior to 1830, Catholic primary schools were quite similar to those found in Protestant neighborhoods, with both sets of institutions developing along lines responsive to the perceived needs of their individual communities.

The Emergence of Secondary Schools for Girls

Although the early parish schools were the precursors of the current Catholic elementary school system (in which 86 percent of the schools are still run by individual parishes), the very first elementary schools were actually founded by female religious as part of the European academy movement. Whereas college or seminary training was viewed as the appropriate terminal education for elite young men, the academy took on this role for young women. These academies charged tuition, providing the principal support for the religious orders conducting them and in turn allowing the orders to sponsor free elementary schools for poor children.

The free schools, however, did not emerge as a major organizational form in the Catholic sector, in large part because of the negative image attached to attending a "school for paupers." As parish elementary schools grew in number, religious orders were more likely to take on teaching in these schools in exchange for a small stipend instead of opening their own schools.

The first female academy (and free school) was founded in New Orleans in 1727 by the Ursuline Sisters from France. Like the Jesuits, the Ursulines had a tradition as a European teaching order, and its members were carefully educated for this task.[19] It was not until 1790 that the next girls' academy, Visitation, appeared near Georgetown.[20] After 1800, academies began to appear with increasing frequency and were a well-established organizational form by 1830.

Like their Protestant counterparts, the Catholic academies were founded primarily for religious and moral reasons. The education of Catholic women, an integral part of the development of a new American culture, emphasized the moral virtues and domestic graces for family life. The early academies taught the four R's, French (owing to the influence of the Ursulines), and other subjects considered proper for an elite young woman's domestic education, such as drawing, music, and needlework. By the 1830s the curriculum had expanded to provide a broader classical education, including Latin, algebra and geometry, chemistry and physics, geography, natural history, and moral philosophy.[21] For their time, the academies had rather progressive ideas about the education of young women.

The establishment and continued existence of these schools depended on the independent contributions and hard work of female religious orders, while the American Church focused its limited resources on supporting the education of men. Although the early female religious orders in America were missionaries from Europe, after the turn of the century new locally founded orders, including the Sisters of Loretto, the Sisters of St. Dominic, and the Sisters of Charity, arose to begin and operate schools. The history of these schools is a story of the enormous personal sacrifice made by numerous communities of religious women, a tradition that lives on at St. Madeline's in the work of the Sisters of St. Joseph of Carondolet.

The Early Leadership of John Carroll

John Carroll, the first Roman Catholic bishop in the United States, played a seminal role in shaping the fledgling American Catholic Church and its schools. Even before he became bishop of Baltimore in 1790, Carroll was responsible for founding the first college-seminary, had encouraged the establishment of girls' academies, and was personally responsible for starting several parish schools. Born into the Catholic aristocracy of Maryland in 1735, Carroll was educated both in America and in Europe before his ordination as a Jesuit. His early activities show him to be both an Americanist and a modernist.[22] For example, he embraced the Enlightenment ideal of science and its potential to enhance human welfare. Contrary to prevailing opinion in Rome and in most European countries, he accepted the separation of church and state as appropriate for America. More broadly, he saw a need for a new understanding about how religion should relate to public life.

Carroll helped to fashion a uniquely American Church, where a spirit of democracy permeated the governance of local Church communities. The first three American bishops were elected by the lower clergy rather than appointed solely by Bishop Carroll. Parishes were controlled by lay trustees. Priests frequently practiced a vernacular liturgy, although this practice was never officially sanctioned. Catholics and Protestants regularly visited each other's churches. Compared with its European counterparts, Catholicism in America was a new experiment for a republican age.

Though in part intellectually motivated, these arrangements were also quite pragmatic. With memories of colonial penal laws still quite fresh, Catholics could be considered one of America's first minority groups. As such, some rapprochement with a dominant and powerful Protestantism was necessary. Political accommodation remained a major issue in American Catholicism throughout the next century, as Catholics periodically came under suspicion for "Popery," "Romanism," and other alleged threats. In addition, because the Church in America had little formal structure and few resources, broad lay involvement and councillor governance arrangements were a logistic necessity. As the institutional base grew, however, this limitation was largely removed.

This first embrace of American Catholicism with the secular world became a casualty to larger social and political events in both the old world and the new. The anticlericalism of the French Revolution prompted a Vatican critique of the principles of reason, liberty, and democracy, and the American Church was subjected to particular scrutiny. Carroll himself also adopted a more conservative stance in his later years. Seeing the Church in America as unwieldy and potentially anarchistic, he sought more centralized clerical control. The initial councillor mode of governance gradually became more monarchical. Prompting tightened ecclesiastical control as well was immigration, which from the beginning of the nineteenth century created an increasingly diverse American Catholic populace in terms of language, culture, and natural loyalties.

Even though these events foreclosed the American Church's first encounter with modernity, the roots of egalitarianism, ecumenism, and democratization had been established by 1800. These forces were largely submerged in terms of official actions of the institutional Church for the next 150 years, but they remained alive in the work and thought of individual religious and lay members.

Establishment and Growth of the System, 1830–1960

In 1830 there was still little awareness among Catholics that they were building a separate educational system, distinct from the "public" one. This idea would certainly have seemed quite foreign at the time, as no such system existed anywhere in the Western world. The distinction between public and private schools remained unclear throughout much of the nineteenth century. Until 1825, Catholic schools in New York City received public aid. The "school wars" during the 1840s in New York and other cities over access to such aid attest to the uncertain nature of this distinction.[23] In frontier regions, the difference between public and private schools remained unclear for a considerably longer time. In rural towns composed entirely of ethnic Catholic settlers, the local school *was* the Catholic school through much of the nineteenth century.[24] Even as a distinct "public" school system began to emerge after 1830, Catholic schools continued to receive support in Massachusetts, Wisconsin, Connecticut, and New Jersey. Public support of Catholic education, such as the Stillwater-Fairbault plan in St. Paul, Minnesota (whereby the teaching of secular subjects in Catholic schools was paid for from public funds), persisted into the 1890s.[25] It was not until 1898 that New York State ruled that an existing arrangement aiding Catholic schools in Poughkeepsie, New York, was illegal.[26]

Fears of the "Romanist" Threat

Although the great waves of Catholic immigration did not begin until the middle of the nineteenth century, the number of Catholic immigrants that had arrived in the United States by 1830, especially in the cities of the Northeast, was perceived as a threat by the Anglo-Saxon Protestant majority. The Napoleonic dictatorship, which stifled the French Revolution, showed the fragility of democratic rule. The growing mass of "unruly foreigners" raised doubts in some about the "moral fiber" of these new American citizens.

America looked to formal schooling as an answer. Informal socialization in the home, existing tuition-charging academies, and free schools for poor children supported by private philanthropy were not sufficient to sustain the nation in these threatening times. To confront the combined forces of immigration and urbanization, the "common school" emerged. As envisioned by its chief advocate, Horace Mann, the common school not only would make education universally available to all children without regard to creed, class, or social background but would also seek to ensure that these children were educated together—"in common." Moreover, Mann intended this education to be a broadly humanistic one. He argued that an effective democracy demanded the full intellectual, social, and moral development of all of its citizens. Only through such a common education could America sustain a harmonious community amidst its growing diversity.[27]

The widely shared understandings that moral education was the bedrock of schooling and that such personal formation could not occur without the support of formal religion, however, posed a problem for Mann. The idea of a diverse sectarian school system, run by Catholic and various Protestant denominations, was dismissed as incapable of providing the necessary cohering influence for American society. Mann's solution was a nondenominational approach, in which a "common core of all religions" would be taught through techniques such as reading from the Bible without comment.

Although Catholics were not opposed to publicly supported schools, the thought that their children would be forced to read the Protestant version of the Bible, to study explicitly anti-Catholic texts, to sing Protestant hymns, and to endure other religious insults quickly led many to conclude that Mann's nondenominational religion was actually Protestant. This belief was amplified by public rhetoric from prominent figures such as Lyman Beecher and Josiah Strong, who believed it imperative to save America from the "forces of darkness" incarnate in Romanism.[28]

Thus one interpretation of the history of Catholic schools is not that Catholics deliberately set out to create a separate system but, rather, that the idea was largely forced upon them by a hostile "public" system under Protestant control. As G. K. Chesterton aptly phrased it, America is a "nation with the soul of a church."[29] Mid-nineteenth-century leaders sought to define that spirit as Protestant, and not Catholic. By way of the schools, they sought to ensure that Protestant institutions and symbols marked American public life. For Catholics to defer to this policy, given the broadly held view that education was fundamentally a moral enterprise, was tantamount to a denial of their faith.

More than just religious differences were at stake: issues of culture and language were also central. America's social elite saw the common schools as socializing foreigners whose presence might otherwise be threatening to them. Public school educators thus saw their task as homogenizing not only religion but other aspects of culture as well, including language. Immigrants were to be assimilated into an Anglo-Saxon tradition.[30] The resultant insensitivity and disdain for ethnic values and language alienated many immigrants and encouraged the establishment of alternative institutions where both their faith and their culture would be valued.

Even so, throughout most of the nineteenth century, the American bishops made repeated efforts at accommodation with the new "public" system. As Catholics continued to encounter hostility and anti-Catholic rhetoric in supposedly nonsectarian public schools, however, the movement toward a separate system gradually grew. The American bishops, assembled at the first Council of Baltimore in 1829, recommended the establishment of schools in connection with churches and permitted the use of parish revenues to pay teachers. Echoing the distress of common school advocates, the bishops voiced a concern about the formation of moral character in the absence of "proper" schooling.

The bishops reaffirmed this exhortation in 1866 at the second Baltimore Council, specifically noting the dangers inherent in the public schools. Over two decades of rebuff by the "public" system were apparently beginning to take their toll. Finally, at the third Baltimore Council in 1884, the bishops commanded Catholic parents to send their children to parochial schools. Bishops and pastors were strictly enjoined to erect a school near each church, if one did not already exist, within two years. Although these joint decrees were never fully realized, they combined to manifest the espoused aim of Catholic education that would stand until the mid-1960s: "every Catholic student in a Catholic school."

The Controversy over Pluralism Within

Creation of a separate school system in the face of Anglo-Saxon Protestant hostility, however, is only part of the story. The failure to achieve accommodation with the emerging public school system was as much attributable to internal quarrels among ethnically diverse American Catholics as to the external Protestant threat. Throughout the nineteenth century, leadership in the American Church had a strong English-Irish bent, starting with Bishop Carroll and extending to later leaders such as James Cardinal Gibbons and Archbishop John Ireland. English-speaking and theologically liberal in orientation, these men emphasized the commonalities between Catholicism and American values and sought a rapprochement with American institutions, particularly the common schools. It was Archbishop Ireland, for example, who had spearheaded the ill-fated Stillwater-Fairbault plan for public support of Catholic schools.

A vision of a distinctly American Catholic Church, of which these accommodations were a part, was not widely shared by subsequent non-English-speaking immigrants. The internal debate among American Catholics eventually focused on the question of whether Catholicism would be American, that is, English speaking and Irish dominated, or would replicate its European roots as a relatively independent, ethnically based, and pluralistic institution.

Conflict over Church control in the face of internal pluralism came to a head around 1890. Peter Paul Cahensly, a deputy in the German Reichstag and a leader in the St. Raphael Society, which looked after the welfare of German emigrants to America, had petitioned Pope Leo XIII in 1891 to create ethnic parishes in America and to appoint Church leaders on the basis of nationality. Cahensly called for the teaching of native languages in addition to English in American schools and supported an institutional respect for different cultures. Cardinal Gibbons vigorously opposed the petition as an unjustified intrusion of Europeans into American affairs. Although Leo XIII eventually rejected Cahensly's specific requests, he did enjoin Cardinal Gibbons to heed the diverse needs of an immigrant Church. The immediate controversy was resolved, but the pluralism issue remained hotly contested in urban dioceses well into the twentieth century.

Also involved were tensions over theological liberalism and conservatism. Leaders such as Gibbons and Ireland espoused a vision of American Catholicism remarkably compatible with post-Vatican II doctrine. The heart of their beliefs was the need for religious ideas to engage culture rather than to stand apart from it. If the Church was to maintain its relevance and vitality in the face of modernity, it must recognize change as fundamental, they argued. Not surprisingly, an ecumenical attitude toward engagement with Protestants was embedded in this view. The accommodationists also tended to support a different view of the institutional Church—a kind of Catholic republicanism—with less rigid distinctions between clergy and laity.

These ideas contrasted sharply with conservative positions that had hardened during the eighteenth and nineteenth centuries over conflicts between the Roman Church and emerging European secular states. American conservatives joined Roman officials in supporting a strong Church authority exercised by a clerical hierarchy. They invoked an image of the Church as "a pastor and his flock." For conservatives, the life rhythm of a good Catholic was to "pay, pray, and obey."

The Roman response to the American controversy came like two blasts from a double-barreled shotgun. Leo XIII issued *Testem Benevoletiae* (A Testament of Esteem) in 1899, which sided with the conservatives on how the Church should be organized and should function. *Testem Benevoletiae* formally censured the "errors of Americanism." The second volley, the 1907 papal encyclical *Pascendi Dominici Gregis* (On the Doctrine of the Modernists), spoke out against the "errors of modernism." The Church should not effect a rapprochement with the modern world—the modern world was the problem. These two papal pronouncements crushed a budding Catholic intellectualism in America and eviscerated an independent Catholic press. Teaching in seminaries came under close scrutiny; books were banned, and "brain rot set in as a climate of fear gripped the academy."[31] Ecclesiastical authority was firmly reestablished.

Ironically, this rebuke of nineteenth-century Catholic liberalism protected the American Church's experiment with educational pluralism. With the papal rejection of the forces of "Americanism" and "modernism," conservatives derived indirect support for the establishment and maintenance of ethnic schools. At the time, many feared that ethnic Catholic schools would promote separatism and permanently establish a divisive ethnic politics threatening to democracy. Events developed quite differently, however, for two reasons. First, most immigrants did not want the total isolation of a ghetto Church. They sought a piece of the economic promise that was America, and therefore they wanted schools to teach the English language and some of the mores of American life. Second, Catholic schools were continually subject to external scrutiny. They had to attest over and over again to their Americanism, lest a suspicious public policy turn virulently against them.

Immigrants valued the ethnic parish school because of its connection to their European past. The school staff shared their ethnicity and religion, with an empathetic understanding of old world ways. Although to some the ethnic schools represented a fortress designed to protect a separate Catholic culture, they actually served more as bridging institutions between two different cultures. The use of English grew rapidly, even in schools originally established with a different language of instruction. While Catholic schools consciously sought to preserve Catholic values and ethnic identities, they also facilitated the assimilation of immigrants into American public life. They served both a preserving and a transforming function.[32] Mary

Perkins Ryan has observed: "The parochial school at that period served to slow up the process of acculturation, to make it less of a traumatic experience—less of a complete, almost instantaneous break with the European past [as was the case in public schools of that time] and all it stood for. The children in the Catholic schools were 'Americanized'—but by teachers of their own race and religion, who clung in great part to the old ways, only slowly adapting to the new."[33] The strongest testament to the wisdom of this practical educational philosophy would not emerge until half a century later. In 1966, Andrew Greeley and Peter Rossi reported that immigrant Catholics had by 1960 reached a social standing in America ahead of Protestants and second only to Jews.[34]

A National Defense in Response to Nativism

Over nine million immigrants, the vast majority of whom were Catholic, streamed into America between 1880 and the onset of World War I. Although they were originally welcomed as "fuel" for a rapidly expanding industrial order, xenophobic fears surrounding America's entrance into the war and the growing squalor and crime in urban slums brought about a wave of anti-Catholic bigotry. The papal proclamations of *Testem Benevoletiae* and *Pascendi Dominici Gregis* amplified concerns about docile, obedient Catholics taking orders from Rome. Parochial schools came in for an especially strong attack. The print media proclaimed the Catholic school "a destroyer of American Patriotism"[35] and the source of urban problems. One editor argued, for example, that a "Romanist minority, trained by nuns and priests . . . , furnishe[s] the majority of our criminals."[36]

Laws enacted by individual states mandated instruction in English and increased control over curriculum, instructional materials, and teacher certification. A number of states restricted attendance at nonpublic schools. The legal right of such schools to exist was in question until 1925, when the Supreme Court decided in *Pierce v. The Society of Sisters* that an Oregon law requiring compulsory attendance in public schools was unconstitutional.

In the face of what they saw as a conspiracy to create a state monopoly on education, the Catholic hierarchy responded with a national defense of parochial schools. One aspect of this defense was accommodation when possible. Bishops renewed efforts to encourage English instruction and to discourage ethnic schools. To demonstrate the positive social and civic contributions of Catholic schools, courses in citizenship and patriotism were added.

Rhetoric was also sharpened. Catholics sought to defend their institutions' right to exist and their purposes as properly American. In 1919, the bishops formed an education department within the National Catholic Welfare Council to present official Church positions on matters of educational policy and more generally to represent the interests of Catholic schools to the public. In 1922 the council's executive secretary, James H. Ryan, wrote a systematic apologetic for Catholic schooling. Noting that the first American schools were religious schools—both Protestant and Catholic—Ryan recalled that tax-supported public schools dated only from the 1850s. As a result, he argued, public schools had no legitimate claim "to being considered the only true American system of education."[37] Through such statements, Catholics reminded the nation that democracy was a religious ideal and aggressively argued that Catholicism embraced the essence of this ideal. The motto "For God and Country" captured the spirit of their counter-crusade.[38]

The external threat to Catholic education also served an internal purpose in facilitating further consolidation of all Catholic institutions, particularly schools. The nativism movement provided bishops with a rationale to rein in ethnic schools. In the process, the ethnic schools became more American and Catholic schools in general came to constitute more of a system. New organizational structures emerged to formalize these arrangements. The Catholic Educational Association, for example, which later changed its name to the National Catholic Educational Association (NCEA), was founded in 1904 as a voluntary association among Catholic educators to discuss basic issues concerning the operation of schools and the improvement of educational practice.

Schooling was increasingly coordinated along diocesan lines. The parish and religious order schools founded in the nineteenth century had largely developed from the initiative of individual clerics and laypersons. As the demands for Catholic schooling escalated far beyond capacity, however, the bishops took a more active role in shaping the system. Around 1890, the bishops began to open new secondary schools, called central or diocesan high schools, which enrolled students from different parishes across the diocese. By 1910, these new institutions were widespread. Also around 1890 the bishops introduced diocesan school boards as a first attempt to coordinate activities. By 1920, in an effort to tighten administrative control further, many dioceses replaced these boards with a superintendent of schools appointed by and responsible to the bishop.

In these moves to formalize and standardize schooling into a system, albeit still a relatively decentralized one, Catholics were responding to larger social forces shaping American life. In the public sector, the efficiency movement in education, the growing science of pedagogy, and efforts to improve teacher preparation typified progressive schooling. Regardless of the distrust they might have for progressive educational philosophy, Catholics didn't want to be left behind. Catholic schools had to be just as good in secular terms as they were in Catholic terms. Similarly, modern ideas about the formal organization of schooling, including the creation of professional bureaucracies, did not go unnoticed by Catholic educators.

A Traditional Academic Curriculum for All Students

Much of the written history of Catholic schooling focuses on how its institutions developed in interaction with a politically dominant Protestant America. In some cases, Catholics directly imitated public initiative, often shaping schools out of a desire to accommodate. Sometimes, however, they took a different course in sharp rejection of the dominant culture. The debate over high school curriculum in the first quarter of this century exemplifies this dynamic.

At the beginning of the twentieth century, Catholic secondary schooling, like public secondary schooling, was limited to a relatively small percentage of the population. As opportunities for Catholic secondary schooling expanded, a more comprehensive educational philosophy, with an expanded life studies curriculum, was increasingly espoused as an alternative to the academic curriculum found in the older boys' preparatory schools and girls' academies.

In considering a new high school curriculum, Catholics were responding to movements in the larger society. The *Cardinal Principles of Secondary Education,* published in 1918 by the National Education Association (NEA), conceived of the high school as a more universal institution with a different, more vocational, emphasis. Although some Catholic high schools embraced the philosophy of the *Cardinal Principles,* this bulwark of the contemporary comprehensive public high school was eventually rejected by Catholics, owing to the interaction of several forces.[39]

Much of the vigorous debate among Catholics about the purposes and methods of their high schools was played out in the proceedings of the National Catholic Educational Association. In the spirit of pragmatism, voices were raised in favor of eliminating Greek from the curriculum, reducing the amount of Latin, and adding commercial and vocational courses. Considerable discussion ensued about the merits of the classics and about the need for more industrial training to better prepare future workers.

The reaction against these pragmatic voices was vigorous and forceful.

Critics argued that the classics were the languages of Western civilization. Their study had moral and aesthetic value; they provided intellectual discipline and encouraged inventiveness. Such a curriculum "trains the mind better."[40] The overwhelming response from NCEA members was that the study of classical humanism served every student well.

This rejection of life studies and vocationalism was predicated on fundamental philosophical premises. Developing the student's ability to reason was a central tenet of Catholic educational philosophy, beginning with the *Ratio Studiorum* and further affirmed in Neoscholastic thought, discussed in the next section. Such intellectual development was deemed necessary in order to grasp fully the established understandings about person, society, and God. Although universal secondary education had expanded the base of people to be educated, the purpose of education should not change. Practical education deviated too far from the central moral aims of schooling.

Institutional status and social class dynamics were also at work in the debate. The NCEA had grown out of the Association of Catholic Colleges of the United States, and these institutions of higher education exerted a major influence on Catholic secondary education through the 1920s.[41] The colleges maintained close relationships with the boys' preparatory schools and girls' academies and tended to deprecate the weak academic programs in parochial and diocesan high schools. The latter schools were determined to prove their worth before the Catholic educational elite: the higher educational institutions. To secure such recognition and respect, diocesan schools increasingly put the college-preparatory curriculum first, with life studies offerings becoming ancillary. Catholic colleges themselves added to this pressure in 1912 by instituting strict academic admissions requirements, including 16 credits in specific academic subjects.

The value of education as a vehicle for social mobility was also increasingly apparent to both Catholic educators and immigrant parents. This idea was raised in early discussions of the Association of Catholic Colleges, as leaders "cried out that Catholic youth should not be the 'hewers of wood and drawers of water,' but should be prepared for the professions or mercantile pursuits."[42] The classical curriculum was the curriculum for the attainment of status. Catholic educators were urged to point out to parents the greater earning power of students who finished high school. An academic education in high school and then college paved the way for social position, the professions, and Catholic leadership in society.

Last, Rome placed its seal of approval on a conservative educational philosophy in 1929 in a statement by Pius XI, *Divini Illius Magistri* (On the

Christian Education of Youth). Arguing that true education is directed toward the ultimate ends, Pius XI cautioned against errors of pragmatism in the curriculum. The Church was a conserver of humanity's cultural heritage. Though supporting efforts to discern what is of worth in modern systems, Pius XI cautioned against "hastily abandoning the old, which the experience of centuries had found expedient and profitable." Two important features were signaled out and affirmed by the Pope: the teaching of Latin and single-sex rather than coeducational schooling.

Although Catholics made some accommodation to the philosophy of the *Cardinal Principles,* they never moved as far or as firmly in that direction as did the public schools. The end result was to reaffirm the position articulated at the third Baltimore Council in 1884: "The beauty of truth, the refining and elevating influences of knowledge, are meant for all, and she [the Church] wishes them to be brought within the reach of all. Knowledge enlarges our capacity both for self-improvement and for promoting the welfare of our fellow men; and in so noble a work the Church wishes every hand to be busy."[43] Catholicism's uneasy relationship to secular society thus continued. Much but not all of the modern world could be embraced, even by Catholic liberals. Practical concerns would increasingly enter its debates and be given their due, but ultimate principles could never be compromised.

Continued Expansion

By the end of the 1920s, the system of Catholic schooling had been fully formed, and significant accommodations of Catholics with American life had been made. Although ethnic parish schools continued into the 1950s, English increasingly became the language of instruction alongside, if not totally replacing, the language of the parish. The institutional growth begun in the second half of the nineteenth century continued, slowed by World War II but not reversed. The Catholic school system that had enrolled 405,000 students in 1880 had grown to 2.5 million students and almost 10,000 schools by 1930. By 1950, there were 11,000 schools and 3.1 million students. In the next fifteen years the system again spurted ahead, reaching a high of over 13,000 Catholic schools educating 5.5 million students.[44] In its peak year, 1965, the Catholic system enrolled about 12 percent of all American elementary and secondary students.[45]

The Prologue's portrayal of St. Madeline's in 1955 describes the daily routines found in most of these schools throughout the first half of this century. Prayer and religious practices punctuated a tightly ordered school day. Frequently called to task by their teachers—usually sisters, but in some instances, brothers and priests—students were pressed to do their best academically. Teachers stressed diligence in study, emphasized recitation, and rewarded neat work. Although Catholic students generally socialized in exclusively Catholic circles, they frequently compared themselves with their public school counterparts. Catholic school students considered themselves as much set apart by the number of books they carried home each night as by the uniforms they wore. Despite the cataclysmic events that reverberated around the globe—two world wars, an economic collapse, and atomic devastation—the rhythm of St. Madeline's remained the same.

1960 to the Present: "The Catholic Moment"

With the election in 1960 of John Fitzgerald Kennedy as the first Roman Catholic president of the United States, American Catholics had clearly come of age. In the context of such acceptance, the protectionist mentality afforded by a ghetto Church and its separate social institutions seemed strangely anachronistic. In an ironic twist, at the very moment when Catholic school enrollment had reached its apogee, Mary Perkins Ryan published a controversial book, *Are Parochial Schools the Answer?* which raised serious questions about the continued need for Catholic schooling. These domestic concerns were in turn swept up and greatly amplified as the second Vatican Council prompted new scrutiny of virtually every Church institution and practice.

In American Catholic schools, central symbols such as statues and sisters dressed in religious garb largely disappeared; the student population changed; teaching staff became increasingly lay; and the religion curriculum was transformed. But perhaps most dramatic of all were the numbers: Catholic schools in the United States lost over half their enrollment between 1965 and 1990. From a high of 5.5 million students in 1965, the Catholic school enrollment dropped to 2.5 million students in 1990. From enrolling 12 percent of the school-age population in 1965, Catholic schools enrolled only 5.4 percent in 1990. The number of schools declined accordingly, from 13,000 in 1965 to about 9,000 in 1990.[46]

Closely linked to these declining enrollments were financial problems, the chief cause of which was the exodus of men and women from religious life. The school system had literally been built on their backs, through the services they contributed in the form of the very low salaries that they accepted. When it became necessary to replace them rapidly with lay teachers, school budgets skyrocketed. In 1967, religious sisters, brothers, and priests constituted 58 percent of the teachers in Catholic elementary and secondary schools. By 1983, this proportion had dropped to 24 percent, and by 1990, it was down to less than 15 percent. In terms of absolute numbers, religious staff in the schools declined from 94,000 in 1967 to 20,000 in 1990, a drop of 79 percent.[47]

The demise of vocations also created problems for the religious orders, which had a further impact on schools. Meeting the health-care and retirement needs of religious members suddenly became pressing concerns for individual orders. Younger religious had left in disproportionate numbers, and new vocations were few. The resultant demographic profile of many old and infirm members often forced the religious who remained active to request that their full teaching salary be returned to their order rather than being mostly contributed back to the school, as in the past.[48]

Dioceses also encountered financial problems that affected schools. As the Church sought to embrace the social justice mission decreed by Vatican II, the demands on its resources grew dramatically. Suddenly there were many more social missions to support. This expansion of mission occurred at the same time that diocesan resources were shrinking, a problem linked to the sharp decline in religious vocations. Although dioceses continued to help some inner-city schools serving high numbers of disadvantaged students (in line with the Church's social justice commitment), diocesan support could not be seen as a major solution.

One obvious response to schools' serious financial problems was to raise tuition. In 1967 the average yearly secondary school tuition was $203. By 1980 it had increased about fivefold, to $970, and by 1988 it had almost doubled again, to $1,875. Even so, lay faculty salaries remained very low, with median salaries of about $20,000 in 1988.[49] With the change from a mostly religious to a mostly lay faculty and with the movement of Catholicism and its schools into the real world, the Church was suddenly the target of its own social justice rhetoric. Teachers began calling for a "living wage" for their ministry.

From the perspective of the "institutional balance sheet," therefore, the 1960s and beyond hardly sound like the "Catholic moment." To appreciate the relevance of such statements requires us to look beyond the numbers to the great intellectual and spiritual renewal that washed over Catholic schools after Vatican II. For despite all of its problems, Bishop Carroll's dream of the American Church, engaged in contemporary culture and conveying a vision of what society could and should be, is now actively pursued.

The Intellectual Tradition Undergirding St. Madeline's

Much of the way of life in St. Madeline's of the 1950s had endured with only minor changes since the Council of Trent in the sixteenth century responded to the Protestant Reformation. In some ways, Trent was a renewing activity for the Church. Changes such as the institution of seminaries to enhance the academic and spiritual formation of priests were meant to address abuses of religious life that had prompted much of the Protestant outcry. In addition, however, Trent centralized authority in the papacy and the institutional Church, a movement whose force would continue to grow over the next three hundred years and would nearly strangle the Church in the process.

The three centuries following Trent also saw a profound transformation in Western society. Among intellectuals, the Enlightenment provided the philosophical underpinning for a growing secularism that had begun to emerge with the Renaissance. On a more popular level, the view of human freedom shaped by democratic revolutions in both Europe and America threatened the patriarchal authority of Rome. The Church remained steadfast, nevertheless, continuing to assert its power in response to the "dangers" of modernity. In 1869 the Church convened another council, Vatican I (1869–1870), to address this issue formally.

Vatican I and the Revival of Scholasticism

Some engagement with modernity was evident in Catholicism in the 1800s. As we have seen, the American Church had flirted with democratic ideas during the colonial period. In Europe, a social Catholicism movement was growing among some members of the laity and individual religious in response to the plight of modern man, the exploited worker. The Church, however, did not approach its task at Vatican I with an adaptive mentality. There was nothing renewing about this council, as the Church took a defensive and repressive stance toward the sociopolitical and intellectual threats from the external world. The council affirmed the reigning pontiff, Pius IX, who had declared that "the Pope cannot and should not be reconciled and come to terms with progress, liberalism, and modern civilization."[50] Modernity, not the Church, was the problem. European intellectuals who did not agree were increasingly subject to papal condemnation and their texts often assigned to the Index of Forbidden Books. The Church deemed whole lines of intellectual inquiry and discussion inadmissible and forbade further work.[51]

Vatican I asserted the dogmatic authority of Church teachings, and lest there be residual confusion about Church powers, the council promulgated the principle of papal infallibility. Vatican I aimed to have the Church act as a total institution for its members in order to insulate them from the threats of modern society. In this light, the American Church's position on education, espoused at the third Baltimore Council, that every Catholic child should attend a Catholic school, takes on a particular salience.

Although much of the language of Vatican I drew on Scholastic philosophy, its proclamations actually rested more on this newly decreed papal authority than on reasoned argument. Not until Leo XIII succeeded Pius IX did the Church finally engage the dilemma posed by modernity. Pope Pius IX had relied on his absolute authority to condemn and serve notice; Leo XIII's thrust was more intellectual. The new Pope encouraged a renewed study of the original works of St. Thomas Aquinas, rather than focusing on his interpreters. Although Leo's intent was to employ reason in order to reaffirm the correctness of Church teachings, Neoscholasticism's resort to reason would open the Church to an encounter with modernity and ultimately to change.

Through its new look at the thirteenth-century writings of Aquinas, Neoscholasticism reconnected with Aristotelian thought, which has served as a major intellectual tradition shaping Catholicism through two millennia.[52] St. Thomas supported the Aristotelian ideal of science, whereby many of the mysteries of human life could eventually be revealed through the application of human reason. The ultimate end—"the Kingdom of God"—was, however, unattainable except through faith. Although science and modern scholarship were powerful tools, only religious faith could direct humans toward the proper ends for the individual and society and sustain them through their repeated encounters with their limitations.[53]

Neoscholasticism brought intense scrutiny to modern ideas about relativism, subjectivism, and individualism. Not a romantic longing back to some "golden age," Neoscholasticism offered a rigorous and a coherent synthesis of human nature, society, and God.[54] It sought to recover timeless truths, what it termed Natural Law, to bring these perennially valid principles to bear on the moral dilemmas of the present day. As this scholarship developed, however, an important acknowledgment emerged. The medieval scholasticism of St. Thomas's era was more nuanced than had long been supposed, and was somewhat at odds with the rigidity of Church teachings affirmed at Vatican I.

In opening up a Catholic scholarship that might effect a rapprochement with modernity, Neoscholasticism accomplished a great deal for the Church. The fruits of science and reasoned inquiry could no longer be denied by mere resort to a "higher authority." By drawing on reasoned arguments from Natural Law in articulating the Church's positions on social and personal morality, rather than simply making proclamations based on divine revelation, Catholic teachings became open to examination and debate.

The high point of Neoscholasticism as an intellectual movement in America came with the writings of Etienne Gilson and Jacques Maritain during the second quarter of the twentieth century. Maritain's writings are especially germane here because he focused on the modern implications of Aquinas for a Christian philosophy of education. Although Maritain's ideas took little immediate root in Catholic elementary or secondary schools, they were a shaping influence on Catholic intellectuals of the 1940s and 1950s and now represent a significant background to contemporary Catholic schooling.

Like any philosopher of education, Maritain began with basic premises about the nature of the individual and society.[55] He rejected both the Enlightenment ideal, which places the individual over society, and the totalitarian responses to the excesses of individualism, which gave undue power to the state. Maritain instead offered the concept of "person-in-society"; he argued that efforts to place either of the phrase's components over the other were inherently deficient.

Maritain took care to distinguish his position from that of philosophical liberalism. In particular, he developed the concepts of the person and the common good, contrasting these with liberal beliefs about the individual and the public good. To the liberal, the individual is a physical being with material wants and needs who seeks pleasure and avoids pain. In liberal thought society is secondary to the individual, and is constructed by individuals in order to provide for their desires. While acknowledging physical needs as basic to mankind, Maritain argued that the person is also socially formed, fundamentally connected to humanity, and in common with all humanity has a spiritual life directed toward some good greater than just individual self-aggrandizement.

At the heart of the person, according to Maritain, are two virtues: love and wisdom. Love is essential in the practical order. It guides humans in living together here on earth, it sustains them in times of adversity, and it grounds their hope for the future. Its principal religious symbol is the life of the man called Jesus. Wisdom dominates the intellectual realm. Through it, persons can discern what is of true value and worthy of a human life. This is symbolically represented in the concept of the Kingdom, as the *telos* toward which all human effort should be pointed. Love as the ethical stance toward the other is in turn grounded through wisdom in a teleological view of the true ends of mankind.

Maritain maintained that both of these virtues are intrinsically social, in that they require a community for their formation and maintenance. In this sense, person and society are necessarily bound together. "Society in the proper sense, human society, is a society of persons. A city worthy of the name is a city of human persons. The social unit is the person."[56]

This view of person and society led Maritain to articulate two fundamental principles of the social order. The first is the primacy of the *common good* as the principal aim of society. Such *good* flows back over all persons by virtue of their membership in the *common*. Schooling, for example, was described in the nineteenth century as a common good. These institutions were to form in every citizen those basic intellectual, moral, social, and political dispositions necessary to sustain a free society.

Such common goods are contrasted with public goods, which, while broadly accessible, have benefits that principally accrue to individuals rather than to the common. In the rhetoric now dominant, schooling is seen as a public good. Schools provide services that should be universally available. Individuals acquire education in order to achieve greater individual economic rewards. Society, except as the conduit for distributing these services, has largely disappeared from the conversation. Even the subtle shift in language from "common" schools in the nineteenth century to "public" schools in the twentieth century demonstrates this point.

Maritain's second principle is the preeminence of the contemplative over the practical life. Variants of this idea have often been invoked by the Church to justify its otherworldly orientation. Maritain, however, argued that such narrow interpretations of Scholasticism were simply incorrect. Thomas did not deny the importance of laboring in the world, but rather emphasized that such practical activity must be directed toward some greater end. Maritain used this idea to criticize the role of modern institutions and the instrumental rationality that directed their action. Although scientific understandings were enormously significant practical developments, it was far from certain that emergent technologies based on these understandings would automatically benefit the human community. He argued that a source of prudence, some larger vision of how "man is bound to things divine," is required.

These basic ideas about person and society infuse Maritain's philosophy of education.[57] According to this philosophy, the primary aim of education is the formation of persons. He shared with progressive secular philosophers such as John Dewey the aim of an independent, self-reliant learner. He also argued, however, for the importance of cultural traditions and their transmission through schooling. Man's labor in the world must be directed toward something greater, and envisioning this telos requires a rootedness in tradition. It is difficult to determine where we may want to go, if we don't have a good sense of where we have been and why this is so.[58]

In addition, Maritain maintained that schooling must also shape basic moral dispositions toward justice, courage, a love of beauty, and—foremost—a passion for truth. Maritain was particularly concerned about an emotivist psychology that viewed all human effort as an essentially covert attempt to advance self-interest. In his view, "at the beginning of human action, insofar as it is human, there is truth, grasped or believed to be grasped, for the sake of truth. Without trust in truth, there is no human effectiveness."[59] Maritain worried that if humans abandoned the pursuit of truth as the unifying principle for society and accepted relativism, then everything would devolve into competing interests and ultimately to the dominance of the most powerful.

A European by birth and writing in the 1930s and 1940s, Maritain was naturally concerned about the preservation of democracy and the role of education in that task. He argued that a society of free men implies agreement about the bases of life in common—the dignity of the human person, human rights, equality, freedom, justice, and law—a common consent to what might be called the "democratic charter." The body politic has the right and duty to promote this democratic charter through schooling. On this account, however, Maritain had difficulty with Horace Mann's nondenominational solution. Because public schools can only use practical and instrumental reason to ground these commitments, the teaching of the charter is greatly weakened.[60]

In Maritain's view, democracy requires more than just a self-interested assent: students must come to love it and have a passion for it. Similarly, "those who teach the democratic charter must stake on it their personal convictions, their consciences, and the depths of their moral lives." Quite simply, "No teaching deprived of conviction can engender conviction."[61] But such commitment seems unlikely if the grounds for this commitment are relegated to the private realm.[62] For these reasons, Maritain saw the growing secularization of education as a threat to the common good.

Similarly, Maritain took exception to the increased vocationalism in schooling and argued instead for a classical humanist emphasis. Such education, once the privy of the social elite, is education for democracy and thus should be universal: "Education directed toward wisdom, centered in the humanities, aimed to develop in people the capacity to think correctly and to enjoy truth and beauty, is education for freedom or liberal education.

Whatever his particular vocation may be or whatever special training his vocation may require, *every human being* is entitled to receive such a properly human and humanistic education."[63]

One central theme unifies Maritain's educational philosophy. Every aspect of schooling, from its basic structure and curriculum to the nature of teachers' work and their roles, should be directed toward advancing the common good and should be informed by some larger conception of a properly human social order. This premise in turn rests on a belief in the dignity of each person and in the power and responsibility of education to elevate mankind "toward things divine."

Through scholarship of this sort, Neoscholasticism moved the Catholic Church toward becoming a "public religion," able to engage contemporary social and political problems.[64] Although the monolith of Neoscholastic thought as the authoritative synthesis of the "Catholic position" has now been shattered,[65] its mark remains. Current scholarship employs multiple rationales to ground social action, but these theories all share Neoscholasticism's insistence on the capacity of human reason to arrive at ethical truth, albeit at times a difficult and uncertain process. Similarly, although contemporary Catholic social ethicists may now deny moral negatives ("Thou shalt not . . ."), they continue to affirm the value of moral norms and principles in place of a situational intuitiveness in public and personal life.[66]

Postmodern thinkers increasingly speak of the need to rekindle a sense of social responsibility and public participation in a diverse and pluralistic American life.[67] In the search for a grounding for this renewed social commitment, these two residuals of Neoscholasticism—the capacity of reason to arrive at truth and the need for moral norms and principles in social life—represent an active, vital, coherent Catholic voice in this extended dialogue.

Although selected Neoscholastic scholars such as Maritain, Gilson, Karl Rahner, and John Courtney Murray offered Catholics a way to engage with modernity, the more conventional and doctrinaire interpreters of Thomas wreaked much havoc. Their scholarship reinforced a hierarchical conception of the institutional Church, in which the magisterium would think and the flock would follow. The Church would be *for* the people but surely not *by* the people. Perhaps the most vivid educational symbol of this extreme authoritarianism was the Baltimore Catechism, a precise exposition of the tenets of the faith that first appeared in 1885. Although the cathecism underwent several subsequent revisions, rote memorization of its questions and answers represented, into the early 1960s, the chief means by which children were to acquire faith. Knowing the catechism was *the* faith experience for three quarters of a century. Practicing the faith involved following its rules.

Further, Neoscholasticism's very strengths were also its weakness. Its aggressive resort to intellectualizing faith diminished the common appeal of the Christian message. The rich imagery of the gospels—of the man called Jesus who was the Kingdom and the Light—was replaced by abstract philosophy. In the immediate term, at least, Neoscholasticism distracted many Catholics from the more concrete imperatives of the gospel message to advance human goodness through hope in the vision of the "final Kingdom."[68] Not until Vatican II did the Church firmly reconnect to these social Christian understandings.

The Emergence of Social Catholicism

Throughout the nineteenth century the institutional Church maintained an otherworldly stance that encouraged individual spirituality and withdrawal from the secular world. It remained largely silent about the human problems arising from the industrial revolution. To the extent that these problems received clerical attention, they were viewed principally as occasions for private charity.

Beginning in the mid-nineteenth century, however, some European lay Catholics and individual clerics began to see the "working-class problem" as a structural issue of social justice that required more than individual charity. These "social Catholics" worked to develop a response that balanced the excesses of the two dominant ideologies of the day: economic liberalism, which overemphasized the individual and ignored the moral implication of the relation of capital to labor; and totalitarian socialism, which gave too much control to the state and devalued the dignity of the person.[69] In response to the first excess, social Catholicism argued against the concentration of wealth and echoed Neoscholasticism's priority of the common good. Social Catholics also stressed the need for ethical judgments that transcended an exclusive emphasis on instrumental rationality. In response to the second excess, social Catholicism favored limiting the powers of the state, which should be subservient to fundamental human rights and liberties, especially religious freedom.[70]

Belatedly, the institutional Church responded to the problems of the worker with *Rerum Novarum* (On Capital and Labor). This papal encyclical was the culmination of numerous individual initiatives that, until 1891, had received virtually no leadership from Rome. The evolution of this encyclical as the official expression of the institutional Church exemplifies what is now termed a "prophetic Church": the spiritual force of laypersons and individual clerics imploring that action be taken by established institutions, including the Church itself, on the human dilemmas of the day.

Although a half century later than Karl Marx in addressing the "worker issue," *Rerum Novarum* was the first occasion on which one of the great forces of world order took up this concern. The encyclical used Neoscholastic teachings to argue both for limitations on private property and for the state's duty to enact social legislation to protect workers from the manifest excesses of laissez-faire capitalism. In practical terms, the document supported trade unionism as a means to effect improvements in the conditions of the working class. In general, *Rerum Novarum* moved the Church morally toward socialism while also expressing distrust of its attendant statism, which seemed likely to infringe on religious rights.

The tone of early social Catholicism was distinctly paternalistic, voicing a desire to return to a simpler rural society based on the principle of the medieval guild coupled with an ecclesiastical vision of the integrative parish that took care of its members' needs. It became increasingly apparent, however, that new forms of social arrangements, such as the trade union, would be needed to confront the new problems of economic and social modernity. It was still generally assumed, however, that such new social institutions should be set up and controlled by the Church.[71] Until *Rerum Novarum,* for example, the idea that Catholic workers might be entrusted with responsibility for running social organizations created for their benefit was unheard of. Further, both of Leo XIII's successors, Pius X and XI, reaffirmed the principle of clerical domination in a hierarchically organized Church expounded at Vatican I. The democratization of the Church would have to await Vatican II, when the concept of the Church as a shepherd and his flock finally gave way to the "people of God."

In speaking out about what were increasingly being defined as secular matters, the Church opened a discussion on the nature of Christian democracy. To traditionalists, including Pius X, the concept of a Christian democracy meant reestablishing a Christian state on a popular foundation—that is, a new rationale for the traditional integrated view of church and state. More progressive thinkers saw in Christian democracy the need to disestablish the Church from secular society and embrace an alternative (and more prophetic) conception of Catholicism in relation to the modern world. From this perspective, the Church is separate from, yet actively engaged in, public affairs. It seeks to introduce Christian understandings about social problems to a broad constituency in ways that permit both believers and nonbelievers to work together toward social justice within secular democratic institutions. It is this latter understanding that would eventually be affirmed as Church policy by Vatican II.

Social Catholicism was active in America. Most American Catholics at the turn of the century were from the working classes. If for no other reason than expediency, the Church had to address the social distresses afflicting its members concentrated in the cities. What began as a crusade of charity emphasizing "individual corporal works of mercy" evolved to a broader focus on social justice by 1920. This movement gave rise both to the tradition of the "labor" priest and to new lay-formed and lay-controlled social organizations such as the Catholic Worker.[72]

Although most priests in the early twentieth century engaged in conventional parish work, activist priests also emerged in many cities. Peter C. Yorke was a charismatic example. Born and educated in Ireland, he immigrated to the United States and took up residence in San Francisco. A major actor in resolving the port strike of 1901, Father Yorke supported the strikers. Appealing to the Natural Law arguments set out in *Rerum Novarum,* Yorke contended that organizing labor unions was a human right and not just a pragmatic concession. Opposing Yorke's effort was the archbishop of San Francisco, who sided with the employers. Similar events had occurred in the late 1880s in New York, where labor priests emerged from local parishes but were opposed by a conservative Catholic hierarchy. This period of labor conflicts offers numerous instances of individual action that enlivened the idea of a prophetic Church acting in opposition to established institutional authority.

John Ryan, a native American born of Irish immigrant parents, lent intellectual leadership to the American version of social Catholicism. Ryan used his position as head of the Social Action Department of the National Catholic Welfare Council to awaken the American Catholic conscience to the demands of the social gospel. Ryan, like Yorke, worked in the Natural Law tradition. He elaborated on *Rerum Novarum*'s ideas about natural human rights to articulate a coherent rationale for modern Catholic social ethics. His writings, linking morality to economics, developed the concepts of the living wage, supported organized labor, and argued for state intervention to effect social change. Unlike other activists of the time, Ryan brought these progressive ideas into the institutional Church itself. In the American bishops' 1919 "Program of Social Reconstruction," which Ryan wrote, the American Church officially lined up behind his views. It was such an amazing turn of events that Upton Sinclair called it nothing less than a "Catholic miracle."[73]

In the 1919 program the bishops aligned themselves with a larger Christian social gospel movement that took issue with the policies of established Protestant churches.[74] These institutions, according to their social gospel critics, had too readily embraced existing economic and social arrangements as just and appropriate. In evoking the stance of a prophetic Church, Catholics saw themselves as challenging these Protestant institutions as the proper interpreters of the "true American spirit" of the founding fathers. John Coleman, a Catholic theologian, writes: "Protestantism—it was argued—diluted the indispensable foundation for America. Only Catholics who maintained a steadfast belief in Natural Law could sustain the bedrock on which America rested. They were the last hope against the barbarian cynics who were undermining American institutions by their naturalism, positivism, and utilitarian individualism. Protestants were seen as untrustworthy guardians of the American heritage."[75]

Perhaps most important, the Catholic attitude concerning poverty had shifted. A traditional resignation toward human affliction and injustice as "God's way" was replaced with an active commitment to redress social injustice. Alongside a strong Catholic tradition of devotionalism and personal religion, Ryan had added a public religion. Although previously Catholics had been seen chiefly as opponents to socialism, Ryan helped them articulate their own vision of social reform.

The bishops' program received little attention in the 1920s, an economic prosperity distracted society from concerns about structural social problems, but the seeds of an American Catholic social ethics planted by Ryan grew over the next several decades. Broadening beyond labor organizing, Catholic social action gradually came to focus on poverty, housing, and racial justice. The 1920s, moreover, saw the emergence of a movement that would loom large in the future—an articulate lay Catholic middle class began taking the initiative for the expanded social gospel.

Best known among the lay activists were Peter Maurin and Dorothy Day, who founded the Catholic Worker movement.[76] Like other less prominent groups, such as Friendship House and Grail, this new organization crystallized around particular human needs, rather than individual parishes, and was run not by the clergy but by resourceful, educated, and independent-minded lay Catholics. Because groups like the Catholic Worker—which provided a newspaper, soup kitchen, shelter, and social support for indigents—were often unresponsive to Church directives, they received no support from the institutional Church. Their leaders were nonetheless active Catholics pursuing the spirit of the social gospel.

A radical Catholic scholarship also grew during the 1920s and 1930s.

Prominent in this work was Paul Hanley Furfey. Trained in social science, Furfey came to reject its instrumentalism as inadequate for bringing about social reform. In *Fire on the Earth,* he argued that the inspirational power of religion was needed both to envision social reform and to change the "hearts of men" to act toward it.[77] While not opposing the efforts of Ryan and others to use Natural Law arguments to change existing social arrangements, Furfey instead took his inspiration from the gospel message. Directing one's effort toward advancing the Kingdom of God implied a radical incompatibility with existing mores and social institutions. Jesus was a social agitator, so social Christianity must be an oppositional movement. Much of the spirit of modern-day liberation theology is grounded in this view.

Furfey's response, in the idea of Christian personalism, was a call to live the life of Christ, to love one's neighbor as oneself.[78] He focused not on large-scale institutional change but on the humane qualities of the hundreds of daily, mundane, face-to-face social interactions that make up human life. Such personalist action is effective, Furfey argued, through the influence it has on others. True social change requires the spiritual force of individuals personally engaging one another, with genuine human caring infusing these encounters.

The organizational complement to Christian personalism was an emphasis on the principle of subsidiarity. Human meaning derives not from bureaucratic structures but from small voluntary associations constructed around the soft and fragile institutions of family, school, neighborhood, and workplace. These institutions act as buffers between the individual and an impersonal, bureaucratic society. The myriad opportunities afforded for human engagement shape a sense of personhood and nurture communal values. Such existing institutions need to be cultivated and new ones need to be promoted. At root here is a theory of social change that contends that "if people cannot be mobilized in the small wood of their neighborhood, they will not be mobilized in the large."[79]

Furfey also saw this social mission as being nurtured by a religious interiority. Participation in the Mass was a powerful symbolic activity. This social context brought people together around the central symbol of personalism, Christ, whose life and death direct all human effort toward advancing the Kingdom of God. There was a role for private contemplation as well. Furfey saw value in planned times for private reflection on daily events in the light of Catholic beliefs.

Active, committed social Catholics such as Dorothy Day and Paul Furfey were a small minority, often scorned by the official Church throughout the first half of this century. Papal encyclicals instead encouraged a devotional Catholicism based on one's private relationship with God. This vertical religion was manifested through devotions to the Black Virgin, Our Lady of Fatima, the Bleeding Heart of Jesus, and various saints. Indulgences, novenas, and religious feasts were encouraged, all under strong clerical direction. Not until the 1960s did Vatican II rebalance the nature of faith toward a horizontal religion that emphasized the responsibility of Catholics to advance social justice in the world and that found the essence of people's faith experience in their social connectedness to those around them.

Although far from widespread, American social Catholicism in the first fifty years of this century helped prepare the ground for a renewed Catholicism. With the Vietnam War, Catholics moved to the forefront of the reform movement. At the highest level of government, the moral exhortations of two active Catholics, Robert Kennedy and Eugene McCarthy, influenced Lyndon Johnson's decision not to run for reelection in 1968. On the intellectual front, Thomas Merton contributed as a major force in the peace movement. And in the streets, Philip and Daniel Berrigan continued the tradition of the labor priests, giving personal witness for social justice and peace. This largely grass-roots activity provided inspiration for renewing the institutional Church as Vatican II emerged.

The Message of Vatican II

It was to universal surprise that Pope John XXIII, within three months of being elected Pope, announced his intention to convene a second Vatican Council. Described as an ecumenical council, Vatican II brought together over 2,500 bishops from around the world to deliberate in intermittent sessions between 1962 and 1965. The end result of their efforts was nothing short of revolutionary, profoundly affecting virtually every aspect of Catholic life. Vatican II has been aptly described as a paradigm shift from medievalism to postmodernity in the images of the Church and its relationship with the world.[80]

Pope John characterized the council's task as one of *aggiornomento,* an updating or reviving of the Church to heed the "signs of the times" and at last to encounter the modern world. His call was answered in one of the major documents of Vatican II, the pastoral constitution *The Church in the Modern World,* formally known by its opening phrase, *Gaudium et Spes.* Its stirring message of engagement with society began: "The joys and hopes, the griefs and the anxieties of the men of this age, especially those who are poor or in any way afflicted, these too are the joys and hopes, the griefs and anxieties of the followers of Christ. Indeed, nothing genuinely human fails to raise an echo in their hearts. For theirs is a community composed of men. United in Christ, they are led by the Holy Spirit in their journey to the kingdom of their Father and they have welcomed the news of salvation which is meant for every man. That is why this community realizes that it is truly and intimately linked with mankind and history."[81] Coming from a Church that for centuries had directed human attention to otherworldly concerns and had often viewed those not of the faith as its mortal enemies, such a statement was remarkable.

At the outset of the council, in a dramatic gesture further symbolizing the outreach of the Church, the assembled bishops addressed a message to all humanity. Identifying themselves as "coming together in unity from every nation under the sun," the bishops called on all people to join them in building a world where peace and justice would prevail.[82] To Protestants, from whom Catholics had been separated for over four hundred years, the ecumenical invitation was even more explicit: come to Rome and participate in the *aggiornomento*.

Over its three-year history, the council produced two major constitutions for the Church—one dogmatic and one pastoral—and fourteen other constitutions, decrees, and declarations.[83] These documents literally transformed the very foundations of Catholicism. Reinterpreting its tradition, the Church pursued two broad purposes: to renew its own institutional life and to involve itself in what Pope John had termed the "spiritual crisis of the modern world."

Some of the documents, such as the *Constitution on the Sacred Liturgy,* had immediate, highly visible effects. The Latin Mass ended, priests came down from the altar and joined the congregation, members of religious orders abandoned medieval garb for modern dress, statues and private devotionalism virtually disappeared as the hallmark of Catholic faith. Other proclamations, in particular *The Church in the Modern World, The Constitution on Divine Revelation,* the declarations on *Religious Freedom, Christian Education,* and *Non-Christian Religions,* and the decrees on *Ecumenism* and on the *Apostolate of the Laity* worked their effect more slowly, but no less profoundly. It is in these texts, and in the human effort they catalyzed, that the guidance for the social transformation of St. Madeline's from 1955 to the present day can be found.

Given the scope of the council's effort and the sheer number of people involved, it is not surprising that subsequent scholarship about Vatican II has uncovered textual ambiguities and unresolved conflicts between conservative and liberal positions. These ambiguities and conflicts are very much present in Church discussions today. Even so, the council spoke unequivocally on five themes:[84] the commitment to *aggiornomento;* a changed concept of Church organization from hierarchical and institutional to the communal imagery of the "people of God"; an affirmation of religious freedom, ecumenism, and dialogue with other religions; an emphasis on the social mission of the Church; and a heightened focus on Jesus as the central figure in a renewed attention to the Bible as the Word of God.

Aggiornomento as adaptation. Vatican II rejected the hostility and suspicion toward the modern world that had characterized Catholicism in the nineteenth and early twentieth centuries. Recognizing that science and modern humanism had spawned many valuable social and technical developments, the Church affirmed their vital role in moving into the future. While Catholic heritage was of great value in this "pilgrimage," the Church should not be allowed to become a museum piece. Rather than focusing on a God-given eternal order, Vatican II encouraged human efforts toward the Kingdom of God on Earth and articulated a new role for the Church in supporting and guiding this work.

In a related vein, the Church also affirmed itself as an organically developing entity. The classicist mentality that had dominated Church thinking since the Protestant Reformation and had been especially reinforced at Vatican I—that the Church moved through history more or less unaffected by it—gave way to the view that religion must "change to meet the needs of the times." In invoking the image of a "pilgrim Church," Vatican II rejected the notion of Catholicism as a pure and perfect institution. Rather, the Church is a human institution for which continued reformation is needed.

Even more revolutionary, the spirit of reformability applied to dogma itself. Although the basic tenets of the Christian faith address enduring human values and, as such, are immutable, the concepts and imagery in which they are expressed have a historicity. If this historicity is not acknowledged and the concepts and symbols themselves are not periodically renewed, the Catholic faith will eventually become irrelevant.[85]

The Church as the "people of God." The concept of the Church as an unequal society, hierarchically organized under strong clerical control, gave way at Vatican II to new imagery. Authoritarian decision making at each level of Church hierarchy—the Pope toward his bishops, the bishops with their pastors, and pastors with their congregations—was replaced by a commitment to dialogue and collegiality at every level and between levels. Lay members of the Church were encouraged to assume leadership in Church affairs—"to exercise their Apostolate both in the Church and in the world, in both the spiritual and temporal order," and to speak freely and openly—"let it be recognized that all the faithful, clerical and lay, possess a lawful freedom of inquiry and thought."[86] Although differences in the competence of individuals were acknowledged, no class of individuals or set of topics was excluded from these two prescriptions.

This commitment to debate and freedom of dissent was characteristic of the council from its very first deliberations.[87] By its conclusion in 1965, the demise of papal absolutism was clearly set. Since the council, many new democratic institutions have emerged to establish these commitments, including synods of bishops, episcopal conferences, and parish, regional, and national councils. Democratization of the Church had, in fact, typified the American agenda beginning with Bishop Carroll in the early 1800s, and was rekindled in the efforts of Ireland and Gibbons later in that century. Although these first two efforts at effecting a new structure for the American Church and facilitating engagement with secular society were rejected by Rome, Vatican II finally accepted the American agenda as the Church's agenda.

Affirmation of religious freedom and ecumenism. For centuries, both Catholics and Protestants had sought to gain control of the apparatus of civil power to effect an integration of church and state. With the *Declaration of Religious Freedom,* Vatican II formally repudiated this idea. The declaration definitively affirmed the separation of church and state as appropriate to the modern world. This separation is philosophically linked with the new conception of the Church as the people of God. In rejecting institutional control over secular affairs, the Church embraced a more prophetic image of its relationship to the modern world: critically engaged in culture, yet also sufficiently removed from it to be willing and able to scrutinize existing social arrangements on the basis of Catholic tradition and heritage.

This declaration was another major contribution of the American Church to deliberations of the council. Its principal proponent was John Courtney Murray, an American Jesuit, who with support from the American bishops (in particular Cardinal Spellman of New York) pushed the document through the council. So controversial was the idea that Murray's opponents had initially managed to bar him from the council.

In addition to affirming the wisdom of the principle of the separation of church and state, the Council also affirmed tolerance for all faiths and rejected any coercion in the sphere of beliefs. The concept of faith as a free choice made over time by an informed, educated conscience replaced the spirit of indoctrination into the mind of the Church, which had been enacted through such instruments as the Baltimore Catechism. The emphasis on universalism that had dominated the Church since the middle ages and was vividly symbolized in the Latin Mass was replaced with an appreciation for the differences among regions and cultures. For the Church to function vitally in the modern world, Catholics in each nation must retain the ability to express Christ's message in ways that are meaningful to them. Here again the American experience, in its 150-year struggle to be one Church embracing many cultures, proved formative in the council's deliberations.

This new respect for pluralism within the Church was carried forward and further broadened in the *Decree on Ecumenism* and the *Declaration on Non-Christian Religions*. After centuries of hostility and sometimes armed conflict, the Church expressed a newfound reverence for the heritage of other Christians, and anathema gave way to dialogue. A corresponding shift occurred in attitudes toward non-Christian religions. Considerable common ground exists among faiths, as each encounters the shared concern of relating religious understandings to modern, secular life. In the spirit of ecumenism, the council proclaimed: "The ties which unite the faithful are stronger than those which separate them. Let there be unity in what is necessary, freedom in what is doubtful, and charity in everything."[88] The days of Crusades and inquisitions, and even the Index of Forbidden Books, seemed very far away.

The social mission of the Church. Since the Reformation, the Catholic Church had viewed its mission primarily as preparing the faithful for eternal life, emphasizing a personal religion with an omnipotent God in heaven. As such, Catholicism was vertical, individualistic, and otherworldly in its focus. Beginning with *Rerum Novarum* and followed forty years later by the encyclical *Quadragesimo Anno* (On the Reconstruction of the Social Order), the Church had begun a commitment to social justice based on Natural Law. The force of this commitment came fully forward at Vatican II, as the Church articulated peace and social justice as the central concerns in carrying out the life of Christ. Rather than a primary emphasis on the hereafter, the Council emphasized that God was immanent in humankind and revealed through its development. As human society moves inexorably toward the realization of the Kingdom of God, the pursuit of peace and social justice is God's work on earth.

This revitalized social mission had important implications for American Catholic schools. As American Catholics had moved in great numbers into the middle class, the last vestiges of the ghetto Church had crumbled in the early 1960s. With this, questions naturally arose about maintaining a separate Catholic school system, given that its traditional mission—protecting and nurturing immigrant Catholics in a hostile new world—was apparently accomplished. In the council's commitment to the pursuit of social justice, however, a renewed sense of purpose would blossom in Catholic schools.

Scriptural inspiration and the Word of God. In each of the major developments from Vatican II, the Church engaged critical concerns about its internal organization and its relationship with the modern world. In reemphasizing the Scriptures and the life of Christ, Vatican II found the antidote to the arcane legalism and excessive devotionalism that had developed in the Church over five centuries. As we have seen, Neoscholasticism left two important legacies for the Church: a belief in the capacity of human reason to arrive at ethical truth and an affirmation of the place of moral norms and principles in public and personal life. In reaffirming the inspirational quality of the Bible, Vatican II recovered a third great strength in addressing modernity: a deep sense of the power of the symbolic as an integrative force in human life.[89]

In returning to the inspiration offered by the life of Christ, the Catholic Church recovered its soul. In tending to the least of God's creatures, Christ served as a model for all Christians. In his revelation of a Kingdom to come, he provided a vision of a social life toward which all human effort should be pointed. In his death and resurrection, he offered enduring hope for mankind, despite suffering, setback, pain, and struggle. Here were ideals worth adopting, images that motivated personal effort toward the pursuit of the greater good.

The Effect of Vatican II on American Catholic Schools

Defining a new and important role for Catholic schools in modern society, Vatican II issued a specific statement on schooling, *The Declaration on Christian Education.* Its humane language sharply reversed the austere and doctrinaire tone of most earlier commentaries on education. Calling for a new school environment "enlivened by the spirit of freedom and charity," the council urged these institutions to act as the "leaven of the human community." Consistent with its embrace of pluralism, the council assigned the task of discerning the implications of its teachings for renewal of schools to episcopal conferences—national meetings among the bishops.

Following this directive, the National Conference of Catholic Bishops (NCCB) in the United States developed a number of statements. *To Teach as Jesus Did,* an important NCCB directive in 1972, fleshed out the council's theme of active, publicly engaged schools. The document articulated a threefold educational ministry: to teach the message of hope contained in the gospel; to build community "not simply as a concept to be taught, but as a reality to be lived"; and "service to all mankind which flows from a sense of Christian community." Schools were thus instruments of social justice that would embody this commitment in every detail of their educational philosophy.

This call to social justice involved confronting America's most important social issue—racism. Although Catholic organizations such as Friendship House had been actively engaged in combating racial injustice for decades, the Church had been relatively complacent about segregation. Particularly in urban areas, the Church's response to this matter became a test of the spirit of Vatican II. Forced busing plans in largely Catholic cities increased interest in Catholic schooling among ethnic whites. At the same time serious financial difficulties were emerging for Catholic schools that higher enrollments could help to solve. Although it stumbled momentarily, the Church moved firmly and aggressively, in many cases against its own members, in resisting a tide of racially motivated enrollments. The bishops would not allow Catholic schools to become havens for separatists and racists.[90]

In addition to resisting "white flight," Catholic schools also sought to redress racial injustice directly. St. Madeline's is a case in point. Despite migration of its traditional clientele to the suburbs, the school chose to remain in Los Angeles and to serve an increasingly non-Catholic and nonwhite population. This general recommitment to urban education occurred even though the religious orders no longer had the sisters needed to staff their far-flung array of schools. Economic logic dictated closing all fast-emptying inner-city institutions, where service needs were great and financial resources few, in favor of maintaining suburban schools, but often this course was not followed. Although many inner-city schools did close, both dioceses and individual religious orders allocated their human and fiscal resources disproportionately toward keeping these institutions open. Deserting the poor and serving a more affluent clientele would be a counterwitness to the gospel.

The number of religious staff continued to decline and the financial pressure on all Catholic institutions (especially schools) continued to grow during the 1970s, but the commitment to the disadvantaged remained firm. In 1979, the Conference of Bishops declared in *Brothers and Sisters to Us:*

> We urgently recommend the continuation and expansion of Catholic schools in the inner cities and other disadvantaged areas. No other form of Christian ministry has been more widely acclaimed or desperately sought by leaders of various racial communities. For a century and a half the Church in the United States has been distinguished by its efforts to educate the poor and disadvantaged, many of whom are not of the Catholic faith. That tradition continues today in—among

other places—Catholic schools, where so many Blacks, Hispanics, Native Americans, and Asians receive a form of education and formation which constitutes a key to greater freedom and dignity. It would be tragic if today, in the face of acute need and even near despair, the Church, for centuries the teacher and guardian of salvation, should withdraw from this work in our own society. No sacrifice can be so great, no price can be so high, no short-range goals can be so important as to warrant the lessening of our commitment to Catholic education in minority neighborhoods.

In addition to encouraging a presence in disadvantaged communities, the legacy of Vatican II also heightened sensitivity about tacit assumptions embedded in daily school life. In drawing on Neoscholasticism, but now with a modern face, the American bishops embraced the educational philosophy of "person-in-community":[91] "The educational efforts of the Church must therefore be directed to forming persons-in-community; for the education of the individual Christian is important not only in his solitary destiny, but also to the destinies of the many communities in which he lives."[92]

This theme of community appears even more strongly in the first post-council document on schools to emanate from Rome, the 1977 statement *The Catholic School.* Its first sentence acknowledges the important role of Catholic schools in the Church's mission as redefined at Vatican II: "Catholic schools aim at forming in the Christian those particular virtues which will enable him to live a new life in Christ and help him to play faithfully his part in building up the Kingdom of God." The Catholic school, organized as a community, is an "irreplaceable source of service to society." Mirroring the mission of the Church, the fostering of community in the Catholic school "is undertaken seriously as working for the building up of the Kingdom of God."[93]

Resolving the question of how the Catholic school ought to function as an agent of religious formation is a critically important element of this document. Prior to Vatican II, religious teaching was almost exclusively didactic, conveying the "deposit of faith" as represented by the catechism. In its most routinized form, instruction was painfully close to indoctrination. In *The Catholic School,* a broader conception of religion permeates school life. To be sure, religion should continue to be taught systematically, but the recommended methods and instructional aims are now quite different. Replacing a declarative transmission of facts, the new approach invites students to engage in a tradition of systematic thought about man, society, and the ultimate purpose of human existence. Reflecting critically on the personal life of Christ plays a central role in this education and illumines important moral questions particularly salient for adolescents striving to discern their place in the world.

The Catholic School also reminds its readers that the Church's commitment to pluralism implies that all teaching should be sensitive to the diverse culture that students bring. As such, schools ought to be welcoming places for such groups as blacks, who are often non-Catholic. When combined with an ethos of "freedom in what is doubtful and charity in everything," the spirit of *The Catholic School* invites not submission but dialogue and encounter. Similarly, *The Catholic School* signals that all aspects of school structure, policies, and daily life provide occasions for Christian personalism. Each encounter offers a teaching moment that can shape students' understandings about "who we are" and "how we should live." Such personalism carries over into the adult work organization for teachers as well, affirming a spirit of dialogue and collegiality as the basis for meaningful work.

THE INTELLECTUAL heritage of the contemporary Catholic school is a rich blend of Neoscholastic principles that are lightened with a humane spirit and deepened with a symbolic richness that was reclaimed at Vatican II. Catholic schools maintain a steadfast belief in the capacity of human reason to arrive at ethical truth. Developing each student's intellectual capacities to ascertain such truth and honing a critical disposition in pursuing it constitutes the central academic purpose of these schools—a purpose common for all students, regardless of their origins or vocational plans.

The dignity of the person rooted in community is also reaffirmed. Through immersion in Catholic religious tradition, the school seeks to develop students' views of life aims to be pursued. Through sharing a common life infused with the symbols and rituals of community, hope for the future and active commitments toward humanity and social solidarity are encouraged.

To be sure, this ethical vision represents an ideal, and reality can be quite different. Our focus in the remainder of this book is on probing this reality. Yet to comprehend contemporary Catholic high schools, one needs to appreciate the mission toward which they are directed and the traditions on which they draw. On any particular occasion, schools, staffs, and students often fall short of these inspirational aims. Nevertheless, these ideals are very much alive—a voice of conscience—in contemporary Catholic schools, offering standards against which actions are judged and shortcomings marked.

❖ 2 ❖

Research Past
and Present

RELATIVELY LITTLE was known about the operation of Catholic high schools as we began our research in the early 1980s. A plethora of commissions, task forces, and individuals investigated the condition of American education (especially secondary education) in the first half of the decade, declared it grossly inadequate, and made many recommendations for its improvement. Catholic schools, however, were seldom included in these investigations. The omission is curious, because many of the recommendations being advanced for the reform of public schools in the early 1980s had actually existed in Catholic schools for some time. Increasing academic course requirements for graduation, community service programs, and extending more control to individual schools, teachers, principals, and parents, for example, were already all common practices in Catholic high schools.

This study seeks to provide empirical evidence on Catholic school organization and its effects. We see this research as an opportunity to extend our knowledge about what makes a good school.[1] Although there are many comparisons of public and Catholic schools in the analysis, our purpose is not to offer critical assessments of the relative worth of these two school types. Rather, we believe that a comparison of alternative organizational forms may help us better understand how various features of school operations contribute to school life.

This chapter introduces our empirical inquiry of Catholic schools. We describe the initial ideas we brought to the project and how we have organized our empirical investigations. We also provide basic information on the seven Catholic high schools that we have studied in depth, and general facts about Catholic high schools that we have drawn from national data sources.[2]

Prior Research on School Effects

Equality of Educational Opportunity, written by James Coleman and others and published in 1966, introduced what came to be called "input/output studies" of school effectiveness. The Coleman report was one of the first large nationwide surveys to measure both educational inputs—consisting of school, family, and student characteristics—and educational outputs, conceived primarily as academic achievement as measured on standardized tests. This research and much of the work that built on it was based on human capital theory, which suggests that an investment in education can promote economic development by increasing the "value" of individuals. The focus on school resources such as staff/child ratio, salary schedules, and number of books in the library had a distinctly economic bent, as did the choice of the input/output model itself.

Educators were disappointed by the results of this research, which concluded that academic achievement was determined more by family background than by school facilities and resources. These findings were subject to considerable debate, but further analyses failed to yield substantially different conclusions.[3] An important and enduring consequence of Coleman's work, however, was to redefine a central educational issue: achieving equality in *outcomes* assumed priority over equal access to educational resources. Influenced by these findings, research on educational equity gradually moved away from scrutiny of the equality of available educational resources toward a focus on the distribution of the outcomes of education and the factors believed to affect those outcomes.

From the point of view of most professional educators, more resources are by definition highly desirable. Resources, however, serve only as means for addressing more central concerns: curriculum, the amount and quality of instruction, selection and maintenance of a talented and committed faculty, providing a positive environment to shape student life, and institutional leadership. As educational research in the 1970s and early 1980s began to focus on these variables, certain attributes associated with effective public schools were identified. These findings were relatively consistent across diverse contexts and research methods.

The large body of research on effective schools, though generally weak in methodological terms, offered some sensible and rather compelling conclusions.[4] This research concentrated first on identifying especially effective schools for disadvantaged students, and then attempted to isolate characteristics that those schools shared. Key features included strong administrative leadership, orderly school climate, high expectations set by teachers for students' performance, an emphasis on the acquisition of basic skills, frequent evaluation of student progress, a high proportion of time spent on instruction, and a conscious effort to create a school environment, or ethos, that incorporated these elements. In addition, effective schools appeared to have leaders who protected or buffered their faculty from administrative details, intrusive external forces, and disruptive student behavior, and thus allowed teachers to concentrate on instruction. More recently, teacher participation in school decision making and parent involvement have been added to this list of descriptors of effective schools.

Over the course of the 1980s, research on the effectiveness of Catholic schools began to appear.[5] James Cibulka and colleagues reported in 1982 on an examination of inner-city private elementary schools, most of which were Catholic.[6] They concluded that the effectiveness of these schools derived from strong institutional leadership, the shared values of the staff about the purposes of the school, a safe and orderly environment, and a clarity of mission and purpose. Cibulka and his colleagues, who gathered only limited data on student achievement, based their conclusion primarily on parents' reports about school quality and their reasons for choosing Catholic schools.

Two other important books published in 1982—*High School Achievement: Public and Private Schools,* by James Coleman, Thomas Hoffer, and Sally Kilgore, and *Minority Students in Catholic Schools,* by Andrew Greeley—proved both seminal and controversial.[7] Coleman, Hoffer, and Kilgore concluded that Catholic schools, in comparison with public schools, produced higher cognitive achievement; that they were less racially segregated; and that variation across students in patterns of achievement was much less dependent upon family background. Greeley's results were in some ways even more powerful. Analyzing the same data base used by Coleman and his colleagues (and the same data base employed in most analyses in this book), Greeley claimed that not only was the achievement of minority students in Catholic schools greater than that of minority students in public schools, but that these differences were greatest for the most disadvantaged youth—students from poor families, those whose parents had a limited education, and those enrolled in nonacademic curricular programs. There was now a body of empirical evidence that the achievement of students in Catholic high schools was less dependent on family background and personal circumstances than was true in the public sector, which led Coleman and his colleagues to conclude that contemporary Catholic schools better approximated the common school ideal. We refer to this hypothesis as the "common school effect."

The conclusions drawn by Coleman, Hoffer, Kilgore, and Greeley were quickly and strongly challenged by a number of social scientists and educational policymakers. That Coleman and his colleagues chose to interpret their empirical findings as providing evidence favoring federal support for tuition tax credits and educational vouchers intensified the debate. Whole issues of the *Harvard Educational Review* and *Sociology of Education* were dedicated to the controversy.[8] Most of the scientific arguments revolved around methodological limitations associated with the *High School and Beyond (HS&B)* data base used both by Coleman and his colleagues and by Greeley. In particular, the initial data from *High School and Beyond* consisted of a single cohort of sophomores and seniors. Without longitudinal data to track experiences and progress of a group of students over time, it is very difficult to draw clear inferences about the effects of schools on student learning. Even in the absence of a controversial political debate, scientific arguments about the validity of the findings were inevitable.

Yet with the release of the first longitudinal information from *High School and Beyond,* the debate continued.[9] All participants concurred that this was a far better source of information for comparing the relative effectiveness of Catholic and public schools, but beyond this the consensus quickly broke down. Even if researchers agreed about the likely size of the Catholic school effects (that is, differences in two-year gains between Catholic and public school students), they disagreed about their significance.[10]

The literature can be summarized quite differently depending upon one's ideological orientation. In our judgment, Christopher Jencks has offered the most balanced summary.[11] The accumulated evidence indicates that average achievement is somewhat higher in Catholic high schools than in public high schools, and it also suggests that Catholic high schools may be especially helpful for disadvantaged students.

Curiously, most of the attention throughout this debate focused on claims about mean achievement differences, an emphasis that in part reflects the long-established tendency among social scientists and now some members of the public to conceptualize school effects in terms of average differences.[12] When viewed from a policy perspective, however, the claims about the weaker relationship between family background and academic outcomes in Catholic schools are equally relevant. Advancing the equality of educational opportunity and outcomes has been a major integrating theme for educational policy since the 1960s. Here, apparently, was a set of schools— Catholic secondary schools—in which the "common school effect" was flourishing. Although questions persisted about the magnitude of these effects and the certainty that should be attached to any claim based on *HS&B*

data, at a minimum a closer look at the operation of these schools seemed warranted.

Unfortunately, the research of Coleman, Hoffer, Kilgore, and Greeley provides only limited information about *how* these Catholic school effects might accrue. Comparison of the average outcomes in public and private schools was these researchers' primary focus, and thus the educational variables that they selected for examination were primarily those on which the two types of schools differed. The original Coleman research suggested that school policies concerning order, discipline, amount of homework, and absenteeism played a major role. Adding to this list of explanatory factors, Greeley highlighted the nature of the governance arrangement for the school and the quality of instruction reported by students. Longitudinal investigations singled out academic courses within Catholic secondary schools as another significant factor.[13] Although these findings were highly suggestive, alone they tell us little about the internal organization of Catholic secondary schools. More generally, we learn little about how aspects of school organization may act either to attenuate or exacerbate the relationship between the background that students bring to high school and their subsequent development. Trying to understand these relationships became the primary focus for both our field studies and our statistical analyses.

General Research Approach

The empirical research reported in Parts II–IV includes both original field research in seven Catholic high schools and statistical analyses of a large and representative sample of data on Catholic high schools included in the *High School and Beyond* survey. Part II relies most heavily on the field observations, and Parts III and IV draw more on the survey analyses.

Organization of the Fieldwork

In two waves of fieldwork, in the fall of 1982 and the spring of 1983, a two-person team visited each school for approximately 10 to 12 person days. During the first visit, the team interviewed staff, students, and parents, observed classroom and general school life, and collected extensive documentation on each school. These activities were organized to address concerns in six broad areas: the school's philosophy and mission, the curriculum and academic structure of the institution, the school organization and staffing, the character of student life within the school, finance and governance, and the Catholic character of the school. The first wave of field research focused on what was interesting in each of these six areas, and asked what was really going on in these schools.

We conceived of the initial visits in broad terms and deliberately explored a larger number of issues than we would eventually treat in detail. We drew up our agenda on the basis of the then existing research on effective schools already summarized, our personal knowledge of Catholic schools, and our previous professional experiences in a variety of educational contexts. We also left ample opportunity at this point for those we were studying to influence our research agenda. Because the primary purpose of this first phase of activity was to generate hypotheses about the essential features of Catholic secondary school organization, we looked for distinctive organizational features while also remaining attentive to unspoken clues about values shared and conflicts hidden.

Processing the evidence generated during the first round of field research involved substantial interpretation. Although making such judgments is useful for elaborating general ideas and more specific research propositions, it can exert a biasing influence if not checked against rigorous empirical evidence. A search for this evidence constituted the primary purpose of the second wave of field research. (Descriptive analyses of the *HS&B* data, which we began simultaneously with school visits, also helped in this regard.) Thus the first wave of fieldwork was exploratory, and the second wave more structured. We returned to the field sites in the spring of 1983 with eighteen specific propositions embedded within six general themes.[14] These themes represented our understanding, at that time, of the organization and outcomes of Catholic secondary schools. Had we written a report at that point, the report would have documented these themes. During the second wave of data collection we concentrated on how we could know whether our understanding was correct and what else might be going on that could explain the evidence we had assembled so far.

The instrumentation for the second wave of field study was tailored around this second set of research questions. Our detailed data collection plan consisted of thematic open-ended and structured interviews, questionnaires, classroom observations using a protocol we had developed, and procedures for document review. Every item in this data collection effort was cross-referenced to one or more of the propositions. During the second round of visits, we interviewed approximately 280 participants, observed over 160 classes, and collected almost 2,000 questionnaires from students, teachers, and parents. These data provide an extensive empirical record of our field research.

Survey Research: Analyses of High School and Beyond

The *High School and Beyond* survey, initiated in 1980 by the National Center for Education Statistics, was designed to build on information that had been regularly collected as part of the Center's National Longitudinal Studies (NLS) program, begun in 1972. Unlike the NLS-72 study, in which data were collected only on high school seniors, *HS&B* also included a sample of students who were sophomores in 1980. The longitudinal data on this cohort are particularly valuable to those interested in research on secondary schools, because they provide an extensive source of information on high school experiences and their impact on students.

The base year (1980) design consisted of a two-stage probability sample. At the first stage, a sample of 1,015 American secondary schools was drawn. Within each of the sampled schools, a random sample of 72 students was selected—36 sophomores and 36 seniors. Several types of schools, including Catholic schools and schools with high proportions of minorities, were deliberately oversampled. In addition to the base-year data collection, follow-up studies were conducted biennially through 1986. All data are available on public-use data tapes from the U.S. Department of Education.[15]

Questionnaire data were collected from both individual students and school principals. Students were surveyed extensively on their individual and family background; high school and employment experiences; future educational, employment, family, and career plans; and their attitudes and behaviors concerning school, family, friends, and personal life. Similarly, the school questionnaire covered a wide range of topics, including school resources, programs and policies, student demographic composition, staffing, and principals' perceptions of their students' attitudes and behaviors. Cognitive achievement tests were also administered to students in vocabulary, reading, mathematics, science, writing, and civics.[16]

Most of the *HS&B* analyses reported in this book use information on the student cohort who were sophomores in 1980 and seniors in 1982. The National Opinion Research Center, charged with the actual data collection, achieved a 94.6 percent participation rate for the 1982 follow-up with this cohort. The follow-up survey included many common items with the base-year data collection, enabling researchers to study change from sophomore to senior year in a wide range of student attitudes, behaviors, and academic outcomes.

Our analyses include all Catholic school students in *HS&B* who were enrolled in the same school for both their sophomore and their senior years.

In order to compare results with the public sector, we also drew an 11 percent random subsample of public schools from *HS&B* and the data on all sampled students with these schools. The latter technique produced a public school and student sample of approximately the same size as that for Catholic schools. It also preserved maximum student sample sizes within these schools, a procedure that is particularly important for the analysis in Part III.

In addition to the main *HS&B* data, the *Administrator and Teacher Survey (ATS)* was collected in 1984 and released for public analysis in 1988.[17] This supplement substantially extends the information on the internal organization of schools, especially on teachers' perspectives about the school and the nature of their work. Because these data were collected on a random subsample of only 401 of the 1,015 schools in the original *HS&B* design and were released relatively late in our research, we did not fully integrate them into all of our work. The investigation of communal school organization in Chapter 11, however, does rely on them.

Although some of the individual questionnaire items from *HS&B* were useful as they stood, others were merged with related items to create composite factors. This process of selecting and constructing variables was guided both by the existing research literature on school effects and by propositions developed during the field research. The *HS&B* file that we constructed contained extensive data on student and family background; school characteristics such as social and racial composition, staffing, resources, and climate; students' attitudes and behaviors related to various aspects of schooling; and a broad array of dependent measures, including academic achievement, educational aspirations, and affective and social development. The actual constructs and variables are detailed as they are introduced (see, for example, Figure 8.1 and Table 11.2). Analysis of these data constitutes the primary evidence employed in Chapters 7–11 and provides supporting evidence for most of the other chapters of the book.

The Field Sites

Site Selection

In our field research we sought to examine the diversity among Catholic secondary schools. Seeking coverage of the major geographic areas where concentrations of Catholic schools exist, we selected schools from six different dioceses: Boston, Baltimore (2 schools), Cleveland, Louisville, San

Antonio, and Los Angeles. Four of these are among the twenty largest dioceses in the United States in terms of Catholic school enrollment.

To help us select specific school sites, we asked the superintendent in each diocese to nominate "good schools" that we might visit. In structuring this inquiry, we deliberately offered superintendents a broad definition of "good," including such elements as high student achievement, a range of academic and extracurricular programs, harmonious social relations among a diverse racial and socioeconomic mix of students, emphasis on values and personal development, high student and teacher morale, and a strong religious character. Because we were interested in schools located in different types of communities (urban, rural, and suburban) and with different mechanisms for school governance (religious order, diocesan, and parish or inter-parish), we requested specific nominations in each of these categories. The superintendents suggested a varied group of schools, including several recommended for reasons other than high achievement. They also provided us with descriptive data about each school—tuition levels, percentage of graduates attending college, academic organization, coeducational or single-sex organization, enrollment, and racial and social class composition.

In choosing the final set of schools, we sought contrasting examples in terms of financial health, size, demographic composition, and governance. We looked for affluent schools and schools with a weak resource base; schools ranging in size from 130 to over 1,500; coeducational and single-sex schools; schools with racial composition varying from all white to racially mixed to all black; and schools in which student enrollment was almost exclusively Catholic and schools in which half the students were non-Catholic. We rejected some schools because of their academically elite reputations. We wanted good schools, but not necessarily the best schools. The sample of seven reflects the diversity that is Catholic secondary schooling in America.

The Seven Schools

Table 2.1 provides a summary of selected school features of our field sites. St. Madeline's was detailed in the Prologue. Brief descriptions of the other six schools follow.[18]

St. Richard's is a coeducational, college-preparatory high school located in a middle-class suburb outside of Boston. Housed in modern glass and concrete buildings and surrounded by athletic fields, it resembles a contemporary suburban public high school. At its 1959 opening, a diocesan order

Table 2.1 Overview of schools in field sample

School	Governance	Location	Enrollment	Sex	Year founded	College attendance	Racial composition	Tuition	Religious faculty	Principal
St. Richard's	Diocesan	Suburban Boston	855	Coed	1959	79%	99% White	$1,420	24%	Lay male
St. Frances'	Private	Urban Baltimore	540	Girls	1865	46%	77% White 22% Black	$1,200	42%	Sister
St. Cornelius'	Diocesan	Urban Cleveland	950	Coed	1969	64%	75% White 19% Black 6% Hispanic	$1,050	18%	Priest
St. Madeleine's	Private	Urban Los Angeles	660	Girls	1889	92%	92% Black 6% Hispanic	$1,050 $1,200*	43%	Sister
St. Edward's	Private	Suburban Louisville	1,500	Boys	1864	90%	98% White	$1,450	18%	Brother
St. Peter's	Inter-parish	Urban San Antonio	350	Coed	1927	88%	35% White 28% Black 36% Hispanic	$900	0%	Lay male
Bishop O'Boyle	Private	Rural Maryland	130	Coed	1829; 1972	95%	90% White	$1,950	7%	Priest

*Non-Catholic

of nuns fully staffed St. Richard's. Now a majority of the teachers are lay, and St. Richard's has had a lay principal since 1979. Thirteen sisters from three different orders, three brothers, and one priest complement the lay staff. The religious order that originally opened the school still provides a majority of the sisters, who live in a convent on the school grounds. The total staff numbers fifty-seven, including two administrators, three full-time counselors, two librarians, and fifty teachers. The 1982–83 faculty salaries ranged between $11,000 and $18,000.

St. Richard's enrollment of approximately 1,000 students, drawn from thirty small surrounding communities, is almost all white. The 1983 enrollment, which matches the school's all-time peak in the early 1960s, represents a dramatic increase from the late 1960s, when enrollment fell to 600. Three-quarters of the graduating seniors are typically accepted at small, nonelite, eastern four-year colleges. The average SAT score at St. Richard's are close to the national norm.

St. Frances', a private girls' school in central Baltimore, was founded in 1865 by an order of American sisters. For its first sixty years, St. Frances' provided largely vocational training in dressmaking, fine sewing, embroidery, tailoring, stenography, and business for needy girls between the ages of twelve and twenty-one.

Located in a four-story red brick school building dating back to the nineteenth century, St. Frances' is maintained in its original form, with rich wood paneling and molding, a massive and elegantly carved central staircase, marble fireplaces, and worn pieces of antique furniture in the public rooms. The 1983 school enrollment of 500 represents a decrease of nearly 200 since the mid-1970s. The student population, primarily working-class girls from inner-city Baltimore, is 77 percent white and 22 percent black. The present curriculum emphasizes both college preparation and entry-level employment skills such as typing and data processing. About half of the graduates go to college, most to small, nonelite local schools in the surrounding area. St. Frances' maintains an all-female staff of sixteen sisters, twenty-two laywomen, and a nonteaching sister/principal. The founding order of nuns continues to own and govern the school.

St. Cornelius', a coeducational diocesan high school, serves low-income, working-class families. Located in the oldest Polish-American community in central Cleveland, the school opened as an elementary institution at the turn of the century. As an ethnic parochial school, it served a Polish immigrant and working-class community in a city with several eastern European immigrant populations. Prospering along with the community, St. Cornelius' parish, with its beautiful Gothic church, convent, rectory, elementary school, high school, and grounds, became the central focus of the Polish community in Cleveland.

During the early 1960s, however, many of the small single-ethnic high schools operated by individual parishes began to experience financial and enrollment problems as the families from which they had traditionally drawn their students left the inner city for middle-class suburbs. The diocese was forced to negotiate mergers among individual parishes to form central/ diocesan high schools. The current St. Cornelius' is a consolidation of four different schools.

In the manner in which it is organized, the courses it offers, and the population it serves, the consolidated St. Cornelius' has broken new ground for a Catholic high school. Students from over fifteen different ethnic parishes are now educated on three different campuses in central Cleveland, using buildings vacated as other schools closed. A complicated master schedule of buses and courses links the campuses. A comprehensive range of college-preparatory, vocational, business, special education, and bilingual courses, comparable to those in public urban high schools, is now offered. Another departure from St. Cornelius' former existence as a white ethnic parish school was the decision to serve a nontraditional student population, including blacks and Hispanics. In 1982–83 the school enrolls nearly 1,000 students, 20 percent of whom are not Catholics. The student body includes nearly 200 blacks and 50 Hispanics. Approximately two-thirds of St. Cornelius' graduates seek postsecondary education, most to small, nonelite local institutions.

The staff of sixty-four includes five administrators, four counselors, two librarians, a nurse, a chaplain, and fifty-one teachers. The faculty consists of a priest, eight sisters, twenty-one laywomen, and twenty-one laymen. The diocese, which has assumed control of the school under consolidation, is responsible for choosing the school's principal. The regular school faculty is supplemented by several public school teachers, paid by public funds, who staff the special education program. The latter is one of the few instances in our fieldwork where we observed public and private schools cooperating closely. Annual salaries in 1982–83 ranged between $11,000 and $24,700. The eight sisters, adhering to a salary schedule for women religious issued by the diocese, received $650 a month for their services that year.

St. Edward's, a private boys' school enrolling over 1,500 students, was founded in 1864 by an order of brothers of European origin. Housed on a spacious twenty-four-acre campus on the outskirts of Louisville, the school has continually served a selective, predominantly white, Catholic, middle-class student body. St. Edward's long history and academic reputation has given it a prominent position in the city and state, and the school boasts many leading citizens, politicians, businessmen, and professionals as alumni. Over 90 percent of its graduates go to college, many to elite eastern schools. Graduates' SAT scores average forty to fifty points above the national norm. The school, which regularly produces the highest number of National Merit Scholarship winners in the state, offers twelve advanced placement (AP) courses.

The staff includes five administrators and sixty-eight teachers (including counselors). The 1982–83 faculty consisted of twelve brothers, forty-two laymen, and twelve laywomen. Salaries, comparable to the local public school schedule, ranged from $12,240 to $24,100. The founding order of brothers has continued to own and administer the school under a board of directors that includes both lay and religious members. The school maintains an active and visible development office that contributes substantial fiscal resources to a sound and carefully managed financial base.

St. Peter's, a coeducational inter-parish school located in central San Antonio, serves 350 students from low-income and working-class families. The school's enrollment of approximately equal proportions of blacks, Hispanics, and whites represents a dramatic demographic change from its earlier history, when the student body was mostly white with a few Hispanic students. Over three-quarters of its graduates seek post-secondary education in small, local four-year and community colleges.

Until the mid-1970s, nuns provided the principal staffing for the school. At that point the order consolidated its commitments and redirected its efforts away from education toward community and social service activities. Because of shrinking membership and increasing retirement and medical expenses, the assignment of sisters to St. Peter's declined rapidly, falling to just one sister in 1982. This change has placed great financial pressure on both the school and the parish, as salary costs have skyrocketed to accommodate the increasing numbers of lay faculty. When the parish could no longer support the school, it sought financial assistance from the diocese. By pooling resources with two small neighboring parishes, the diocese transformed St. Peter's into an inter-parish school. Although the immediate financial crisis has been temporarily postponed, the financial condition of the school remains precarious.

St. Peter's offers both general and academic programs, but because of its small size it has a curriculum that is limited in its number of advanced offerings. The total staff includes an administrator, a counselor, a librarian, and eighteen teachers. The teachers—eight laymen and ten laywomen—

earned salaries that ranged between $8,500 and $18,000 in 1982–83. The single sister, who provides nonteaching services as the school's accountant/ treasurer, represents the only religious presence on the campus, where lay faculty teach even religion. At the time of our visit, the school did not have a priest to serve as chaplain.

Because of its precarious financial base, the school's continued survival depends on an extensive subsidy from the surrounding community. This support is attributable in large part to the shared sense that the integrated student body and emphasis on multicultural harmony found at St. Peter's offers an important standard for other institutions in San Antonio.

Bishop O'Boyle—a private, coeducational high school nestled in the rolling countryside of semi-rural Frederick County, Maryland, near the Catoctin Mountains and the Shenandoah and Potomac rivers—traces its history back to 1829, when Jesuit priests founded a literary institute there. Since that time the school has undergone two name changes, three governance changes, and a brief departure from its original mission as a Catholic school.

Shortly after its founding as a Jesuit boys' school, Bishop O'Boyle was converted to a coeducational school staffed and operated by nuns. That governance arrangement continued until 1972, when the school moved from downtown Frederick to a colonial mansion outside the city. The sisters then handed control to a lay board, which subsequently defined the school as a "Catholic institution in origin and traditions but ecumenical in spirit." After a few years of instability in the mid-1970s—when the mission, philosophy, Catholic affiliation, and enrollment appeared to waver— Bishop O'Boyle reverted to a more traditional Catholic coeducational preparatory school structure.

With a lay board and a priest as headmaster, the school currently enrolls 130 mostly middle- and upper-class white students. The curriculum prepares 95 percent of its graduates to enter a variety of public and private colleges on the eastern seaboard, including elite Ivy League schools. Although the school's tuition, almost $2,000 in 1982–83, was the highest of the schools in our field sample, Bishop O'Boyle remains in a precarious financial situation because of its low enrollment. The salaries of lay faculty and the demands of repairing and remodeling a charming but decaying building dating from 1740 add to the school's financial uncertainty. The staff consists of the priest who serves as a teaching headmaster and thirteen lay teachers, four men and nine women. The 1982–83 salaries ranged between $10,000 and $20,000.

★   ★   ★

IN SUM, OUR FIELD sample includes the range of governance structures (private, diocesan, parish), gender groupings (coeducational and single-sex), enrollments (from close to 100 to 1,500), historical traditions (founding from 1829 to 1969), racial composition (from almost all-minority to all-white, with several integrated institutions), academic and social selectivity, religious presence (from almost entirely lay to close to half religious faculty and administration), and financial stability (from precarious to very solid) extant in Catholic secondary schools.

Statistical Profile

We began our examination of the contemporary Catholic high school with two comparative portraits of St. Madeline's. We now seek to enlarge the picture from another vantage point: a statistical profile of Catholic school students, faculty, major resources, and organizational features.[19]

Students

The Catholic school of the mid-1950s was almost exclusively white and typically dominated by a single European ethnic group. Regardless of ethnic group—most frequently Irish, German, Italian, or Polish—students were virtually all Catholic. Over the next three decades, however, enrollment patterns in Catholic schools changed considerably. Of the students enrolled in Catholic secondary schools in 1970, 8.2 percent were members of a minority group; by 1983 the proportion had risen to 17.3 percent and by 1990 to 22.2 percent.[20] During this same period non–Catholic enrollment quintupled, from 2.6 percent to 14.3 percent. The percentage of Hispanics in Catholic secondary schools now exceeds that in the public sector. In aggregate, blacks remain somewhat underrepresented in Catholic schools, largely because only a small proportion of blacks in the United States are Catholic.[21] When religious preference is taken into account in estimating enrollment rates, blacks attend Catholic secondary schools in higher proportions than do whites or Hispanics.[22]

There is a considerable flow of students in both directions between the Catholic and the public sectors, a point on which we expand in Chapter 7. Only about three-fifths of the students in Catholic secondary schools completed grades 1 through 8 in a Catholic elementary school. About one-fifth of Catholic secondary school students enter the sector for the first time at grade 9. The remaining fifth have had a mixture of Catholic and public elementary experience.

A 1983 survey focused on Catholic high schools serving low-income students, institutions where more than 20 percent of the pupils were from families whose income that year was less than $10,000.[23] Such schools, which represent close to 10 percent of all Catholic high schools, are likely to be rather small (under 500 students), are most common in urban areas, and tend to have high percentages of minority and non-Catholic students. Although St. Madeline's is not representative of the entire Catholic sector, neither is it atypical. In virtually any major city, Catholic schools like St. Madeline's, with high proportions of minority students and even a majority of students who are non-Catholic, can be found.

Consider a brief statistical comparison of public and Catholic secondary school students (see Table 2.2). The typical Catholic high school student is likely to reside in a home where the level of parents' education is somewhat higher than that of parents of public school students, and where there are more education-related possessions such as books and typewriters. Catholic

Table 2.2 Comparison of public and Catholic high school students

Descriptor	Public schools	Catholic schools
Average family income, 1982	$27,851	$33,596
Average years of parental education (higher of both)	13.9	14.9
Percentage black	12.2	6.6
Percentage Hispanic	6.3	7.4
Percentage other minorities	2.4	1.4
Percentage Catholic	30.7	89.4
Number of children in household	3.4	3.7
Percentage who attended Catholic elementary school, grades 1–8	3.3	61.0
Percentage of households headed by a single parent	27.6	16.0
Percentage of households with		
Daily newspaper	82.5	90.9
Place for student to study	46.4	53.7
Typewriter	75.6	86.6
Electric dishwasher	56.7	66.9
More than 50 books	86.0	87.4
Calculator	82.3	87.4

Source: Data from *High School and Beyond.*

school students tend to come from somewhat larger families, and the percentage of households headed by a single parent is lower (16 percent versus 28 percent in the public sector).

In general, Catholic high school students are somewhat more advantaged than their public school counterparts. The average family income for Catholic school students in 1982 was $33,596; for the public sector it was $27,851. These average income differences primarily reflect the fact that the very poor (those with family incomes under $10,000) are underrepresented. The majority of Catholic high school students, 58 percent, came from families whose incomes ranged between $10,000 and $30,000. Affluent students, whose family incomes were in excess of $50,000, actually appear slightly underrepresented in the Catholic sector.[24]

The underrepresentation of the very poor in Catholic schools is more manifest at the secondary level. For elementary schools, the social class composition of the two sectors is more similar.[25] A primary explanation for this phenomenon, discussed in Chapter 7, is the higher tuition rates for secondary schools. The higher rates result both from the generally higher costs of secondary education and from differences in the mechanisms for financing Catholic elementary and secondary schools.[26] Our analysis indicates that despite the existence of some financial aid programs for needy students, family income represents a barrier for access to Catholic secondary schools for the very poor.

Overall, the differences between students in Catholic and public high schools on traditional student background measures are not large. Although much has been made of these differences in the controversies surrounding the conclusions offered by Coleman, Hoffer, and Kilgore, for the most part the two sectors serve largely overlapping student populations. The statistics suggest that Catholic high schools educate a very broad cross section of what Arthur Powell and colleagues termed "the unspecial"[27]—students who are neither exceptionally needy nor exceptionally affluent.

Faculty

The changing composition of the school faculty has been a highly visible element in the transformation of Catholic schools since the 1960s. Many schools now have all-lay faculties, and projections suggest that by the turn of the century this will be the norm. The implications of this change are profound, raising questions about both the financial viability of Catholic schools and the continuation of the "Catholic character" of these institutions.

A comparative statistical overview of Catholic secondary school teachers in the early 1980s indicates that these teachers are more likely to be female and less likely to be members of a minority than their public school counterparts (see Table 2.3). Although Catholic school teachers are considerably younger and have less teaching experience, they are as well educated as those in the public sector. Surprisingly, almost 60 percent of Catholic school teachers have had at least one year of teaching experience in public schools. As with students, there seems to be a considerable flow of teachers between public and Catholic schools.

Teachers' salaries represent an important difference between the sectors. In the early 1980s, the public school advantage in starting salaries was about $3,000. The average public school teacher earned $6,000 more than his or her Catholic school counterpart. Although these average salary differences in part reflect the greater length of tenure of the average teacher, they also result from the relatively low levels at which Catholic school salaries top off. In fact, the greatest difference between public and Catholic school salaries occur in the salaries of the most experienced teachers.

Even though these summary statistical data may hide some important qualitative differences, nonetheless they do allow us to see that Catholic school teachers today are different from what we know of their 1950s counterparts. In general, there are many more lay teachers, they are better educated, and they are much more likely to have had teaching experience

Table 2.3 Comparison of public and Catholic high school faculties

Descriptor	Public schools	Catholic schools
Percentage minority	8.4	5.4
Years experience	17.4	12.4
Percentage new teachers	2.5	4.3
Percentage male	62.0	47.0
Percentage under age 35	26.0	42.0
Percentage with advanced degrees (masters and beyond)	49.6	51.8
Average starting salary, 1982 (bachelor's degree)	$14,045	$11,121
Average salary, 1982	$22,667	$16,325

Sources: For percentage minority, percentage under age 35, average starting salary, and average salary: NCEA (1985), 38ff. For years experience, percentage new teachers, and percentage with advanced degrees: *High School and Beyond.* For percentage male: Lee and Smith (1990).

in the public sector. They are neither poorly trained nor "culturally isolated," terms often used in the past to describe the staff in Catholic schools.

School Characteristics

The largest concentration of Catholic high schools is in the New England and Middle Atlantic states, where 35 percent of these institutions are located. Catholic high schools are also quite prevalent in the Great Lakes area (26 percent) and the Pacific coastal states (16 percent). There are few Catholic schools in the South, except in urban areas such as Miami, New Orleans, and San Antonio. The same is true for the Rocky Mountain states.[28]

Most Catholic high schools are urban; 61 percent are located in cities with more than 100,000 inhabitants. Less than 18 percent of Catholic high schools are found in small towns and rural areas. Twenty-two percent of the schools are located in areas where more than a quarter of the local population is black, and 15 percent of the schools are in areas where more than a quarter of the residents are Hispanic.[29] Many Catholic schools, however, tend to draw students from a fairly wide geographic area. Although 14 percent of students live within walking distance of the school, 21 percent commute from more than ten miles away.

Although the data in Table 2.2 indicate that there are substantial proportions of minorities and economically disadvantaged students in Catholic schools, they do not indicate how these students are distributed across schools. The system could, for example, be highly stratified, with minorities and the poor isolated from their more advantaged counterparts. Coleman and his colleagues found just the opposite, however. Minorities are more evenly distributed among Catholic schools than within the public sector. The same pattern holds true for family income.[30] The typical Catholic school is more internally diverse with regard to race and income than the typical public school. Although there are individual exceptions, any global characterization of the Catholic sector as racially or economically segregated is ill-founded.

In terms of their physical plant, Catholic secondary school facilities are relatively new. Of the high school buildings currently in use, less than 5 percent were erected prior to 1900, and 18 percent were built between 1901 and the onset of the Great Depression in 1929. School construction proceeded slowly between 1930 and the end of World War II, with only 6 percent of current facilities having been erected during this period. School construction projects revived during the postwar baby boom, when 32 percent of current facilities were built. Construction peaked in the early 1960s, during which another 32 percent of current facilities were built. Half of all facilities currently in use were completed after 1956. Few, however, have been built since 1970.

The typical secondary school is reasonably well equipped with core academic resources (see Table 2.4). Virtually all schools have libraries with a number of volumes that compares favorably with libraries in public schools of similar size. Other common facilities include a computer resource center; biology, chemistry, and physics laboratories; audiovisual facilities; an art room or studio; and a chapel. Resources for vocational education, however, present quite a different picture. Most schools have a typing center, but almost none have specialized skill facilities in such areas as wood or metal shop.

Data on staff resources in public and Catholic secondary schools during the early 1980s indicate that teaching resources are rather similar between the two sectors (see Table 2.5). The student to teacher ratio is 18 to 1 in Catholic secondary schools, 16 to 1 in public high schools. Bigger differences between the sectors occur for specialized staff such as remedial teachers and psychologists. These positions, as well as teacher aides and other support staff, are much less common in Catholic than in public schools.

These data reveal a major organizational difference between Catholic and public secondary schools. The internal structure of the typical Catholic

Table 2.4 Specialized instructional facilities in Catholic high schools

Facility	Schools with this facility (%)
Library	98
Art room or studio	86
Photography lab	67
Computer center	90
Audiovisual/media center	83
Biology lab	93
Chemistry lab	89
Physics lab	75
Chapel	85
Typing lab	92
Wood shop	9
Metal shop	4

Source: Data from NCEA (1985), 95.

Table 2.5 Comparison of staff resources in public and Catholic high schools

Descriptor	Public schools	Catholic schools
Ratio of students to staff	15	16
Ratio of students to teachers	16	18
Ratio of students to librarians and media specialists	597	340
Ratio of students to remedial specialists	504	891
Ratio of students to psychologists	2,025	4,579
Ratio of students to teacher aides	349	2,549

Source: Data from Coleman, Hoffer, and Kilgore (1982), 79.

secondary school is less differentiated than its public school equivalent. This phenomenon is manifested in a number of ways, one of which is school staffing. The specialization of staff and more complex school organization, commonplace in large public secondary schools, is atypical in Catholic schools. The contemporary Catholic secondary school is characterized by a more traditional school organizational form: a teacher in a classroom with a group of students. This is similar to the 1950s organization, except that class sizes are now smaller.[31]

Distinctive Features

Much of what we have described so far points to commonalities among public and Catholic schools. The data on instructional facilities, however, begin to focus our attention on some important differences between the two sectors. They provide specific evidence of the greater academic orientation of Catholic secondary schools, a pattern also seen in comparisons of course offerings (see Table 2.6). Catholic schools are somewhat more likely to offer advanced academic courses, and much less likely to offer vocational courses.

The track placements of students further demonstrate the academic emphasis of Catholic schools (see Figure 2.1). A large majority of Catholic school students (72 percent) are engaged in an academic program; only 10 percent concentrate on vocational studies. In contrast, students in the public sector are distributed approximately equally across the three tracks.

School size is another distinctive difference. The average Catholic high school enrolls 546 students; the average public school has 845 students. The figure for public schools may appear low to those whose vision of the modal

Table 2.6 Comparison of course offerings in public and Catholic high schools

Course offerings	Public schools (%)	Catholic schools (%)
Second-year Algebra	97	99
Calculus	47	80
Chemistry	96	98
Physics	90	93
Third-year Spanish	46	83
Third-year German	20	20
Home economics	97	50
Auto mechanics	50	8
Wood or machine shop	89	4

Source: Data from *High School and Beyond;* see also NCEA (1985), 53ff.

secondary institution is the comprehensive high school. But almost 30 percent of the high schools in both sectors are very small, enrolling fewer than 300 students (see Figure 2.2). The major difference between the sectors is the relative absence of large Catholic secondary schools. Over 85 percent of Catholic secondary schools enroll fewer than 900 students. In the public sector, however, 40 percent of the schools have enrollments greater than 900 and 5 percent of the schools have more than 2,000 students. Size is related to location in the public sector, with small public schools typically found in rural areas and large schools concentrated in cities.

The consequences of secondary school size are complex and often misunderstood. Two interrelated factors are at work, the first of which is eco-

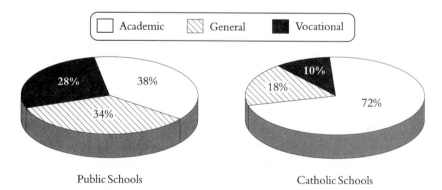

Figure 2.1 Proportion of students in different curricular tracks in Catholic and public high schools. Modified from Lee and Bryk (1988).

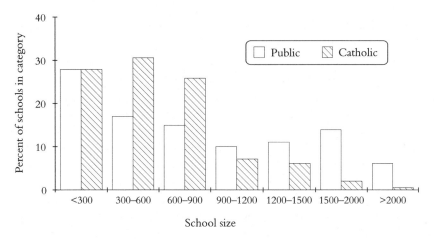

Figure 2.2 Comparative sizes of public and Catholic schools. Data from *High School and Beyond.*

nomic. Unless the school is particularly well financed, a small secondary institution (enrollment less than 300) finds it difficult to provide a full range of more specialized instructional facilities such as science laboratories and resource centers. In this regard, economies of scale are realized by larger schools.[32] Closely related to this are concerns about the breadth and depth of curricular offerings. In both the public and the Catholic sectors, larger schools are able to offer a more diverse array of courses, a topic we return to in Chapter 4.

These gains in efficiency resulting from increasing school size are counterbalanced, however, against a second concern—the consequences for the nature of the social relations within the institution. As detailed in Chapters 5 and 11, the smaller size of Catholic schools facilitates personal social interactions among students and faculty which, in turn, contribute to a sense of community within the school.[33] Students in small schools are more likely to gain experience in leadership or executive positions. They are also more likely to report that their teachers are interested in them and that they, in turn, are interested in schoolwork. Similarly, teachers in such schools are more likely to feel satisfied about their work and to be willing to expend greater personal effort.[34]

Thus there may be an ideal school size: neither too large to inhibit a strong sense of community nor too small to prohibit a full curriculum with adequate instructional facilities.[35] Although the precise "ideal size" is arguable, it is clear that the relatively small size of Catholic secondary schools is a significant feature of their organization, one whose consequences will be considered in Chapters 8, 10, and 11.

Finally, perhaps the most distinctive difference between public and Catholic secondary schools is the prevalence of single-sex education in the Catholic sector. Although 54 percent of Catholic high schools are coeducational, 20 percent are boys' schools and 26 percent are for girls only. In the public sector, by comparison, virtually no schools are single-sex. There has been a general movement over the past twenty years away from single-sex secondary schooling in both sectors, but surprisingly little is known about the relative efficacy of this alternative organizational form. We suspect that many will find surprising the results on this topic presented in Chapter 9; at a minimum, they suggest that this organizational form merits more consideration.

❖ II ❖
INSTITUTIONAL ANALYSIS

❖ 3 ❖

Classroom Life

THE LARGEST SINGLE portion of teachers' and students' school lives is spent in classrooms, engaged with both the subject matter and each other. We begin with sketches of two Catholic high school teachers and their classes. In their efforts, we observe many features common to instruction in Catholic high schools. Through their words and actions, we begin to comprehend the deep personal commitment of many teachers and the response of their students.

Teachers and Teaching

Mrs. Susan Cramer

Susan Cramer, herself a graduate of St. Madeline's, began teaching there in 1965, right after she graduated from Marymount College, a small liberal arts college for women in Los Angeles. Although many changes have occurred at St. Madeline's since her graduation, the mission of preparing students for college has remained the same. Cramer speaks warmly of her role as a St. Madeline's teacher: "I love it and want to be here. I feel I give students what they will need for life—what's good for them—the arts, literature, and writing skills. I try to envision what their lives will be like after they have graduated, and so I emphasize a strong background in communication skills as well as their total development as young women. I'm concerned that they know how important it is to develop a positive sense of themselves and to understand the contribution they can make to society."

We observed her eleventh-grade American literature classroom. As the students entered, Cramer arranged a batch of papers at her desk in the front of the class. A slight woman of medium height with her long brown hair pulled back, she looked proficient and businesslike, an image supported by her tortoise-shell glasses, high-collared white blouse, and gray skirt. All twenty-one students were seated by the time the bell rang. Cramer took roll, listing the names of two absent students on a small sheet of paper that a student then posted at the door of the classroom. With little introduction, Cramer plunged her students into a lively discussion of *The Great Gatsby*. She posed a question and, as students raised their hands, pointed to them to elicit their responses.

Cramer: In many ways, Myrtle and George are the antithesis of Tom and Daisy. Does anyone know what I mean by "antithesis"?

Student 1: I think it means the opposite.

Cramer: Yes, that's right. They are the opposite and different. How do you see them as different?

Student 1: Well, they live in different parts of Long Island, and Myrtle and George are poor while Tom and Daisy are very wealthy.

Cramer: Good. Do you see any ways in which they are alike?

Student 2: [Blurts out an answer, then sheepishly raises her hand and waits to be recognized.] Each couple was having marriage problems.

Cramer: Good. Now, let's look at Fitzgerald's view of how money affects people and influences their lives. What did money do for Daisy?

Student 3: Money made her happy.

Cramer: Did it, though? How do you support your statement?

Student 3: The book says she came from a wealthy family, and she married Tom who was rich. Money gave her power. She could do things that were impossible for the poor.

Cramer: Yes, that's true. Money allows the rich to think about themselves and their lives in ways that are different from other people. That's a major theme in Fitzgerald's writing. You can look for it in other characters and other books. Money brings happiness to some people, like Daisy, and seems to destroy others, like Gatsby. Fitzgerald once wrote about the rich in this way: "They were a race apart, with a better seat in life's grandstand. Their existence was somehow more beautiful and more intense than that of ordinary mortals." Do you think that's true? Why?

The discussion continued as Cramer gently prodded her students: "Give examples . . . support your views . . . be specific." Students focused on the expressions "race apart," "life's grandstand," and "ordinary mortals." Gradually the evidence emerged, and the argument took shape.

Cramer next guided the students to demonstrate their understanding of the novel's themes. She also retrieved those students whose attention had wandered and reinforced her standards of speech and oral presentation.

Cramer: Think about it. I want a thematic statement. I want more than a couple of people to answer. What's the meaning here?

Student 4: Does it have to do with living in the present?

Cramer: You're on the right track. Anyone else?

Student 5: I think it means the past is dead or something.

Cramer: Very good, but let's eliminate the "or something."

Student 5: The past is dead and one should never try to repeat it.

Cramer: Excellent!

Student 2: How about . . . how can you live in the present when you are trying to live out the past?

Cramer: Good, I think you understand the theme, and you are expressing it well. One of the most fascinating things about Fitzgerald is his view of time past and his search for the beautiful moment that will never fade. I think of his writing as a surgeon operating on himself. [She says this with great excitement and enthusiasm.]

The animated dialogue continued until the class bell rang. By the end of the fifty-minute period, each student had contributed her ideas at least once and had responded to the thoughts of her classmates. Arguments were set forth, debated, and rebutted. There was an air of involvement and satisfaction. Cramer's demeanor throughout remained unhurried but purposeful. Without seeming rushed, she firmly led her students through the material she had planned.

Cramer described her classes and the English curriculum as "courses that teach students to succeed in college, to express themselves orally and in writing, and to make them aware of how they speak." She felt strongly that for these young women, no less than for her own St. Madeline's classmates a generation earlier, the school provides opportunities to develop full, productive lives. Although few of the girls' parents are college graduates, she encourages each student to aspire to higher education and to a career in the media, business, or the professions. Her classroom pedagogy reflects official departmental policy on the use of standard English: "All the members of the department correct students when they use the black dialect and non-standard English. We approach it in a positive way, but we want the students to know the difference between slang and formal language. After all, we are preparing these girls for a world beyond their home culture."

Cramer teaches five classes per day—two regular sections and one honors section of American Literature for juniors, a senior creative writing class, and a sophomore composition group. Although she also serves as department chair, she receives no extra free periods to compensate for this added responsibility. Her day typically begins with a stop in the faculty room for a cup of coffee at 7:15. After a brief chat with the teachers who have gathered there, she generally enters her classroom about twenty minutes before the homeroom period begins at 8:00. In addition to teaching five classes, she often spends her free period on departmental business, such as observing a new faculty member. She usually returns to her classroom from 2:30 to 3:00 to help individual students after school. She also spends several hours each week advising students on the school newspaper: "I want to encourage them to write outside of class, and moderating the newspaper gives me a chance to work with students who want to expand their writing skills. It also enables me to get to know some of them better. The girls and I often make lasting friendships through this activity." After a stop in the faculty room to check her mailbox and the bulletin board, she heads home at about 4:00. Like other St. Madeline's teachers, however, she also participates in frequent evening and weekend activities at the school, which include parent orientation sessions, parent conferences, student dances, and attending an occasional field hockey or basketball game.

Cramer requires each of her 125 students to produce at least one weekly writing assignment. Some assignments are brief (perhaps no more than a few well-developed paragraphs); others are more extended—book reviews, essays, or critiques of literature students have read. Each week the eleventh-grade class is assigned a list of new vocabulary words, on which students are quizzed regularly. Regular homework and testing are also an essential part of Cramer's teaching: "I may seem a bit old-fashioned, but I can't understand how students can learn to write without doing frequent writing assignments, and the same is true for reading and vocabulary work. All my assignments have a purpose, and I usually check students' homework for completeness. Homework complements what I do in the classroom."

Cramer believes that students should read literature closely and thoughtfully. Her eleventh graders read from an American literature text as well as such works as *The Great Gatsby, The Crucible, The Scarlet Letter, Death of a*

Salesman, and *The Grapes of Wrath.* In the *Gatsby* class we observed, she challenged and even pushed students to think about what they had read and how it related to major themes in Fitzgerald's work. Her own strong interest in literature and her incisive questioning kept almost all of her students engaged. Students commented, "She makes literature come alive for us." "Because Mrs. Cramer is very demanding, I pay attention through-out the class. In the end, I find that I really learn a lot from her classes."

Although Cramer was warm and friendly with her students, her business-like teaching style did not allow the student-teacher relationship to become too intimate. Nor did she permit extraneous questions or personal stories to distract her from her teaching tasks: "I would describe my teaching style as formal. I don't talk about my personal life; maybe I should. I teach in a traditional manner, teacher-centered with student input. I feel more comfortable with lecture and discussion teaching. I'm not big on group activities and spontaneous sharing."

Cramer commented on her work as a teacher in a Catholic high school: "Being a good teacher is my major responsibility. Beyond that, I take a longer view on what we are doing here. I'm concerned about convincing my students that they can achieve in what they set out to accomplish. Being black and women could reinforce their minority status. That's why I'm a role model for them. The religious values that I learned at St. Madeline's have influenced my life. I want to pass those on." She described one of her college history professors as the teacher who most influenced her: "He conveyed his interest and love for the subject matter to all of us. He was a well-organized content specialist who integrated history into the larger context of human endeavors. He knew history, respected its discipline, and loved to transmit its values and insights to his students." Her own view of good teaching involves planning, expertise, and commitment, and she values order and organization in her classes. "At the beginning of each semester, I set goals for each class in terms of the content covered and the assignments I will give. Each class follows a well-defined pattern."

A typical introduction to the day's lesson includes an overview: "Here is where we are going today. I want you to see how it relates to what we have just done." After establishing the transition between yesterday's class and today's, she devotes the majority of class time to new material. A few minutes are reserved at the end to answer questions, summarize the day's class, and clarify assignments. Cramer rarely deviates from this pattern. She insists that students take notes and supervises the way that they do it. "They can't just wing it. This is a college-prep school. I feel that I have an obligation to teach them how to take notes and to make sure that they do."

Cramer invests serious effort to remain knowledgeable in her field. "I'm always reading and trying to attend conferences to get ideas on how to present material in new ways. Even though I've taught for a number of years and have a master's degree, I want to improve in my craft."

Her students sense her commitment to teaching. One senior said, "She knows what she's talking about. She knows her students. She demands a lot from you and gives you hard assignments, but I wish I were in her class again." Another student commented on her expectations for the class: "A lot of us thought that this was too much. I can't handle it. But she was easy to talk to, and she would say, 'Oh, I know you can do it or else you wouldn't be at this school.'" Another student talked of being the fourth member of her family to have Cramer as an English teacher. The sisters swapped stories about class standards, the challenging reading and writing assignments, and their appreciation of the experience. In their own words, "they had been Cramerized"—a badge of merit proudly worn.

Brother Antonio

Brother Antonio, in his early fifties, has been a teacher for twenty-seven years, and for the last nine years he has taught mathematics at St. Edward's High School. Proud of being a teacher, he takes the responsibility seriously. Thin and slightly balding, with aquiline features hinting of his Italian heritage, he speaks forcefully in a flat Boston accent that is vaguely incongruent with his Louisville, Kentucky, surroundings.

A busy man with little time for idle chatter or personal leisure, Brother Antonio keeps a demanding schedule. He arrives at St. Edward's at 7:30 every weekday morning. He teaches four classes, chairs the mathematics department, and coaches athletics. His teaching responsibilities include two accelerated Algebra I/II classes, and one class each of Algebra I and Mathematics I. The freshmen in his Algebra I/II honors sections will complete two courses of algebra in a single year, which enables them to take three semesters of calculus before graduation. The Algebra I section is a standard freshman algebra class; Mathematics I treats pre-algebra topics for students with weak mathematics skills.

In the two weekly periods assigned for his responsibilities as the department chair, Brother Antonio observes and evaluates other teachers as well as working individually with students who seek his help. He leaves his office at 3:00 each afternoon for the gym, where he dons coaching apparel. He typically remains there until about 6:00. In the fall, he coaches the cross country team; in the spring it is track. Brother Antonio's evenings are devoted to grading papers, preparing for the next day's classes, and working for the Interscholastic Athletic Association. On weekends and during the summer, he works as a track official at regional and state tournaments and conducts clinics for high school track coaches.

Brother Antonio's efficiency and high energy are evident in class, where his quick speech seems directed toward squeezing every instructional moment out of each period. We observed an Algebra I/II class with 36 honors freshmen boys. Using Houghton Mifflin's *Algebra I: Structure and Method* text, the class worked on both simplifying radicals in monomial and binomial expressions and rationalizing denominators to combine algebraic expressions.

Br. Antonio: OK, men, let's try these. We led you down the path to multiply two expressions with radicals. Now, let's multiply binomial expressions with radicals.

Student 1: Can we use FOIL? [Acronym for multiplying terms in a binomial: *F*irst, *O*uter, *I*nner, *L*ast.]

Br. Antonio: Yes, you can use FOIL.

Student 2: You can't multiply with a radical like $(x - 3)(x + 3)$.

Br. Antonio: Yes, you can. Try it . . .

Student 3: Is the answer "$x + 9$"?

Br. Antonio: Work it out. Give everyone a chance to work at it . . . [Students consult with each other as they work out the problem.]

Br. Antonio: I need a volunteer to do numbers 1, 2, and 3 at the board. OK, Jim, you do number 1. Tom, you do number 2. No [pointing to two students enthusiastically waving their hands], both of you can't do number 3. You go to the board, Stephen.

Br. Antonio: How do you multiply $(x + 7)(x - 7)$, William Cooper?

Student 4: $x^2 - 49$.

Br. Antonio: Good. Now is there any difference in form between $(x + 7)(x - 7)$ and this problem $(x + 4)(x - 4)$?

Student 4: Not really. They're both the product of the sum and difference of two numbers.

Br. Antonio: That's right. And what's the form for the product of the sum and difference of two numbers?

Student 5: $a^2 - b^2$.

Br. Antonio: That's it! Any questions on this?

Student 6: What if you have $(a - b)(b - a)$?

Br. Antonio: Tom, what would you do in that case?

Student 7: You can still use FOIL. I think it will work.

Br. Antonio: Right . . . Do you see that?

Student 6: Yeah, I see it now.

When the students completed their problems at the chalkboard, Brother Antonio checked the work by questioning the students who had stayed at their desks:

Br. Antonio: OK, how about number 6? Anybody want to challenge number 6? Is this part correct up to here, Roberts? What do you think? . . . What did he do wrong?

Student 7: It's not the same way that I did it, but it's right. I think he used another method.

Br. Antonio: Good. We don't have to use the same methods for these. He did more work than he had to, but his method and answer are correct.

As is his custom every day at the end of class, Brother Antonio assigned a dozen or so problems from the text as that night's homework.

Brother Antonio questions his students constantly, challenging them to think about problems in different ways, even when their answers are correct. He encourages them to work together and to help one another. He enjoys asking difficult questions and takes pride in helping students clarify their understanding. He stresses alternative methods for solving each problem. Students with strong intuition are encouraged to follow their instincts. Those with good analytical skills must use them. Working to solve sets of equations involving two variables, students in the class we observed used strategies that included trial and error, substitution, graphing, and reduction to a single variable.

The boys in Brother Antonio's class are alert and involved. Although the crowded room is rarely quiet, conversation is focused and controlled. Even when presenting new material, Brother Antonio uses a question-and-answer strategy. His pace varies from class to class, but his style is consistent— teacher and students working together. Brother Antonio talked about his expectations for graduates of St. Edward's: "The graduate should be able to study by himself. He should have good problem-solving skills. I think he should know how to organize and find information that he needs for his work. It's not enough for students to be able to repeat what teachers tell them. To prepare students for the future, it's important that they become skilled in the process of inquiring and learning." He also discussed the social mission of the school:

> By the time a student graduates, he should be able to work coopera-
> tively with others. I'm concerned that each student recognize his
> responsibility to society and develop a sense of justice and compassion
> for others. Our off-campus retreats and the senior service program try
> to instill this in the students. In my classes, I insist that the kids show
> respect for each other. Many high school kids get sarcastic and use
> put-downs toward their classmates. That's one thing I won't allow in
> my classes. I also think that religion coursework and the opportunity
> to practice one's beliefs are important parts of a complete education
> too.

The two most memorable teachers from Brother Antonio's own education were religious brothers with strong personalities, both of whom were
well versed in the subjects they taught. "My high school geometry teacher
set high standards. He made us stretch to reach those standards. He refused
to accept our excuses when we complained about the amount of homework
or the difficulty of the proofs." Recalling his eighth-grade teacher: "He
was always prepared for class, and rarely wasted a minute. In those days,
classes were big; I think we had over 45 students in our class. I always felt
like I had learned a lot when I left for the day."

Driven by a conviction about the importance of what he teaches his
students and his responsibility to do it well, Brother Antonio carefully plans
his instruction to maximize teaching time and student involvement. A strict
disciplinarian who tolerates neither disruptive behavior nor disinterest, he
also demands that students do their best. Students appreciate Brother Antonio for encouraging them to think, and they generally describe his classes
in positive terms:

> He's a teacher who constantly motivates you to learn. He doesn't want
> you to take his word for it, but to prove it for yourself. I like the way
> he encourages us to work together in solving problems.

> He's smart. He knows his math and he knows what he wants us to
> learn in each class.

> I like the way that he lets us answer in our own words. I feel like I'm
> involved in each class.

Although we did not observe harshness in his discipline, students recounted with a certain glee an incident in which Brother Antonio found a

student studying another subject during his class. Walking quietly over to the hapless offender's desk, Brother Antonio seized his book and hurled it out the classroom window. In a similar vein, several students recounted in mock horror Antonio's threats of the "claw," the "eyeball popper," and the "woody woodpecker"—all possible ways a teacher could "encourage," with a firm grasp between the neck and collarbone, a wayward student to attend to the lesson at hand. These stories, which seem to have taken on mythic proportions, are definitely a part of Brother Antonio's lore and are passed on by upperclassmen to each new freshman class.

Describing his role as department chair, Brother Antonio spoke about the need to upgrade the skills of the teachers he supervised. Toward this end, he observes each teacher on several occasions each year. He spends additional time with teachers who are having difficulties with subject matter, in managing classes, or in working effectively with students. He encourages teachers to continue their professional development during the summer. Occasionally, even with close supervision and support, a teacher does not meet Brother Antonio's expectations. When this happens, the teacher is counseled that if his or her teaching does not improve, Antonio will not recommend contract renewal to the principal. During the previous year, one untenured math teacher—and three other untenured teachers—had not been rehired at St. Edward's for this reason. Brother Antonio is nevertheless quite positive about his fellow faculty members. He commented favorably on the amount of time they spent talking about "our program" and "what we are trying to accomplish": "We work hard to improve the curriculum. When parents and students suggest changes, we consider them and implement them if we think they meet the needs of the students and fit into our programs. The faculty is good. They work hard to change and improve what they're doing."

On teaching at St. Edward's, Brother Antonio said, "I really like it. I can't believe that I've been here for nine years. I get a lot of satisfaction out of working with the kids in class and in sports. I feel like I am making a difference in their lives."

General Features of Instruction

Use of Instructional Materials

In the classes we visited, teachers relied extensively on textbooks as the major instructional source, especially in mathematics, science, and foreign language courses. In English, social studies, and religion classes we were more likely to find some teacher-produced materials being used. Most instruction took place in conventional classrooms, although we noted a few classes in such makeshift settings as a corner of an auditorium or part of a basement cafeteria. The traditional seating pattern in the classrooms placed students in rows of desks or tables facing the teacher in the front. An occasional class had a seminar arrangement, with students and teacher seated in a small circle facing each other, but the sheer number of students made this seating plan infeasible for most classes.[1] Although the physical resources within classrooms were modest, teachers had access to the basic instructional materials required to perform their job: books, audiovisual equipment, maps, globes, posters, and charts.

Teachers chose various approaches to decorating their rooms. Bulletin boards often displayed posters, diagrams, and color pictures relevant to the current instructional unit. Items encouraging a strong school spirit were common, as were slogans expressing pride in the school: "We are the Royal Family!" (at St. Peter's, where the team nickname is the Royals). Posters exhorted attendance at school events: "May the Force Be with Us against Aquinas Prep on Friday! Get Your Ticket for THE GAME Today." Students' art projects, their collages for religion classes, and examples of their writing were also prominently exhibited in classrooms. These displays conveyed two clear images: we are a community, and your individual contributions are valued here.

Classroom Activities

During our second round of field research, we employed a structured observation protocol to document teachers' use of class time in fifty-seven classrooms within our seven field sites. Substantial proportions of classroom time were spent in discussion, teachers' introduction of new material in the form of lectures and demonstrations, review of previous homework, and in-class writing assignments (see Table 3.1). Virtually all of these activities were directed by the teacher and involved the whole class. Student-led discussion and cooperative work among students in small groups were uncommon. External interruptions such as public address announcements or classroom visitors were also rare. Similar time-use statistics have been reported elsewhere. A recent large-scale survey of Catholic high schools serving low-income youth showed a heavy emphasis on teacher-directed activities with the whole class. A large survey of public high school classrooms reported a similar allotment of time.[2]

Virtually every class we visited used some amount of time for the teacher

Table 3.1 Amount of time spent on various classroom activities in Catholic high schools (based on observed classes in field-sample schools)

Activity	Time spent (in minutes)	Time spent (%)
Discussion	12.4	27.0
Instruction, new material	10.3	22.5
Homework review	6.7	14.6
Assigned work in class	5.9	12.9
Clerical	2.6	5.7
Quiz, drill	2.1	4.9
Review of quiz, drill	1.8	3.9
Oral reading	1.8	3.9
Review of previous work	1.6	3.5
Silent reading	0.5	1.1
PA announcements	0.1	0.2
Total	45.8	100.0

to lecture the whole group. In most classes some individual coaching of students by the teacher occurred, typically during drill and practice activities based on in-class worksheets or homework. Although some classroom discussion time (particularly in English, religion, and social studies) involved give-and-take as portrayed in our sketch of Susan Cramer's literature class, much of the discussion had a recitation quality; teachers asked questions to which students were expected to respond with the "correct" answer.

Regular testing and assigned homework are basic components of teaching. Teachers typically gave at least one quiz per week. The data in Table 3.1 actually underreport the amount of class time devoted to testing activities, because in order to maximize the information gained during our field research, we did not observe classrooms in which a full-period test was under way. All testing time referred to in Table 3.1 was devoted to short quizzes. Data from surveyed teachers indicated that full-period tests occur, on average, every two or three weeks.[3]

About two-thirds of the teachers in our field sites reported assigning homework at least three times a week, and over half the students reported spending more than five hours per week on homework. Data from *High School and Beyond* reported in Chapter 8 indicate that such responses are typical of Catholic secondary school students. Most teachers (62 percent) indicated that they "always" or "usually" graded the homework they had assigned.

Student Engagement

Assessing the engagement of students in classroom instruction can be an elusive task, because it involves assessing cognitive processes that are not directly observable. We approached this problem in two ways. First, we looked for indicators of noninvolvement in classroom activities, such as students whose heads were on their desks or who were staring out the window; students who were without books, paper, or pencils; or students who talked to others during class instruction. Second, we noted signs of active student participation, such as contributing to class discussions, working out problems at the board, reading aloud from the text, or asking questions. At two predetermined points, 10 minutes into each class and 10 minutes before the end of each class, we recorded what each student was doing. In the fifty-seven classes we observed, almost 90 percent of the students were engaged at the initial checkpoint, and slightly under 80 percent were engaged at the later assessment.

These data suggest a high level of student engagement in classroom instruction.[4] Even more important, however, is that the relatively small proportion of students not engaged in class activities refrained from interfering with the engagement of others. Across all the classes we visited, we did not observe a single incident of disruptive student behavior. Teacher questionnaire data suggest that the absence of disruption is a general characteristic of classroom life within these schools. Fewer than 5 percent of the teachers reported *any* of the following problems: student fights in class, students under the influence of alcohol or drugs, physical or verbal abuse of students, students ridiculing other students, and excessive absences or tardiness. Failure to do homework and minor infractions were cited by fewer than 15 percent of the teachers as regular problems within their classes.

Data from *High School and Beyond* allow us to generalize these findings about the infrequency of disruptive behavior in Catholic high schools (see Figure 3.1). The incidence of students' cutting classes, refusing to obey instructions, talking back to teachers, and instigating physical attacks on teachers is very low, both in comparison with public schools and in absolute terms.

The absence of disruptive behavior is further complemented by student attitudes that are very positive about their schools and teachers. The vast majority of students express a strong interest in school (both on their part and on the part of their friends), believe that the academic quality of their

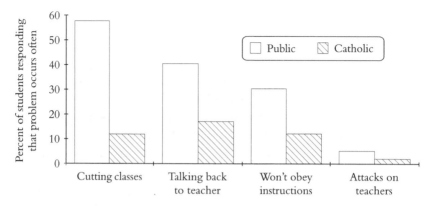

Figure 3.1 Student reports about classroom discipline problems: Percentage of students who indicate that these problems occur "often." Data from *High School and Beyond.*

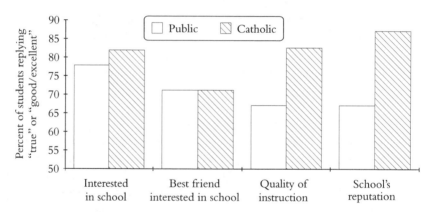

Figure 3.2 Student reports about their interest in school and school ratings (good or excellent). Data from *High School and Beyond.*

school is either good or excellent, and agree almost unanimously that their school has a good reputation within the community (see Figure 3.2). Moreover, despite the rather ordinary character of instruction in many Catholic school classrooms, students describe their teachers as unusually patient, respectful, and happy with their work (see Figure 3.3).

The sketches with which we began this chapter are thus also generalizable in another important regard: they demonstrate that mutual respect among students and teachers characterizes these schools and classrooms. Teachers are firm and committed to high standards in classroom work, but they

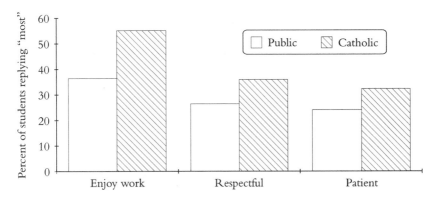

Figure 3.3 Student reports about their teachers. Data from *High School and Beyond*.

simultaneously display a strong personal interest in students, both in and outside of the classroom. Both their language and their behavior bespeak a strong sense of commitment to individual students and to a school life permeated with Christian personalism.

The Character of Work

Teachers' Work Load

Teachers in our field schools reported spending an average of 8.25 hours at their schools each day. Typically, a teacher arrives shortly after 7:30 A.M. and leaves at approximately 3:45 in the afternoon. He or she normally teaches five 45-minute periods per day, which might include a single section in one course and two sections each in two others. In addition to the almost 4 hours of class each day, teachers might spend about 45 minutes on class preparation, approximately an hour on lunch and other personal business, and 30 minutes in passing between classes. The remainder of the typical teacher's time on campus is spent correcting papers and working with students individually.

After the instructional day, many teachers coach athletic teams or supervise other extracurricular activities. Half of the teachers in the schools we visited took responsibility for at least one after-school activity, which might consume another 6 hours per week of their time. For those with coaching responsibility, the time demands were somewhat greater, averaging nearly 11 hours per week during the athletic season. Half of the teachers also averaged over 8 hours per week on school-related responsibilities such as bingo, fund-raising, and parents' meetings. More generally, over 80 percent of our field-sampled teachers reported that they frequently worked with individual students beyond the school day, either before or after school. Similarly, over 80 percent were actively involved in attending extracurricular activities such as athletics, drama, or music presentations.

In addition to over 40 hours at school, teachers reported devoting an extra 8 to 10 hours per week at home on correcting papers, reading for class assignments, preparing for class and other school-related work. The combination of regular teaching, extracurricular activities, and home preparation time meant that many teachers in our field sites were spending well over 50 hours per week on their work. Similar data have been reported for Catholic secondary schools serving low-income youth; about a third of the teachers in that sample of 106 Catholic high schools indicated that they devoted more than 55 hours per week to school responsibilities.[5]

A brief look at a typical day for a Catholic secondary school teacher— in this case, Margie McDaniel, a second-year English teacher at St. Peter's—helps to pull these numbers together into a more coherent picture. Arriving at school at 7:45, McDaniel begins her teaching day with homeroom at 8:15. Between 8:30 and 9:20, she teaches an English I class for students of average ability. Her next instructional period, a remedial reading section for fifteen students, begins immediately thereafter. During her free period (10:10 to 11:00), she corrects papers or prepares materials for one of her later classes. The period from 11:00 to 11:50 finds her teaching an honors section of English I. Lunch with faculty colleagues consumes only 20 minutes, with the remaining half hour of the lunch break usually spent meeting with students from one of the activities for which she takes responsibility. Her second section of English I begins at 12:40, followed immediately by a regular English II section.

The seasons dictate the remainder of her afternoon schedule. In the winter she coaches the girls' varsity basketball team from 2:45 to 4:15, which is normally followed by an hour or so of administrative chores associated with her position as girls' athletic director. The fall finds her coaching junior varsity volleyball; in the spring she assists with softball. On the few days without athletic practice, she might spend a few afternoon hours on her duties as English department chair. Rarely does she leave St. Peter's before 5 P.M., and on many occasions she is there well into the evening, either for athletic events or for parents' meetings. In addition, McDaniel often spends some portion of her weekend time at the school for various extracurricular activities.

Despite this large commitment of time, McDaniel was enthusiastic about her teaching and coaching at St. Peter's, and especially about the school's community spirit. Knowing the students both academically and personally and influencing their personal growth has been rewarding. Although the hectic schedule sometimes overwhelms her, she claims to have gained both organizational skills and the ability to use time productively.

Teachers frequently offered comments linking positive testimony about school life with remarks about how stressful it could be. In particular, they mentioned the daily demands of correcting papers, admonishing students, monitoring cafeterias and hallways, meeting with parents, and extended workdays. While expressing a real love for their work, they also worried about how long they could keep up the pace.

Even so, interviews and surveys from teachers in our field schools suggest a high level of job satisfaction among Catholic high school teachers, observations that are corroborated by survey data from NCEA (1986) and from *HS&B*.[6] Compared with their public school counterparts, Catholic high school teachers are more likely to be satisfied with their work, to feel personally efficacious, and to feel that good performance is recognized. They are also much less likely to report that their job requires excessive time for administrative tasks. Most of these teachers would advise young people to pursue teaching careers. The teachers' major discordant perception involves their salaries—Catholic school teachers are only half as likely as public school teachers to report that teaching allows them to earn a decent income. Because the average salaries in Catholic high schools are only about 70 percent of those in public schools, this response is not surprising.

Role Perspectives

Another distinctive feature of teaching in Catholic high schools is the view teachers have of their work. In general, teachers see their role in broad terms, involving considerably more than just specialized instruction in a subject area. These teachers are as concerned about the kind of person that each student becomes as about how much a student knows. Many teachers describe their work as a kind of ministry and their role as one of shaping young adults. We observed numerous instances of teacher behaviors consistent with these reports. Frequent personal accounts from both students and parents provided further corroboration.

We interviewed teachers about their views of their role within the school, their reason for teaching in a Catholic school, and their feelings about their work. To tell this story, we rely heavily on their comments. Virtually every teacher saw his or her work as extending beyond the five-class, seven-hour day. Although committed to teaching, class preparation, and the importance of the instructional programs, they also emphasized the personal values and the sense of community at their schools. A woman religious teacher at St. Cornelius' described her work: "I don't view it as a job. What I see here, and one of the reasons our religious community is here, is for the education of the poor . . . I think the importance of this work is not only in the academics but also because we teach personal values and are concerned about meeting students' other needs as part of what we do."

A faculty member at St. Edward's responded to our questions:

> I see what we do as teachers on three levels. We are role models, in that we are living examples of the beliefs that are taught in religion classes. We also have an obligation to teach values. I used to think that I was a Spanish and French teacher. Now I know that my values are at least as important as the content I teach. Finally, I remind myself that we play a four-year part in these students' lifetimes . . . What we have to transmit is a vision for the future to help them mold themselves into the kind of persons they want to become.

A faculty member at St. Frances' spoke about the importance of integrating life with learning in her classes: "As far as I'm concerned . . . besides the background on literature, grammar, and the like, we discuss life and the problems that students are likely to encounter. It is just as important that they learn about life while they are here as that they learn about academics."

Teachers in Catholic high schools see themselves as role models for their students. One teacher stated quite succinctly a view that was expressed by many others: "Even if teachers don't teach religion, we teach by our lives. Basically, this school is a good environment, and we teach by our example and who we are. We strive to make students more conscious of the world around them and how they fit into it."

Some teachers spoke about their work as "helping people, being involved, and feeling fulfilled as a result," an important part of which involves supporting students with troubled families. Principals and counselors frequently commented on the growing number of students whose families were experiencing divorce, unemployment, or other problems. One teacher described the surrogate-parent role that teachers and schools served for some students: "It's amazing when you hear them talk about their families. It's like they don't have any stability at home. Their life here at the school is about the only thing that is stable in their environment. I feel at times that we function almost like parents for some students."

In broad terms, many faculty view their multiple roles with the school—

teacher, coach, counselor, and adult model—as a form of ministry.[7] The character of the social encounters that results from this view is pervasive and readily apparent. A field observer in another study of Catholic schools echoed our experience: "There's a feeling here that is hard to miss if you spend any time here . . . a tremendous rapport between students and faculty. The faculty is extremely concerned about the kids, not only academically. A number of people are involved in other areas nobody even knows about. I think at any one time probably the whole faculty is involved in something, for somebody."[8] This is personalism lived, day in and day out.

THE CHARACTER OF instruction in Catholic high schools appears quite traditional in format, setting, use of materials, and pedagogy. We observed some examples of excellent teaching, but, on average, the technical aspects of teaching in Catholic high schools can be described as "ordinary." Although we saw more emphasis on testing and homework than appears to be the case in public high schools, in most other respects the teaching techniques employed in Catholic secondary schools are quite similar to what have been reported for public schools.

The first surprise for us in our fieldwork findings was students' positive reactions to this rather ordinary teaching and their high levels of engagement with classroom activities. The prevailing professional rhetoric at the time we undertook these visits argued that a more appealing and diverse curriculum and more scintillating instruction were necessary in order to promote greater student engagement in learning. Neither of these two desiderata was especially prevalent in Catholic high schools, yet engagement was occurring. Trying to make sense of this observation eventually led us to a new dimension of inquiry, focusing on the quality of human relations within the school, and to the evolution of a set of ideas about communal school organization.

Similarly, the roles teachers assumed in Catholic high schools were broader and the perspectives they offered on their work different from what we had expected. The typical teacher's work load was heavy, including multiple class preparations and extensive extracurricular involvement. Low salaries were a major source of dissatisfaction, especially given the commitments involved. Nonetheless, these teachers spoke very positively about their work and the considerable psychic rewards it afforded them.[9] To them, teaching values and shaping the lives of young people by their actions and their example was as important as the subject matter presented in classes. This broad concern and extended teacher role was not lost on students, who saw their instructors as interested in them, as patient and understanding, yet also as firm and committed to high standards. Such teacher personalism, which seemed to pervade the myriad social encounters within the schools, was infectious, pulling students strongly toward engagement in school life.

Initially we saw little connection between our observations of teacher commitment and student engagement. Although both were quite common in all the schools we visited, we did not at first understand or link them. As our work proceeded, however, we came to appreciate the influence of tradition in these schools. We also slowly began to see these events as subsidiarity at work—fomenting social ties, building social solidarity— where both the academic structure and the communal organization of the school were key contributors.

❖ 4 ❖

Curriculum and
Academic Organization

BEGINNING IN THE early 1960s, broad changes were introduced in the curriculum of U.S. high schools.[1] The first phase of curriculum development grew out of post-Sputnik fears that the nation's secondary schools were not challenging its most talented students. In response high schools added new courses at the top end, such as calculus, and substantially upgraded the content of others, particularly in the physical and biological sciences. These developments set in motion a general movement toward offering college-level courses (and college credit) as advanced electives in the high school. The resulting curriculum in many school districts gradually began to appear more akin to that of a small college than to what just a few years earlier would have been viewed as quite sufficient for a good high school.[2]

Shortly thereafter, concerns grew about the lack of relevance and sensitivity of the school curriculum to the needs of disadvantaged students. The addition of remedial programs at the high school level, particularly in reading and basic mathematics, was one visible response. A more pervasive but less well studied phenomenon was the growth of the "general track" within public secondary schools.[3] This alternative offers a less-demanding curriculum to students who do not wish to pursue either the wholly college-preparatory program of the academic track or the career training offered in the vocational track.

Curriculum developments here were quite profound. On the one hand, there was a proliferation of personal development courses, with such titles as "Leisure and Recreational Activities" or "Personal Grooming and Fashion," as schools offered an expanded range of nonacademic and underdemanding electives to students. Adjustments were also made in the traditional academic areas in which credits were required for high school graduation, such as mathematics and English. "Checkbook Mathematics" could substitute for algebra. A course on contemporary mystery stories might replace a survey of English literature.

In general, Catholic schools were subject to the same social forces as their public school counterparts in the 1960s and 1970s, and they too introduced innovations into the curriculum to respond to the needs of both talented and academically disadvantaged students. Many Catholic schools also experimented with new curriculum content, individual study projects, and new ways of scheduling classes and allocating time. These changes were not nearly as far-reaching as in public schools, however, nor did they ever take deep root.[4] The academic structure of the Catholic schools we visited in the mid-1980s remained closely coupled to their traditional mission of simultaneously fostering the intellectual development and the character development of all their students.

All of our field-site schools had at least some advanced academic offerings. Calculus was offered in each school. A fourth year of foreign language, usually French or Spanish, was common. The curriculum content of courses in biology, physics, and chemistry was modernized in response to curricular development in these areas in the recent decades, including more emphasis on learning through experimentation. At the other end of the curriculum, each of the seven schools offered some form of remedial instruction in reading and mathematics. We did not encounter, however, anything comparable to the diverse elective offerings associated with the average public school curriculum. Although records indicate that the curriculum of nonacademic courses expanded in at least some of our field sites during the late 1960s and early 1970s, most of this had disappeared by the time of our visits.

Curriculum Structure

Each of the field-site schools placed a heavy emphasis on standard academic courses: mathematics, science, English, social studies, and western European languages. Although most of the schools offered a range of academic electives, the course of study expected for every student was largely specified. These required courses ranged from a low of 14 (of 21 needed for graduation) at one school to a high of 20 (of 22 needed for graduation) at another. The core academic curriculum, which varied somewhat among the schools, typically included: four credits in English; three credits in social studies (usually Western civilization, non-Western cultures, and United States history); two credits in mathematics (usually algebra and geometry); two credits in science (typically biology and a physical science); and two credits in foreign language, with French, Spanish, and German the most common options.[5] (A "credit" is a one-year course that meets approximately five 45-minute periods per week. This is often referred to as a "Carnegie unit.") In addition, the schools required all students to take four credits in religion.

National course enrollment information from *High School and Beyond* supports the generalization of our field observations to the entire Catholic sector. Catholic school students take considerably more academic courses than do their public high school counterparts (see Table 4.1). The typical student in a Catholic secondary school takes an average of over a year more mathematics and a half year more foreign language. Other analyses have shown that Catholic secondary school graduates average 16 credits in core academic subjects compared with 13 credits for public school graduates.[6]

One obvious reason for these differences in course enrollments is the difference in curricular track placements between public and Catholic schools. Seventy-two percent of Catholic school students are in a college-preparatory program, while only 38 percent of public schools students are enrolled in this track (see Figure 2.2). The comparable figures for vocational programs are 10 percent and 28 percent, respectively. It might seem logical, then, to conclude that a major reason Catholic high school students take more academic courses is simply that a larger proportion of students are enrolled in academic programs that require such courses for graduation.

Our analyses indicate, however, that there is more to this story. We compared the academic course enrollment patterns for students within the same curricular track in the two sectors (see Table 4.2). For students in the academic track, the course enrollment differences between public and Catholic schools in mathematics, science, and foreign language are not large. Catholic school students take 0.4 years more mathematics, 0.3 years more foreign language, and no more physical science. Much more pro-

Table 4.1 Average number of academic courses taken by public and Catholic high school students

Courses taken	Public schools	Catholic schools
Foreign language	1.10	1.72
Physics and chemistry	0.55	0.82
Mathematics	2.07	3.19

Source: Data from *High School and Beyond.*

Table 4.2 Catholic and public high schools: Sum of academic and nonacademic courses taken within academic track, by sector

Courses taken	Public schools			Catholic schools		
	Academic track	General track	Vocational track	Academic track	General track	Vocational track
Math, yrs.[a]	3.20	1.54	1.22	3.58	2.59	2.23
Science, yrs.	1.03	0.31	0.20	1.00	0.47	0.22
Foreign language, yrs.	1.38	.97	.87	1.69	1.44	.72
English, yrs.	3.15	2.95	2.87	3.19	3.21	3.17
Social studies, sem.	2.34	2.25	2.18	2.44	2.38	2.25
Business, sem.	3.36	3.87	4.83	2.85	3.59	4.23
Vocational, sem.	2.09	2.88	3.06	1.44	2.03	2.26

Source: Data from Lee and Bryk (1988), 85.

a. Mathematics courses are the sum of Algebra I, Geometry, Algebra II and Trigonometry, Pre-calculus, and Calculus.

nounced differences are observed when we compare the vocational and general tracks. General track students in Catholic schools take a full year more of mathematics and almost a half year more of foreign language than do their public school counterparts. Similarly, vocational track students in Catholic school take an extra year of mathematics. Although science and social studies enrollment is about equal in the two sectors, vocational and general track students in Catholic schools are also taking a slightly greater number of English courses. This extra academic emphasis in Catholic schools is accompanied by reduced enrollment in business and vocational courses.

The greater academic course enrollment in Catholic high schools is thus not confined primarily to students in the college-preparatory track: the differences between sectors in courses taken are much greater among students enrolled in nonacademic programs. Catholic school students in the academic track take 12 percent more academic courses than do their public school counterparts; comparable figures for Catholic school students in vocational and general tracks are 38 percent and 95 percent, respectively. The greater enrollment in academic courses in the Catholic sector thus results from two factors: the substantially greater percentage of students enrolled in the academic track in Catholic schools, and the greater emphasis on academic coursework for students not in academic programs.[7]

A Closer Look at the Curriculum

We limited our investigations of curriculum in field-site schools to the areas of mathematics, English, and religious studies. We chose mathematics and

English because of their central role in schooling; religious studies was examined because it is the most obvious sign of the Catholic character of these schools. The numerous data sources employed in our fieldwork allowed us to develop a rich base of information on curriculum in the seven schools we visited.[8]

A major organizational problem in developing secondary school curriculum is how to accommodate the diversity in students' skills as they enter high school. The response of the field-sample schools to this problem seems to depend on three factors: the nature of the ability distribution of entering students, the size of the institution, and the resources available. Because our field sites were selected to ensure variation along each of these dimensions, we encountered some predictable differences in curricular offerings. We also found considerable commonality in the schools' academic programs, which derives from a widely held belief among Catholic secondary school educators that a traditional academic curriculum is appropriate for most adolescents. At root here, as discussed in Chapter 1, is an educational philosophy of person-in-community that sees the full intellectual development of each person as a fundamental human right and as the central aim of education.

Mathematics

A three-year sequence consisting of Algebra I, Geometry, and Algebra II/ Trigonometry made up the core of the mathematics in each school. This sequence was designed for the average student—one who had covered arithmetic and pre-algebra by the end of the eighth grade. Variations were introduced to accommodate both talented students and those whose prior academic preparation left them poorly equipped to succeed in standard high school work.

Students in Algebra I studied equations with one and two variables, exponents, radicals, quadratic equations, and linear graphing. The tenth-grade course, Plane Geometry, included the theorems of Euclidean geometry with special emphasis on constructions, congruence, similarity, and applications of the Pythagorean theorem. The ability to solve problems and document proofs with previously learned theorems was stressed. Algebra II and Trigonometry, usually offered in the eleventh grade, extended the Algebra I treatment of linear and quadratic equations and treated new material on graphing of first- and second-degree equations, conic sections, irrational and complex numbers, logarithms, trigonometric functions and identities, and series and sequences.

In schools with a high proportion of average students, such as St. Madeline's, the great majority enrolled in this three-course sequence. St. Madeline's used the same text for all sections of the sequence—students were randomly grouped into classes, and the pace of instruction varied only slightly among the various sections at each grade level.

For less able students, all of the schools made some accommodation, which usually involved both remedial work in freshman and sophomore year and some adjustment to the pace and intensity of instruction. A portion of the freshman class in each school was typically required to complete remedial work in basic computational operations, percentages, decimals, fractions, and practical applications of mathematics. At St. Peter's, the school with the least affluent students among our field sites, approximately 40 percent of the ninth graders were enrolled in such a course. Classroom instruction in this course emphasized drill work on computational fundamentals, and teachers employed a programmed text with a variety of individualized work that they regularly checked. In subsequent years these students would move into sections of Pre-Algebra, Algebra, and at least some would move on to Geometry. St. Madeline's approached instruction for underprepared students by spreading the content of the standard Algebra I course over two years with remedial work integrated within the context of a slower pacing of the normal algebra instruction. Students from the two-year Algebra I sequence who enrolled in a third year of mathematics took Geometry.

Although the initial academic experiences of these students were somewhat different from those of their better-prepared peers, the structure of their academic program was based on a common school goal: to move all students as far as possible through the traditional content of high school mathematics. There was more emphasis on drill work as part of remedial classroom instruction, but expectations about homework and the level of student effort remained similar to those found in sections for average students.[9] Practical mathematics courses, such as Consumer Mathematics, which stressed the concepts and mathematics of simple and compound interest, margins of profit, and income tax calculations, and Career Mathematics, a treatment of mathematics in surveying, banking, investment, insurance, purchasing, and other areas, were offered at several schools. These courses were available, however, only as senior-year electives rather than as an alternative track to the core sequence.

Catholic high schools also made accommodations for the more talented students. A typical approach was to collapse Algebra I, Geometry, and Algebra II/Trigonometry into two years, in order to prepare students for Analysis in grade 11 and Calculus or other advanced electives in grade 12. Small schools with limited fiscal resources and where the majority of students typically entered poorly prepared had a particularly difficult time responding to the needs of the relatively few students capable of pursuing advanced work. As a result, schools such as St. Frances' and St. Peter's relied primarily on independent study and tutoring for such students.

It is thus in curriculum offerings for talented students, more than anywhere else, that larger school size and a more extensive resource base appear especially important. St. Edward's is a case in point. Its student population of 1,500, nearly three times the size of the average Catholic high school, its greater financial resources, and its large proportion of well-motivated and well-prepared mathematics students meant that it was both practical and, in fact, necessary to provide a wide range of advanced mathematics offerings. In addition to two advanced placement calculus courses, the school offered advanced courses in linear programming, probability and statistics, and five one-semester courses in computer programming, ranging from introductory programming to an advanced placement course that included FORTRAN and PASCAL.

English

Each school required four years of English for graduation. These required courses typically integrated writing skills, vocabulary usage, grammar, and the reading and analysis of literature. The emphasis shifted from grammar and basic writing skills at grades 9 and 10 to reading and analysis of more complex works of literature in the upper grades. The level of teachers' expectations and the difficulty of homework assignments also increased over this four-year period. The required writing in the ninth grade involved short passages of narrative and exposition. By grade 12, students were expected to engage in extensive literary analysis and produce a research paper. The treatment of literature in the ninth grade typically involved a survey introduction to several genres; the eleventh- and twelfth-year classes focused in more detail on classic works of both British and American authors.

Each school relied on several texts, some of which were used throughout the four-year program. Typically, a student had at least four books: a textbook or series of paperbacks specific to the literature area covered that year; a writing text that detailed the processes of writing, including, for example, brainstorming for topics, the revision process, and samples of students' work to critique; a grammar text that was used for all four years; and a vocabulary text that usually spanned two grade levels, 9–10 and 11–12.

The St. Richard's English program was typical of those of the schools we studied. Ninth-grade English emphasized narrative and descriptive writing. Each week, students might produce two or three paragraphs on topics such as hobbies, interests, school subjects, a hero or heroine, their greatest accomplishment, or traits they valued in a best friend. Grammar, including drill for proper usage, was a regular part of the classwork; students studied and reviewed the rules of grammar with examples from their own writing or the writing text. Vocabulary development was addressed in a paperback, such as *How to Build a Better Vocabulary* or *Thirty Days to a More Powerful Vocabulary*. Teachers typically devoted parts of one or two classes each week to vocabulary development; students were asked to memorize the words, their spelling, and to use each word in a sentence. Ninth-grade literature introduced four literary genres—poetry, drama, the short story, and the novel—and included some Greek and Roman mythology. During the course of the year, students typically read *The Iliad, The Adventures of Huckleberry Finn, To Kill A Mockingbird, Julius Caesar,* and several O. Henry short stories. With one or two reading assignments a week, students usually completed between ten and fourteen works of varying length in a year. About 35 percent of class time was spent on reading and study skills, 25 percent on grammar exercises, and about 20 percent on writing skills and vocabulary development.

Tenth graders continued their work on grammar, vocabulary, and literary genres begun in their first year, with increasing emphasis on critical writing. Writing assignments, which became longer and more involved, included the analysis and critique of short stories and poetry as well as essays articulating a coherent point of view on a controversial topic. Vocabulary and grammar drills continued, but were less in number than in grade 9. Four field-site schools employed *Warriner's Complete Book of English Grammar* as a class text for the first two years of high school, and students retained it as a reference in the eleventh and twelfth grades. Except for students needing remediation, reading and study skills were emphasized less in the second year, when students typically read works such as *My Antonia, A Separate Peace,* the Poe short stories "The Cask of Amontillado" and "The Pit and the Pendulum," a play (typically *Julius Caesar*), and the poetry of Langston Hughes.

A typical eleventh-grade English course surveyed American literature from the colonial period to the twentieth century. The relationship between historical events and social contexts received special emphasis, as well as the styles and interests of twentieth-century authors in *The Great Gatsby, The Grapes of Wrath, The Sound and the Fury, Our Town,* and similar works. Teachers of American history and junior-year English might assign complementary readings to highlight historical relationships. Typical readings included *The Scarlet Letter, The Red Badge of Courage,* and *Main Street.* The focus of the year's work was on critical and analytical writing, with weekly essays and one or two critical papers assigned each quarter. Vocabulary development at this level was geared toward preparing students for nationally administered college entrance tests (PSAT and SAT). Reading and discussion consumed as much as 40 percent of weekly class time: writing accounted for another 35 percent. The remainder of the time was divided between grammar and vocabulary work.

Senior English focused mainly on literature, from the Anglo-Saxon period to the twentieth century. Students read classics such as *Beowulf, The Canterbury Tales, Paradise Lost, Jane Eyre, Hamlet, Of Human Bondage,* and the poetry of Wordsworth and the Romantics. The mechanics of English and vocabulary development were no longer stressed. College-bound students were assigned a research paper, expected to be about fifteen pages in length, typed, and to include footnotes and bibliography. This paper, which represented the culmination of writing activities for the year, typically involved literary criticism; students might be asked to compare and contrast two or three authors or several works by the same author. The purpose of the research papers was to develop students' analytic skills in reviewing critics' and commentators' work, while also providing opportunities for displaying original thinking.

Some accommodation was made in response to the differing skill levels of students as they entered high school. St. Edward's English program was the most differentiated in terms of students' abilities. Based on entrance examination results and students' eighth-grade records, St. Edward's placed ninth graders in one of eleven sections—two honors sections, seven college-preparatory sections, and the remaining two special (remedial) sections. After the ninth grade, students' English sections were adjusted, based on interest and performance. Regardless of level, all sections emphasized the reading of literary classics and the mechanics of writing, grammar, and word usage. Students in the honors sections received more demanding assignments involving extra reading and writing.

The philosophy of remedial instruction in Catholic high schools is exemplified by the intensive remedial English program at St. Edward's in which seventy freshmen were divided among a team of four teachers. These students received ninety minutes of English instruction every day, including extra time devoted to reading skills, the improvement of writing skills, and grammar in addition to the regular ninth-grade curriculum. For most students, this "special program," as it was called, continued in the tenth grade. By grade 11, the number of students in need of remediation was approximately halved, and virtually all students reached the standard college-preparatory level by their senior year.

A low-budget version of this approach was pursued at St. Cornelius', where weaker students enrolled in a developmental reading course in ninth grade in addition to regular ninth-grade English. In subsequent years these students moved into the standard college-preparatory English sequence. Other than the freshman remedial program, English electives at St. Cornelius' were restricted to creative writing, speech, and journalism. These courses were available to students as upper-division electives in addition to the standard English sequence.

In general, each school offered a limited number of English courses beyond the core four-year sequence. These courses were designed primarily as senior-year options for honors students seeking advanced work, although an occasional elective for the non–college bound student might be offered. For example, a St. Richard's English elective that focused on careers in writing usually attracted approximately 10 percent of the senior class.

Religion

The religion curriculum, which is the most visible way in which Catholic schools differ from their public counterparts, has experienced significant change since the 1960s in its teaching personnel, content, language, and pedagogy.

Prior to 1965, religion was invariably the first class of the day in Catholic high schools. The class's prominent place in the schedule was intended to reinforce the preeminent position of religion in school and in a student's life. Religion classes were taught exclusively by religious, either priests, sisters, or brothers, and emphasized the dogmatic teachings of the Church, including the mystery of the Trinity, the role of Jesus as the Son of God and redeemer of the human race, the role of Mary as the mother of Jesus, the saints, the purpose of the sacraments, and the structure of the Church (in which bishops serve as direct successors to Jesus' apostles and the Pope serves as the successor of St. Peter). The use of the Old Testament was largely restricted to the creation story and the lineage of Jesus from Adam through Noah, Abraham, Moses, David, and Solomon. The major prophets, Isaiah and Jeremiah, were examined as foreshadowers of the Messiah. Other scripture was used sparingly, mostly as a support for the principles being taught.

Though not taught directly in high school, the Baltimore Catechism was the organizing guide for all religious instruction. A popular four-volume religion text of the period, *Our Quest for Happiness,*[10] used a narrative historical approach to communicate the major teachings of Catholicism to high school students. The series integrated the teaching of dogma, morals, and admonitions of the Church such as the prescriptions for attending Mass on holy days of obligation or abstaining from eating meat on Fridays. The wording of the text, though an improvement over earlier books, was strongly prescriptive and rigidly doctrinaire by today's standards. Its tone reflected the orientation of a ghetto Church under siege by an unfriendly world.

Pre-1965 religion classes emphasized rote memorization of Church doctrine and laws. Students read a religious textbook, memorized and recited answers to questions that were posed in the catechism, and provided answers to prescribed questions at the end of each chapter. The formation of conscience and the value of personal opinion were subordinated to internalizing the official Church position on a wide range of questions, from divorce and euthanasia to prescriptions for receiving the sacrament of Penance during a ten-week period around Easter and avoiding even entering the houses (much less the churches) of worshipers of other faiths.

Among the most notable changes in contemporary Catholic high schools is in the personnel who teach religion—60 percent of the religion faculty members and over one-third of the religion department chairs are now lay people.[11] The period immediately following Vatican II, roughly 1968 through 1976, saw greater turnover among religion teachers than anywhere else in Catholic high schools.[12] The earlier emphasis on Church doctrine and the personal relationship between God and the individual was rebalanced with a recognition of the importance of human relationships and issues of social justice. Many older religious staff members preferred to teach in their disciplinary specialty and to allow those trained in post-Vatican II theology to conduct religious instruction.[13]

The religion curriculum in the field-sample schools generally consisted of three full-year required courses and a choice of semester-long electives in the senior year. All of the schools required four religion credits for graduation for all students, whether or not they were Catholic. Discussion group teaching was the most common classroom strategy that we observed. In these discussions, students shared their views, and teachers' questions probed differences in students' opinions, with textbook readings typically used to orient the discussion. At St. Madeline's, for example, we observed ninth-grade students discussing sexuality, abortion, and venereal disease after reading a section in their supplementary text, *Choice and Conscience: Abortion in Perspective.*[14] Teachers also lectured and, on occasion, used films and guest speakers. Religion classes involved regular reading assignments and some writing assignments. Students were rarely grouped according to ability, except when such grouping occurred because of scheduling constraints.

The religion sequence a St. Edward's, similar to what we encountered at four other schools, exemplifies religious instruction in a progressive Catholic high school. The focus of Religion I encouraged students to examine and reflect on their lives in relation to the world about them and to consider the role that faith and belief in a personal God might play within this context. These objectives were addressed through the study of the Old Testament as the expression of a community's wonder about God. Religion II focused on the Christian's relationship to himself, other people, and God. Examination of the New Testament was used to discuss the life of Jesus. The course discussed such issues as peer pressure, obedience versus freedom, and sexuality as examples of challenges faced by teenagers in living their faith. The sacraments, the liturgy of the Church, and students' role within a vital contemporary Christian community were also studied.

Religion III treated moral behavior and personal responsibility for making moral decisions. Students' own moral values were probed in the context of Church teachings. Notions about sin, personal redemption, and reconciliation were situated within the demands of a moral life, emphasizing the formation and use of conscience. The course then applied these principles to specific issues on both a global level (for example, nuclear disarmament) and a personal level (for example, sexuality).

A series of semester-long senior electives constituted Religion IV. At St. Edward's, these included "Christian Lifestyles" (a study of marriage and other lifestyles), "Belief and Unbelief" (an investigation into the ultimate ontological questions), "Contemporary Catholic Faith" (an examination of the roots of Catholic faith including tradition and heritage), "The Meaning of Life" (an inquiry into values that may guide the student in a choice of a personal philosophy), and "Death and Dying" (an examination of the issues and concerns surrounding the reality of faith). Other schools among our field sites offered electives on broad-based moral and ethical topics such as the Holocaust, conscience, prayer, and the history of religions. Community service work was available as an elective course in all of the schools we visited and was a particularly popular choice.

This type of religious studies program is grounded in the premise that faith is a developmental process, the end state of which can only be achieved through individual free choice. The aim is to develop and nurture personal conscience as a guide to personal action, and as a result, teaching by rote or imposition is seen as distorting the concept of faith.[15] This view contrasts sharply with the pre-Vatican II orientation that Catholics must learn the "mind of the Church." In contemporary religion classes, students are typically asked to analyze and interpret situations and to apply basic principles to complex social and moral problems. From a pedagogical point of view, the development of skills in analysis and synthesis has replaced the former emphasis on memorization, recall, and comprehension.

On balance, not all of the field-sample schools shared this orientation toward religious instruction. The religion curriculum at both St. Frances' and St. Peter's was more traditional, placing heavier emphasis on the notion of faith as received truth. These programs assumed that baptized Catholics had already acquired religious faith, so that religion classes were meant to provide the opportunity to study its attributes and understand its depth. In the religion classes we visited at these schools, a teacher might present a lesson on the morality of divorce, and students were asked to answer questions from a text that spelled out the Church's position. Less discussion meant that the relationship of students' personal concerns and experiences to the lesson were probed less frequently. In general, lecturing was the dominant teaching technique in these schools' religion classes.

Who Takes What?

The commonality in students' academic experiences within Catholic secondary schools is not just in the number of academic courses taken. As we investigated actual course content, we found a substantial core of subject matter shared by all students. In contrast, field studies on public schools document the very different intellectual experiences that students can have in even nominally similar courses within the same school.[16] Unlike the course of study for Catholic school students—which is largely determined by the school—the set of courses public school students take is negotiated through a complex set of social interactions among teachers, guidance counselors, and the students themselves. These negotiations typically result in structuring inequities into students' academic experiences: students with weaker academic and social backgrounds "choose" quite undemanding courses.

Although the curriculum in Catholic high schools differentiates to some degree according to variations in students' prior preparation, the actual academic experiences of students remain relatively similar across classes of differing ability levels. Standard indicators of academic preparation— entrance examination scores, elementary school teacher recommendations, and elementary school grades—are generally used in the initial assignment of students to remedial, general, or honors sections. As students proceed through high school, however, their accumulated academic record determines subsequent placements. Our review of records in the field sites indicated that students moved both up into more difficult sections as well as down into somewhat less challenging courses.[17]

Flexible policies for assigning students to classes in most of the field-sample schools meant that students were seldom kept out of classes they wanted to take. Of all the schools we studied, St. Edward's had the most extensive grouping by ability and was also the most academically rigorous school. Traditionally, this school had placed students in sections upon entry to grade 9 on the basis of results from entrance examinations and elementary school records, and this placement continued with the same sections for all of their classes for the next four years. At the time of our visits, a new computerized scheduling system was helping to remove this restriction. Students could now shift in and out of honors classes according to the subject, rather than having to enroll in all honors or all regular academic classes. In this case, a technological innovation allowed a less rigid tracking practice.

Finally, even within this school—the most academically stratified of those we observed—the resource allocation patterns worked to diminish the effects of stratification. St. Edward's assigned extra staff, including some of its most experienced teachers, to work with students who had the greatest learning needs. Unlike many public schools, the honors sections at St. Edward's had the largest enrollments, some with as many as forty students, whereas the remedial classes in the special program for freshmen and sophomores averaged between fifteen and twenty per class.

Institutional Effects of Academic Organization

We have shown that the curricular structure of Catholic secondary schools is relatively homogeneous, with students sharing a common core of intellectual experiences. We hypothesize that this constrained academic structure works to mitigate the differentiation normally occurring in high schools and thus contributes to the common school effect. More specifically, we contend that the academic organization of the high school is the major mechanism through which initial background differences among students are eventually transformed into achievement differences. If this proposition is true, we expect that the stronger relationships in the public sector between background characteristics and academic outcomes reported by Coleman and his colleagues and Greeley will disappear once we control for key student academic experiences such as track placement and which courses are taken. This question is investigated in Chapter 10.

There is, however, a prior concern to which we now turn. It could be argued that the different, and potentially more advantageous, academic organization of Catholic high schools is nothing more that a selection phenomenon—that the organization is possible because more able and academically ambitious students choose to attend Catholic schools and pursue more academic coursework on their own initiative.[18] In response to this concern, we undertook several analyses of *High School and Beyond* data to examine whether the observed academic experiences of students in Catholic schools could simply be explained as a matter of student and family selection, or whether we could discern school policy effects even after taking account of student selectivity.

Specifically, we considered two questions: Is track placement primarily a school-affected decision or a matter of student/family choice? Does the pattern of courses students take indicate institutional effects, or is this too just a reflection of background differences among students? Our field observations of deliberate school policies governing construction of the curriculum and assignment of students to it support strong institutional effects. But perhaps we were just observing differential student and family choice under a market system. Unless we are convinced that there is more at work than individual choice, there is little reason to pursue questions about the consequences of alternative academic organizations of high schools.

Track Placement: Assigned or Chosen?

Tracking in secondary schools is a complex process, a complete investigation of which would require a very sophisticated research design. Our task at this point is more modest. We seek to examine available evidence in *High School and Beyond* to discern the likelihood of institutional effects on students' track placements. We bring three quite different analyses to bear on this issue. Each analysis has its own weaknesses, but there is no reason to believe that they share a common source of bias. If each analysis points to the same conclusion, the validity of that conclusion is greatly strengthened.

A first and relatively simple approach considers student reports about the placement process. In particular, the 1980 *HS&B* sophomores were asked: "Were you assigned to the [curriculum track] program you are now in, or did you choose it yourself?" Because there are such large differences between sectors in the proportion of students in various tracks, it is instructive to examine these reports separately by track.

We may compare the proportion of Catholic and public school students in each of three curricular tracks who report that they were assigned to that track (see Figure 4.1). In general, Catholic school students are more likely to report that they were assigned to the track in which they are currently enrolled. More important, the between-sector differences are most pronounced in the academic track. Students in Catholic schools, who are twice as likely to be in that track in the first place, are also more than twice as likely as their counterparts in public schools to be *assigned* to this program. The reports from students, therefore, support the contention that Catholic schools play a more active role in guiding students toward an academic course of study. These reports also indicate that in public schools, the selection of a college-preparatory program is especially subject to student/ family choice.

A second piece of evidence is found in the match-up between track enrollment and college plans. Enrolling in the academic curriculum track is generally considered appropriate, perhaps even essential, behavior for students who plan to attend college.[19] Therefore, comparing students' intentions about college with their actual track placement provides an important indicator of both the efficiency of the process that allocates students to tracks and the degree of congruence in the school environment between students' aspirations and actual academic behavior.

Simple cross tabulations of the proportions of students with college ambitions at various stages in their high school careers by academic track

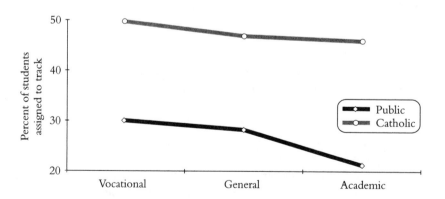

Figure 4.1 Proportion of students in each curriculum track reporting they were assigned to track by the school. Data from *High School and Beyond*.

provide useful evidence here. In particular, we consider reports from *HS&B* students about their educational aspirations at three points: a retrospective report about the plans they had while in grade 8; their plans midway in their high school career (end of grade 10); and their plans as they prepare to graduate (end of grade 12). Students in both sectors describe themselves as somewhat more educationally ambitious before they entered high school than they were at sophomore year (see Table 4.3). Over this period, there is a 7 percent decline in the proportion of students planning to go to college in both Catholic and public schools. This suggests a "cooling out" phenomenon as students confront the reality of academic work. The overall trend in college plans, however, is different in the two sectors. There is a steady downward drift in postsecondary plans from grade 8 through grade 12 among public school students, but the data suggest a slight increase among Catholic school students in educational aspirations over the last two years of high school.[20]

Focusing on the congruity between educational aspirations and academic activities, we find a much closer fit in Catholic schools. Seventy-one percent of Catholic high school students indicate that they had college ambitions in grade 8, and 72 percent of students in that sector are enrolled in the academic track in grade 10. In the sophomore year, the proportion of students in the academic track is even slightly greater than those who state that they plan to go to college (72 percent versus 64 percent).

The public school reports suggest some incongruity. Although 53 percent of public high school students indicate that they planned to attend college

Table 4.3 Public and Catholic schools: Percentage of students who state they had plans to attend college in grades 8, 10, and 12 compared with proportion in academic track

	Public schools	Catholic schools
Percentage of students reporting college plans in		
Grade 8	52.5	70.9
Grade 10	45.0	64.0
Grade 12	41.4	66.5
Percentage of students in academic track in grade 10	38.0	71.5

Source: Data from Lee and Bryk (1988), 83.

when they were in grade 8, only 38 percent are in the college-preparatory track at grade 10. This means that a significant number of public high school students who had college plans were not enrolled in high school programs structured to reflect those ambitions. Somehow a sizable proportion (15 percent) of educationally motivated students in public schools are "leaking" out of the programmatic environment necessary to realize their academic plans.

This analysis provides further evidence suggesting an institutional pull by Catholic schools toward academic pursuits. This again contrasts with public schools, where some incongruity exists between students' academic efforts and their educational aspirations. In public high schools, a continuous process of discouragement appears to be at work, as increasing numbers of students abandon postsecondary educational plans.

A third piece of evidence involves the track placements for those students who transfer from Catholic elementary school to public high school at grades 9 or 10 (C→P). These students have been exposed to elementary schooling similar to that of the majority of students in Catholic secondary schools. As a result, examination of this subgroup of students provides at least a partial control for prior educational experiences.[21] That these students *had* been in Catholic schools shows that at one time their families evidenced values associated with selecting private schooling of this sort, and this fact strengthens the analysis against claims of selection bias on this account.

In certain respects the C→P students resemble their public school peers. Of the C→P subgroup, 40.6 percent are in the academic track as opposed to 38 percent of the entire sector. Approximately 50 percent of C→P students report college ambitions in grade 8. The average socioeconomic status for this subgroup is also very similar to that of the public sector as a whole. In other respects, however, the C→P group more closely resembles Catholic high school students: fewer C→P students are minority students (11 percent) and fewer are non-Catholics (8.7 percent)—and even these students rate themselves as quite religious.

Using a prediction equation technique, we estimated the proportion of the students in the C→P group who *would* have been in an academic track had they chosen a Catholic high school.[22] Comparing these predictions with the actual proportion of students who enrolled in an academic program provides an estimate of the Catholic school "track advantage." The prediction equation indicates that 60.2 percent of the students in the C→P transfer group *would have been* in an academic track *if* they had stayed in the Catholic sector. Compared with the actual academic track enrollment for this group—40.6 percent—we find a difference of 19.6 percent. This difference, almost a 50 percent increase in the likelihood of being assigned to an academic track, is both a substantively and a statistically significant effect.[23]

Here too we find evidence supporting the contention that Catholic high schools exert an institutional pull on their students toward academic work. Students with comparable academic and family backgrounds are much more likely to be in an academic track if they attend a Catholic school. Both the *HS&B* analyses and the field observations point in the same direction. Assignment to track in Catholic high schools is more directly controlled by the school and not as much influenced by student choice or whim.

Course Enrollment: A Consequence of School Organization or Student Choice?

Students in public schools are afforded considerable discretion in their choice of courses. The expansion over the last two decades in the number and type of courses offered is a key factor here. Public high school students are typically presented with a smorgasbord of outwardly appealing courses that may entice some students away from more traditional academic offerings. Our field observations suggest a different situation within Catholic high schools. The course offerings are not as broad, and the largest portion of a student's course of study is set by school graduation requirements. Analyses of *HS&B* data provide further support for this contention.

We examined the number of course offerings in Catholic and public secondary schools in three academic areas (mathematics, science, and foreign language) and two nonacademic areas (personal development and business). In both sectors larger schools tend to offer more courses, regardless of subject-matter area. This is primarily a matter of logistics. In larger schools, more classes must be organized in each subject area. Although in principle a school could just add more sections of the same course, the data indicate that there is a disproportionate tendency in larger schools to rely on increasing offerings rather than adding sections to accommodate larger enrollments.

This expansion of curriculum accompanying larger school size works somewhat differently, however, in the two sectors. Although the relationship between school size and course offerings in mathematics and science is reasonably similar in Catholic and public schools (Figures 4.2 and 4.3), Catholic schools tend to offer considerably more foreign language courses across all size groups (see Figure 4.4). This partially explains the data presented earlier indicating that Catholic high school students enroll in more language courses—that is, they take more courses because there are more to take. In contrast, public schools generally provide a greater number of

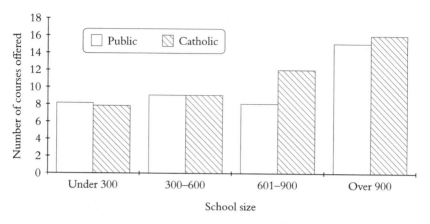

Figure 4.2 Number of courses offered in mathematics in Catholic and public schools. Data from *High School and Beyond.*

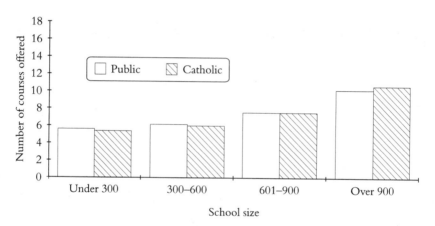

Figure 4.3 Number of courses offered in science in Catholic and public schools. Data from *High School and Beyond.*

offerings in nonacademic areas (see Figures 4.5 and 4.6).[24] Although Catholic schools provide courses in these subjects, the number of offerings does not increase with school size at the same rate as in the public sector. When logistics permit a curriculum expansion in Catholic schools, it is most likely to occur in academic subject areas and not elsewhere.

These analyses provide further empirical support for the inference that Catholic schools take a proactive stance encouraging academic coursework among their students. Here too, however, there is still the competing explanation of student choice. Might not the greater number of academic

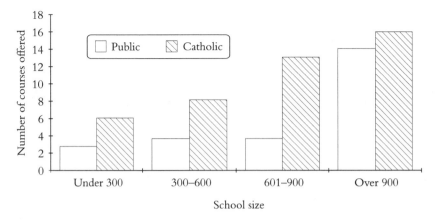

Figure 4.4 Number of courses offered in foreign language in Catholic and public schools. Data from *High School and Beyond*.

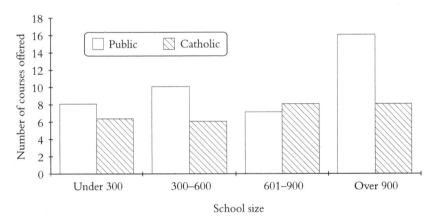

Figure 4.5 Number of courses offered in personal development in Catholic and public schools. Data from *High School and Beyond*.

courses and greater enrollment by Catholic school students in such courses simply reflect the somewhat more advantaged nature of the students who attend Catholic schools, given that we know that social class is related to academic course enrollment and aspirations in both sectors?

This question suggests a closer scrutiny of course enrollments across sectors and, in particular, a comparison of public and Catholic school students with similar backgrounds and the same achievement levels at sophomore year. If the Catholic school "academic course-taking advantage" persists even after adjusting for the differences among students on these

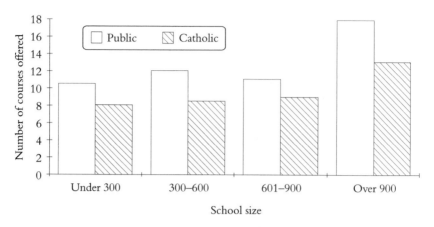

Figure 4.6 Number of courses offered in business in Catholic and public schools. Data from *High School and Beyond.*

factors, then the empirical evidence lends even more support for a school effects explanation. For several reasons, the best place to pursue this question with *HS&B* data is in the area of mathematics instruction. First, the mathematics test has been shown to be the most reliable *HS&B* measure.[25] Second, it contains the most items (38), and visual examination suggests that its content bears some relationship to specific secondary school instruction. Third, the main *HS&B* information source on curriculum is course titles, which tend to be more informative in mathematics than in other areas.

In this analysis we combined the Catholic and public school samples to investigate, separately for each curriculum track, the effect of school sector on enrollment in advanced mathematics courses. Here the sector effect represents the difference between Catholic and public school students in taking advanced courses *after* being adjusted for differences in academic background, social class, minority status, remedial placement, and sophomore-year mathematics achievement.[26] The results are presented in Table 4.4. In all three tracks, students in Catholic schools take more advanced math courses. The standardized effect estimates for Catholic school sector in Table 4.4 are reexpressed in Figure 4.7 in terms of the number of extra math courses taken by Catholic school students. As in the unadjusted data in Table 4.2, the biggest differences between the sectors are for those students who are in the nonacademic tracks, where the Catholic school "math-course advantage" is more than half a year.

All of the analyses on both track placement and course enrollments indicate a considerably greater academic emphasis in Catholic high schools

Table 4.4 Standardized regression coefficients for the model predicting enrollment in advanced mathematics courses, separately for each curriculum track (combined Catholic and public high school sample)

Independent variables	Curriculum track		
	Academic	General	Vocational
Catholic sector effect	.14***	.25***	.25***
Academic background	.11***	.20***	.14***
Social class	.06**	.09**	.07
Minority group	−.01	.04	.00
Remedial program	−.10***	−.08**	.05
Sophomore mathematics achievement	.47***	.43***	.36***
% of variance explained (R^2)	33	41	29
Sample size	2,176	1,009	738

Source: Data from Lee and Bryk (1988), 86.

Note: Combining the Catholic and public samples into a single analytic unit, with a dummy variable (Catholic = 1, public = 0), assumes that there are no significant interactions between school sector and background variables. In these regressions, there were statistically significant interactions (as a group) only for the vocational track sample. However, the results show a similar pattern across all three curriculum tracks.

**$p \leq .01$. ***$p \leq .001$.

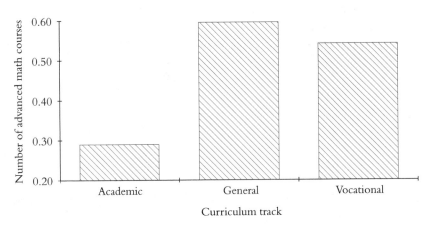

Figure 4.7 Catholic school advantage in advanced math course enrollment, adjusted for background and tenth grade math achievement. Data from *High School and Beyond.*

for all students, regardless of curriculum track. These empirical results support a conclusion that there are important differences in the academic organization of Catholic and public secondary schools. Moreover, there is substantial evidence that these differences are deliberately created as a matter of policy.

ALTHOUGH CATHOLIC schools explored curriculum innovation during the 1970s, these "academic reforms" never became institutionalized. After a brief period of experimentation, schools returned to a conventional class-period organization, heightened academic standards, and a renewed emphasis on a common core of academic subjects. It is thus not surprising that HS&B data indicate that students in Catholic schools take more traditional academic courses than do their counterparts in public schools.

Simple examination of course enrollments can be misleading, however; students may have very different experiences in courses with similar titles in the same school. Although Catholic schools make some accommodation in curriculum offerings both for less well prepared and for more talented students, the subsequent differentiation among students' actual academic experiences remains modest in comparison with public high schools. In the schools we visited, students shared a broad core of intellectual experiences. The common goal for students—regardless of ability, interests, or aspirations—was to move them as far as possible through a traditional academic program. We deduce that Catholic high schools take a direct, active role in deciding what their students *should* learn and deliberately create an academic structure to advance this aim.

This academic organization provides a strong contrast with characterizations of contemporary public high schools as "shopping malls," where market forces and free choice dominate. On the one hand, the expansion of the curriculum in the public high school has given students a greater degree of choice in their program of study. Some of the specialty programs in large comprehensive public high schools are impressive by any standard, with few rivals within the Catholic sector. The quality of experience for students exposed to such programs is, in all likelihood, outstanding. On the other hand, the extensive specialization and student choice within public high schools have obscured (but not eliminated) what was more obvious under an assigned tracking system—that less advantaged young people are more likely to enroll in nonacademic courses. Even here, however, such developments have "solved" an institutional problem: to the extent that students choose their courses (for good or bad) and are held responsible for the consequence of those choices, schools are less accountable for social inequities in students' exposure to academic knowledge.

In contrast, we posit that the Catholic high school, with its strong emphasis on a common core of academic experience and only modest levels of student choice, attenuates some of the powerful differentiating influences at work in public secondary schools. Such an academic organization, moreover, exerts a strong integrating force on both students and adults, binding them together in a common round of school life that encourages each person's best efforts.

❖ 5 ❖

Communal
Organization

St. Frances', located in inner-city Baltimore, boasts two imposing brick buildings set amid a cluster of modest turn-of-the-century rowhouses. The high school's main building, a four-story edifice, was built late in the nineteenth century. Next to it stands the "new building," a gymnasium and classroom annex, constructed in 1930. A black-topped school yard almost the size of a square city block surrounds these two structures. A barbed-wire fence along the back of the campus offers protection from unwelcome intrusions of the city. Security is a conspicuous concern. The doors remain locked, requiring visitors to ring a bell for admission. Only after being visually screened and identified were we admitted to the school premises. Safety requires constant vigilance in the world outside St. Frances'.

The atmosphere inside, however, stands in sharp contrast to the exterior surroundings. The neighborhood's shabbiness, the loud noise of traffic, and the threat of violence are left behind. The large main lobby of the school is graciously appointed. Off the main lobby is a sitting room furnished with antique furniture and an elegant but worn oriental rug. The elaborate and highly polished banisters of the massive oak staircase lead to the upper floors, and each staircase landing is framed by a vibrant stained-glass window. The marble floors, worn in the center from a century of use, suggest a timeless elegance. Despite the age of the facilities and the evidence of wear and tear, it is clear that both students and adults care about the school buildings in which they work.

Even more striking about St. Frances' is the way people interact. The halls ring with students' animated conversations. In pairs or small groups, sitting on the floor or perched on chairs and sofas, they exchange information about the day's events. Friends or teachers who pass are typically greeted by an embrace, a kiss on the cheek, a friendly pat on the back, or at least a smile and a quick "hello." Warm and informal interactions suggest a genuine sense of human caring. As at St. Madeline's, the St. Frances' students and faculty agree: this school feels like home. The strong sense of stability and affection conveyed by this environment represents a psychological contrast as pronounced as the physical contrast between the school and the city outside.

Anyone who has recently spent time inside Catholic high schools finds it difficult to ignore the distinctive atmosphere in many of them. In seeking to understand this special character, we have concluded that the description used by both students and adults—"we are a community"—captures the essence of the schools' social organization.

Although the importance of a sense of community has been frequently noted in writings about good high schools,[1] the essential features of such schools have remained largely unidentified. The rhythms of life within the Catholic schools we visited were rather different from the impersonal and bureaucratic routines that characterized the public secondary schools with which we were familiar. In light of the intellectual heritage of these schools, we gradually became convinced that Catholic schools represented a very different organizational form, which we term "communal."

It became increasingly evident that a full account of the operations of Catholic schools would need to build on, but also extend, the features of classroom interaction and academic organization already discussed. This expanded framework would need to include: the role of a school's tradition and values; the nature of the social interactions among students, faculty, administrators, and, to a lesser degree, parents; and the ways in which such interactions draw individuals into a shared school life. Accordingly, we considered in more detail four features of Catholic high schools that appeared central: the definition of the boundaries that constitute the community; the system of organizational beliefs that structures a shared purpose; the social activities that give life to these beliefs; and the formal organizational roles that facilitate this social dynamic.

We posit that when these organizational features join together, far-reaching effects accrue. Work within such contexts benefits both teachers and students. Faculty are encouraged to commit their best efforts to their uncertain and taxing profession; students are motivated to engage in academic study even if its immediate value is not obvious. Here we elaborate the basic features of the communal organization found in Catholic high schools. We return to these ideas in Chapter 11, where we empirically test these effects on teacher commitment and student engagement.

A Definition of Boundaries

The orderly environment within Catholic schools reflects a philosophical belief in schools as sites for contemplation and thinking.[2] This perspective requires schools to create within their environs "times of peace, islands of grace, and places of quiet."[3] Organizing space in ways that invite study and private thought contributes a tranquil atmosphere that balances a lively and vibrant student social life. Even in the largest of our field sites, St. Edward's, whose physical plant resembles that of a modern suburban high school, pride in the school environment was evident. In the clean and well-maintained buildings, the incidence of vandalism was very low.[4] Students and faculty actively participated in keeping their school orderly and neat.

This sense of respect and responsibility carried over into these schools' social environment. As we entered our field-site schools, teachers and students immediately identified us as guests and greeted us with friendliness and hospitality. The school buildings and campuses were clearly not public places, but were "owned" by the students and teachers, who welcomed us into their home.

The concept of a community, however, is more complex than mere physical space. It also implies membership in a set of traditions and mores that reflect the group's purpose. Particularly important in this regard are the mechanisms that control the entry and exit of individuals into and out of the community.

Admission and Termination of Students

In general, Catholic high schools are not highly selective in their admissions. The typical school reports accepting 88 percent of the students who apply, and only about a third of the schools maintain a waiting list.[5] Indeed, the school does not operate as the principal selection mechanism; the real control rests with the students and their families through their decision to apply for admission. The voluntary nature of this action is important, because it signifies a willingness to join the community and to accept its values. This choice is the first step in building a relationship of trust between the school and the student and his or her family.

There are general requirements for admission to most Catholic high schools. About 70 percent of the principals report that their schools require either standardized achievement scores or school-constructed tests. Most schools also request an interview with prospective students and their parents, a letter of recommendation from the applicant's elementary school, and previous academic records. Religious affiliation is not a routine consideration. Less than a fourth of Catholic high school principals reported that a student's religious background is considered in the admission decision.

Principals in the field sites said that they looked for students with the potential to succeed in their school. No single factor was preeminent in the admission decision, and all information on applicants was evaluated. Principals occasionally took risks in individual cases. Nearly one-fifth of Catholic high school principals reported having accepted students during the previous year who had been expelled from public schools for either disciplinary or academic reasons.[6] An encouraging recommendation or a good interview with a student and his or her parents might convince a principal that an applicant had more potential than an otherwise dismal record would indicate. In commenting on the decision to admit a high-risk student, principals spoke of the importance of communicating the school's expectations explicitly to both student and parents. Principals also indicated that such students were likely to receive extra assistance from teachers and counselors during their first year of transition into the school.

Contrary to widespread belief, very few students are expelled from Catholic high schools for either academic or disciplinary reasons. On average, Catholic high schools dismiss fewer than two students per year, and fewer than three students per year are suspended for any reason.[7]

Virtually every Catholic high school has a written code of conduct that includes a dress code, standards for social behavior among students and faculty, and a list of prohibited behaviors (for example, alcohol and drug possession and use, smoking, leaving the school grounds during the day). In the majority of schools, a first serious offense (such as possession or use of alcohol or an illicit drug, theft, physical injury to another student, or verbal abuse of a teacher) is met with suspension. Repeated offenses can be expected to result in expulsion.[8] This set of standards is widely understood among parents, students, and school personnel. Extreme antisocial behavior is not tolerated and occurs rarely. Because the school's standards are made clear to students and parents as a part of the admission process, a decision to enroll in a Catholic high school constitutes an assent to this code of behavior. The position of the school is thus articulated clearly and is implicitly, if not explicitly, endorsed by parents.

Although Catholic schools have control over their student population by means of admissions and expulsion procedures, the direct use of these controls is not extensive. To be sure, there are norms for student conduct that the school community actively respects and protects. Nonetheless, Catholic schools maintain such understandings while at the same time remaining relatively open institutions with a membership that is quite diverse racially, socially, and even religiously. The operant social dynamic is conditioned both by the school's explicit philosophy and by the voluntary choice on the part of students and parents to join the community. These interactions, which are rather similar in all Catholic high schools, forge a base of commitment between the student and family and the school.

Personnel Selection and Termination

In choosing staff, principals in the Catholic high schools we visited reported that they looked for individuals who had a strong academic background, who enjoyed working with teenagers, and who were supportive of the school's philosophy. They preferred candidates who were also willing to coach, supervise extracurricular activities, and be available to students beyond regular school hours. Principals often related the hiring of staff to concerns about the school's culture. They saw new teachers not just as filling particular openings in departments but also as members of the larger faculty, committed to building a community within the school. Most of the teachers in the field-site schools were graduates of either Catholic elementary or secondary schools, and nearly a fifth had graduated from the school at which they were teaching.

In general, Catholic school principals enjoy considerable discretion in the hiring and firing of faculty. Over 95 percent of the principals reported that they made the final decision on new teachers.[9] This is markedly different from their public school counterparts, who are much more likely to complain that "central office control" and "excessive transfers from other schools" act as substantial barriers to recruiting excellent teachers for their schools.[10]

Similarly, few Catholic high schools have a tenure policy for their faculties. Whereas 88 percent of public high schools offer tenure, only 26 percent of Catholic high schools do so.[11] As a result, Catholic school principals face substantially fewer obstacles in dismissing a teacher for poor performance. Termination procedures in the public sector are far more complex and much more time consuming. It has been estimated that a dismissal proceeding in the public sector, including development of documentation and case preparation, requires three times as long as in Catholic schools.[12]

Not surprisingly, given salary levels and tenure policies, there is a somewhat greater turnover of teachers in Catholic than in public schools. *High School and Beyond* data indicate an annual teacher turnover rate of 12 percent in the Catholic sector, compared with 9 percent for public schools. Over

15 percent of Catholic secondary schools have annual turnover rates in excess of 20 percent. Statistics on faculty stability provide similar evidence. Whereas 18 percent of the faculty in Catholic schools have taught in their current school for more than ten years, the comparable figure in public schools is 36 percent.

Observations in our field-site schools provide some perspective on these statistics. Three distinct types of individuals made up the faculties of the Catholic high schools we visited. The first group consists of highly committed professional teachers who view their work within their schools as careers. In the past, members of this category were almost entirely religious: sisters, priests, and brothers. More recently, increasing numbers of lay individuals are making career commitments to Catholic school teaching. It is particularly these individuals for whom the relatively low salaries in Catholic schools are problematic.

The second group consists primarily of young laypeople who choose to teach in a Catholic school for a few years after college. Many of these individuals see teaching as an important social and educational ministry, and as a way perhaps to give something back for what they may have received during their own schooling. These teachers tend to use this period in their lives to clarify career or graduate school goals before moving to other pursuits. For a few young women, teaching still constitutes the traditional short-term employment before beginning to raise a family.

The third category, composed mainly of women, is made up of individuals who move into teaching in Catholic schools (or, perhaps, return to it) after their own children are in school or even grown. The work schedule, the supplement to family income, and a general respect for the social value and mission of Catholic schooling are primary motivations for this group.

This typology suggests that only for the first group—the professional teacher—is a career an important concern. In the past this group was mostly religious staff, and therefore the economic issues attendant to a possible loss of employment were not real. For the other two groups, neither economic gain nor career development are likely to be major concerns. Because the motivations for working in a Catholic school are principally intrinsic and psychic for these groups, an unfulfilling teaching experience is usually sufficient reason to move on.

Catholic school principals have been able, at least in the recent past, to attract a lay faculty who share their vision for the school. As a result, new teachers are likely to have much in common with their faculty colleagues and to identify quickly with the school's mission. Given the extended commitment of time and considerable financial sacrifice required, those who continue to teach in Catholic schools are there because they choose to be. The personal commitment behind such a choice is an asset to the school community.

Shared Organizational Beliefs

An Academic Core for All

We found strong support among the faculty in the field sites for an academic core curriculum for all students. The idea that all students should take a core of academic courses was shared by both religious and lay faculty (80 and 85 percent, respectively), who also agreed that all students should master such a curriculum (77 and 76 percent, respectively). Interestingly, teachers appeared to distinguish between *what* ought to be learned and *why* it should be learned. Given the strong support for a common academic core shown above, it is somewhat surprising that so few teachers (only 29 percent of religious and 33 percent of lay faculty) agreed that all students should follow a college-preparatory program. The apparent message is that an academic core curriculum is appropriate for all students, regardless of their postsecondary plans.

These beliefs are reflected in the formal organization of the curriculum, discussed in Chapter 4. Such beliefs also seem to motivate the policies governing the assignment of teachers to courses. We found it quite common for individual faculty members to teach sections ranging from remedial to honors. Although seniority plays a significant role in course assignments within the public sector,[13] department heads and principals in our field-site schools indicated that Catholic high schools make these decisions primarily on the basis of the skills, interests, and aptitudes of teachers. Teachers often used such language as "an opportunity to serve" to describe the teaching of remedial classes. No one described such work as a consequence of his or her low status within the organization.[14]

An emphasis on academic pursuits, with a school and classroom environment that is structured toward these ends, is a common characteristic of Catholic secondary schools. In the field-site schools 58 percent of religious and 63 percent of lay faculty assigned homework at least three times per week, for example, and most teachers also indicated that they "frequently" or "always" graded the homework. Testing was described as a regular part of their teaching by 87 percent of religious and 90 percent of lay teachers. This academic focus is also reflected in a national survey of Catholic high school principals; 69 percent described the classroom environments in their schools as "very structured," and 77 percent characterized the school day as "very structured."[15] Nearly unanimous are principals, teachers, and students, who agree that "all students are expected to do homework," that "all teachers press students to do their best," and that "all students place a high priority on learning."[16] Such high levels of academic expectations and environmental press are as prevalent in inner-city schools serving high proportions of minority and disadvantaged youth as in suburban schools.[17]

Formation of Personal Character

In the Catholic schools we visited, established procedures guided the handling of offenses serious enough to warrant suspension or expulsion. These rudiments of due process are routine in most Catholic high schools.[18] Although on the surface these procedures resemble those found in the public sector, the motivating force is quite different.

Field studies report that public schools have extensive codes of conduct and elaborate systems for adjudicating misconduct.[19] Philosophically, the intent of these structures is to protect individual students' rights while securing the necessary order for academic learning to occur. Beyond safeguarding this basic social order in schools, however, the contemporary public high school appears relatively silent about any larger socialization aims. The latter is a very recent phenomenon; through World War II, the formation of moral character was viewed as a central purpose of public schooling.[20]

Closely tied to this development is a fundamental change in the nature of adult authority in public high schools. The traditional notion that a teacher acts in place of a parent, *in loco parentis,* has been reduced to a more limited and regulated role.[21] Much of this change grew out of legislative and judicial efforts beginning in the 1960s to redress infringements of student rights and thereby to create more just school environments. Students, however, tend to offer rather dismal evaluations of their schools' effectiveness in this regard; the vast majority of public school students view discipline as neither strict nor fair.[22]

In the Catholic schools we visited, the approach to student conduct was much richer than maintenance of a minimal social order. Through both formal philosophy statements and routine day-to-day encounters, the schools articulated an explicitly moral understanding of the purposes of education. In terms of students' academic efforts, the emphasis was on developing a sense of personal responsibility and a commitment to hard work.[23] Under this philosophy, students' failure to give their best efforts belittled both the sacrifices of their parents in paying tuition and also the efforts of their teachers, who were working hard on their behalf. Although many of the teachers we interviewed lamented the disturbing social problems that even students from "good" families encountered at home, the teachers were reluctant to evoke family background as an excuse for poor performance. Though students' home lives might be chaotic, when they were in school "their job is to learn and mine is to teach them," said one instructor.

These Catholic schools consciously sought to shape the kind of people students would become—to engage in what might be called "character building." The adults regularly and comfortably discussed the basic principles for which the school stood: truthfulness, caring, social responsibility. In confronting particular incidents of misconduct, the school staff discussed with the student the meaning of membership in the school community and how the student's personal behavior had violated its norms: "You are a member of this community, and your behavior affects others." Although obeying rules was important, this was true mainly because of the larger principles the rules embodied. Responding to infractions of the rules often afforded public opportunities to teach the beliefs of the community.

Responsibility for character formation was shared broadly among the faculty and was as much a part of their job as the courses they taught or the extracurricular activities they supervised. As in public schools, there were formal structures for disciplinary matters. Typically, an assistant principal had broad responsibility for both school discipline and the adjudication of incidents of serious misconduct. When specialized expertise was needed, such as treating a student's drug problem, efforts were made to obtain it outside the school. Even so, the whole faculty remained involved in shaping the moral tone of the school and in serving as day-to-day role models. Although no national data exist to cross-check our field observations on this topic, other case studies of Catholic schools offer corroborating accounts.[24]

School Mission

Not surprisingly, Catholic school teachers expressed a strong commitment to their students' academic *and* personal development. Eighty-nine percent of a national sample of Catholic high school teachers supported the view that "major emphasis should be placed on mastery of reading, writing, and mathematics skills." Similar endorsements were offered for "critical thinking skills" (83 percent), "intellectual curiosity" (81 percent), and "a healthy self-concept" (89 percent). There was also substantial support for the development of "compassion" (79 percent), "tolerance" (69 percent), and a "commitment to justice" (68 percent). The priority given these social values exceeded support for more traditional religious development, such as building a "knowledge of Catholic doctrine" (52 percent), "acceptance of Catholic teachings on moral values" (52 percent), and "clear understanding of the Bible" (49 percent).[25]

Responses to queries about students' religious formation also supported the emphasis on the social and personal aspects of student development. Teachers' statements about their most important objectives included: "to help students develop a compassion for other people" (82 percent felt that this was either "extremely" or "very" important); "to help students see the relevance of a Christian value system in their daily lives" (71 percent); and "to help promote a sense of community within my school" (70 percent). The traditional components of religious formation—inculcating a commitment to Church doctrine and moral teachings—were given a lower priority.[26]

Lay and religious faculty differed somewhat in their views on religious formation, particularly about Church teachings on issues of personal morality. Religious faculty rated objectives such as "building a faith commitment," "encouraging participation in the sacraments," and "acceptance of Catholic teachings" considerably higher than did their lay colleagues. Religious faculty were also more likely to support the Church's stand against sex outside of marriage, birth control, and abortion.

Substantial division on matters of personal morality has persisted within the American Catholic Church since the promulgation of *Humanae Vitae,* the controversial papal encyclical on birth control, in the late 1960s. These divisions rarely surface as a source of overt conflict, however, which is important for the operation of schools. Such internal differences coexist with a solid core of principles upon which the faculty do agree: that education is fundamentally a moral enterprise; that the person is composed of both intellect and will; and that both of these components are properly the focus of teachers' efforts.

A Set of Shared Activities

Core Academic Curriculum

A Catholic school's belief system is enacted through a variety of activities. Foremost is the core academic curriculum, detailed in Chapter 4. The procedures employed in organizing students and teachers into courses tend to minimize the stratifying effects that occur through conventional forms of curriculum organization common in public secondary schools. In general, the organization of academic life in Catholic schools provides a common ground of shared experiences for students and faculty alike.

Extensive Extracurricular Involvement

The extracurriculum provides additional occasions in which to put school beliefs into practice. Extensive student-faculty interaction occurs in athletics, school clubs, and other school-based activities. Catholic school teachers are more involved in these activities and spend more out-of-classroom time engaged with students than their public school counterparts (see Chapter 11). The relatively small size of Catholic high schools (an average enrollment of 546, versus 845 in the public sector) is supportive in this regard. Previous research has documented the constrained opportunity for student involvement in extracurricular activities in big schools.[27] Similarly, as teachers become more specialized in large schools, a smaller proportion of them are drawn into such activities.[28]

As already noted, principals explicitly look for faculty willing to undertake this extended role. Teachers in the field sites, though sometimes lamenting the amount of time spent in these activities, saw them as occasions for moral teaching and for building personal relationships that enhanced classroom work. Against this background, the student reports in *High School and Beyond* about the high levels of teacher interest in them are not surprising.[29]

More generally, we found broad participation in extracurricular activities by both students and faculty in the schools we visited. Students often remained at school as late as five or six o'clock to watch or take part in athletic events, to complete laboratory work, to seek academic help from teachers, or to conduct research in the library. St. Richard's, for example, also served as a place for teenagers to gather on weekends. Several hundred students might attend a basketball game in the gym on a Friday evening in the winter. The next morning, several dozen students might be on campus to decorate the cafeteria for a dance that evening which most of St. Richard's students would attend. Other students would return on Sunday to clean up after the dance or to take part in a Sunday liturgy. St. Richard's served as a social as well as an academic center in its students' lives. Even without weekend events, students often used the school as a meeting place before a movie or a visit to a classmate's home.

Religious Activities

The religious activities of Catholic high schools consciously aim to unite adults and students around the school. Through liturgies, retreats, and community service programs, the Catholic school conveys important organizational values and gives vitality to the idea of membership and social responsibility within a larger community.

Liturgies. Daily attendance at Mass held a central place in the life of students in Catholic high schools of the 1950s. The rapid decline in the availability of priests, beginning in the late 1960s, meant that many schools no longer had access to a full-time chaplain. Celebration of the Mass has thus become an occasional event, but one that remains important nonetheless.

The form of this ritual has changed significantly since Vatican II, most prominently through the introduction of English as the language of liturgy. Although the traditional Latin Mass had a solemn power that encouraged private reflections and contemplation of one's relationship to God, this vertical religion is now rebalanced with a heightened horizontality. Symbols of community such as the sign of peace, when the members of the congregation greet each other with a handshake, have been added. The material elements drawn into the celebration—readings, instrumental music, dance, song, artistic illustrations—invite broader and more active social participation. The meaning of the Mass, the central ritual of Catholic faith, has remained unchanged, however. In eating the bread and drinking the wine of the communion Eucharist, participants are called to share Christ's life and vision and are exhorted to "go and live this faith." While a very personal religious activity, the Mass is also public, in that it invites a response from participants about their common endeavors.[30]

Students in our field sites reported that even after all of the changes brought about by Vatican II, the Mass often feels rather formal. On occasion, however, it hits the mark, stimulating a sense of personal meaning and belonging that links students and adults not only to one another but to a tradition of two millennia.[31]

In addition to changes in the Mass, new liturgical services such as prayer readings, communal reconciliation services, celebration of the rhythms of the liturgical year, and song programs have been added to further enliven the spirit of solidarity encouraged by Vatican II. These activities provide opportunities for school members to assemble and reflect together, sometimes as a whole school, on other occasions perhaps as a homeroom or class. These services may occur in a school chapel; smaller groups might convene in a classroom, an outdoor setting, or a student's home nearby.

Retreat programs. School retreats have experienced equally dramatic changes. The contemporary retreat program bears little resemblance to the activity it replaced—the "days of recollection." In these earlier programs, several hundred students would be assembled in a school chapel or auditorium to be addressed by specially trained priests. Their inspirational talks, often rich in fire and brimstone and replete with warnings about the temptations of the flesh and the pain that awaited those committed to the everlasting fires of hell, were followed by long periods of required silence during which students were directed to consider their personal morality.

In contrast, contemporary programs reflect the spirit of Vatican II in both their focus and their organization. Social morality, the advancement of social justice, and the formation of caring relationships among students, teachers, and parents are organizing themes. Rather than something that is done *for* students, retreats are now a shared undertaking in which there is broad participation preparing for and carrying out the program. Retreats are times to talk about personal concerns, to listen to others, and to reflect on one's life. This new focus is a concrete example of the theological shift in the concept of the Church—from a pre-Vatican II notion of followership, captured in the image of the shepherd and his flock, to the idea of community, captured in the image of the "people of God."

Contemporary retreat programs are typically held at a pastoral off-campus site designed to invite reflection. Away from home, students are encouraged to step back from their daily lives to think about their relationships with friends and family. Retreats aim participants away from the self-absorption of adolescence to a wider perspective on their world and the values worthy of a human life.

A well-developed retreat program can become one of a school's central activities. In the field-site schools, students typically described the junior or senior retreat as a peak experience of their high school years. Such retreats, which could last three or four days, usually involved several faculty members. At St. Edward's, for example, a team of fourteen—five faculty (one a priest), seven alumni, and two senior leaders—were involved in a typical program. Over the course of the year, fifty-four of the eighty staff worked as retreat leaders, bus drivers, substitute teachers, or follow-up directors. Such broad involvement of adults reflects the importance attached to retreats within the school's life. They offer another important opportunity for school staff to shape the kind of people students will become.

Community service programs. A new addition to the spiritual life of Catholic high schools appeared in the aftermath of Vatican II. Over 90 percent of Catholic schools now provide opportunities for both on-campus and off-campus volunteer service.[32] About half of these schools offer credit for off-campus activities. Although very few schools *require* community service for graduation, a large proportion of students are nonetheless involved.

The range of activities is quite diverse. At Bishop O'Boyle, for example, freshmen and sophomores regularly visited a local nursing home to talk with patients and run errands for them. Many older students worked in an inner-city soup kitchen, where they assisted in preparing and distributing meals. Bishop O'Boyle is relatively close to the city, but most of its students had never seen real poverty. Stories students told suggested that their community service experiences had prompted them to question some of what they had previously taken for granted in their lives.

These service programs signify Catholic schools' commitment to a just social community. One board member of a field-site school remarked, "A school should not call itself Catholic if it doesn't have a volunteer service program." The director of the program at St. Edward's commented: "I'm a believer in service. It's important for students to realize that the things they do make a difference. We can heal people and make their lives better. We can raise the awareness of others. Physical contact is vital for Christianity. Some of our students are sheltered from poverty and from people of different races. This program is important because it makes them more aware."

Service programs thus represent another deliberate attempt by Catholic schools to act out their commitment to community. The programs often start with people voluntarily helping one another within the school. Such activity demonstrates the shared commitment to the forming of persons-in-community. Moving out beyond the confines of the school, these programs reach out to strangers in need in the larger community.

The Formal Organization of the Community

Shared understandings about what students should learn and how adults and students should behave grounds a communal school organization. These beliefs are also visible in the formal structure of adult roles and responsibilities.

Distinctive Aspects of the Principalship

The role of the principal in the governance of Catholic schools is detailed in the next chapter, but an important aspect of this role—as communal leader—merits mention here. In a national survey, Catholic school principals described their top goal as "building community among faculty, students, and parents."[33] The idea of community building recurred in our interviews with field-site principals, who spoke about their responsibility to shape school life and to live out school ideals in their own work. They routinely drew on these images in conversations with students, faculty, and parents; in the objectives they set for the school; in the tasks they undertook for themselves and those they delegated; and in how they used their time. These principals also spoke about the "charism" of their founding religious order and of the inspiration this offered their faculty. Recounting the often heroic efforts of those who proceeded them offered sustenance to others within their school community.

Viewing themselves as agents of change committed to communal aims, these principals rarely described their work in instrumental language: the principalship was not spoken of as a "career opportunity." *High School and Beyond* data confirm this difference between public and Catholic school leaders. When asked about their motivation for seeking the principalship, public school principals were much more likely than their Catholic school counterparts to report a preference for administrative responsibilities and a desire to further their careers and to move up to a higher post. In contrast, Catholic school principals expressed more interest in being able to influence school policy.[34]

This perspective on leadership is also recognized by teachers in Catholic schools who, much more frequently than their public school counterparts, describe their principals as encouraging, supportive, and reinforcing.[35] Catholic school principals are less likely to be seen as evaluators and supervisors than as professional colleagues. Such perceptions are also consistent with a view of the school as a community. This contrasts with more formal organizations, where leadership is likely to be described in bureaucratic or even autocratic terms. An important consequence of this role definition is that principals spend less time on procedural concerns and can devote more energy to building personal relationships among students, teachers, and parents.[36]

The Pastoral Minister: A Special Role

Although principals highly value building community within the school, much more of their daily activity than they would like is spent on such mundane problems as delinquent tuitions, student misconduct, and difficulties in bus schedules. Addressing these managerial needs often distracts principals from their efforts to nurture their school. In contrast, the primary responsibility of the pastoral minister or school chaplain involves tending to the personal needs of school members—both adults and students—as well as to the overall character of the school community.[37] These individuals, who function as extensions of the principal, animate the communal life of the school. In the post-Vatican II Church, however, new responsibilities accompany this role, whether filled by a priest (that is, a conventional chaplain) or, as is increasingly the case, by a layperson, called a pastoral minister, who may be either male or female.

For example, in addition to formal religious functions, other activities of Father Hartwick at St. Edward's regularly brought him into contact with large numbers of students and faculty. A substantial portion of his time was set aside for individual counseling, and he also conducted regular small discussion groups on issues of concern to students. During our visits he worked with three different groups of students about their parents' recent divorces. His formal responsibilities included supervision of retreat and community service programs. Father Hartwick served as counselor and friend to the faculty as well. He saw these interactions as central to his role: "The faculty need my ministry, too. I find that they appreciate my contribution to the school and enjoy talking with me about both issues in their personal lives and their work around the school. It's good for me as well, since it offers me a chance to talk with colleagues about our mission here at St. Edward's."

Although much of Father Hartwick's work—offering Mass, hearing confessions, conducting individual and group counseling—resembles a traditional chaplaincy, the full scope is broader now than in the past and includes a problem agenda set by both students and faculty. There is still concern for vertical religious expression, but Father Hartwick's efforts are also broadly social, focusing on the problems of daily life encountered by community members and their families, both inside and outside of the school.

An Extended Teacher Role

As discussed in Chapter 3, Catholic school faculty typically take on multiple responsibilities: classroom teacher, coach, counselor, and adult role model. This broadly defined role creates many opportunities for faculty and student encounters. Through these social interactions, teachers convey an "intrusive interest" in students' personal lives that extends beyond the classroom door into virtually every facet of school life.[38] In some cases it extends even to students' homes and families. In these interactions with teachers, students encounter a full person, not just a subject-matter specialist, a guidance specialist, a discipline specialist, or some other technical expert. The interaction is personal rather than bureaucratic.

From a purely logistical perspective, the small size of Catholic high schools combined with their limited fiscal resources presses faculty into multiple activities. There are many tasks to be accomplished, and resources to hire specialists to undertake them are scarce. But this is also a consciously chosen role, as evidenced in the language used by teachers in talking about their work. In our field interviews, teachers often used such terms as "ministry," "vocation," or "calling" to describe their activities.[39] This conception of teaching is apparently widely shared in Catholic high schools. In a survey of teachers in Catholic schools serving low-income students, for example, the three most common reasons given for teaching in a Catholic high school were: "a desire to teach in this kind of environment," "a view of teaching as ministry," and "a love of teaching."[40]

The extended role for high school teachers thus arises as a deliberate enactment of the principle of Christian personalism, set in the context of the larger social justice mission of the school. This role is based on the belief that both individual and social change are rooted in the spiritual force that derives from genuine social engagement. An educational environment that promotes social justice requires not only the development of students' intellects but also the nurturance of voices of conscience. Such dispositions are formed through social experience in a just and caring community, in which personalism characterizes social relations and solidarity orders and supports organizational life. In such an environment, people know, trust, and care about one another.

We found strong endorsement of this extended faculty role in our interviews with parents, who spoke enthusiastically about their children's teachers. Terms such as "dedicated," "committed," and "involved in the lives of their students" were frequently used. Almost 90 percent of the parents we interviewed characterized teachers' interest in students as either "good" or "excellent." One parent summarized: "They [the teachers in this school] are generally exceptional people."

Reflecting on these observations, we wondered how schools go about developing faculty members who think about their work in such terms. We found few formal procedures to orient new staff to the school's mission. Rather, the key seemed to be in the hiring process. The composition of Catholic school faculties reflects both self-selection by teachers in applying to work there and the explicit intention on the part of the principals to "build a staff consistent with the school's values." Over 50 percent of the new lay teachers who have entered Catholic schools over the last two decades have had a Catholic elementary, secondary, or postsecondary education, and the vast majority of these teachers have experienced Catholic schooling at all three levels. Most lay teachers are young (over 80 percent are less than forty-four years of age), and thus have been educated during the post-Vatican II period.[41] These facts about teachers' educational background are important, because research on teaching suggests that the most important formative influence on teachers is how they themselves were taught.[42] We conclude that the teacher culture in Catholic high schools is in large measure a natural inheritance of the broader religious renewal in the American Catholic Church following Vatican II.

The transformation of Catholic schools into post-Vatican II lay institutions also benefited greatly from the general shortage of available teaching positions in public schools during the 1970s. In 1983, principals reported few serious problems in attracting good candidates. They were able to attract new teachers who were technically competent and whose values were consistent with those of the institution, despite the low salaries and considerable responsibilities. Should labor market conditions change, however, Catholic schools could find it difficult to maintain such faculties in the future.[43]

WE HAVE ASSEMBLED a diverse array of information from field observations, in-depth interviews, and survey reports about the distinctive beliefs, activities, and structures that typify the contemporary Catholic high school, and we have attempted to link these observations with the intellectual tradition that undergirds Catholic schools. Important to understanding life within these schools is the idea of the Catholic high school as a community. This concept integrates a variety of organizational phenomena, including the boundary conditions that tend to induce institutional affiliation; the shared beliefs that bring coherence and lend meaning to daily school life; the organizational activities that enliven and validate these beliefs; and the institutional roles that formally affirm the broadly espoused commitment to school community.

Narrowly construed, institutional boundaries are the physical limits that define a school building. Also at work, however, are traditions and mores that operationally define membership in the community. These boundary conditions, both physical and psychic, serve the important function of clearly marking both the rights and the responsibilities of school participation. By accepting membership, faculty, students, and parents make a personal commitment to the organization. Failure to meet this organizational commitment means the potential loss of membership.

Although procedures exist controlling both student and faculty membership in Catholic schools (and are common to all private schools), these policies are seldom restrictive in operation and Catholic school communities remain quite open. The student composition of today's Catholic schools is much more racially and religiously diverse than in the 1950s. It is not unusual to find students in inner-city Catholic high schools who have previously encountered academic or disciplinary problems in a public high school. Similarly, Catholic high school teachers now bring a breadth of background and perspectives to their schools previously unknown in this sector.

The contemporary Catholic high school bears little resemblance to such total institutions as military and fundamentalist academies. Although these institutions are also formed as communities, their social cohesion is obtained through a closedness that requires both highly restrictive admission and free-wheeling expulsion procedures, as well as an emphasis on indoctrinating students in the institution's ideology.[44] There is a distinctive set of organizational beliefs that typifies the Catholic high school, to be sure, but we would characterize these beliefs as expansive, liberating, and humanizing rather than narrow, restrictive, and closed.

The commitment to a core academic program for all students represents an important manifestation of this belief structure. This commitment is grounded in a concept of the person that maintains that developing the ability to reason is the common inheritance of all men and women—it is what makes them distinctly human. In religious terms, all are made in the image and likeness of God. More important than individual aptitude or background is the willingness to commit one's best effort. This notion was captured in a saying overheard in St. Madeline's: "No one fails here who works hard." This contrasts sharply with the operant motto within many public high schools, where "no one fails who shows up."[45]

Strong attention to students' social and personal development accompanies this academic orientation. The adults in Catholic schools accept the responsibility to shape adolescents' lives through personal interaction and individual example. This interest in character formation stands in sharp contrast to a prevalent ideology in public high schools that students should be treated as adults, free to make their own choices and also, implicitly, responsible for the consequences of those choices. In such an ideology, the failure to choose wisely is seen as the personal failure of an individual student rather than the collective responsibility of an institution.[46]

The educational beliefs extant in Catholic high schools are rooted in basic religious understandings, revitalized through Vatican II. These beliefs draw on fundamental Christian virtues of faith, hope, and love. Through faith, participants reach beyond the destructive press of individual material interest. Hope sustains them in the pursuit of worthy aims that will never be fully realized. Finally, love is the force in personal relationships that radiates outward toward others in shared commitments toward social responsibility and justice.

To be sure, these virtues are not a precise social scientific description of average behavior within schools. They are classic institutional norms, in that they motivate and inspire human behavior toward a different world. They have the essential character of all living traditions: the ability to bring meaning to action and thereby transcend the instrumental intent of action. They represent the ideals to which members of the community aspire, while at the same time recognizing that they may never fully achieve them. They are descriptions not of "what is" but, rather, of that toward which "we ought to be pointed."

Such a belief structure stands in a sharp contrast to Gerald Grant's poignant description of life at Hamilton High, a comprehensive urban high school, where the major norm consists of learning how to manipulate the rule system to maximize self-interest.[47] These beliefs are also markedly different from the portrayal offered by Sara Lawrence Lightfoot of Highland Park, an affluent suburban high school,[48] where the primary emphasis is on individual success defined as academic achievement now in order to ensure economic success later. Intellectual values are materialistic, and school operations are distinctly bureaucratic, legalistic, and instrumental. The bonding of students to the school is weak, and there is little altruism of spirit.

But beliefs alone, without tangible concomitants, are little more than empty myth. The belief system of the Catholic high school infuses the basic organization of the school and is regularly acted out in its daily life. Beyond the core curriculum, such shared religious activities as liturgies, retreats, and community service programs further contribute to this common foundation, as does the extensive engagement of both students and faculty in the extracurricular life of the school. An important facilitating factor, the relatively small size of Catholic high schools, makes them more conducive to informal social interactions among both students and faculty. Finally, an extended teacher role that moves beyond academic expertise to see adults as active agents of personal development contributes to the communal experience.

When the factors we have described here coalesce, organizational coherence results. The structure and the activities that occur in such places can be interpreted and understood within the context of the prevailing belief system. Life within such a school makes sense to its members.

We close this chapter with a bit of the language of Catholic schools, in this instance a school philosophy statement. Although not from one of the schools we studied in depth and perhaps more eloquently crafted than most, this statement captures the spirit and sense of commitment to Catholic schools which we have tried to describe.[49]

The Philosophy of St. Ignatius High School

St. Ignatius is a four-year boys' Catholic and Jesuit college preparatory high school. The aim of the entire St. Ignatius community—administrators, faculty, staff, parents and students—is the spiritual, academic, emotional, and physical development of the students.

During his four years at St. Ignatius High School, a student should grow in a personal relationship with Jesus Christ. He should come to realize that he is invited to follow Jesus and work with Him to build God's kingdom on earth. Just as the motto of all Jesuits is "For the Greater Glory of God," the student should come to the same orientation of making choices that honor God by doing the greater or better good.

Specifically, the student should be marked by a number of characteristics. A St. Ignatius student is one who is open to growth. He seeks opportunities to stretch his mind, imagination, feelings and religious commitment.

A St. Ignatius student is intellectually competent. He possesses an appropriate mastery of the fundamental tools of learning. He discovers his emerging intellectual skills for more advanced levels of learning.

A St. Ignatius student is loving. He is able to move beyond self-interest or self-centeredness in his relationships with others.

A St. Ignatius student is a person of faith. He has a basic knowledge of the major doctrines and practices and spirituality of the Catholic Church. He strengthens his relationship with a religious tradition and community. What is said here, respectful of the conscience of the individual, also applies to students of other religious backgrounds.

A St. Ignatius student is committed to doing justice. He recognizes the potential within himself for doing injustice, as well as the injustices in some of the surrounding social structures. He is preparing himself to become a competent, concerned, and responsible member of the world, national, local, and family communities. Thus he is beginning to appreciate the fact that Christian morality not only involves the individual conscience, but demands that each person work actively—in society—to positively promote social justice. In summary a St. Ignatius man is a man for others.

Strong in spirit, rich in the language of renewal from Vatican II, this philosophy remains firmly rooted in tradition: a focus on Christ's life as a model for social interaction; an acknowledgment of the individual, the individual conscience, and the implicit declaration that true faith can occur only as a result of a reasoned choice by an informed conscience; a commitment to unity of the person—body, mind, and spirit; and a belief that education must develop each person's ability to reason as well as the necessary habits of mind and heart that deepen personal life and enrich the social world. Above all, the philosophy proclaims a commitment to reach out to others, an active social responsibility to promote the greater good. Each Catholic high school attempts, in its own way, to make this rich and complex tradition meaningful to young people. Students should know the message, experience it while in school, and ultimately go live it as adults.

❖ 6 ❖

Governance

SEVERAL FACTS complicate any discussion of the governance of Catholic high schools. First, the nature of their fiscal and legal authority varies, depending upon the particular type of Catholic school. Some schools, known as diocesan or central high schools, are operated by dioceses. Others are run by individual parishes or as collaborations among parishes. The largest number are sponsored by individual religious orders and are referred to as private schools.[1] In diocesan schools, formal responsibility resides with the diocese and ultimately with the bishop, who is the religious and executive leader of the diocese. Authority in parish schools is vested in the pastor, who serves as the chief executive officer for the parish. In private schools, responsibility may be vested either in the religious order that sponsors the school or, as is increasingly common, in a board of directors appointed by the founding religious order.

Second, the interpretation and implementation of the governance system vary substantially across dioceses, depending upon the orientation and interests of the individual bishop. Under canon law, the bishop maintains authority over all Catholic schools within his diocese. Although this authority applies most forcefully in the area of Church teachings, the bishop's influence can also extend beyond this domain, because his opinion carries significant weight on most matters. In general bishops refrain from involvement in the day-to-day affairs of operating schools, but they are more likely to take a visible role when controversial issues such as closing financially troubled schools arise.

Third, variations in the organizational control of the religious orders who provide staff for schools add another dimension to the picture. A few orders, known as diocesan congregations, fall under the direct supervision of the bishop. For schools staffed by such congregations, the line of authority between the bishop and the congregation, and thereby to the school, is clear and geographically proximate. For other religious orders, such as the Jesuits, the line of authority begins with a papal agency in Rome. These papal congregations are subdivided by geographic area into what are typically referred to as provinces. Bishops maintain canonical powers over schools operated by papal congregations, but only in extraordinary circumstances do they actually exercise any direct influence. On balance, it is somewhat surprising that in this system of overlapping jurisdictions the incidence of conflict is rare.

Fourth, Vatican II opened to laypersons new opportunities to exercise responsibility for Catholic institutions. With regard to schools, several constitutional elements—such as diocesan pastoral councils, parish councils, and local school boards—have been grafted onto the system within the past two decades. Some of these arrangements exist for individual schools; others are diocese-wide and may set policies that affect a large number of schools.

The governance structure of St. Richard's is typical of diocesan schools. Its major decision-making body, a diocese-wide board, has both religious and lay members appointed by the bishop. The board is charged with recommending policies to the bishop in such areas as faculty salaries, employee benefits, school calendars, tenure policies, tuition and fees, and discipline codes. Although the board officially operates in an advisory capacity, the bishop normally follows the recommendations the board offers. Promulgated policies apply to all diocesan schools under the bishop's control. The appointment of principals in diocesan schools also comes under the authority of this board.

Many diocesan high schools also have a local advisory board. At St. Richard's, the advisory board meets regularly to discuss the school budget and academic programs and to provide support for school fund-raising projects. Although the diocese technically maintains fiscal and legal control of St. Richard's, it does not subsidize the school. Should the school's financial situation become unstable, the diocese would be liable for any deficit incurred, and might move to close the school. As long as the school manages to balance its budget, however, decisions about routine financial matters normally rest with the principal and the local advisory board. Neither diocesan nor local school boards are much involved in such academic matters as curriculum and supervision of instruction; generally these responsibilities are handled by the principal and school staff. As a result, even diocesan schools are relatively autonomous organizations.

In private Catholic high schools such as St. Madeline's and St. Edward's, the key governing body is the school's board of directors. These boards, typically composed of both religious and lay members, have powers similar to boards found in schools that belong to the National Association of Independent Schools. They have authority to select the principal, to set tuitions and faculty salaries, to establish other financial policies, and to oversee the academic, religious, and extracurricular programs of the school. Most diocesan policies, such as faculty salary schedules, do not apply to private schools. Contact between individual private schools and the diocese is generally cordial but limited.

Organizational control in private schools rests primarily in the principal and the board of directors. Virtually all institutional policies are made there. Religious orders maintain considerable influence through their appointment of the board members, who in turn select the principal. In the choice of principal, preference is given to members of the religious congregation that sponsors the school. The religious orders also provide administrative and technical support services in planning, development, spiritual leadership, financial control, legal advice, and personnel selection. The strength of many private high schools directly reflects the contributions of the sponsoring religious order.

Most governance matters in parish schools are resolved in the interactions among pastor, principal, parish council, and parish school board (if these latter two exist). An organizational chart would be somewhat misleading, because much of the decision making is quite informal. The pastor's opinion is accorded a great deal of deference. A positive relationship between the principal and the pastor is usually a key to smooth governance in these schools. Like diocesan schools, however, parish schools operate within the policies formulated by the diocesan board.

The Central Administrative Role of the Principal

Research on effective schools has emphasized the importance of leadership in the principal's role.[2] In each school we visited, regardless of the particular type of governance arrangement, the principal acted as the chief administrative officer.[3] Although limited to a single institution, the responsibilities involved are equivalent in range and nature to an administrative combination of public school principal and superintendent. The Catholic school principal bears responsibility for financial management, development and fund-raising, public and alumni relations, faculty selection and supervision, student recruitment, and in many cases, discipline and instructional leadership. The principal must also maintain amicable relationships with the diocese, the neighboring parishes, the religious order, the local community, and the parent body. Serving as teacher, advisor, coach, mentor, counselor, disciplinarian, reconciler, strategist, leader, manager, conserver, recruiter, and spokesperson, many Catholic school principals operate like owners of small businesses. No task is too big or too small for the principal to undertake, and the variety seems endless.[4]

A brief portrayal of a typical workday for Father Kevin O'Leary, the principal of St. Cornelius', illuminates this diverse and challenging role.[5] Recall that this high school is located in inner-city Cleveland, within sight (and smell) of several large steel mills. The school serves students from white ethnic, black, and Puerto Rican working-class families, most of whom are Catholic. The presence of these students at St. Cornelius' represents their families' willingness to sacrifice financially to provide a good education for their children, in a city whose public schools are beset with problems.

A Principal's Typical Day

Father O'Leary begins his day by celebrating the 7:00 Mass at a convent for the Carmelite Sisters, where he serves as chaplain. After a brief breakfast and a twenty-minute drive to school, he arrives at St. Cornelius' by 8:15 A.M. Quickly greeting his secretary, he pours a cup of coffee and drops in to see the dean of students. During the next 30 minutes, they review recent disciplinary problems. O'Leary involves himself in these activities because he views the school's response to discipline problems as a guidance function. Through his own actions, he encourages students to recognize their responsibilities both to themselves and to the school community. Although most of the problems concern classroom misbehavior, truancy, and fighting, on occasion more serious concerns arise, such as the selling of drugs on campus. For O'Leary, these events threaten the basic order of the school and require careful deliberation. Expulsion is the usual penalty for selling drugs on campus, but O'Leary first talks with the parents and students before committing himself to such a serious course of action.

At 9:00, we find O'Leary with the business manager, reviewing the financial records of freshmen and sophomores whose monthly tuition payments are in arrears. He directs the business manager to grant two-week extensions to all of the cases they have reviewed, with the proviso that students whose parents fall behind the new schedule will be suspended from classes until their accounts are settled. Even with these procedures, O'Leary knows that he will excuse some special cases: "Sometimes I get discouraged over the collection of tuition. It takes so much of my time, and the problem never goes away. With the recession in the steel industry, our parents are really in a tough situation. As soon as we collect tuition for one month, the next month's is past due, and the list seems longer each month. The business manager does his best, but the parents respond more quickly to my calls. It's another case where the principal has to be involved for anything to happen."

O'Leary takes a few minutes to return telephone calls and scan the correspondence piled up on his desk. From 10:25 to 11:00, he begins drafting his monthly newsletter to parents. This month he intends to high-light some of the school's successes. He takes time each day to talk with students, and he especially keeps an eye out for those who may be having difficulty. Some of St. Cornelius' students have been previously expelled from public schools or have had problems with the law. Looking after these students requires constant attention. Somehow many of these troubled young people manage to pull their lives together while at St. Cornelius', an accomplishment O'Leary regards as an especially important model for other students. "The high-risk students who make the grade academically and socially here make me feel especially good about what we're doing."

O'Leary's last office activity of the morning is calling the archbishop to invite him to celebrate Mass at the school before Thanksgiving. The archbishop seems enthusiastic, agreeing to check his calendar and call back to confirm the date and time. As we discussed in Chapter 5, nurturing the spiritual life of the school is an important aspect of O'Leary's work. A Mass offered by the archbishop is a special event providing an occasion to assemble the entire school community. The archbishop's visit will also provide visibility for St. Cornelius' in the greater Cleveland area, publicity that may have ancillary benefits in such areas as fund-raising and student recruitment.

The rest of the morning is spent getting out of the office and being visible around the school. O'Leary greets teachers and students in the corridors. He stops in some classes for a few minutes and then moves on. During a cafeteria lunch, he joins some senior athletes, inquiring about their classes and plans for the future. Because many St. Cornelius' parents did not complete high school and thus may be unfamiliar with the intricacies of postsecondary education, O'Leary makes a point of discussing educational options with students whenever possible. Chatting briefly with faculty members before classes resume, he suggests to a teacher who is experiencing a scheduling conflict that he see the assistant principal to remedy the situation. He asks a new English teacher about a student who just transferred into her class from a public school. "How's Mary Ageron doing? Is she adjusting all right?" He asks Jerry Dvorac, a long-time faculty member, "How'd your football game turn out yesterday afternoon?"

An important part of O'Leary's work is using what he observes and hears in the cafeteria and the corridors to sense the tone and mood of the school. Brief conversations with faculty sometimes uncover sources of anxiety and problems that he might be able to ameliorate. Our interviews with teachers at St. Cornelius' revealed their appreciation of such informal contacts with their principal. These encounters provide the faculty with an easy way to advise O'Leary on a wide variety of matters—from the progress of students on academic and disciplinary probation to needed repairs for classrooms, hallways, and the gym. The personal banter "feels good," they say. O'Leary often jots notes in order to attend promptly to any concerns raised during these brief exchanges. Back in his office at 1:05, O'Leary calls three board members on the Development Subcommittee to check on their progress in soliciting support for his new financial aid proposal. One member had spoken with a local foundation director interested in sponsoring low-income students in racially diverse Catholic schools. The other two plan to call friends familiar with potentially supportive corporations and foundations.

Professional meetings outside of the school building are also a regular part of O'Leary's schedule. The previous week saw him at the Urban Principals' Association; today he has a meeting with other principals at the diocesan education office several miles across town. The agenda includes enrollment record-keeping for the diocese, new diocesan policies for teacher supervision and tenure, and a discussion of staff development programs on nuclear disarmament and global awareness. Although he complains that such meetings take valuable time away from school, O'Leary also enjoys the opportunity to meet with colleagues. As the meeting concludes and he heads back to school at 3:45, however, he wonders whether the time has been well spent in this particular instance.

On his return, O'Leary finds the administrative team—three faculty members who also serve as part-time assistant principals for curriculum and supervision, scheduling, and discipline—gathered for their weekly meeting. After O'Leary briefly summarizes the meeting he just left, he and the administrators swing into the agenda: reviewing students on academic and disciplinary probation; setting up special conferences with parents about two failing students; discussing athletic eligibility rules; and reviewing bus transportation between campuses that causes tardiness. While administrative team members frequently acknowledge the constraints under which they operate, the mood of this collaborative problem-solving session is still upbeat. As the session concludes, around 6:20 P.M., O'Leary puts some paperwork and professional reading in his briefcase and heads for his car.

Patterns in the Daily Schedule

The day's activity illustrates three sets of concerns that Catholic high school principals must routinely confront: managing operations and personnel, building personal relations, and providing spiritual leadership. Like all secondary schools, Catholic schools have become more complex organizations, with the number of managerial tasks increasing over the past twenty-five years.[6] A substantial portion of the principal's day is devoted to immediate concerns: discipline problems, physical plant needs, and course scheduling. In addition, long-range planning and development have become increasingly important, as individual Catholic secondary schools are now responsible for their own fiscal solvency. Financial management tasks, including collecting tuition and fund-raising to supplement the school's revenues, consume a significant part of any principal's workday as well.

In reality, the job involves more work than a single person can accomplish. Even in small schools with few financial resources, such as St. Peter's, there is some support staff to share these responsibilities. Sorting out tasks among these individuals depends on both the personal interests of the principal and the capabilities of other available staff. The individual characteristics of each school also determine how principals spend their time. Because of the constrained resources at St. Cornelius', members of the administrative team teach, coach, and supervise extracurricular activities. As a result, the support for institutional management is lean, with a share of rather mundane chores falling by default on O'Leary's shoulders. Because the cash flow at St. Cornelius' is always tight, calling about delinquent tuitions is not a trivial part of his job.

In contrast, the principal at St. Edward's, Brother Plodzik, has a specialized administrative team of six full-time professionals: three assistant principals for academic affairs, personnel, and discipline; a plant manager; a director of development; and a business manager. This expanded administrative structure reflects the greater resources of St. Edward's. Brother Plodzik's involvement in financial affairs is primarily limited to development efforts for a capital campaign. His administrative staff attends to the day-to-day aspects of finance, plant maintenance, renovation, discipline, and routine personnel functions. In general, very little of Brother Plodzik's time is consumed by managerial details, which frees him to consider long-term aspects of academic leadership and school development.

Another important dimension to the work of Catholic high school principals involved personal relationships.[7] Over half of principals' time is spent in telephone calls, meetings, conferences, and informal discussions with faculty and students. Talking with parents about admission procedures, disciplinary problems, and other issues makes regular demands on the work schedule. Communication with local pastors, diocesan officials, and members of the community also takes time. Although many of these interactions occur within the context of daily tasks, each exchange provides the principal with an opportunity to build personal relations inside and outside of the school. The principals in our field sites described the forging of these relationships as an important part of their job.

Commitment to building personal relationships is closely intertwined with principals' third general concern: fostering a sense of community. As we detailed in the last chapter, the forging of a school community is far from accidental. The principal has an opportunity here to meld his or her personal vision of the school with its tradition. Father O'Leary, for example, sees the social mission of St. Cornelius' as service to a racially and ethnically diverse student population in a low-income urban setting: "I took this job because I believed in what this school could do. Since I have been principal, I've tried to develop this vision of St. Cornelius' as a school where every kid has a chance to succeed, regardless of the background. We accept kids that no other school would take a chance on, and many of them have done very well personally and academically."

O'Leary's comments convey a personal urgency about the school's mission. In all our field-site schools principals made a deliberate effort to collectivize this commitment. Their language provided clues to how they thought of their work and their schools. Principals often referred to their assistants, for example, as the "administrative team." They commonly spoke of "things *we* have accomplished" in reference to the school's successes. We often heard principals use the expression "*our* school." Building a sense of shared responsibility toward the school mission and its students was a deliberate aim.

The affiliation and commitment that Catholic high school principals feel also has its negative side. The number and complexity of the tasks they face and the demands of their various publics make them susceptible to overextension and exhaustion. Father O'Leary reflected: "I get feedback on the good job we've done. I appreciate it because the drain on me personally has been great. All I've done is eat, sleep, and drink school for the past three years. This could be my personal problem. We've achieved success, but I'm not sure that I would do it the same way again." Each day is balanced between a strong belief in the worth of the school's purpose and doubts about the efficacy of particular activities or the availability of adequate resources to address important ends.[8]

Although much of the work of Catholic school principals is similar to that of their public school counterparts, we conclude that the nature of school leadership has a distinctive character here. Both public and Catholic school principals value academic excellence and students' educational attainment. For principals in Catholic schools, however, there is also an important spiritual dimension to leadership that is apt to be absent from the concerns of public school administrators.[9] This spirituality is manifest in the language of community that principals use to describe their schools and in their actions, as they work to achieve the goal of community.

External and Internal Influences on Governance

In terms of the external governance, most Catholic secondary schools are directly influenced by three groups: the religious order that provides staff for the school; the diocese that holds canonical authority over the school; and an individual board of directors. On the internal side, a major management concern for principals is faculty relations. The process of transforming Catholic schools into lay institutions has raised some new issues in this domain.

External Governance Shell

Religious orders. Traditionally, of course, religious orders played a critical role in the development of Catholic high schools. They constructed and staffed virtually *all* Catholic secondary schools, owning them in the fullest sense of the word. Following Vatican II, however, the situation changed. The rapid decline in the membership of religious orders meant fewer teachers to staff schools. The impact of the declining numbers was further exacerbated by the expanded social role undertaken by the Catholic Church. After Vatican II, many religious orders moved into ministries other than education, including social work, pastoral care, and ministry to the elderly. The cumulative effect of these two simultaneous developments was to reduce sharply the traditional pool of human resources available to schools.

This change involved more than just numbers. Religious orders began to reconceptualize their responsibilities toward schools in terms of "sponsoring" them rather than "owning" them. The notion of sponsorship represented a reappraisal of what religious orders might reasonably hope to accomplish in the years ahead. Given their diminished financial and human resources, it was clear that the orders could no longer staff and fund schools as they had in the past. Instead, they began to channel their efforts into providing the leadership necessary to secure a future for the schools they had developed.

The shift from ownership to sponsorship of schools also had important implications for individual religious staff members. First, the nature of the employment relationship between religious members and the school began to shift from "contributed services" to personal service contracts similar to those used with lay faculty. Second, instead of being assigned to a particular school operated by their order, many religious members were given the option of applying to schools in which they might wish to serve. As a result, a Catholic school might now be staffed by religious members from several different orders. This was the case in five of our seven field-sample schools.

Even with the change from ownership to sponsorship, religious orders still maintained considerable influence over school operations by retaining control of key roles, including the appointment of principals and school board members. The majority of principalships in Catholic high school (61 percent in 1988) still come from religious orders, an arrangement that provides schools some distinct benefits. Administrative operating costs are often reduced, because religious staff generally return some part of their salary to the school. The presence of religious staff in administrative positions also affirms, for parents and alumni, a continuity of the school's religious heritage.

In principle, many religious orders see sponsorship as a transitional strategy in the transformation of Catholic schools into all-lay institutions. Sponsorship means more than simply maintaining control; it also involves careful planning, and developing lay leaders to take the place of religious staff. But not all religious orders have such foresight. The experience of two of our field-sample schools illustrates the kinds of problems that can develop in the transition to lay status.

Despite the existence of a lay board at St. Peter's, a religious order had directed *all* long-range planning and institutional management up until 1980. The sudden and unexpected departure of the religious staff in 1982 left the school quite vulnerable. Central support was unavailable to provide needed services formerly supplied by the religious order. We found St. Peter's, a few months after the departure of the religious order, faced with declining enrollment, a growing financial crisis, and a lack of experienced leaders. This combination of problems suggested that the school faced an uncertain future.

Although the situation at St. Frances' was more stable than at St. Peter's, disturbing conditions were nevertheless evident. The school relied heavily on the expertise and resources of its sponsoring order, which was appropriately described as "running" the school. Although most of the faculty were lay, all administrative positions were held by religious staff. Further, the lay staff believed that the school belonged to the sisters—financially and metaphorically. The religious order, sensing its own financial vulnerability, had just hired an accounting firm to review its assets and liabilities. In our interview, the religious order provincial expressed some doubt about the order's ability to sustain the school. Should they decide to relinquish control, St. Frances' could quickly find itself in the same precarious state as St. Peter's.

Dioceses. The responsibilities of diocesan superintendents and diocesan central offices to Catholic schools under their purview have also changed considerably since the 1960s. Dioceses largely financed the school-building boom of the 1950s and 1960s, when projects were often more spontaneous than planned. An individual bishop could initiate a major building campaign without any clear mechanism to finance it. Not surprisingly, with the rapid changes in the mid-1960s, dioceses became increasingly reluctant to open more schools. Indeed, financial pressures from declining enrollments and rising costs forced some dioceses to close schools that they had just built.

Because dioceses, like the religious orders, no longer had the resources to subsidize a large school system, they too were obliged to rethink their approach to schools. As a result, dioceses transferred to individual schools fiscal responsibility for generating sufficient revenues to maintain their own operations. Diocesan subsidies were still extended to some schools, particularly those located in the inner city, but schools that could not balance their own budgets were forced to close.

Diocesan officials have also redefined their educational responsibilities toward schools. In an attempt to fill the breach created by religious order retrenchment, dioceses have sought to enhance their support services available to schools. This development is particularly important for both parish and diocesan schools, where the loss of religious staff has been greater and where strong religious order sponsorship is less likely.[10] Diocesan offices of education are now a major source for leadership training for administrators and boards, legal and financial advice, assistance on curriculum, and other professional services. Similarly, diocesan boards of education have attempted to provide policy assistance to all schools within their diocese that might seek this service.

Nevertheless, the small staffs and limited resources of diocesan central offices constrain their ability to respond to many requests. In one diocese we visited, which had 40,000 students in Catholic schools, a single professional handled curriculum and staff development. In general, the diocesan resources available to support education have not increased commensurate with the growing demands being placed upon them.

School boards. The development of boards for individual schools within the last two decades is one of the most important changes in the governance of Catholic high schools. Few schools had boards of directors prior to 1970; over three-quarters of Catholic high schools have them twenty years later.[11] These boards have become increasingly influential in school affairs.[12] Vatican II declarations that encourage a broader involvement of laypersons in Church institutions provide the philosophical underpinning for this school board movement. On the practical side, the increased involvement of laity fills the void left by the declining reach of religious orders and dioceses.

An example of a well-functioning board was found at St. Edward's High School. Established in 1971, the original board was composed entirely of religious members appointed by the sponsoring religious order. Lay members, introduced in 1978, gradually increased in number until they constituted a majority in 1983. The board meets formally twice a year to consider a broad range of policy issues. Its major responsibilities are financial: setting tuition, determining faculty salaries and benefits, and managing development campaigns. In the decade between 1973 and 1983, the board raised over two million dollars. It was also instrumental in developing a policy of teacher salary equity with local public schools—very unusual for the Catholic sector.

Beyond these formal board activities, individual members contribute considerable time and expertise. Many are personally involved in fundraising efforts. A subgroup of individuals has advised the principal in restructuring the school's financial affairs. With the board's encouragement, the school hired a professional business manager, who is charged with plant management, financial budgeting and control, and institutional planning. Board members provide technical assistance in these areas, as well, and they have developed an extensive network of contacts with the local business community.

The existence of a school board, however, does not guarantee such a positive result. The board at St. Edward's has had a relatively long history. Its formation and development have required careful planning on the part of the religious order. The school was also fortunate in that its early lay members were prominent citizens in the community who contributed exceptional service. In contrast, although the school boards of two other schools in the field sample had also been in existence for several years, they did not appear to exert much influence on their schools. Moreover, boards can occasionally become a problem for school principals, if individual members attempt to move beyond their assigned role into less familiar aspects of administrative and pedagogical decision making. School boards can thus provide principals with valuable support, but they also constitute an external resource that requires careful management.

Decision Making inside the School

In a national survey of Catholic high schools, principals were asked about their perceptions regarding school decision making on a range of issues (see Table 6.1). A striking feature of their responses is that principals see themselves as having primary influence on all matters except for hiring their replacements. These reports corroborate our field observations that board authority is vested in this position.

According to the surveyed principals, school boards have considerable influence over matters pertaining to the budget, choosing a new principal, and setting policy about admissions criteria and school goals. Boards, however, tend to defer to the principal and school staff on instructional matters and personnel.

These survey reports also confirm our field observations that dioceses and religious orders concentrate on the appointment of the key school leader. Once appointed, however, principals enjoy considerable autonomy. Although this mechanism affords diocesan and religious order officials with considerable institutional influence, neither dioceses nor religious orders directly regulate school affairs.

The data in Table 6.1 also indicate a considerable voice for faculty in setting curriculum and school goals. These findings were supported by questionnaire data from our field sites. Over 95 percent of the teachers indicated that they had considerable control over their own teaching, and 60 percent reported considerable influence in curricular matters.[13] In contrast, teachers' influence is minimal in areas such as disciplinary policy, the hiring and review of teachers, and budgeting. These field-site data are corroborated in a national survey of Catholic high school teachers, less than 5 percent of whom indicated that they exerted significant influence on determining the school budget, establishing school graduation requirements, setting admissions policies, or hiring new teachers.[14]

Teachers had little knowledge of their schools' financial matters and were poorly informed about the financial condition of their institutions.[15] The

Table 6.1 Catholic high school principals' perceptions of who makes final decision: Percentage of principals reporting each agent as final decision maker

	Agent reported as final decision maker				
Issue	School board	Diocesan or order official	Principal or other school administrator	Teachers	Parish pastor
Allocating school budget	46	19	60	4	9
Changing curriculum or graduation requirements	22	9	85	31	2
Determining overall curriculum	15	8	88	36	1
Hiring new teachers	7	6	95	8	3
Nonrenewing of teachers	12	6	93	3	3
Renewing teachers' contracts	10	6	93	2	4
Selecting the principal	41	61	7	3	9
Setting admissions criteria	25	9	83	15	3
Setting school goals and objectives	31	10	85	41	4
Suspending or expelling a student	6	4	97	9	4
Terminating teacher contracts	16	8	91	2	4
Average percentage	21	14	80	14	4

Source: Data from NCEA (1985), 88.

Note: Percentages may total more than 100, because respondents were allowed to check more than one box.

latter is particularly salient in the context of teachers' perceptions about the school's effort with regard to their salaries. Only a third of the teachers in our field schools agreed with the statement, "My salary was the most the school could afford." Moreover, teachers held such perceptions even in schools where the financial picture was quite bleak, such as St. Peter's, St. Cornelius', and St. Frances'. These views extend well beyond our field sites. In a national study of Catholic high schools with high proportions of low-income students (that is, schools like St. Peter's, St. Cornelius', and St.

Frances'), approximately half of the lay teachers did not believe that their schools were making the maximal effort on teachers' salaries.[16]

We find teachers' lack of knowledge about their school's financial difficulties disquieting, especially in light of their otherwise very positive attitudes about their schools. When viewed in the context of the pervasive financial difficulties faced by Catholic schools, the large gulf between teacher understandings of the fiscal situation and the actual figures confronting the principals, school boards, and diocesan and religious order officials who manage the financial affairs is troubling. As might be expected, this "credibility gap" appears to be somewhat stronger among lay than among then religious faculty.[17]

In this context it is reasonable to expect organizational conflict over salaries and perhaps increased movement toward unionization. We encountered little evidence of this, however, in our field research. Nationally, less than 25 percent of Catholic high schools principals report that there is increasing interest in unionization at their school.[18] Further, *High School and Beyond* data indicate a very low incidence of conflict among teachers or between teachers and administrators in Catholic secondary schools. Such conflicts occur with much greater frequency in public schools.[19] This was yet another instance of a field observation that invited further reflection. What accounts for the lack of conflict among adults within Catholic schools, particularly given the low salaries and the disenfranchisement of lay faculty concerning financial matters?

Our observations and interviews suggest that the answer lies in tacit understandings at work in these schools. Many lay teachers spoke of kinship with and respect for the religious members of the faculty, some of whom they may have earlier admired as their own teachers. The religious staff were described as "good people," "dedicated to education," and "committed to the personal development of each student." One teacher said, "The professional pride and teaching tradition of the sisters at this school are incredible. I feel like I can breathe it in the classrooms and hallways!" Such comments suggest that many religious members are highly respected and are accorded some deference for their deep commitment to teaching and learning. The considerable contributions, both past and present, of religious order members to their schools and students are constantly acknowledged by their lay colleagues.

We surmised from these field reports that deference to religious order members is an important factor governing discourse among adults in a Catholic school community. Although this deference has surely contributed to the domestic tranquility of Catholic schools, it also has a disabling quality.

It encourages lay faculty and board members to think that because religious orders have provided for the schools so capably in the past, the future will be no different. It is virtually certain, however, that the retrenchment of the religious orders, in both membership and fiscal resources, signals a shrinking reach. If Catholic schools are to continue to be vital social institutions, both their leadership and an increasing portion of their resources must come from laypersons.

The reverse also appears true. With growing responsibilities among the lay faculty, the institutional influence of religious members is likely to weaken. Its demise may call into question the justification for the existing social order. One possibility is that deference to religious members may simply be transferred to the organizational roles that religious members have filled in the past—the principalship and board of directors. This evolution is uncertain, however, as the intellectual foundations for the role of the layperson in the Catholic Church have been reshaped significantly by Vatican II. As a new conception of the Church—more democratic, less hierarchical—emerges around the concept of the "people of God," more emphasis is accorded to the development and nourishment of individual conscience as a guide to personal action. In a more democratic environment, uncritical deference to traditional authority seems somewhat incongruous.

CATHOLIC SECONDARY schools are best conceived of as a loose federation rather than as an integrated system. Most schools are financially autonomous and responsible for generating income sufficient to balance their own budgets. In addition, although external governance structures are complex and varied, most schools have considerable control over their internal operations.

A common feature of Catholic secondary schools is the central role of the school principal. This position requires considerable expertise in such diverse areas as personnel, finances, community relations, curriculum and supervision, and organizational leadership. We find a curious paradox in principals' behaviors and aspirations. They uniformly identify the need to exercise leadership in building the community of the school as the most important aspect of their jobs, but mundane managerial tasks actually claim large portions of their time. Demands are particularly marked for principals in schools with limited financial resources, because they have fewer support staff. The efforts required to maintain plant and financial operations often allow little time for activities focused directly on developing the school community. This was certainly the case at St. Peter's, where the school's day-to-day survival was the principal's almost exclusive concern.

Unlike public schools, where external influences substantially increased in the 1970s and 1980s,[20] the external governance shell of the individual Catholic secondary school remains relatively thin. Many religious orders now sponsor Catholic schools rather than run them. The choice of words, while subtle, realistically conveys the limited reach of most religious orders today. In principle the bishop maintains a broad base of authority over the Catholic schools within his diocese, but in practice this authority is exercised only in extraordinary instances. The growth in numbers and importance of individual school boards has brought much needed expertise and assistance in financial matters, planning, and fund-raising.

In some ways the external shell is *too* thin. The small size of many Catholic secondary schools, coupled with their sparse administrative structures, makes it very difficult for individual schools to gain access to the wide range of administrative services and instructional supports needed to maintain and develop them. The services provided by religious orders have contracted over the past two decades because of their declining membership and increasing fiscal constraints. In an attempt to fill this void, diocesan offices of education have expanded their role somewhat. Nevertheless, substantial needs remain as Catholic schools now engage in national movements to update instructional programs, renew the staff's professional knowledge and skills, and promote more authentic forms of instruction.

Respect and deference to members of religious orders have also shaped the decision-making structure of Catholic schools. In the future, however, it seems likely that the influence of this governing principle will decline.[21] The expanding responsibilities of lay faculty and board members is part of a larger process of rethinking school operations that has been under way for some time. In many ways, the reshaping of Catholic school governance is a critical test of the principles advanced at Vatican II. Although the image of the Church as the "people of God" offers inspiration, will committed laywomen and laymen continue to answer this call to service? Reshaping the governance structure of Catholic schools is also a decisive test for the institutional Church. Will it reaffirm the principle of subsidiarity, helping not only to support healthy institutions but also to nurture those in need of assistance? Or, at a time of considerable retrenchment within the Church, will it reach too far and seek to control too much?

In addition to the manifest processes of decision making and sources of influence in Catholic secondary schools, two other important control mechanisms are also at work. The first is the "invisible hand of the market." Prior to the mid-1960s, Catholic schools were subsidized substantially by Church funds from parishes, dioceses, and religious orders, to whom they were directly accountable. Today, Catholic schools must be much more market sensitive, in that virtually all schools depend heavily on tuition income and most are not overenrolled. The days when a steady stream of Catholic parents automatically sent their children to Catholic schools have long since passed. For most families, Catholic and non-Catholic alike, the decision to enroll a child is a deliberate act.

A related source of influence on the operations of contemporary Catholic schools, therefore, is a public which must be satisfied that a Catholic education is worth the substantial expense incurred. This influence is certainly felt by school leaders, especially principals and board members, who are entrusted with maintaining stable fiscal operations. Catholic school history is clearly punctuated by important lessons from its market. Early in this century, the comprehensive high school movement failed to take deep root in Catholic high schools in part because many parents wanted an academic program for their children and the social mobility it promised. Similarly, the 1970s experiment with instructional innovations folded quickly, as parents grew concerned and school enrollments dropped.

Likewise, the shaping influences of the distinctive beliefs, norms, and values operative in Catholic schools should not be underestimated.[22] This constitutes a second broad control mechanism. Whether we look at the formal organizational roles of teachers, the community-building rhetoric of principals, or the character of the day-to-day social relations in the schools, the ideology of Vatican II molds school life in powerful ways. This ideology acts as an institutional anchor as schools confront their market environments—orienting them toward engagement with contemporary culture, but also confident in their vision of the "Kingdom to come." It is, to borrow a phrase from Michael Novak, an "openness with roots."[23]

A complex set of control mechanisms thus guides the affairs of Catholic secondary schools. Formal governance mechanisms couple with important institutional ties to religious orders and parishes. These structures, in turn, are embedded in a larger context of market concerns and a distinctive school ideology. Our field investigations and historical inquiry have convinced us that without either of these important shaping forces—markets and ideology—the contemporary Catholic school would be a very different place.

❖ III ❖
DIVERSITY AMONG CATHOLIC SCHOOLS

❖ 7 ❖

The Transition to High School

ENTRY INTO high school represents a significant life change for many students, yet very little attention has been devoted to this transition point, and none to a comparison of students in public and Catholic schools. Fortunately, a limited set of questions on students' elementary school experience in the first follow-up data from *High School and Beyond* makes possible some investigation of this topic. Students were asked to specify which type of school (public, Catholic, or non–Catholic private) they attended in each of their elementary and middle-school years. This chapter makes use of these data, as well as information gathered about Catholic elementary schools as part of our visits to the seven field sites, in focusing on entry into (and exit out of) Catholic and public schools. We examine the probability that students will transfer into and out of Catholic schools during elementary school (and at which grade levels such transfers are particularly likely) and the characteristics and motivation of students who transfer. We also consider students' selection among schools *within* the Catholic sector, or which students choose which Catholic high schools. Discerning the factors influencing these choice processes provides some insight into this critical juncture in students' educational lives, when decisions may have consequences that will endure well beyond high school.

Movement of Students among Catholic and Public Schools

The transition into high school in the public sector varies across communities. Typically, elementary school attendance ends at grade 5 or 6. Several elementary schools within a community may then send students to a centralized middle, intermediate, or junior high school (grades 6 or 7 through grades 8 or 9). By tenth grade, virtually all students are in high school. The Catholic sector, in contrast, is more uniformly organized. The predominant structure consists of elementary schooling extending through grade 8 (there are few separate middle schools), and secondary schooling, which begins at grade 9.[1] In this chapter, we use the term "elementary school" to include all experiences until high school entry.

It was clear from our field research that differences between Catholic elementary and secondary schools in their governance and finance mechanisms give Catholic education a somewhat different cast at the elementary and secondary levels. The vast majority of Catholic elementary schools (over 85 percent) are affiliated with individual parishes and tend to be located relatively near students' homes. Enrollment in these schools is usually open to all children of the parish, and often many nonparishioners, including non-Catholics, also attend. Although tuition rates are sometimes higher for nonparishioners than for parish members, elementary school programs are subsidized by general parish revenues. In many cases, these subsidies make up a significant proportion of schools' operating funds.

In contrast, the parish school is relatively rare at the secondary level (12.9 percent). Most high schools are sponsored either by religious orders or by dioceses, and they may draw students from very diverse geographic areas. St. Edward's, for example, enrolls students from the greater Louisville metropolitan area. In general, enrollment at the secondary level is somewhat more selective than at the elementary level, and this is particularly true for schools like St. Edward's, which enjoy a reputation for high academic quality and have several applicants for every available place.

The governance differences between Catholic elementary and secondary schools also have important financial implications. The typical Catholic high school does not benefit from a parish subsidy, because most schools are not affiliated with a single parish or a specific set of parishes. Catholic secondary schools are expected to generate sufficient revenues to cover expenses through their own means. Although high schools may engage in fund-raising and may receive a small subsidy in the form of contributed services from the religious staff, tuition is the major source of revenue. Tuition thus represents a far larger proportion of the total school income than is the case for elementary schools. The consequence of these governance differences, combined with the greater costs associated with maintaining high school facilities and programs, are high school tuition fees that are on average about three times higher than those for elementary schools.[2]

The Likelihood of Cross-Sector Transfer

Not surprisingly, the Catholic sector loses a considerable proportion of its students between eighth and ninth grades, when students normally enter high school; this juncture is the most likely point for a Catholic school student to transfer into the public sector. Almost two-fifths of Catholic eighth graders do not go on to a Catholic secondary school. Although there are also substantial transfers from the public into the Catholic sector at this point, the net loss is still about a fifth of the sector. More specifically, 1.3 percent of the total enrollment in the public sector transfers to Catholic schools at ninth grade and 37.9 percent of Catholic elementary school students move to a public school (see Table 7.1).

The next most likely transfer point is between third and fourth grade (1.1 percent of public school students transfer into the Catholic sector and 9.8 percent of Catholic students transfer out). Transfers from the Catholic to the public sector are relatively stable (from 6.3 to 10.3 percent) from second through sixth grade. Fewer students transfer between seventh and eighth grade (4.1 percent).

For transfer from public into Catholic schools, it is somewhat more likely that younger children will transfer (about 1 percent a year in the first three

Table 7.1 The probability of transferring between the Catholic and public school sectors at each elementary grade level

Grade level transition	Public to Catholic sector	Catholic to public sector
Grade 1 to 2	0.008	0.085
Grade 2 to 3	0.009	0.103
Grade 3 to 4	0.011	0.098
Grade 4 to 5	0.006	0.066
Grade 5 to 6	0.005	0.088
Grade 6 to 7	0.006	0.063
Grade 7 to 8	0.003	0.041
Grade 8 to 9	0.013	0.379

Source: Data from *High School and Beyond.*

Note: There is some degree of multiple transfer between sectors. In the Catholic sector, 7.4 percent of the sample transferred more than once during elementary school, and in the public sector, the comparable figure is 4.5 percent. The figures in this table are therefore not strictly additive. In a separate analysis, we found that a total of 38.9 percent of students in the Catholic sector and 13.7 percent of students in the public sector indicated that they transferred sectors sometime in their elementary school years.

grades). In the middle grades the probability of transfer is low (about 0.5 percent per year).

Although the Catholic sector represents a large proportion (about 58 percent) of the total number of students enrolled in nonpublic education at the elementary and secondary levels, its students represent a small proportion of the total numbers enrolled in American schools.[3] The effects of the high transition probabilities out of the Catholic sector and very low probabilities of transfer from the public sector are thus not as large when viewed from the perspective of the actual numbers of students involved in the moves.[4]

Another way to look at the information on cross-sector transfers is to consider specific hypothetical examples. If a student is in Catholic elementary school at some particular grade, what is the probability that he or she will be enrolled in either Catholic or public high school as a senior? How do these probabilities compare with those for students in public elementary schools at each grade? (see Tables 7.2 and 7.3).

Almost overwhelmingly, students who begin their education in the public sector remain there (see Table 7.3). Over 97 percent of the students in public schools at twelfth grade were in a public school at first grade. In contrast, students who start in Catholic schools are much less likely to finish their education in a Catholic school (see Table 7.2). As students advance through the grades, the probability of remaining in the Catholic sector increases until high school graduation. The process, however, is not nearly as certain as in the public sector. Of those students who are in a Catholic high school at grade 12, less than 40 percent attended first grade in a

Table 7.2 Probability that a student in Catholic elementary school in a given grade will be in the public or Catholic sector at grade 12

In Catholic school at elementary grade	Sector at grade 12	
	Public	Catholic
Grade 1	0.606	0.394
Grade 2	0.589	0.411
Grade 3	0.562	0.438
Grade 4	0.546	0.454
Grade 5	0.522	0.478
Grade 6	0.494	0.506
Grade 7	0.465	0.535
Grade 8	0.444	0.556
Grade 9	0.106	0.894

Source: Data from *High School and Beyond.*

Table 7.3 Probability that a student in public elementary school in a given grade will be in the public or Catholic sector at grade 12

In public school at elementary grade	Sector at grade 12	
	Public	Catholic
Grade 1	0.974	0.026
Grade 2	0.976	0.024
Grade 3	0.976	0.024
Grade 4	0.978	0.022
Grade 5	0.980	0.020
Grade 6	0.981	0.019
Grade 7	0.984	0.016
Grade 8	0.985	0.015
Grade 9	0.997	0.003

Source: Data from *High School and Beyond.*

Catholic school and only 56 percent were in a Catholic school at eighth grade. By ninth grade, however, the proportion jumps to 90 percent.[5] These results confirm our earlier observation that the juncture between elementary and secondary school represents a major transition point in the Catholic sector.

Choice Patterns for Public and Catholic Schools

High school entry represents a school change for virtually all students. Although most students in the United States attend a public elementary or middle school and continue into a public high school, there are four logical and distinct groupings of students we wish to consider:[6]

1. Students who transfer from public elementary to Catholic high schools (P→C);
2. Students who move from Catholic elementary to Catholic high schools (C→C);
3. Students who transfer from Catholic elementary to public high schools (C→P); and
4. Students who move from public elementary to public high schools (P→P).

Two of these groups (1 and 3) make a conscious choice to change sectors. The other two groups (2 and 4), although they probably change schools, choose to remain in the same sector for their elementary and secondary school experiences. Comparing the average characteristics of these four groups provides some insight into the type of students who *change* at this natural transition point. Examining characteristics of the schools chosen by these four groups helps us discern something about their motivation for transfer.

Three sets of comparisons are useful here: comparison with the group left behind, comparison with the group that transferees join in their new schools, and comparison of the group transferring into a sector with those transferring out. That is, how are the students who transfer into Catholic schools at the beginning of their secondary school career (the P→C group) different from those who continue into Catholic high school from Catholic elementary school (the C→C group)? How do P→C students differ from their counterparts who continue in the public sector (P→P)? How do the Catholic-to-public transfer students (the C→P group) differ from those who transfer from public to Catholic schools (P→C) at the same point?[7]

In general, students who transfer from public into Catholic high schools are more affluent, less religious, better prepared academically, and have higher educational aspirations than students in the other three groups. These students (the P→C group, column 1 of Table 7.4) transfer into Catholic high schools where average achievement, average social class, and reported quality of instruction are all relatively high. In contrast, those students who transfer from Catholic elementary schools into public high schools (the C→P group, column 3 of Table 7.4) are less affluent and less academically able than those who remain in the Catholic sector (C→C group).

Students who transfer into the Catholic sector (P→C) are of a higher social class than the students they are joining (C→C) and are of a considerably higher social class than those who transfer out of the Catholic sector (C→P). The average family income in the P→C group is about $3,000 more than the family income of those continuing in the Catholic sector, and over $6,000 more than that of the Catholic elementary school students who transfer into a public school (C→P). A larger proportion of those students who transfer into Catholic schools are minorities (15 percent) than either the continuing Catholic group or the group that transfers out. The minority composition for this P→C transfer group is similar to that of the stable public school group (P→P). The P→C group contains 4 percent more males than those who transfer out (C→P), and 9 percent more males than the group continuing on from Catholic elementary schools. Although more non-Catholics transfer into Catholic secondary schools than out, the P→C group is still 79 percent Catholic.

In terms of the types of schools chosen by transferring students, the public-to-Catholic group attends schools whose average sophomore-year achievement level is over one-half standard deviation higher than in the schools selected by the Catholic-to-public transfer group, and is also slightly higher than the average achievement level of high schools chosen by those students continuing in the Catholic sector. Of all three groups, the P→C students enroll in the most affluent schools and the schools with relatively low minority enrollment (10.1 percent), even though the composition of the P→C group has a relatively high proportion of minorities (14.9 percent). In contrast, while the C→P transfer group is only 10.6 percent minority, they are transferring into schools whose average enrollment is 18.4 percent minority. Transferees into the Catholic sector (P→C) also attend schools where instructional quality is rated by students considerably higher than in the schools chosen by the C→P transfer students. The schools selected by P→C students are also smaller and are more likely to require an entrance exam for admission than the schools the three other groups attend.

The academic behaviors of transfer students while in high school are also informative. In general, the public-to-Catholic group evidences more academically oriented activity than the Catholic-to-public group. They spend an average of two hours more per week on homework, have fewer unexcused absences, watch less television, and are more likely to associate with academically oriented friends. They are also much more likely to be in an honors curriculum by senior year, but equally likely to have enrolled in remedial courses (in either English or mathematics) in either their freshman or sophomore year. Their track placement is 35 percent more likely to be academic, and 15 percent less likely to be vocational, than that of their C→P counterparts—a striking difference.

In general, public-to-Catholic students follow a more academic course of study than Catholic school students transferring into public schools. P→C students take an additional year of mathematics, about one-third year more science, and fewer vocational and business courses than their C→P counterparts. The transfers from public schools also display more academically oriented behavior than those who stay in the Catholic sector, although the differences here are not large.

The academic achievement in Catholic high schools of transfers from public school is also higher. The P→C students have considerably better test scores at sophomore year than those who transfer from Catholic to public schools, and somewhat better scores than their new (C→C) classmates. The gains in academic achievement between sophomore and senior year are roughly comparable for the P→C and C→C groups, with transfer students gaining more in mathematics and somewhat less in science and

Table 7.4 Means for groups transferring sector or remaining in Catholic and public high schools

Variable	Public to Catholic (P→C) $n = 286$	Stay in Catholic (C→C) $n = 1,103$	Catholic to public (C→P) $n = 796$	Stay in public (P→P) $n = 1,684$
Student Background				
Social class[a]	0.28	0.08	−0.19	−0.20
% Black	4.3	2.7	4.0	9.0
% Hispanic	10.6	6.4	6.6	6.4
Family size	2.5	3.1	3.5	2.8
% Female	47.0	56.2	51.1	50.9
% Who repeated elem. grade	11.5	6.4	12.0	12.6
% College plans, gr. 8	73.7	72.4	48.8	54.1
% Non-Catholic	21.1	7.3	8.7	70.9
Religiousness[a]	−0.10	0.32	0.06	−0.80
Family income, 1980	$28,261	$25,449	$22,092	$22,458
Characteristics of High School Chosen				
Average achievement	56.47	55.14	51.07	50.32
School's social class	0.21	0.06	−0.31	−0.26
% Minority students	10.1	13.2	18.4	16.1
Quality of instruction[a]	0.73	0.42	−0.46	−0.49
School size	765	827	1,450	1,238
% Requiring entrance exam	84.2	74.6	0.0	5.1
Academic Attitudes and Behaviors				
Television, hrs./day	3.03	3.39	3.47	3.65
Homework, hrs./wk.	6.46	5.66	4.41	4.10
Days absent (unexcused), 3 mos.	1.47	1.35	2.20	2.36
Peer attitudes to good grades[a]	0.34	0.11	−0.09	−0.04
% Remedial program	8.3	7.8	8.3	7.9
% Honors program	17.3	12.2	5.5	6.4
% College-prep track	75.4	61.4	40.0	35.1
% General track	20.1	34.0	39.3	47.0
% Vocational track	5.2	5.2	20.0	18.2
Math courses, yrs.	3.50	3.24	2.38	2.15
Science courses, yrs.	0.93	0.90	0.76	0.68
Vocational courses, sem.	1.50	1.53	2.48	2.32
Business courses, sem.	1.31	1.74	2.78	2.50

Table 7.4 (continued)

Variable	Public to Catholic (P→C) n = 286	Stay in Catholic (C→C) n = 1,103	Catholic to public (C→P) n = 796	Stay in public (P→P) n = 1,684
Outcomes of Schooling				
Sophomore Year Achievement[b]				
Reading	9.24	8.71	7.62	7.19
Mathematics	18.20	17.06	14.36	13.49
Science	11.16	10.03	9.59	9.29
Writing	10.97	10.77	9.09	8.79
Senior Year Achievement[b]				
Reading	10.94	10.41	8.88	8.41
Mathematics	21.73	20.19	16.86	15.47
Science	12.10	11.25	10.85	10.23
Writing	12.64	12.77	11.03	10.36
Sophomore-to-Senior Gains[c]				
Reading gain	1.70	1.69	1.24	1.21
Mathematics gain	3.52	3.09	2.47	1.98
Science gain	0.96	1.22	1.28	0.94
Writing gain	1.68	2.00	1.94	1.63

Source: Data from *High School and Beyond.*

Note: For a further description of variables, see Table 8.1. Sample sizes are unweighted. Three of the four groups (P→C, C→C, and C→P) include all cases in the *High School and Beyond* file who were in the same high schools for both sophomore and senior years. The P→P group is a subsample. If it were weighted up to its "real" sample size in the *HS&B* file, it would contain 18,820 cases.

a. These variables are standardized and weighted on the Catholic sample (Catholic mean = 0, Catholic s.d. = 1).

b. The achievement scores reported here are the *HS&B* formula scores, which are number correct, adjusted for guessing. The four achievement tests contain the following numbers of items: reading–19; mathematics–38; science–20; writing–17.

c. Gains are computed by subtracting the sophomore-year score from the senior-year score. However, there are other ways of computing gain that adjust for the fact that those whose initial score is lowest often gain most. (See Bryk et al., 1984, p. 62, notes 14 and 15.) For this reason, we have used a covariance method for computing gains in our regression analyses presented in Chapter 8.

writing. In comparison, the students who transfer from Catholic elementary to public high schools gain considerably less than the P→C group between sophomore and senior year in reading and mathematics achievement, but somewhat more in science and writing.

As we look across the various statistical comparisons involving transfer students from the public sector, one reason for choosing a Catholic high school seems to stand out—a desire for a demanding academic experience. As a group, these are educationally ambitious students, who by and large are transferring into high-achievement schools that are relatively selective (84 percent have an entrance exam). The schools into which these students transfer have more affluent students, and there is more emphasis on taking academic courses. The vast majority of P→C students enroll in an academic program. Transferees from public schools rate the Catholic high schools they have selected quite positively, and their ratings appear valid given the relatively high achievement levels in these schools. Even though a large majority of P→C students are Catholic, they describe themselves as less religious than either the C→C or C→P groups. They are therefore probably not choosing a Catholic school primarily because of its religious orientation, although the data also suggest that they are not likely to be strongly opposed to this feature either.

In contrast, the motivation of students who transfer out of the Catholic sector after eighth grade appears somewhat more complex. Here, too, religious considerations do not appear to be a major issue. These students actually consider themselves more religious than either the P→C or the C→C group, and less than 9 percent of them are non-Catholic. Yet they are choosing to leave the Catholic sector in which they were heretofore educated.

We know that C→P students are moving into less academically competitive environments. They are much less likely to have college plans at the point of high school entry than their Catholic elementary school counterparts (C→C) remaining in the Catholic sector. Their educational ambitions, in fact, are similar to those of the public school group (P→P). C→P students are likely to attend a large nonselective public school where the average achievement is considerably below that found in the Catholic sector. These students are more likely to enroll in a general or vocational program, and to take considerably more vocational and business courses, than either of the Catholic high school groups. In general, the academic profile of the C→P transfers is fairly similar to that of the students they are joining in the public sector (P→P).

Thus, as was true for the P→C transfers, academic reasons also appear to influence the decision of students who choose to move from a Catholic elementary to a public secondary school. The profile of the typical C→P student is the logical complement to that of his or her P→C counterpart. Unlike the students transferring *into* the Catholic sector who were less religious, better academically prepared, and selecting a more academically oriented environment, the students transferring *out of* the Catholic sector at the end of elementary school are more religious, appear less academically successful, have lower educational aspirations, and are more likely to pursue a general or vocational course of study.

The *HS&B* data also suggest another reason that students transfer out of Catholic schools, one that we heard about in our field research as well. The substantially higher tuition charges of Catholic secondary schools, as compared with Catholic elementary schools, constitute a barrier to access for students from poor families. The group of students transferring into the Catholic sector has a family income higher than that of any other group, and is thus in the best position to afford the tuition charged by Catholic secondary schools. In contrast, students transferring out of Catholic schools have the lowest family income of the four groups. Their social class rating is comparable to that of the stable public school group and considerably lower than that of either group attending Catholic high school. The fact that C→P students are leaving tuition-charging schools for tuition-free schools cannot be overlooked.

The results of a multivariate discriminant analysis provide further statistical support for this argument.[8] The analysis was used to predict the choice of a public or Catholic high school by students enrolled in Catholic elementary schools. The analysis indicates that low family discretionary income (that is, income adjusted for a basic subsistence level and family size) is a strong deterrent to choosing to attend a Catholic high school.[9] Other factors that predict transfer to public high school include larger family size and non-Catholic religious status. Factors that influence the decision to attend a Catholic high school include higher parental education and greater educational ambition.

Our evidence thus suggests that there are two major factors involved in the decision to leave the Catholic sector at the end of elementary school: (1) an economic barrier to attending a Catholic secondary school posed by substantially higher secondary school tuition; and/or (2) an orientation of students and their families toward less academic pursuits. Religious concerns do not seem to be a primary consideration. As for those who move into the Catholic sector from public elementary schools, it seems fairly clear that they are choosing to make this transfer primarily for academic reasons—to attend a more academically oriented school. By and large, the P→C group is not economically disadvantaged. Their average social class is comparable to that of students who continue within Catholic schools, and they have substantially greater resources than those who transfer out.

Thus, we see a reshaping of the Catholic student population at high school entry into a smaller and more selective group—more academically oriented and somewhat more advantaged—than is characteristic of Catholic elementary school students. This process of transition also involves a recognition of the different academic demands of various schools. Even so, as we noted in Chapter 5, the entry process into Catholic high schools is not especially selective. In most instances, the major element of selectivity consists of self-selection—parents and students choosing to apply first to the sector and then to a particular school.

Selection within the Catholic Secondary Sector: Who Goes Where?

Because most Catholic schools are located in metropolitan areas, many students who select Catholic secondary education are confronted by a variety of high schools in their area among which they may choose. These institutions differ in terms of gender grouping (single sex or coeducational), governance structure (religious order, diocesan, parish, or inter-parish), and academic and religious emphasis, school size, and location. What factors influence the choice among specific types of Catholic high schools?

Gender Grouping and Governance Types

Catholic secondary schools can be grouped into five distinct categories that represent a combination of the sex composition of the school (boys only, girls only, or coed) and the school's sponsorship (religious order, diocese and other). In principle there are six possible groupings, but one combination—coed schools sponsored by a religious order—is rare. Only 2 of the 83 schools in the HS&B sample fit this description. Most religious order schools trace their origins back to a time when coeducation was viewed as harmful by Church leaders. Almost all of the religious order schools that are now coeducational began as single-sex schools and converted only recently.

Table 7.5 displays basic descriptive information on these five types of schools and the students enrolled in them. Students attending religious order schools tend to be more affluent and to have higher achievement and college aspirations. These schools generally charge higher tuitions and attract larger proportions of students transferring from public elementary schools. In comparison, students in coeducational schools tend to be more religious and are more likely to have attended a Catholic elementary school.

There are also substantial differences associated with the sex composition of the schools. Regardless of the source of school sponsorship, girls' school students tend to spend more time on homework and watch less television. They have fewer discipline problems and exhibit a more positive attitude toward classes. Boys in either type of boys' school are more likely to have leadership roles in their schools and to take more courses in mathematics and science.

Girls' non–religious order schools are distinct in several ways from the other four school types. The average social class and income levels are considerably lower—even lower than the national average for public schools.[10] The students' attitude toward academics in girls' non–religious order schools is also less positive. Over half of the girls in these schools are enrolled in a vocational or general program, a marked difference from the general pattern in the Catholic sector, where almost three-quarters of students are in the academic program. The levels of achievement and college aspirations in these schools are the lowest among the five groups and are quite similar to public school averages.

In order to consider students' school choices by gender and governance type further, we again used discriminant analysis. The analysis identified two separate factors that relate student background to the type of school selected.[11] The first taps issues of social class. This factor identifies a group of relatively affluent students who are more likely to have attended public elementary schools. Such students are most likely to select boys' religious order schools and least likely to choose girls' non–religious order schools. The second factor focuses on a religious dimension: students who express positive views about religion, come from larger and two-parent families, are less likely to be black, and have attended Catholic elementary schools. Such students are more likely to be found in coeducational schools.

Social Composition, Resources, and Climate

To investigate the question of who goes where, schools may also be characterized in terms of their social composition, resources, and various aspects of their climate. We use logistic regression techniques to illuminate the relationship between particular school descriptors (for example, having a strong academic climate) and the characteristics of the students enrolled.[12] The findings from these analyses are displayed in Table 7.6, in which each column identifies the characteristics of the students who are most likely to be found in a particular kind of school. The relationships identified here are adjusted for one another. That is, the effect of student social class on attendance at a school characterized by high academic achievement is net of race/ethnicity, academic background, and the other background factors listed at the left of the table. The plus and minus signs indicate the direction and magnitude of the relationships between student background factors and the characteristics of schools where these students are *more* (indicated by

Table 7.5 Mean differences among five types of Catholic schools for selected variables

Variable	Boys' religious order	Boys' diocesan and other	Girls' religious order	Girls' diocesan and other	Coed Catholic schools	Total Catholic sample
Student Background	(n = 286)	(n = 258)	(n = 392)	(n = 219)	(n = 900)	(n = 2,050)
Family income, 1982	$37,896	$31,791	$35,306	$25,431	$33,757	$33,596
Social class[a]	0.27	0.09	0.17	−0.71	0.01	0.00
Religiousness[a]	−0.17	0.09	0.02	−0.35	0.11	0.00
Parental involvement with school[a]	0.01	−0.08	0.15	0.03	0.05	0.00
Parental engagement with student[a]	−0.03	0.01	−0.04	−0.32	0.07	0.00
% Black	7.6	6.9	2.8	2.7	3.7	4.2
% Hispanic	12.5	9.2	9.1	14.9	7.2	8.9
% Catholic elementary experience	52.4	50.6	46.1	69.9	61.7	57.2
% Non-Catholic	11.6	9.1	12.6	14.5	12.0	12.1
School Characteristics	(n = 11)	(n = 10)	(n = 17)	(n = 11)	(n = 34)	(n = 83)
School size	830	767	470	577	502	546
Student/faculty ratio	20.1	19.4	15.9	18.3	18.0	17.8
% Annual faculty turnover	10.4	9.5	14.9	6.6	12.8	12.4
% Faculty at school 10+ years	30.5	31.3	17.4	22.3	14.7	18.4
% Faculty with advanced degrees	53.8	68.6	44.2	37.0	36.6	42.3
Tuition, 1980	$1,101	$993	$1,049	$695	$687	$833
Per-pupil expenditure, 1980	$1,634	$1,354	$1,312	$796	$1,320	$1,310
First step on salary scale, 1980	$8,754	$9,187	$8,483	$8,365	$8,669	$8,635
% Students in vocational program	2.3	4.8	6.3	34.3	10.3	10.2
% Students in general program	13.5	18.7	16.2	24.2	18.9	18.3
% Students in academic program	84.3	76.5	77.4	41.4	70.7	71.5

Student Engagement with the School

Homework, hrs./wk.	5.86	5.00	7.53	6.18	5.56	6.14
Days absent (unexcused), 3 mos.	2.29	2.15	1.85	2.22	2.28	2.22
Television, hrs./day	2.68	2.32	2.09	2.54	2.92	2.45
Readiness for class[a]	0.08	-0.16	0.13	0.05	-0.04	0.00
Incidence of discipline problems[a]	0.31	-0.02	-0.04	-0.15	-0.03	0.00
% in leadership positions	53.9	55.4	40.9	41.7	46.5	47.3
Interest in academics[a]	0.07	0.09	0.20	-0.21	0.04	0.00
Mathematics courses, yrs.	3.79	3.71	3.36	2.75	3.12	3.19
Science courses, yrs.	1.15	1.07	0.73	0.62	0.78	0.82
Foreign language courses, yrs.	2.36	1.33	1.79	1.07	1.40	1.72

Outcomes of Schooling

Senior achievement composite[b]	58.5	57.0	56.3	53.5	55.2	55.8
% Planning to graduate from college	83.3	75.1	74.5	44.0	62.4	66.5

Source: Data from Bryk et al. (1984), 43.

Note: For a further description of variables, see Table 8.1. Sample sizes are unweighted.

a. Standardized variables centered on weighted means and standard deviations from total Catholic sample, mean = 0, s.d. = 1.

b. An academic achievement composite created by HS&B consisting of senior year achievement in vocabulary, reading, and mathematics. It is scaled to a mean = 50 and s.d. = 10 for the entire HS&B sample.

Table 7.6 Aspects of student and family background related to characteristics of schools

Explanatory variables	High average social class	Low incidence discipline problems	Strong academic climate[a]	High academic achievement	Strong religious climate[a]	More fiscal resources[a]	More faculty resources[a]	Perceived high-quality teaching[b]
Academic background				+++		++		
Catholic elementary experience	−−				+++			
Female	−−	+++	+++	−−−	+++		−	−
Black	−−	−		−			−−−	−−
Hispanic								
Non-Catholic		+++		−	−		+	
Student's social class	+++		+++	+++		+++	+++	+++
Financial sacrifice	+++		+++	+++		+++	+++	+++
Religiousness					+++		−−−	
Single-parent household	−			−		+		
Family size					+++	−−	−−−	
Home ownership				++		+		−−

Source: Data from *High School and Beyond*.

Note: These analyses use logistic regression methods. The dependent measures compare the lower and upper thirds on each distribution. The "+" and "−" entries in this table are based on the nominal significance levels of each variable in the final logistic regression models.

a. These school indicators are factor composites of the individual variables identified in Table 8.1 for each respective construct.

b. The perceived quality of teaching indicator aggregates students' reports about the quality of instruction and certain desirable characteristics of their teachers (e.g., patient, fair, return work promptly).

+, − p ≤ .05.   ++, −− p ≤ .01.   +++, −−− p ≤ .001.

"+") or *less* (indicated by "−") likely to be found. Multiple plus or minus signs indicate stronger relationships. For example, females and non-Catholic students are more likely to attend schools where the incidence of discipline problems is low (see the second column in Table 7.6). Black students, however, are less likely to attend such schools. In terms of schools with high average achievement, females, blacks, and students from Catholic elementary school are less likely to enroll. Such schools instead attract students from a higher social class, students with a strong academic background, and students whose families are willing to sacrifice financially to pay the tuition.

A pattern of results emerges in these logistic regression analyses similar to the discriminant analyses reported earlier. Higher family social class and a greater degree of family financial sacrifice predict attendance at schools with a strong academic climate, relatively high levels of fiscal and faculty resources, and high perceived teaching quality and academic achievement. In general, students from Catholic elementary schools (the C→C group) are less likely to choose schools of this sort. Such schools are more likely to be sponsored by religious orders and to be single-sex institutions (from Table 7.5). A different set of background characteristics is associated with selecting schools with a strong religious climate: Catholic elementary school experience, personal religiousness, being Catholic, being female, and coming from a large family. These schools are somewhat more likely to be coeducational and to be sponsored by dioceses or parishes (Table 7.5).

There are also differences related to gender in the type of Catholic secondary school attended. Boys are somewhat more likely to attend high-achieving schools with more affluent classmates and greater faculty resources; girls are more likely to be found in schools with a strong religious climate, fewer discipline problems, and a positive academic climate. In part, these results suggest that families may apply different criteria in selecting a secondary school for their male and female children. We also know from our field work, however, that boys' and girls' schools have different organizational structures and different normative environments, and thus we suspect that the relationships observed here are based as much on institutional design as on family choice.

At the point at which students enter high school, many of them make a deliberate choice in regard to their schooling. A closer look at these decisions supplies important background information to help understand the effects of Catholic schools explored in the next two chapters.

Our analyses suggest that students who transfer from public elementary schools choose a Catholic high school primarily for academic reasons. These students are more likely to enroll in an academically oriented single-sex school. In this regard, the choice of a Catholic secondary school may be viewed as pursuing an option not generally available in the public sector— a single-sex secondary education. Because gender-segregated schooling is still widely available in the Catholic sector, we focus special attention on this organizational form in Chapter 9.

Those who transfer from Catholic elementary to public high schools appear to have two reasons for doing so: financial and academic. The higher tuitions at secondary schools act as deterrents to the choice of Catholic high school for children from less affluent families. There is also evidence that the lower-achieving students in Catholic elementary schools choose to move to a public high school where the academic orientation is less demanding and where there is greater opportunity for enrolling in business and vocational courses.

The variation among Catholic high schools can be characterized along two dimensions, academic and religious, that reflect their dominant features. Students who select an academically oriented Catholic secondary school are more likely to be male, from a higher social class, from a public elementary school, from a family willing to make a greater financial sacrifice to pay tuition, and to have a stronger academic background. Catholic schools characterized by a stronger religious emphasis with fewer discipline problems are more often selected by females, by students from Catholic elementary schools, and by less affluent students.

❖ 8 ❖

Variations in
Internal Operations

WHAT HAPPENS to students after they enroll in high school? Here, our analyses examine how students' personal characteristics combine with school factors to influence their experiences in Catholic high schools and the consequences that flow from these experiences.

The Analytic Model

We considered an extensive set of variables and constructs in our investigation (see Table 8.1). These variables may be organized into four clusters that represent a logical progression: (1) students' background (personal, family, and academic); (2) school characteristics; (3) students' academic attitudes, behaviors, and school activities; and (4) a diverse set of outcomes of secondary schooling, both academic and nonacademic.

The sheer length of the list of variables in Table 8.1 hints at the complexity of any examination of school process. To assist us in this task, we have constructed a general model (see Figure 8.1) that links the clusters described above. In formulating this model, we relied heavily on previous research in the public sector and on our field observations within the Catholic sector. Because there had been little previous research investigating these relationships within Catholic schools, we deliberately chose a broad analytic framework to guide the exploration.

The analyses that follow attempt to identify sturdy statistical relationships present in these data. Because we are interested primarily in the "major" trends, our description of these analyses is rather general. We do present sufficient details in the various tables and chapter notes, however, to provide

Table 8.1 Variables identifying major constructs and factors

Factors	Constructs	Variable description	Variable name
Personal, family, and academic background	Academic background	A composite variable consisting of College ambitions in grade 8 Repeated elementary school grade(s) Remedial group placement at high school Entrance exam required for high school entry	Academic background
	Elementary school experience	Catholic, public, or mixed	Catholic elementary experience
	Demographic characteristics	Sex Race (Hispanic, black, white) Religion (Catholic, non-Catholic)	Female Black, Hispanic Non-Catholic
	Social class	A composite variable consisting of Family income Parental education Parental occupation Selected household possessions	Student's social class
	Financial sacrifice	School tuition as percentage of family income	Financial sacrifice
	Religiousness	A composite variable consisting of Frequency of attendance at religious services Student thinks of self as religious person	Religiousness
	Family resources	One or two parents in household Number of siblings Home ownership	Single-parent household Family size Home ownership
	Parental support	Parental engagement with student (monitor school work, speak with student about personal matters, know student's whereabouts)	Parental engagement with student
		Parental involvement in school matters (PTA, parent-teacher conferences, school projects)	Parental involvement with school

School characteristics		
School social context	Average social class level	School's social class
	Social class diversity of school	Social class diversity
	Percentage black enrollment	% Black students
	Percentage Hispanic enrollment	% Hispanic students
Disciplinary climate	Principal's report of discipline problems	School discipline problems
	Incidence of discipline problems (school average)	School disciplinary climate
	Students' reports about frequency of abusive behavior (school average)	Abusive behavior in school
Academic climate	Students' attitude toward academics (school average)	Students' academic attitude
	Students' use of time for academic purposes (e.g., more homework, less TV, less paid work)	Students' academic use of time
	Peer attitudes toward academics	Peers' academic attitude
Fiscal resources	Tuition (1980)	Tuition
	Per-pupil expenditure (1980)	Per-pupil expenditure
	School size	School size
	Student/faculty ratio	Student/faculty ratio
Faculty resources	Starting salary level (1980)	Starting faculty salary
	Percentage of faculty with advanced degrees	% Faculty with advanced degrees
	Percentage of teachers at school ten years or longer (faculty stability)	% Faculty > 10 years at School
	Percentage of faculty who leave each year other than retirement (faculty turnover)	% Annual faculty turnover
	Principal's reports about problems with staff	Incidence of staff problems
School religious climate	Percentage non-Catholic enrollment	% Non-Catholic students
	Percentage from Catholic elementary schools	% Catholic elementary students
Academic organization	Diversity of academic tracks (academic, general, vocational)	Multiple academic tracks
	Ability grouping in grade 12	Ability grouping
	Hours of instruction per year	Hours of instructions

Table 8.1 (continued)

Factors	Constructs	Variable description	Variable name
Students' academic attitudes, behavior, and courses taken	Academic attitudes	Student interest in academics	Interest in academics
		Student attitude toward getting good grades	Attitude toward good grades
	Behaviors relating to academics	Number of unexcused absences in a three–month period	Number of unexcused absences
		Hours per week spent on homework	Homework, hrs./wk.
		Hours per weekday spent watching television	Television, hrs./day
		Student's disciplinary record	Incidence of discipline problems
		Readiness for instruction (arrive on time with books, supplies)	Readiness for instruction
	Co-curricular school activities	Participation in athletics	Athletic participation
		Leadership positions held in co–curricular activities	Leadership experiences
		Executive experiences, such as opportunities to address class groups	Executive experiences
	Course enrollment	Years of math courses	Years of mathematics
		Years of chemistry and physics	Years of science
		Years of social studies and history	Years of social studies
		Number of business courses	Number of business courses
		Years of foreign language courses	Years of foreign language
		Number of vocational courses	Number of vocational courses
		Remedial math or English Program (senior year)	Remedial program enrollment
		Honors math or English Program (senior year)	Honors program enrollment

Outcomes of schooling		
Academic achievement	Reading Mathematics Science Writing } measured in both sophomore and senior years	Reading achievement Mathematics achievement Science achievement Writing achievement
Affective and social development	Locus of control (student's sense of control over social environment)	Locus of control
	Self-concept Community orientation Family orientation Attitude about women's role in career and family } composite measures based on mean of sophomore and senior year responses	Self-concept Community orientation Family orientation Traditional role of women
College orientation	Level of educational aspirations (measured in the senior year)	Educational plans

Source: Modified from Bryk et al. (1984), 40–41.

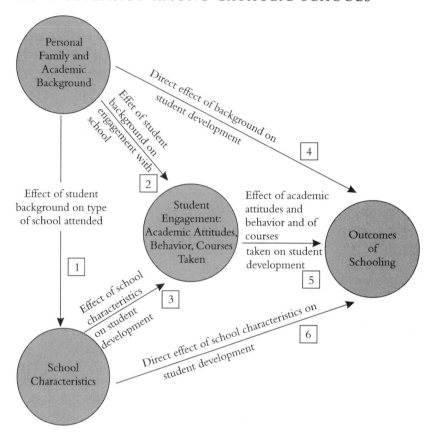

Figure 8.1 Analytic model for analysis of student development. Modified from Bryk et al. (1984), p. 48.

the reader interested in more technical details with a basis for evaluating our conclusions.

Our primary interest here is how aspects of Catholic schools influence the educational development of the students who attend them. Identifying such school effects on student outcomes is complicated by the differences in the types of students who attend different kinds of schools. The family and academic background of a student influences the kind of secondary school that he or she might select (represented by arrow 1 in Figure 8.1). This background also has some direct effect on the student's school performance (arrow 4). As a result, any simple comparison of achievement levels across schools becomes difficult to interpret. For example, suppose we compare two schools. The achievement is high in one, but low in the other. Assume further that the school with high achievement has abundant resources and highly qualified teachers, and tends to enroll students from more affluent families. In contrast, the school characterized by low achievement has fewer resources and enrolls students from more disadvantaged families. To what, then, should we attribute the observed differences in average achievement between the two schools? Are we seeing the effects of variations in school policies and resources, or are we seeing differences that result from the characteristics of the students who happen to attend the two schools? Most likely we are seeing a combination of both.

There are other complications in attempting to understand school effects. Students' engagement in school life—the attitudes and behaviors they display, the academic and extracurricular activities in which they engage—plays a central role in their educational development. How both family background and school characteristics affect students' learning depends, to some extent, on the degree to which these factors influence the nature of this engagement. It is for this reason that the student engagement factor is located at the center of our analytic model. The various elements that constitute this factor have strong effects on the outcomes of schooling (arrow 5). Further, many of the effects on student development of both family background and school factors work through these elements (arrows 2 and 3, respectively).

The model displayed in Figure 8.1 is a representation of an analytic technique known as *path analysis*. The aim of path analysis is to identify the direction and magnitude of "paths," both direct and indirect, by which one variable, such as a student's social class, relates to another, such as senior-year mathematics achievement. In using path analysis to examine school effects on student development, we must consider more than just direct linkages between school factors and achievement (arrow 6). In fact, an exclusive focus on arrow 6 would be misdirected. The analyses to be discussed indicate that much of the effect that Catholic schools have on student development occurs through a two-stage process.[1] School characteristics influence the nature and intensity of students' engagement, which in turn is the most powerful causal factor influencing the outcomes of schooling. Analytically, this requires first identifying the important student engagement variables, and then determining how students' background and school characteristics influence these variables. The focus is therefore on arrows 2, 3, and 5 in our analytic model.

Statistical methods such as path analysis provide some help in sorting out these relationships.[2] These techniques allow us to take into account the fact that any relationship of interest—for example, the association between a school's tuition rates and students' science achievement—sits within a network of many other relationships. Science achievement, for example, is influenced both by students' academic background and by the number of science courses they have taken, factors that are also related to one another. Path analyses permit us to assess the unique contribution of each measure of student background, school resources, and student engagement to the various outcomes of schooling, while simultaneously taking into account the other relationships that are also present in the data. The large number of variables in our school process model precludes a full recounting of all the details. Instead, we discuss the results in terms of two major questions: How do student background and school characteristics combine to influence the nature of students' engagement in school (arrows 2 and 3)? How do background, school characteristics, and student engagement factors combine to influence the outcomes of schooling (arrows 4, 5, and 6)?

A caveat is in order. Statistical analyses search for relationships among individual variables. They address questions such as whether the level of per-pupil expenditure for a school is associated with student achievement in mathematics, after controlling for average differences in family income across schools. From a substantive point of view, however, we are typically interested in assessing the strength of the relationships among more general constructs, such as what effect school fiscal resources have on academic achievement. Although statistical analyses can be very helpful in establishing associations among individual variables, drawing conclusions about relationships among constructs from a set of statistical associations is a more complex task and inevitably involves at least a modest degree of interpretation and inference. It is in drawing conclusions that we rely upon our field observations. They provide a basis for understanding a very complex set of statistical evidence.

Effects of Student Background and School Characteristics on Students' Engagement

We know from the previous chapter (Table 7.6) that students' family background and academic preparation prior to high school entry play a significant role in the selection of a particular Catholic secondary school. How much do these characteristics influence students' engagement with their school, once differences due to student-school matching have been taken into account? We also wish to determine whether features of schools have direct effects on student engagement, once personal characteristics are taken into account. The results are reported separately for three categories of student engagement: attitudes and behaviors at sophomore year, course enrollment patterns throughout high school, and co-curricular participation.

Attitudes and Behaviors at Sophomore Year

The relative influence of school factors (arrow 3 in Figure 8.1) and personal background (arrow 2) on students' engagement in schooling depends upon the particular variable in question. Table 8.2 presents results for students' academic attitudes reported at sophomore year. As before, the plus and minus signs indicate the direction and magnitude of the relationships of background and school variables with each of the student engagement measures. The R^2 statistics indicate the proportion of variance in the particular outcome that is explained by the entire set of predictor variables (the students' background and school measures, in this case). Although these statistics can sometimes be misleading because they depend in part upon the reliability of the outcome measure, they nonetheless provide some information about the adequacy of the final fitted models.[3]

We focus on two measures of students' attitudes: their interest in academics and their attitudes toward other students who get good grades. Positive responses on these attitudinal measures are more prevalent among female students, religiously oriented students, and those with a strong academic background. Parents' engagement with their children is also associated with positive academic attitudes. Minority status, financial sacrifice, and being Catholic are not related to these attitudes. Students from single-parent families, however, display fewer positive school-related attitudes. After adjusting for differences among schools in the types of students enrolled in them, certain school characteristics are also related to students' academic attitudes. In particular, the statistical associations displayed in Table 8.2 indicate that a favorable school climate is linked to positive student attitudes. For example, students are more likely to report positive academic attitudes if they attend a school where their peers are academically oriented. However, neither school size nor school resources is related to academic attitudes, nor are such features as the average social class of the school or the percentage of minority enrollment.

Table 8.3 presents results for selected student behaviors that are related to academic achievement: absenteeism, time spent on homework and watching television, the incidence of discipline problems, and students' readiness for instruction (coming to class with books, paper, and pencils). Both student background and school features have especially strong relationships with the amount of time students spend on homework ($R^2 = 17.8$ percent). Students with stronger academic background, female students, and those who consider themselves religious spend more time on homework. Students also report more time spent on homework when their parents are personally engaged with them. The academic climate of the school is also

Table 8.2 Aspects of background and schools related to student attitudes at sophomore year

Explanatory variable	Interest in academics	Attitude toward getting good grades
Student Background		
Academic background	+++	+
Catholic elementary experience		
Female	++	+++
Black		
Hispanic		
Non-Catholic		
Student's social class	++	
Financial sacrifice		
Religiousness	+++	++
Single-parent household	––	–
Family size		
Home ownership		
Parental engagement with student	+++	+++
Parental involvement with school		
School Characteristics		
School's social class		
Social class diversity		
% Black students		
% Hispanic students		
School discipline problems		
School disciplinary climate	–	
Abusive behavior in school		
Students' academic attitude	++	++
Students' academic use of time	++	
Peers' academic attitude	+++	+++
Tuition		
Per-pupil expenditure	+	
School size		
Student/faculty ratio		
% Faculty with advanced degrees		
% Faculty > 10 years at school		
% Annual faculty turnover	+	
Incidence of staff problems		
% Non-Catholic students		
% Catholic elementary students		
Multiple academic tracks		
Ability grouping		
Hours of instruction	–	
% of variance explained (R^2)	19.2	12.9

Source: Data from *High School and Beyond.*

related to the amount of homework students do. More time on homework is reported in schools where students' attitudes about academics are positive. Students also do more homework in schools with stable faculties and few problems with staff. A similar set of relationships appears with the variable tapping readiness for instruction.

Two of the student behaviors we examine here—unexcused absenteeism and disciplinary problems—represent negative activities. The relationship of student background to these two behaviors is similar to that described for homework and readiness for instruction, but in the opposite direction. That is, less parental engagement and less religiousness are associated with more problems in discipline and attendance. Such behaviors are more prevalent among male than female students. Another negative behavior is time spent watching television, which is greater among black students and those from families of lower social class. All three of these behaviors that detract from academic pursuits are more likely to occur among students who attend schools with weaker academic environments.

In general, personal background and school factors are both related to students' attitudes and behaviors in highly predictable ways. Students with stronger academic and family backgrounds are more likely to display attitudes and behaviors conducive to the academic aims of schooling. In terms of the effects of school characteristics, students are more likely to display positive academic attitudes and behaviors if they attend schools with positive academic climates. Conversely, negative student behaviors associated with lower achievement are more commonly exhibited in schools with weaker academic environments. A number of significant relations appear to connect positive student behaviors with various measures of schools' fiscal and human resources and their academic organization. These results, however, are not especially strong.

Enrollment in High School Courses

No behavior is more central to a student's academic life than the choice of which courses to take. In Chapter 4, we discussed the curriculum and course content in Catholic high schools as well as the programs of study typically encountered by students. We now examine in more detail how variations in students' backgrounds and school characteristics relate to their programs of study. The specific outcome variables considered in these analyses include the number of courses students take in mathematics, science, business, and vocational areas as well as their placement in remedial and honors programs. Although the subject-matter areas considered here

Table 8.3 Aspects of background and schools related to academic behaviors at sophomore year

Explanatory variable	Unexcused absences	TV (hrs./day)	Homework (hrs./week)	Working for pay	Discipline problems	Readiness for instruction
Student Background						
Academic background	-	+	+++	-	-	
Catholic elementary experience		+		--		
Female		+++	+++	---	--	+++
Black		+++				
Hispanic						
Non-Catholic						
Student's social class		--	+	-		
Financial sacrifice						
Religiousness	--		+++		-	++
Single-parent household			-			-
Family size						
Home ownership				+		
Parental engagement with student	---		+++	-	--	+++
Parental involvement with school			+			-

School Characteristics						
School's social class						
Social class diversity		−	−		−	−
% Black students						
% Hispanic students						
School discipline problems						
School disciplinary climate		−			+++	
Abusive behavior in school			++			
Students' academic attitude			++			++
Students' academic use of time		−−−			−−−	−−
Peers' academic attitudes	−−	−−	+		−−	+++
Tuition					−	
Per-pupil expenditure					−	
School size			+	+		
Student/faculty ratio					−	
% Faculty with advanced degrees		++	+			
% Faculty > 10 years at school			+			+
% Annual faculty turnover			−			
Incidence of staff problems						
% Non-Catholic students			−			−−
% Catholic elementary students					+	
Multiple academic tracks					−	
Ability grouping						
Hours of instruction						
% of variance explained (R²)	7.3	11.2	17.8	7.3	13.6	11.2

Source: Data from High School and Beyond.

are not especially specific, they provide the best indicators available in *HS&B* to differentiate academic and nonacademic courses of study. The number of courses taken in mathematics and science are good indicators of the intensity of a student's academic program. We have found, however, that the numbers of courses taken in English and social studies are less informative. Taking more math or science courses can usually be interpreted as indicating increased student interaction with advanced subject matter, but this is not necessarily true in other curricular areas. Results of these analyses are presented in Table 8.4.

Course enrollments are generally explained by our analytic model more fully than were the academic attitudes and behaviors presented earlier, as indicated by the higher proportion of variance explained. The relative contribution of school characteristics is also greater for courses taken.

In general, students of higher social class and those with stronger academic backgrounds are more likely to be enrolled in honors programs, and they also take more advanced academic courses. Conversely, these students are less likely either to be in remedial courses or to be pursuing business and vocational offerings. Girls' course-taking activities are a noteworthy exception to this pattern. Female students in Catholic high schools are considerably less likely to take mathematics and science courses, but they are no more likely to take vocational courses. As was also the case for academic attitudes and behaviors, we again find significant relationships for student religiousness. Religiously oriented students are more likely to be in an honors program, to take more science courses, and to engage in fewer vocational offerings.

Several school characteristics are strongly related to enrollment in math and science courses. For example, again we find that a strong academic climate is important, as is a stable faculty. Lower course enrollments in math and science occur in schools with more staff problems. In contrast, students attending schools with high tuitions and schools with less socially diverse student bodies display greater academic course enrollment patterns. Not surprisingly, a less intense academic climate is associated with more vocational courses taken.

The pattern of results for the measure of multiple curriculum tracks also merits comment. In Catholic high schools with multiple tracks, an emphasis on less academic pursuits (as seen in more business and vocational courses taken) exists side by side with a higher proportion of students enrolled in honors programs. These statistical findings are consistent with the idea that tracking is the major differentiating mechanism for student academic experiences within schools. To encounter statistical evidence of such internal differentiating effects within the Catholic sector is interesting, because curriculum tracking is less pervasive and less rigid among Catholic schools than is the case in the public sector (see Chapter 4). The effect on students of the particular curriculum tracks in which they enroll will be examined in more detail in Chapter 10.

Co-Curricular Participation

Co-curricular activities are another important component of student experiences within the modern Catholic high school. Participation in these activities is less well explained by student background and school characteristics (see Table 8.5). For the entire set of outcomes measuring co-curricular activities, parental involvement in the school is strongly related to student participation. This parent involvement factor includes measures of attendance at PTA meetings and parent-teacher conferences, visiting classes, and volunteering at the school. These activities are different from those included in the measure of parental engagement in children's learning, which taps parents' supervision of students' schoolwork and knowledge of students' personal activities.

In terms of other student characteristics, girls are less likely to participate in athletics and other extracurricular activities, but are more likely to have executive experiences (such as speaking before large groups). Students of a higher social class and those with stronger academic backgrounds tend to be more involved in co-curricular activities, especially executive and leadership experiences.

In terms of school characteristics related to students' co-curricular participation, two patterns merit comment. Student participation is greater in schools where peer academic attitudes are strong and where per-pupil expenditures are high. The latter indicates a school resource effect that we also observed in our field studies. More extracurricular opportunities were offered in Catholic schools with greater fiscal resources. Given that many Catholic high schools operate on very constrained budgets, it is not surprising that extracurricular options are limited in such schools.

Effects of Student Background, School Characteristics, and Students' Engagement on Student Development

Tables 8.6 through 8.8 report results for a range of student development measures: academic achievement (in sophomore and senior year), educational aspirations (senior year only), and social and affective development

Table 8.4 Aspects of background and schools related to courses taken, measured at senior year

Explanatory variable	Courses taken				Program placement	
	Math	Science	Business	Vocational	Remedial	Honors
Student Background						
Academic background	+++	+++	---	---	---	+++
Catholic elementary experience						
Female	---	---	-			
Black					+++	
Hispanic						
Non-Catholic					+	
Student's social class	+++	+++	---	-	-	+++
Financial sacrifice						
Religiousness	-	+		---		++
Single-parent household						
Family size						
Home ownership				+		
Parental engagement with student	+					
Parental involvement with school				+		

School Characteristics

School Characteristics						
School's social class	––					
Social class diversity		–	+++	–––		
% Black students						––
% Hispanic students				–	––	
School discipline problems	+					
School disciplinary climate						
Abusive behavior in school						
Students' academic attitude	+++		+++	–		
Students' academic use of time	+++		+++		–	
Peers' academic attitudes	+++	++	–––	––		+
Tuition	+++	+				+
Per-pupil expenditure	–––		++			
School size				++		
Student/faculty ratio						
% Faculty with advanced degrees	+++	+++	–––	–––		
% Faculty > 10 years at school	+++		–			
% Annual faculty turnover				++		
Incidence of staff problems	–––	–––	–––			
% Non-Catholic students	––		–––			+++
% Catholic elementary students		++	+++			+++
Multiple academic tracks	––		–––	+++		+++
Ability grouping			–––			
Hours of instruction				–		
% of variance explained (R^2)	28.1	21.3	18.7	17.2	14.8	13.9

Source: Data from *High School and Beyond.*

Table 8.5 Aspects of background and schools related to co-curricular behaviors, measured at senior year

Explanatory variable	Athletic participation	Leadership experience	Extracurricular activities	Executive experience
Student Background				
Academic background		++		+++
Catholic elementary experience				
Female	---		---	++
Black				
Hispanic				
Non-Catholic				
Student's social class		++	+	+
Financial sacrifice				
Religiousness				++
Single-parent household				
Family size	++		+	
Home ownership				
Parental engagement with student				++
Parental involvement with school	+++	+++	+++	+++
School Characteristics				
School's social class				
Social class diversity				
% Black students				
% Hispanic students				+
School discipline problems				+++
School disciplinary climate				
Abusive behavior in school				
Students' academic attitude				
Students' academic use of time				
Peers' academic attitude	+	+	+	
Tuition				
Per-pupil expenditure		+		+++
School size				
Student/faculty ratio				
% Faculty with advanced degrees				++
% Faculty > 10 years at school	-		--	
% Annual faculty turnover		-		
Incidence of staff problems				-
% Non-Catholic students				
% Catholic elementary students				
Multiple academic tracks				
Ability grouping				
Hours of instruction				
% of variance explained (R^2)	7.4	9.4	12.2	16.1

Source: Data from *High School and Beyond.*

(a composite across the two years). It should be noted that these analyses differ from the previous ones in this chapter in that they include the set of measures of student engagement (as predictor variables) in addition to the background and school characteristics included in previous analyses. With these measures we can examine arrows 4, 5, and 6 in Figure 8.1.

Academic Achievement

Achievement at sophomore year. Students' academic background and social class have substantial direct effects on achievement at sophomore year (see Table 8.6). The degree of family financial sacrifice associated with a student's attendance at a Catholic secondary school is also an important predictor, with higher achievement expected from students whose families expend a larger percentage of their disposable income for school tuition. Female students score higher in writing and lower in mathematics and science. Students educated in Catholic elementary schools are higher in reading and writing achievement at sophomore year, but lower in science. Race/ethnicity, non-Catholic status, religiousness, and parental engagement and involvement have no significant direct effects on sophomore achievement.

In terms of the influence of student engagement, students' time use is important. Those who spend a great deal of time watching television, have unexcused absences from school, or exhibit other discipline problems are likely to have lower achievement in tenth grade. An interest in academics and more time spent on homework are linked with academic success. Working for pay while in high school, however, is unrelated to tenth-grade achievement.

Certain school factors also influence sophomore-year achievement. Students attending relatively larger schools with more stable faculties, with few staff problems, and a positive disciplinary climate are likely to show higher test scores. Academic achievement in mathematics, science, and writing is lower for students who attend schools that use more ability grouping.

Academic achievement at senior year. By the time students have reached their last year of high school, the prediction pattern has changed considerably (see Table 8.7). By far the most important contributors to academic achievement at this point are measures of students' engagement with school, specifically their academic courses and co-curricular activities. Taking more mathematics and science courses and enrolling in an honors program have strong direct effects on achievement across all curricular areas, not just in math and science. The strong effects of math and science course-taking is explainable by the fact that more able students generally take advanced

Table 8.6 Aspects of background, schools, and student engagement related to academic achievement at sophomore year

Explanatory variable	Reading	Mathematics	Science	Writing
Student Background				
Academic background	+++	+++	+++	+++
Catholic elementary experience	++		−	++
Female		---	---	+++
Black				
Hispanic				
Non-Catholic				
Student's social class	+++		+++	+++
Financial sacrifice	+++	+++	++	+++
Religiousness				
Single-parent household	−			
Family size		+		
Home ownership		++		
Parental engagement with student				
Parental involvement with school				
School Characteristics				
School's social class		+++	+++	
Social class diversity				
% Black students				
% Hispanic students				
School discipline problems			---	---
Students' academic attitude				
Students' academic use of time				
Peers' academic attitude				
Per-pupil expenditure				
School size		+	+	+++
Student/faculty ratio				
% Faculty with advanced degrees				
% Faculty > 10 years at school	+++	+++	+++	+++
% Annual faculty turnover				
Incidence of staff problems	---	---	---	−
% Non-Catholic students		+		
% Catholic elementary students				
Multiple academic tracks				
Ability grouping		--	---	---
Hours of instruction				

Table 8.6 *(continued)*

Explanatory variable	Reading	Mathematics	Science	Writing
Students' Engagement with School				
Interest in academics	+++	+++	+	++
Attitude toward good grades				
Number of unexcused absences		−		−
Homework, hrs./wk.		+		
Television, hrs./day	−−−	−−−	−−−	−−−
Paid work, hrs./wk.				
Number of discipline problems		−−−	−−−	−−−
Readiness for instruction				
% of variance explained (R^2)	25.4	27.0	26.1	30.3

Source: Modified from Bryk et al. (1984), 56.

Note: School disciplinary climate, abusive behavior in school, and tuition have been dropped because no significant effects appear here or in either of the following two tables.

courses in all academic areas. Executive and leadership experiences, such as speaking before a group and presiding over a school club, are also positively associated with achievement. Athletic participation, however, has a negative effect.

An important finding from these analyses is that the direct effects of students' attitudes and their use of time are substantially diminished by senior year. It is not that these considerations are no longer important; rather, by senior year their effects are manifested *through* actual student engagement with school activities, both academic and co-curricular. That is, the effects of students' attitudes and behaviors on achievement are largely indirect, working primarily through the ways that these attitudes and behaviors influence student engagement with academic courses and the co-curricular programs of the school. The pattern of influences of family and personal background on senior-year outcomes is quite similar to that at sophomore year, albeit somewhat weaker. Again, these relationships become indirect, acting through student engagement.

The pattern of effects associated with school characteristics remains relatively constant from sophomore to senior year. A positive disciplinary climate is, again, directly linked to high achievement. Senior achievement levels are also higher for students attending schools with more stable staffs and higher per-pupil expenditures. These findings suggest that the quality of some Catholic secondary schools appears to suffer as a result of limited fiscal resources.

Two other features that are often used as measures of school quality—student-teacher ratios and the amount of scheduled instruction—show no

Table 8.7 Aspects of background, schools, and student engagement related to academic achievement and educational aspirations at senior year

Explanatory variable	Reading	Mathematics	Science	Writing	Educational aspirations
Student Background					
Academic background	+++	+		+++	+++
Catholic elementary experience			−−	+++	−−
Female		−−−	−−−	+++	
Black					+
Hispanic					
Non-Catholic		−	−		
Student's social class			++	++	+++
Financial sacrifice	+	+++		+++	
Religiousness					
Single-parent household					
Family size					
Home ownership					
Parental engagement with student					
Parental involvement with school					
School Characteristics					
School's social class	+	+	+++		++
Social class diversity			−		
% Black students					
% Hispanic students					+
School discipline problems	−−		−−−	−−	
Students' academic attitude					
Students' academic use of time					
Peers' academic attitude					
Per-pupil expenditure		++		++	
School size					
Student/faculty ratio					
% Faculty with advanced degrees			−−−		
% Faculty > 10 years at school	+++	++	++	++	
% Annual faculty turnover					
Incidence of staff problems					
% Non-Catholic students					−−
% Catholic elementary students					
Multiple academic tracks			+		
Ability grouping			−−		
Hours of instruction					

Table 8.7 (continued)

Explanatory variable	Reading	Mathematics	Science	Writing	Educational aspirations
Students' Engagement with School					
Interest in academics					
Attitude toward good grades					
Number of unexcused absences		--	++		-
Homework, hrs./wk.			--		+++
Television, hrs./day			-		
Paid work, hrs./wk.					
Number of discipline problems	---				-
Readiness for instruction					
Athletic participation	---	---	---		+
Leadership experiences		++			+++
Executive experiences	++		+++	++	+++
Years of mathematics	+++	+++	+++	+++	+++
Years of science	+++	+++	+++	+++	++
Years of social studies					
Number of business courses					
Number of vocational courses	--	-	-	--	--
Remedial program enrollment	---	---	---	---	
Honors program enrollment	+++	+++	+++	+++	+
% of variance explained (R^2)	35.4	54.7	36.9	37.3	39.7

Source: Modified from Bryk et al. (1984), 58–59.

consistent pattern of effects in Catholic schools. These results should not be interpreted, however, as indicating that these school features have no effect on student achievement. The problem here is an analytic one: both of these variables are confounded with school type. Boys' religious order schools have less scheduled instruction and higher student-teacher ratios, but also have higher achievement. The higher achievement is in large measure due to the stronger academic and family background of their students and the greater fiscal resources in these schools, as discussed in Chapter 7. Although our statistical methods are intended to tease out structural relationships from spurious ones, on some occasions, it remains unclear how accurate the final results actually are.[4]

Educational Aspirations at Senior Year

Student social class, as well as the average social class of the school, is a strong predictor of students' aspirations for higher education. Academic background also significantly influences such aspirations. Students with a complete Catholic elementary school experience are less likely to have aspirations for postsecondary education. Students' use of time, as well as their co-curricular and coursework activities, are all strongly associated with aspirations for higher education. More time spent on homework, less absenteeism, and fewer discipline problems are also related to higher aspirations. The same is true for leadership, executive experiences, and participation in athletics. Enrollment in an honors program and more mathematics and science courses contribute in like fashion. In general, the factors associated with high aspirations are similar to those that directly influence academic achievement. The major exception to this pattern is athletic participation, which is negatively related to achievement but positively linked with postsecondary aspirations.[5]

Social and Affective Development

Statistical models of student outcomes have somewhat less explanatory power in the social and affective domains than for the other outcome areas we have explored. This is due both to the difficulty in obtaining good measures for these constructs (the reliabilities of social and affective outcome measures are generally lower than for academic achievement) and to the relatively instability of the phenomena. Further, because we designed our analytic model to focus on academic aspects of the school experience, it is not necessarily the best model for examining affective and social outcomes. The results of our analyses in this outcome domain are also less consistent, in part because these outcomes are not strongly related to one another. As there are fewer general patterns here, our summary comments on the results presented in Table 8.8 are particularly selective.

Parents' involvement, both with the school and especially with their children's academic endeavors, has strong influences on affective outcomes. When parental engagement is high, students report a strong sense of control over their environment (locus of control), a more positive self-concept, a stronger community and family orientation, but they also report more stereotypic attitudes about women's roles.[6] Religiousness displays a pattern similar to parental engagement on the measures of community and family orientation and the traditional role of women. Various important predictors of academic outcomes, including academic background, elementary school experience, the level of family financial sacrifice, social class, and courses taken, play very little role here.

There are also substantial gender and race differences on affective and social outcomes. Girls have a higher sense of control over their environment

Table 8.8 Aspects of background, schools, and student engagement related to social and affective development at senior year

Explanatory variable	Locus of control	Self-concept	Community orientation	Family orientation	Traditional role of women
Student Background					
Academic background	+++				
Catholic elementary experience					
Female	++	--	-	+	--
Black	+++		++	--	--
Hispanic	-				
Non-Catholic					
Student's social class					
Financial sacrifice		--			
Religiousness			+	+++	+
Single-parent household				+	
Family size					+
Home ownership					
Parental engagement with student	+++	+++	+	+++	+
Parental involvement with school			+		+

Table 8.8 (continued)

Explanatory variable	Locus of control	Self-concept	Community orientation	Family orientation	Traditional role of women
School Characteristics					
School's social class			−		
Social class diversity					
% Black students					
% Hispanic students					
School discipline problems		−−			
Students' academic attitude					
Students' academic use of time					
Peers' academic attitude					
Per-pupil expenditure					
School size					
Student/faculty ratio					
% Faculty with advanced degrees					
% Faculty > 10 years at school					
% Annual faculty turnover					
Incidence of staff problems					
% Non-Catholic students					
% Catholic elementary students					++
Multiple academic tracks		++	+		
Ability grouping					
Hours of instruction					

Students' Engagement with School

	23.8	12.1	14.4	16.4	22.1
Interest in academics	++		+++		
Attitude toward good grades		+	++	++	
Number of unexcused absences			+		
Homework, hrs./wk.			++	++	
Television, hrs./day	–––				–
Paid work, hrs./wk.			+	++	
Number of discipline problems	–			––	
Readiness for instruction					
Athletic participation					
Leadership experiences	++		++		
Executive experiences	++	+	++	–	
Years of mathematics	++				
Years of science					
Years of social studies					
Number of business courses					
Number of vocational courses					
Remedial program enrollment					+++
Honors program enrollment				––	
% of variance explained (R^2)	23.8	12.1	14.4	16.4	22.1

Source: Modified from Bryk et al. (1984), 59.
Note: For explanation of "traditional role of women" measure, see note 6.

(locus of control), but a lower self-concept. They also have a stronger sense of family, but are much less supportive of a traditional role for women. Blacks are higher on locus of control and community orientation, but are less oriented toward family and display less traditional attitudes about women's roles.

There is an extensive array of significant statistical relations between the various measures of engagement—students' academic attitudes, behaviors, and course enrollments—and these social and affective outcomes. The specific variables that come into play depend upon the particular outcome. There are no consistent patterns, however, across the set of student engagement variables. In terms of the school characteristics we have considered, there is little evidence of direct school effects on affective or social outcomes.

The Relative Effects of Background, School, and Student Engagement

We now turn to a comparison of the *relative* effects of the major constructs in our model—student background, school characteristics, and students' engagement in school life—on the student outcome domains considered in this chapter: academic achievement, educational aspirations, and affective and social development. This procedure involves quantifying the strength of the relationships indicated by the various arrows in the analytic model previously presented in Figure 8.1. These results are displayed in Figure 8.2. Each panel in Figure 8.2 represents a synthesis of results across the various outcome measures within each of the major outcome domains. The width of the arrows and the numbers attached to them indicate the relative strength of the relationship between any two clusters. For example, background has a sizable effect on sophomore academic achievement (notice the wide arrow with a value of .107 in panel A), but a greatly reduced effect by the senior year (the comparable arrow in panel B is much narrower).

The major difference between the models for academic achievement in the sophomore and senior years (panel A versus panel B) is that the latter model includes data on courses taken and co-curricular activities within the student engagement construct. The effect of engagement on senior achievement is the strongest single relationship in all four of our models (an effect of .179). Given that taking courses and participating in the co-curriculum are the major planned activities of a school, there is a certain reassuring simplicity in this finding.

The role of personal, family, and academic background, so powerful in predicting sophomore achievement, is greatly diminished once we take into account students' engagement with the school. Although background has a weaker direct effect on senior achievement, it continues to play an important indirect role through its influence over the degree to which students engage in school life. The strength of the latter relationship increases slightly from sophomore to senior year. In addition, as discussed in Chapter 7, background influences the type of school attended. Student background thus influences student academic outcomes in Catholic schools through three different mechanisms: directly; indirectly, through student engagement behaviors; and indirectly, through the type of school attended.

The results for educational aspirations (panel D in Figure 8.2) are similar to those for predicting senior-year academic achievement (panel B). The student engagement cluster is, again, most important. The direct effects of school features on aspirations are similar to the effects of personal, family, and academic background.

In the social and affective domains, however, the pattern is quite different (panel C). Personal, family, and academic background has a larger direct effect on these outcomes. In addition, background has an indirect effect through its influence over the type of school attended and the nature of students' engagement with that school. The effect of student engagement on these social and affective outcomes is weaker than for academic outcomes, but it is still present. The effects of school characteristics on social and affective development work primarily through their influence over students' attitudes, behaviors, and involvement in academic and cocurricular activities.

A Synthesis of the Effects of Student Background and School Characteristics

The presentation of results thus far has been organized around logical groupings of outcome variables. We now reverse the organization to consider findings concerning the direct and indirect effects of the various factors that define student background and school characteristics. Our summary is selective, although the results in Tables 8.2 through 8.8 permit readers to examine results for particular factors of interest other than those we have chosen to highlight here.

Social Class and Financial Sacrifice

The social class and financial sacrifice constructs are closely related. Although they share many important relationships, there are also some key differences.

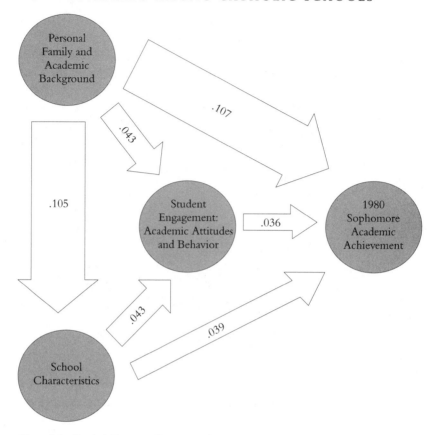

Figure 8.2, Panel A Factors affecting academic achievement for sophomores.
Technical note: Each panel is actually a synthesis of results across the several
variables within each outcome construct. The same set of background,
school, and student engagement variables was employed in each analysis
in attempting to predict the various outcomes of schooling. The numbers
on each arrow are unique explained variances associated with one factor
as it predicts the other. The actual number is an average across the several
regressions associated with each outcome factor. Modified from Bryk et
al. (1984), p. 55.

We saw in Chapter 7 that both higher social class and a family's willingness
to sacrifice financially for its child's education were associated with attending
Catholic schools with stronger academic and disciplinary climates and with
greater human and fiscal resources. As results in this chapter have indicated,
social class and financial sacrifice are directly and positively linked to academic achievement at both sophomore year and senior year, although only

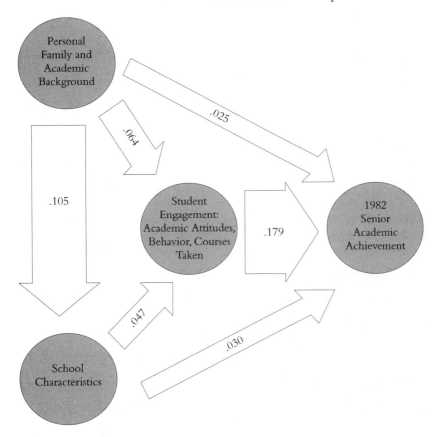

Figure 8.2, Panel B Factors affecting academic achievement for seniors.

social class is related directly to educational aspirations. One important difference in the relations involving social class and finance sacrifice stands out. Social class is directly linked to what students actually do in school, but financial sacrifice is not. Upper-class students display more positive attitudes and behaviors, take more advanced academic courses, and more actively engage in extracurricular activities. No similar pattern appears for financial sacrifice.

The effects of social class are thus multifaceted within the Catholic sector. Higher social class influences a student's academic outcomes through three mechanisms: it increases the probability of attending a good Catholic school; it encourages more productive student attitudes, behavior, and course-taking; and it also has a direct effect on students' academic outcomes. A

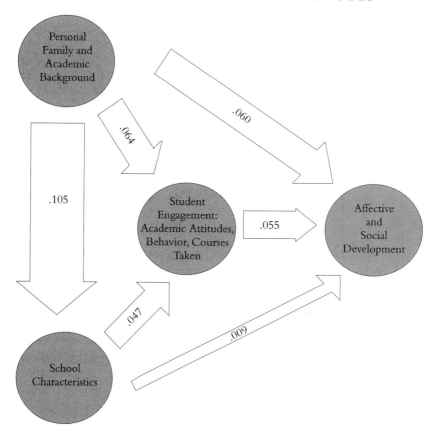

Figure 8.2, Panel C Factors affecting affective and social development.

family's willingness to sacrifice influences the choice of a good school and has a residual direct effect on achievement. It is, however, unrelated to engagement.

In attempting to interpret these relational differences, we note that the financial sacrifice variable is most relevant for lower-class and lower middle-class families, for whom the cost of attending a Catholic high school may constitute a real sacrifice. These statistical results suggest that Catholic schools attract some students from disadvantaged families in which the parents are deeply committed to providing their children with better life opportunities than they had for themselves. These parents are willing to sacrifice today's pleasures in the interest of their child. They know enough to seek out a good school for their child and are willing to support its cost, but they must depend largely on the school to structure an overall

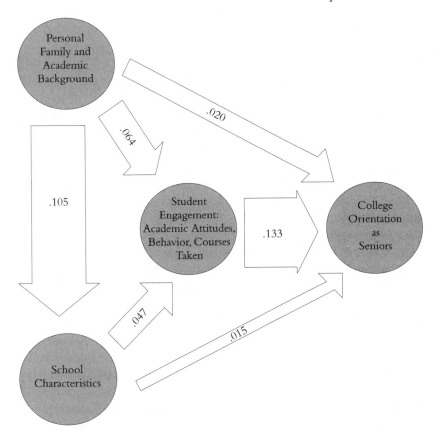

Figure 8.2, Panel D Factors affecting college orientation as seniors.

environment and a specific set of experiences to educate their child appropriately. Such families tend to lack the more general cultural resources available to students from higher-class families, resources that promote individual students' effective pursuit of opportunities that a school can provide. In short, the ultimate educational outcome for students from "sacrificing families" seems to depend to a greater degree on the stance of the institution, because many of these students lack the personal background and cultural experience to help them choose wisely on their own.

The negative effect of financial sacrifice on students' self-concept is also interesting. This finding suggests that although students from "sacrificing families" are successful academically, they may feel somewhat uncertain about themselves and may not be well integrated into a school life that their more affluent classmates seem to embrace readily. These are children in transition—they are the recipients of a powerful family and institutional force thrusting them forward into a social world quite different from that of their parents and quite different from the environment in which they are being raised.[7] They are apparently succeeding, but not without some costs in terms of personal stress and uncertainty. In this process the school is called to play a pivotal role, as a social agent helping to bridge the two worlds in which these children live.

Religiousness

Students with a strong religious orientation are more likely to be actively engaged in school life. They hold more positive academic attitudes, are more likely to exhibit constructive school behaviors (for example, do more homework, appear in class ready for instruction, undertake executive experiences around the school), and avoid social misbehavior (unexcused absenteeism and discipline problems). Religiousness is not directly related to academic achievement or educational aspirations, however. This means that the effects of students' religious orientation on academic outcomes is largely indirect, exercised mainly through its tendency to heighten students' engagement with school life.

Religious orientation is directly connected, however, to several of the social outcomes that we investigated. Students who describe themselves as religious are likely to exhibit more positive attitudes toward community and family, but they also hold more stereotypic views about women's roles. These attitudes reflect traditional Catholic values.

Catholic Elementary School Experience

Recall from Chapter 7 that the elementary school background of students attending Catholic high schools is quite varied, with only about 60 percent having spent all of their elementary school years in the Catholic sector. Evidence about the linkage between different kinds of elementary school experience and high school engagement and outcomes is complex. For example, although students from Catholic elementary schools are less likely to have unexplained absences or to work for pay while in high school, they also spend more time watching television. These students' achievement levels in reading and writing are higher at the end of their sophomore year, but their achievement in science is significantly lower. The effects of Catholic elementary school experience on academic outcomes are generally smaller at senior year; however, they are still positive for writing and negative for science. Students from Catholic elementary schools also report lower educational aspirations. We found no large effects on any of the social and affective outcomes.

Science and Catholic Schools

Our analyses of *High School and Beyond* corroborate earlier findings of slightly higher science achievement for public high school students' than for their Catholic high school counterparts.[8] The Catholic elementary school seems a likely cause for these differences. Students who transferred from public elementary or middle schools into the Catholic sector at high school entry have higher science achievement as sophomores than do students who have been educated in Catholic elementary schools. Further, these differences persist through senior year.

Our field research suggests that the limited resources in Catholic elementary schools are acutely evident in the area of science (where expensive laboratory space and equipment, as well as better trained faculty, are required). The organization of Catholic elementary schools as kindergarten through grade 8 institutions, combined with their small size, adds to the problem. Both the departmental organization and the additional resources typically available in public middle schools seem to be distinct advantages for science education. Although specific benefits accrue from each organizational structure, it seems that the small size and absence of specialization in many Catholic elementary schools detracts from high-quality instruction in science. Our analyses also suggest that the quality of science education can be a problem in some smaller Catholic high schools, particularly those with limited fiscal resources and an enrollment of many students from less advantaged families.

Parental Roles

The two measures of parents' roles included in our analysis—parental engagement and involvement—are quite different from one another, and they display very different patterns of statistical association. The first taps parents' engagement in their child's academic activities; the second measures parental involvement in the organizational life of the school. In general, parents' personal engagement with their children's education appears to be the more important consideration for students' learning. This variable exhibits positive relationships to such measures as students' interest in academics and good grades, doing more homework, being ready for instruction, and taking more math courses and fewer vocational courses. Parental engagement is also associated with less unexplained absenteeism and fewer discipline problems. Like religiousness, parental engagement is not directly associated with academic outcomes at either the sophomore or the senior year. It appears that both of these personal and family background factors effect a positive disposition in students toward the academic mission of the school and thereby facilitate the schools' efforts to impart knowledge. Parental engagement is also strongly linked to both of the affective outcomes we examined—locus of control and self-concept. Similarly, students from families whose parents are especially engaged in their education are more likely to be positively oriented toward both community and family and to hold traditional views about the appropriate role for women. Families appear to exert a strong influence on how Catholic school students feel about themselves and the social commitments they maintain.

Parental involvement with school organizational matters, however, is generally unrelated to academic outcomes. Although children of parents exhibiting such involvement do more homework, they also take more vocational courses. Such students are also more likely to engage in co-curricular activities and to have more leadership experiences. These findings offer a dual interpretation. From one angle, they imply that parents who are active tend to promote volunteerism among their own children. From a different perspective, these same results may be interpreted as indicating that when students become actively involved in the school, this involvement tends to draw their parents along into the school life as a consequence. It seems likely that both processes are occurring.

School Characteristics

As we noted earlier, the relationship of school characteristics to student outcomes is logically different from the effects of student background on these outcomes. School characteristics affect student outcomes by structuring different experiences for students. That is, school effects on student outcomes are by their nature indirect, being mediated through the cluster of constructs that we have termed "student engagement with schooling." The magnitude of the direct effects of school characteristics on student outcomes in Figure 8.2 is therefore small. In fact, we interpret the presence of a residual direct path as indicating that some other important school processes were not included in our analyses.

Among the school measures we were able to construct from *High School and Beyond,* the most important characteristics are the academic and disciplinary climate of the school. A positive school climate can engage students' attitudes and behaviors toward academic pursuits. These statistical associations confirm field observations about the importance of the normative environments of Catholic high schools. Moreover, these results probably underestimate the true significance of a school's normative environment, because the estimated relations are only within the Catholic sector. The true effects are likely to be much stronger in a broader cross section of schools, where there is more variation between schools on these measures.

Although we expected few statistically significant direct links from school characteristics to student outcomes, two associations emerged that merit comment. First, in schools where the incidence of staff problems is higher, students' behaviors are less oriented toward academics and sophomore achievement is lower. These results support a claim that the nature of teachers' commitment can play an important role in students' social and academic pursuits. We take up this topic in more detail in Chapter 11.

Second, schools with a stable teaching force exhibit higher achievement in all curricular areas at both sophomore year and senior year. As we mentioned in Chapter 3, some Catholic high schools have high teacher turnover and low levels of faculty stability, both of which appear to be caused largely by low salaries. This evidence suggests that in the absence of a stable core of teachers, students' academic achievement may suffer.

In general, the school characteristics discussed in chapters 3–6 are incompletely represented in the analyses presented in this chapter because the *HS&B* data did not include some relevant information. The *ATS* supplement to *HS&B*, used in analyses presented in Chapter 11, permits a fuller investigation of these concerns. Although surveying a smaller number of schools, this supplement contains considerable information about teachers' beliefs, the organization of their work, their working conditions, and the nature of their commitment to their schools.

WE DEVELOPED THE school process model employed in this chapter based on earlier research on effective public schools, and then refined it through a myriad of smaller exploratory analyses with the *High School and Beyond* data on Catholic schools. We have used this model to examine the internal processes of Catholic high schools, with students' background and experiences as the principal focus of the analysis. At least one aspect of public high schools that is crucial to their operations is not a major factor in our model: curriculum tracking. This is not surprising, given that almost three-quarters of the students in Catholic high schools pursue an academic program and even nonacademic students take many academic courses. The importance of the courses students take, however, has been underlined by the results presented here. Even within the Catholic sector, where students' academic experiences are more homogeneous, differences among students in courses of study are by far the most important predictors of senior-year achievement. These results highlight the influence of students' academic programs on subsequent achievement and set the stage for our investigation, in Chapter 10, of whether the social distribution of achievement in U.S. high schools is largely shaped by their academic organization.

Another obvious difference between secondary schools in the two sectors—school size—was shown to have little influence on student outcomes within the Catholic sector. In a few instances we actually encountered positive effects for large schools. This result ran counter to one of the propositions emerging from our field research—that smaller school size represents a positive feature of Catholic high schools as compared with their public counterparts.[9] We caution against misinterpreting the statistical results on school size presented so far, however, because our analyses have focused on variation in size *within the Catholic sector*. As discussed earlier, some of the most marginal Catholic high schools are quite small (less than 300 students). In such institutions, the limited fiscal and human resources can overpower the social advantages that accrue from the greater personalism possible within a small organization. The larger Catholic high school may experience the academic benefits of increasing size while still maintaining positive social relations. But the "larger" Catholic high school, with enrollments from 700 to 1,200, is still small compared with the large public high school, where enrollments can be several thousand. The effects of size in the public sector are quite likely to be very different from what we have presented in this chapter. The analyses offered in Chapters 10 and 11, where we compare public and Catholic schools directly, bear on this observation.

❖ 9 ❖

Single-Sex versus
Coeducational Schools

WHEN SECONDARY schooling—both public and private—began, students were segregated by sex. The shift to coeducation by U.S. public schools occurred with relatively little controversy. Such developments were driven largely by efficiency concerns of local school boards rather than by any deliberate educational philosophy. The lack of debate over what Europeans considered a major educational shift is puzzling,[1] especially because the move to coeducation in public schools was not accompanied by any broad social changes in women's roles.

As we discussed in Chapter 1, the early Catholic schools offered the sexes different types of preparation. The first Catholic boys' schools focused on preparing young men for the priesthood; the girls' schools taught those Christian graces believed most appropriate for marriage and motherhood. Around the turn of the twentieth century two forces began to change the nature of Catholic high schools: enrollments began to increase, reflecting increasing demand for education; and as more Catholic colleges opened, the function of Catholic secondary schools began to shift toward preparing students for passage to Catholic higher education. Slowly, training for boys became more broadly academic than the classical training appropriate for the priesthood. Related developments occurred in girls' schools.

Even though the mission of Catholic high schools broadened in the first half of this century, they remained almost entirely single-sex institutions until after World War II. It was widely argued that coeducation provided opportunities for young men and women to work in a more socially relaxed atmosphere and better prepared students for their future lives, but Catholic educators resisted such arguments. The Church's viewpoint on coeducation was stated forcefully by Pope Pius XI in 1929 in his encyclical *Christian Education of Youth*:

> False and also harmful to Christian education is the so-called method of "coeducation." This too, by many of its supporters, is founded upon naturalism and the denial of original sin: but by all, upon a deplorable confusion of ideas that mistakes a leveling promiscuity and equality, for the legitimate association of the sexes . . . These principles [denying the idea of coeducation], with due regard to time and place, must, in accordance with Christian prudence, be applied to all schools, particularly in the most delicate and decisive period of formation, that namely, of adolescence.[2]

Although in theory Catholic educators had to conform to the Pope's teachings on this issue, the financial hardship of providing separate schools for the sexes allowed for exceptions. A coeducational school could be tolerated, for example, when a community could afford only a single Catholic school. Even here, however, coeducation was frequently circum- vented by an organizational form called "co-institution," which entailed the operation of essentially separate schools for the sexes within a common building, with shared library and laboratory facilities.[3]

Philosophical opposition to coeducation persisted through the 1950s. As late as 1957, the Sacred Congregation of Religious issued a detailed state- ment concluding that coeducation was naturally dangerous to high school youth. In the 1960s, however, as broad changes beset Catholic schools, a movement toward coeducation began to spread. New schools were often coeducational, and many existing single-sex schools began accepting stu- dents of the opposite sex. In a recent study of Catholic high schools, one- sixth of the schools indicated that they had changed from being single-sex to coed within the last two decades.[4]

For those high schools that remained single-sex, the renewal of American Catholic institutions spawned by Vatican II had substantial effects. At St. Madeline's, as described in the Prologue, an emphasis on the development of women's full potential was melded to a traditional ethic of personal commitment to family and community. As a result, St. Madeline's of the 1980s was a very different institution from what it had been in the 1950s. We had ample reason to suspect that such schools might have a powerful influence on the young women whom they educated. Similarly, although the account is less dramatic, the boys' school that we visited, St. Edward's, was also a very strong institution that placed a distinctive mark on its students. These field observations encouraged us to examine the relative benefits of single-sex and coeducational Catholic secondary schools more systematically. Although now somewhat reduced in availability, the single-sex option remains prevalent and is still a major source of variability among Catholic high schools.

School Characteristics

In 1983, just over 20 percent of Catholic secondary schools were boys' schools and just over 25 percent were girls' schools, making the single-sex proportion 46 percent overall. Although more recent data are harder to establish, it appears that the proportion of boys' schools had declined by 2 or 3 percent by the late 1980s, with the proportion of girls' schools remaining constant.[5] As we saw in Chapter 7, boys' schools enroll the most advantaged students and girls' schools the least. In terms of staff resources, student-faculty ratios are highest in boys' schools, lowest in girls' schools. Boys' school faculties are somewhat more educated and more stable (both in longevity of employment and in annual turnover rates). In terms of fiscal resources, starting salaries are highest in boys' schools and lowest in girls' schools. Tuition levels are also higher in single-sex than in coed schools. Per-pupil expenditures are highest in boys' schools, but lowest in girls' schools.

Boys' and girls' schools also deploy their human and fiscal resources differently. Boys' schools, for example, are considerably larger than girls' schools and operate larger classes. When combined with a relatively high per-pupil expenditure by Catholic school standards, these features allow boys' schools to pay teachers higher salaries. In comparison, girls' schools pay lower salaries. They are also smaller in size and have a more favorable student-teacher ratio. In essence, boys' schools strive for economic efficiency—larger schools focusing almost exclusively on delivering an academic program to students in relatively large groups. The girls' schools are smaller institutions with smaller classes and more intimate, personal environments.[6]

Past Evidence on Single-Sex Schooling

The 1960s and 1970s witnessed a rapid movement away from single-sex schooling, both within and outside the Catholic sector and at both secondary and postsecondary institutions. Single-sex education was increasingly viewed as a barrier to successful adolescent socialization. As the demand for single-sex education began to decline, institutions either closed or converted to coeducation in order to stabilize enrollments.[7]

Ironically, this trend occurred at precisely the time that research on postsecondary institutions was beginning to document positive effects for single-sex education, particularly for young women. Researchers have reported that graduates of women's colleges are more likely than their coed college counterparts to complete their bachelor's degrees, to advance to graduate school, and to attain leadership positions.[8] Several advantages of women's colleges have been cited: a more favorable climate for students, which supports the serious engagement of women in academic work;[9] more circumscribed heterosexual activity, which eliminates some distraction from schooling; a greater identification with the community on the part of both students and faculty; and female faculty who support and encourage women in a fashion rare in coeducational institutions, where male students typically receive more serious academic consideration.[10]

Because American single-sex education is now confined exclusively to the private sector, most research on single-sex secondary schools has been conducted outside of the United States.[11] Many of these studies are of modest research quality, due to small and nonrandom samples of schools and a lack of statistical controls for differing selectivity among schools. Many studies are also quite dated and thus do not reflect changing attitudes about sex roles in recent decades. Studies conducted in the 1960s and 1970s reflect the social context of that period, when schools were often seen as oppressive institutions and reformers argued for making students' lives more enjoyable. Coeducational schools were found to offer more opportunities for positive social contact across the sexes, whereas single-sex schools (especially for girls) emphasized control and discipline[12] and a more academic orientation.[13] Interestingly, order and discipline, which are now seen as characteristics of 'good' schools, were interpreted as negative features within this research stream.[14] It is also noteworthy that studies reported that girls' school students evidenced less sex-stereotyped attitudes and behaviors.[15]

As we began our study, there was almost no research on the relative effectiveness of single-sex and coed schools in terms of students' academic achievement.[16] Fortunately, *High School and Beyond* provides excellent data for investigating this question; the school and student samples are relatively large and randomly selected compared with previous research on this topic.

The Effects of Catholic Single-Sex Schools

The data presented in Chapter 7 describe the entire Catholic sample of single-sex and coeducational schools included in *HS&B*. We learned in our field research, however, that there is a small subset of Catholic high schools at which vocational training is a primary institutional purpose. In seeking to compare the relative effectiveness of different types of schools, it is important to ascertain that all schools in the sample are addressing similar instructional purposes. Because vocational schools are atypical of the Catholic sector as a whole, we have eliminated the few vocational schools and their students from the analysis reported in this chapter.[17] The resulting analytic sample of schools and students presents a nearly ideal natural experiment. We have a relatively large national sample of schools, with similar institutional purposes (traditional academic programs), and students whose characteristics are similar in most ways.

Background Differences

The four groups of students used in these analyses (boys and girls in single-sex and coed schools) are well matched (see Table 9.1). There are, however,

Table 9.1 Characteristics of analytic sample

Variables	Girls in coed schools	Girls in girls' schools	Boys in coed schools	Boys in boys' schools
Academic Tracks				
% Academic	78.2	76.7	72.0	80.5
% General	13.7	17.4	21.6	16.2
% Vocational	8.1	5.8	6.4	3.3
Personal and Family Background				
Social class[a]	0.09	0.12	0.19	0.23
% Black	4.6	2.7	3.3	7.1
% Hispanic	6.4	10.1	4.0	8.5
% Single-parent family	20.1	16.1	14.3	12.4
Financial sacrifice[a]	0.08	0.09	0.07	0.09
Religious Characteristics				
% Non-Catholic	8.1	9.9	8.5	7.8
Religiousness[a]	0.41	0.13	0.35	0.07
Elementary school experience				
% All-Catholic	62.3	55.6	64.5	54.2
% All-public	16.2	23.1	16.6	27.6
Academic Background				
% Repeated elementary grade	4.8	6.7	9.3	8.2
% College plans, gr. 8	76.6	76.4	68.0	77.4

Source: Modified from Lee and Bryk (1986), 385.

a. These are weighted standardized composite variables, with mean = 0, s.d. = 1.

some personal and family background differences worth noting. In general, boys are somewhat more likely to have repeated a grade in elementary school; girls in coed schools are particularly unlikely to have done this. Although plans for college attendance at entry into high school are quite similar across the four groups, students in boys' schools come from more advantaged families. The level of families' financial sacrifice (as represented by tuition as a proportion of discretionary family income) is slightly higher in single-sex schools than in coed schools, probably as a result of single-sex schools' higher tuitions. These students' families are making a somewhat greater sacrifice to send their children to a single-sex school, which suggests that such families may be placing a higher value on education for their children.

The proportion of non-Catholics is evenly distributed across the four groups. Students in coeducational schools, however, consider themselves more religious than those in either type of single-sex school. Students' religiousness parallels their elementary school experience, with those who attended Catholic elementary schools scoring considerably higher on this measure. As we stated in Chapter 7, students who transfer from the public to the Catholic sector for high school are more likely to choose single-sex schools; those from Catholic elementary schools are more likely to be found in coeducational schools. Both of these trends are stronger for boys than for girls. Minority students, especially boys, are somewhat more likely to be in single-sex schools. Girls in coed schools are somewhat more likely to come from single-parent homes.

A picture thus emerges showing somewhat different types of students in the four groups in our analytic sample. Although boys' schools have the highest minority enrollment, their students are also more advantaged than their coed school counterparts in terms of social class. Girls' school students are less advantaged than those in boys' schools and generally are more similar to girls in coed schools. Overall, the degree of confounding between each gender in the two types of schools in this natural experiment is slight, although somewhat stronger for boys.

Analytic Approach

We report separate cross-sectional results at sophomore and senior year as well as sophomore-to-senior change. There are several reasons for present-ing both types of analyses. First, some of the outcome variables of interest were measured only at either sophomore or senior year. Second, for certain outcomes, such as attitudes toward academics or the time spent on home-work, it is reasonable to hypothesize that these attitudes and behaviors are formed early in the secondary school experience and then remain relatively constant throughout the secondary years. For these outcomes, the sophomore-year measures are especially important. Third, measures of sophomore-to-senior gain do not fully capture a school's effect on its students. Because Catholic secondary schools typically begin at grade 9, student status at the end of the sophomore year includes two years of a school-specific effect. The sophomore results are thus not pure "preprogram measures," and adjusting for sophomore year standing removes a substantial portion of the single-sex school effect that is now expected to accumulate between sophomore and senior year.[18] Hence there is good reason to believe that relying only on change analyses would underestimate the true school effects. It is also widely assumed, however, that the statistical adjustments employed with cross-sectional analyses underadjust for preexisting differences between groups. This implies a likely overestimation of the school effects if we consider only the sophomore- or senior-year results. The combination of cross-sectional and longitudinal analyses thus provides a degree of balance to these potentially competing biases.

Because there are some differences among the types of students who attend Catholic coeducational and single-sex schools, we have introduced a number of statistical adjustments. All effect estimates reported in the next section are adjusted for three sets of variables: student background, academic curriculum track, and school social context.[19] We also modify our reporting format, shifting from the positive/negative summaries used in previous chapters to an accounting of "standardized effect sizes." Positive/negative summaries are quite adequate for the largely descriptive and exploratory purposes of our earlier chapters, but they do not convey sufficient information to judge the substantive significance of any finding; nor do they facilitate a direct comparison of the relative size of effects among the various outcomes. The standardized effect sizes reported in Tables 9.2–9.4 represent the average difference (in standard deviation units) between students in single-sex and coed schools, after taking into account the influence of personal and family background, track placement, and school social context. Positive effects represent an advantage for single-sex schooling. Because previous research has demonstrated different effects for young men and women in the two types of schools, we present separate results for the two genders.

Effects on Attitudes, Behaviors, and Course Enrollment

Students in girls' schools are more likely to associate with academically oriented peers and to express positive interests in both mathematics and

English (see Table 9.2). Although the boys' school effects on academic attitudes are also generally positive, they are not statistically significant. Students in boys' schools are more likely than their counterparts in coed schools to hold positive attitudes about socially active peers and athletes. These effects do not appear, however, for girls' schools.

With regard to school-related behaviors, students in single-sex schools spend significantly more time on homework, and this is especially true for girls. Students in boys' schools enroll in a larger number of mathematics and science courses, and they are less likely than their counterparts in coed schools to enroll in vocational courses. The course enrollment pattern for

Table 9.2 Estimated effects of attending a single-sex school on student attitudes, behaviors, and course enrollment

Variable	Females	Males
School-Related Attitudes		
Interest in mathematics	0.23★	0.12
Interest in English	0.26★	0.14
Association with academically oriented peers	0.23★	0.04
Attitude toward socially active peers	0.10	0.26★
Attitude toward student athletes	−0.18	0.30★
School-Related Behaviors		
Incidence of discipline problems	−0.03	−0.15
Unexcused absences	−0.11	−0.19
Homework, hrs./wk.	0.36★★★	0.23★
Television, hrs./day	−0.15	0.17
Course Enrollment		
Mathematics	0.16★	0.46★★★
Science	−0.02	0.40★★★
Vocational	0.11	−0.26★
Social studies	0.12	−0.05

Source: Modified from Lee and Bryk (1986), 388.

Note: Effects were calculated with ordinary least squares regression, and include adjustments for personal and family background, religious characteristics, academic background, and academic curricular track. Group mean differences on these variables are described in Table 9.1. Additional adjustments were made for the social composition of the school (average school social class, percentage of black students, and percentage of Hispanic students). All effect sizes reported in this chapter are in standard deviation units, and were calculated by dividing the unstandardized regression coefficient for the single-sex dummy variable by the standard deviation of the appropriate dependent variable among students of that gender in coeducational schools.

The asterisks indicate nominal statistical levels (★$p < .05$; ★★$p < .01$; ★★★$p < .001$), using one-tailed tests of significance. A correction factor of 1.5 has been introduced for the design factor associated with the two-stage probability sampling plan (Coleman et al., 1982). These conventions apply to all significance tests reported in this chapter.

girls is more similar across the two school types. Girls in single-sex schools take more mathematics courses and take slightly more vocational offerings and social science courses than their coed school counterparts.

Effects on Academic Achievement

We examined single-sex school effects on achievement in reading, mathematics, science, and writing separately at sophomore and senior year, as well as gains in these areas over the last two years of high school (see Table 9.3). In general, attending single-sex schools positively affects academic achievement. Every one of the statistically significant effects on achievement favors single-sex schools.

Again, the pattern of effects is different for males and females. The estimated boys' school effects are largest at sophomore year, and though still positive, are somewhat diminished by senior year. Boys' schools students

Table 9.3 Estimated effects of attending a single-sex school on student achievement at sophomore and senior year and on sophomore-to-senior achievement gains

Variable	Females	Males
Reading Achievement		
Sophomore year	0.11	0.20★
Senior year	0.21★	0.18
Reading gain[a]	0.14★	0.05
Mathematics Achievement		
Sophomore year	−0.04	0.26★★
Senior year	0.01	0.18★
Mathematics gain	0.04	0.00
Science Achievement		
Sophomore year	−0.05	0.01
Senior year	0.17	0.01
Science gain	0.20★★	0.01
Writing Achievement		
Sophomore year	0.01	0.24★
Senior year	0.08	0.08
Writing gain	0.07	−0.05

Source: Modified from Lee and Bryk (1986), 389.

a. For gains, we employed a covariance model, with senior-year status as an outcome and sophomore status as a control variable in addition to the control variables listed in the note to Table 9.2.

★$p < .05$.   ★★$p < .01$. See also note to Table 9.2.

do not display any statistically significant sophomore-to-senior gains in achievement. For students in girls' schools, however, the estimated effects increase in size from sophomore to senior year, with gains in reading and science achievement that are statistically significant. The girls' school effects on academic achievement are particularly salient in light of the fact that these students are not taking more academic courses than their coed school counterparts (except in mathematics, where no gain is seen; see Table 9.2). As a result, the effects cannot be attributed to more academic courses taken, which is the major explanatory factor for secondary school achievement (as documented in Chapter 8). By discounting such alternative hypotheses, an explanation based on the environment and social organization of an all-girls' school appears more plausible.

Effects on Educational Aspirations and Affective Outcomes

For nonacademic outcomes—educational aspirations, locus of control, self-concept, and sex-role attitudes—the estimated effects generally favor single-sex schools, with larger effects accruing for students in girls' schools (see Table 9.4). The estimated girls' school effect on educational aspirations is statistically significant at sophomore and senior year, and for the sophomore-to-senior gain. Girls' schools also display a statistically significant positive effect in senior-year locus of control and sophomore-year self-concept. None of the estimated boys' school effects is statistically significant.

The final outcome, which measures students' views about women's roles, is a composite of attitudes about the compatibility of work and motherhood, the traditional role of men as achievers, and whether most women are satisfied with home and child care rather than careers (the same measure reported on in Chapter 8). A positive effect on this measure indicates a more stereotypic attitude about women's roles. We find that girls' school students are considerably less likely to evidence stereotyped sex-role attitudes than comparable girls in coed schools. Further, the attitudes among students in girls' schools show a significant decline in stereotyping from sophomore to senior year. Interestingly, although students in boys' schools hold slightly more sex-stereotypic views than their coed school counterparts at sophomore year, this difference disappears by senior year. Sex-stereotyped attitudes apparently are not an inevitable consequence of an all-male environment, at least as such environments are realized in Catholic schools.

We consider the results on sex-role stereotyping among our most interesting findings. Although the traditional purpose of girls' schools was to provide an appropriate finishing experience for Catholic women in their

Table 9.4 Estimated effects of attending a single-sex school on educational aspirations, locus of control, self-concept, and sex-role stereotyping

Variable	Females	Males
Educational Aspirations		
Sophomore year	0.19★	0.13
Senior year	0.23★★	0.11
Aspirations gain[a]	0.15★	0.07
Locus of Control		
Sophomore year	0.16	0.18
Senior year	0.21★	−0.04
Locus gain	0.14	−0.12
Self-Concept		
Sophomore year	0.18★	0.08
Senior year	0.10	0.12
Concept gain	0.02	0.09
Sex-Role Stereotyping[b]		
Sophomore year	−0.16	0.15
Senior year	−0.25★	−0.03
Stereotyping gain	−0.17★	−0.09

Source: Lee and Bryk (1986), 390.

a. For gains, we employed a covariance model, with senior-year status as an outcome and sophomore status as a control variable in addition to the control variables listed in the note to Table 9.2.

b. This is the "traditional role of women" measure used in Chapter 8. The variable has been renamed here to be more informative in the context of the issues discussed in this chapter.

★$p < .05$. ★★$p < .01$. See also note to Table 9.2.

future roles as wives and mothers, this aim no longer dominates students' education in these schools. The former goal has been replaced by a proactive orientation toward gender equity. A more traditional view is still emphasized in some schools, as we observed at St. Frances, but the analyses suggest that the norms of St. Madeline's have become more commonplace. The 1980s portrait of St. Madeline's in the Prologue appears to capture broad and general features of contemporary Catholic girls' schools as empowering environments for young women.

Are These Effects Large or Small?

The reporting of research results in standardized effect sizes is becoming increasingly common, because it provides a convenient metric for comparing results across different outcomes and studies. Moreover, the substantive significance of these estimated effects can be assessed by reference to some external standards. In the current case, two standards are particularly appropriate.[20]

The first standard is based on the average amount of learning for public school students during a year of instruction. It has been shown that this gain is approximately equivalent to a standardized effect size of 0.10.[21] This standard provides us with a way to interpret any estimated effect in terms of an increment to student learning that is associated with attendance at a single-sex school. For example, recall from Table 9.3 that the girls' school effect on the gain in science achievement is 0.20. This means that attendance at a girls' school doubles the learning in science for Catholic school girls over the course of their junior and senior years. While girls in coed schools are making two years of progress, their single-sex counterparts are making four. By this standard, the reported effects would have to be judged as substantively very important.

A second approach to evaluating the significance of the estimated effects focuses on the fact that single-sex school organization is a school-level factor. This suggests that we consider the estimated effects relative to the amount of variation naturally occurring between schools. If the latter were large, it would indicate that the estimated single-sex school effects might be of limited importance relative to other school characteristics that might be studied.

For each of the statistically significant effects reported in Tables 9.2–9.4, we have estimated the amount of between-school variability on these outcomes and then recomputed the effect size estimates based on this standard. The results are presented in Table 9.5, along with the corresponding student-level effect sizes previously reported. Over half of the effect sizes based on the between-school variation are in excess of 1.0.[22] To put these numbers in some perspective, a 1.0 effect size added to a "typical" Catholic school would move its outcomes from the 50th percentile (half the schools are better and half are worse) to about the 83rd percentile (only 17 percent of the schools are better). A 1.65 effect size would move a "typical" school to the 95th percentile. When viewed against the total variation naturally occurring among schools, the estimated single-sex effects thus appear very substantial indeed.

Other Possible Explanations of the Observed Effects

When attempting to draw causal inferences from nonexperimental research, plausible alternative explanations might be offered for any set of results. The most frequently encountered objection is a selection hypothesis; that is, the

Table 9.5 Comparison of estimated effect sizes in terms of student- versus school-level variability

Variable	Effect size based on variability among students	Effect size based on variability among schools
Females		
Interest in mathematics	0.23★	1.35
Interest in English	0.26★	1.95
Association with academically oriented peers	0.23★	—
Homework, soph.	0.36★★★	0.96
Mathematics courses	0.16★	0.67
Reading achievement, senior	0.21★	0.84
Reading achievement gain	0.14★	0.81
Science achievement gain	0.20★★	1.03
Educ. aspirations, soph.	0.19★★	2.14
Educ. aspirations, senior	0.23★	—
Educ. aspirations gain	0.15★	1.44
Locus of control, senior	0.21★	1.14
Sex-role stereotyping, senior	−0.25★	−1.16
Sex-role stereotyping gain	−0.17★	−1.13
Males		
Attitude toward socially active peers	0.26★★	—
Attitude toward student athletes	0.30★	1.82
Homework, soph.	0.23★	0.51
Mathematics courses	0.46★★★	1.31
Science courses	0.40★★★	1.15
Vocational courses	−0.26★	−1.39
Reading achievement, soph.	0.20★	0.84
Math achievement, soph.	0.26★★	1.19
Writing achievement, soph.	0.24★	0.93
Mathematics achievement, senior	0.18★	0.75

Source: Lee and Bryk (1986), 391.

Note: The effect sizes in column 1 are identical to those reported in Tables 9.2, 9.3, and 9.4. The statistical significance of these effects are taken from those tables. The effect sizes given in column 2 were calculated by dividing the unstandardized regression coefficient for the single-sex dummy variable by an estimate of the standard deviation between schools on the corresponding dependent variable. The latter were estimated using restricted maximum likelihood estimation. For some dependent measures, a point estimate of zero was obtained for between-school variance. These are marked by (—) in the table.

★$p < .05$.   ★★$p < .01$.   ★★★$p < .001$. See also note to Table 9.2.

individuals within the groups vary in important ways besides the exposure to a different program. In response to this concern, we have introduced in our analyses statistical adjustments for individual background and track placement and for school context differences—the sorts of factors usually cited in selection hypotheses.

In general, the pattern of results after adjustments is not substantially different from unadjusted mean differences on these outcomes. This holds true whether we consider the cross-sectional results at sophomore and senior year or the longitudinal analyses. Although it is always possible that students and parents are choosing single-sex schools for reasons other than those that we have already taken into account, the evidence assembled here, coupled with our field observations, provides strong support for the conclusion that there are significant outcome differences favoring attendance in single-sex over coed schools in the Catholic sector. The estimated effects are especially strong and pervasive for girls. Our analyses also suggest possible effects for boys' schools, although the evidence here is not as strong.

To what do we attribute the observed effects associated with attending single-sex Catholic schools? Are these advantages a result of factors intrinsic to this form of school organization? Could the effects be due to some other set of considerations, such as school resources and academic policies, which just happen to be associated with single-sex Catholic schools?

We have already mentioned a number of differences between single-sex and coed schools in terms of their structure and resources. Girls' schools are smaller and have smaller classes than coed schools. The boys' schools have more resources, as measured by the proportion of the faculty with advanced degrees, by lower teacher turnover, and by more stable faculties. The girls' schools, in contrast, are the least well positioned on these variables. A similar pattern emerges when we focus attention on fiscal resources. Boys' schools have the highest per-pupil expenditure, but the girls' schools have the lowest. In short, the distribution of resources among Catholic schools is complex, and neither single-sex nor coed schools have a clear and overwhelming advantage.

Further, although we know from Chapter 8 that there are important substantive relationships involving tangible resources, their effects on academic outcomes are mostly indirect. As a result, there is no evidence that resources could account for the effects associated with single-sex schooling presented here. The most powerful factors affecting academic outcomes have been shown to be students' enrollment in academic courses. The most pervasive effects documented above, however, have been for girls' schools, and their students are not enrolling in more academic courses than their coed school counterparts.[23]

In both boys' and girls' schools, students rate their schools and the quality of teaching in them much more positively than do their counterparts in coed schools.[24] How to interpret these data, however, remains an open question. One explanation is that this set of schools, labeled "single-sex," just happens to have unusually effective staffs. It seems more likely, however, that single-sex schools produce not only positive environments for learning but also positive environments for teaching. (In fact, the analyses presented in Chapter 11 demonstrate that these two factors are intimately intertwined in a mutually reinforcing relationship.) From this vantage point, the positive reports about teaching and school quality provide just more evidence of single-sex school organization effects rather than a competing explanation for these effects.[25] We have even further support, then, that something important is occurring in Catholic single-sex schools.

A CURSORY EXAMINATION of our findings indicates a broad base of positive effects for single-sex schools across a diverse array of educational outcomes. Whether considering academic achievement in specific curriculum areas at sophomore or senior year, gains in academic achievement over the two years, future educational plans, affective measures of locus of control or self-concept, sex-role stereotyping, or attitudes and behaviors related to academics, single-sex schools appear to deliver specific advantages to their students. Are these schools better, somehow, in ways that are unrelated to their single-sex organization? It is possible, although we have not been able to discern a set of factors that is not at least indirectly tied to the single-sex organizational form. On the basis of the empirical evidence assembled here, we conclude that a single-sex school organizational effect is the most plausible explanation for the observed results.

Although this book focuses on students' experiences in their high schools, our findings on single-sex schools prompted us to undertake some follow-up analyses as these students moved into college and beyond.[26] It was found that attending a single-sex high school had sustained, positive effects. Again, the effects were stronger for graduates of girls' schools. These students continued to have higher educational aspirations and attended more selective four-year colleges than their academic qualifications would lead one to expect. Students from all-girls' high schools also continued to hold less stereotypic attitudes, were more likely to be politically active in college, and were especially satisfied with their college experience. No differences were found on these outcomes for men from either coed or single-sex high schools. Both male and female students from single-sex high schools were especially likely to have plans for attending graduate school, especially in the field of law.

These results indicate that something positive is occurring in single-sex Catholic high schools. In general, the results appear stronger for girls than boys. Although some may question whether the observed boys' school effects are sufficiently large and pervasive to declare an overall organizational effect, the results for girls' schools are quite convincing.

As has been suggested about single-sex postsecondary education, single-sex secondary schooling may in fact serve to sensitize young women to their occupational and societal potential in an atmosphere free of some of the social pressures that adolescent females experience in the presence of the opposite sex. Adolescence is a critical period for the formation of attitudes about oneself. The results here support the contention that some separation of students' academic and social environments may remove distractions that can interfere with the academic development of students. Although the aims of schooling are varied, academic pursuits rightly belong at the top of the list. If the positive benefits of social contact, widely cited as an advantage of coeducational schooling, act to undermine the academic development of some students, particularly female students, then considerably more thought about the social organization of secondary education seems warranted.

Our results also raise questions about the appropriateness of "students' satisfaction with the school environment" as a major criterion for evaluating schools. This factor has been a primary focus in much of the previous research on single-sex schooling, and that students prefer to attend coeducational schools has been a central element in the argument for the adoption of a coeducational policy. Although student satisfaction is an important consideration (particularly in private schools, which depend on enrollment and tuition for their very existence), when uncoupled from concerns about academic attitudes, school behavior, and achievement, it offers only a partial and somewhat distorted view of schooling. In particular, if improving the social environment is accompanied by a general decline in academic behavior and performance, then a failure to recognize these unintended negative consequences is very troublesome.[27]

It is far from clear, however, that this presumed tension between social and academic purposes is valid. In particular, the results in this chapter indicate that stronger academic attitudes and behaviors, as well as higher achievement in Catholic single-sex schools, are accompanied by very positive reports from students about their schools. These results suggest that a positive social environment can accompany high academic achievement—the two are not contradictory.

In an era when single-sex secondary schools are often considered an anachronism and when these schools are often being merged with opposite-sex schools to create coeducational institutions thought to be more economically and socially viable, it is striking that there has been so little empirical investigation of this form of school organization. For this reason, the particularly strong and pervasive effects for students in Catholic girls' schools merit special attention. It would be one of the great ironies of educational reform if, in equalizing opportunities for young women by breaking down access barriers to the boys' schools with greater resources and more facilities, we are inadvertently destroying one of our great resources—a set of educational institutions especially conducive to young women's learning.

The results of this chapter ought at least to encourage educators to ask whether secondary education in the United States is being enriched or impoverished by the gradual disappearance of single-sex schooling. To be sure, the relevant policy consideration is not whether all secondary schools (or even all Catholic secondary schools) should be single-sex. Rather, public policy should focus on finding ways to preserve existing single-sex schools and to encourage their development in other contexts where the option does not currently exist.

❖ IV ❖
EFFECTS

❖ 10 ❖

The Impact of
Academic Organization

Is THE SOCIAL distribution of academic achievement more equalized in the Catholic sector because of the ways in which schooling is organized there? To be precise, our aim is not to document sector effects but, rather, to understand better their possible causes. In this regard public–Catholic sector comparisons provide a useful natural experiment, because the student outcome differences between the sectors are quite large in some cases. In this chapter we build statistical models to explain this variability. An important test of the adequacy of our models is whether they can actually account for the observed sector differences. That is, if our models are able to explain the sector effects as a part of a larger and more general process of explaining variability among schools, this result will strengthen our overall argument that the distinctive features identified in Catholic high schools are causally connected to observed outcomes.

We have chosen to focus on the social distribution of mathematics achievement for several reasons. First, past research on mathematics learning has demonstrated that this curricular area is most strongly related to schooling and least related to home factors. Second, the best information in *High School and Beyond* about specific courses that students have taken is available in mathematics. In addition, mathematics is the longest and most reliable of the *HS&B* tests.[1]

In terms of the social characteristics of students, we are principally interested here in students' social class and race/ethnicity. It is, however, also important to examine students' academic background in a study of the social distribution of achievement, because prior research has demonstrated that many of the effects of students' race and social class work indirectly through students' academic status at high school entry.

A simple empirical representation of the social distribution of achievement is the regression line between a background characteristic of interest, such as social class, and the specific outcome of interest, such as mathematics achievement. This line is defined by two pieces of information that together summarize the distribution of achievement with regard to social class. The first piece of information consists of the steepness or slope of the line. This captures the actual strength of the relationship. In Figure 10.1, the flatter slope associated with the Catholic sector indicates that achievement is less strongly related to social class in this sector.

The second important feature of the regression line is the intercept, which in this particular case represents the average math score for middle-class students (that is, the predicted outcome for students with an SES rating of 0). Examination of Figure 10.1 shows that average math achievement is also considerably higher for Catholic than for public schools (intercepts of 23.23 and 20.40 for Catholic and public schools, respectively). Thus we find that the average level of mathematics achievement is higher in Catholic schools and that the variation in students' achievement is less strongly related

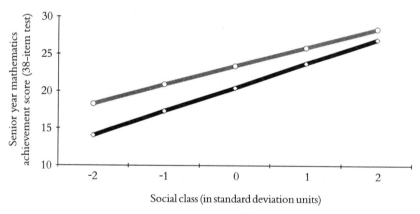

School Sector	Correlation SES/Achievement	Slope	Intercept	Sample Size
▬⊙▬ Catholic	.24	2.50	23.23	2035
▬⊙▬ Public	.33	3.23	20.40	1614

Figure 10.1 Catholic and public schools: Slope and intercept differences for the relationship between social class and mathematics achievement.

to student social class. These two pieces of information indicate a more equitable social distribution of achievement in the Catholic sector.

In a similar fashion, we can graphically represent the linkage between race/ethnicity and achievement. If Catholic schools are more effective for minority students, then differences in achievement between white and minority students should be smaller there. This pattern is found in Figure 10.2. Not only are achievement differences between white and minority students at sophomore year smaller in Catholic than in public schools, but these between-sector differences become even more pronounced by senior year. That is, the achievement advantage of white over minority students, which we term the "minority gap," increases in public high schools during the last two years of schooling, whereas the minority gap actually decreases in Catholic schools.

To place the information in Figures 10.1 and 10.2 in perspective, we have recomputed the Catholic school advantages in terms of the metric, introduced in Chapter 9, of the average amount of learning from a year of high school. By senior year, lower middle-class students attending Catholic schools are achieving 4.5 years ahead of their counterparts in the public

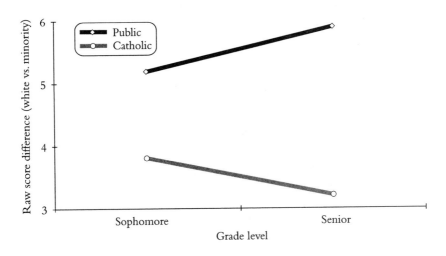

Figure 10.2 Mathematics achievement difference between white and minority students at sophomore and senior years (38 item test).

sector. In contrast, for upper middle-class students, the advantage is 2.4 years.[2] These results are consistent with the display of Figure 10.1; the largest between-sector differences accrue for the most disadvantaged students.

Table 10.1 presents the size of the minority gaps in terms of years of learning. Over the two years between sophomore and senior year, white students in the public sector gain 2.1 years in mathematics achievement. In the Catholic sector, white students gain somewhat more (2.5 years). For minority students the differences between the two sectors are bigger. In public schools, the average gain is 1.5 years. In Catholic schools, however, minorities are gaining 3.3 years—more than any other group, including their white classmates. They are learning at a rate approximately 65 percent faster than that of average public sector students and more than 100 percent faster than that of their minority counterparts in public schools.

It should be added that these results are overly simplistic, in that they look at each aspect of the social distribution of achievement separately. They consequently fail to take into account the existence of other relations that may be operating, such as the effect of students' academic background and the interrelationship of social class and race/ethnicity. These unadjusted sector differences are offered here mainly to illustrate the basic idea of a social distribution of achievement and, more specifically, to provide at least an intuitive understanding of what it means to say that the social distribution of achievement is more equitable in the Catholic sector. Many of the technical difficulties with the simple representations just presented are addressed through the use of more sophisticated statistical methods later in this chapter. Nevertheless, the basic pattern already described still holds—mathematics achievement is less dependent on students' social and racial background in Catholic schools than in public schools. In the remainder of this chapter, we investigate why this might be so.

Table 10.1   Amount of mathematics learning between sophomore and senior year (expressed in terms of years of learning)

	White students	Minority students
Catholic schools	2.5 years	3.3 years
Public schools	2.1 years	1.5 years

Source: Data from High School and Beyond.

Note: These figures are sophomore-to-senior raw gains in mathematics for each group, divided by half of the average growth in mathematics by public school students during the last two years of high school. Following Hoffer, Greeley, and Coleman (1985), this procedure converts raw gains into "years of learning."

In Chapter 4, we demonstrated that students in Catholic schools are much more likely to be exposed to academic subject matter than are their public school counterparts. Although these differences are partly related to the kinds of students attending these schools, the evidence strongly supports the conclusion of sector-specific effects on the placement of students in academic tracks and on academic coursework, regardless of track. In Chapter 8, we demonstrated that students' academic experiences are the most important factors explaining their achievement (see Figure 8.2, panel B). After these influences are taken into account, the direct relationship between family background and achievement becomes trivial. These findings suggest that much of the difference between Catholic and public schools in the social distribution of achievement results from differences in the processes through which student background characteristics first are linked to student academic experiences and then are eventually translated into academic achievement.

Our first analytic approach to investigating this proposition involves the use of path analysis. We examine whether the differences in the social distribution of achievement in the two sectors can be accounted for by a differential set of relations involving track placement and enrollment in academic courses—core academic processes found in all secondary schools.

One difficulty with these path analyses is that they do not provide any direct evidence about how specific characteristics of schools as organizations shape the distribution of these academic experiences among the students within them. That is, the path analyses do not allow an easy way to model explicitly how organizational features condition the link between the characteristics that students bring to the schools and the students' eventual academic achievement. In our second set of analyses, we use a more sophisticated statistical technique—hierarchical linear modeling—to address this concern more directly.

Path Model

The theoretical model for this analysis of the social distribution of academic achievement is displayed in Figure 10.3. The model flows from left to right. The student background factors (academic background,[3] social class, and minority status) are shown at the left of the model. The second set of variables captures key aspects of students' early academic experiences—whether students are placed in an academic track[4] or are exposed to remedial mathematics in grades 9 and 10. Next we consider tenth-grade achievement and how this, in combination with the other factors already

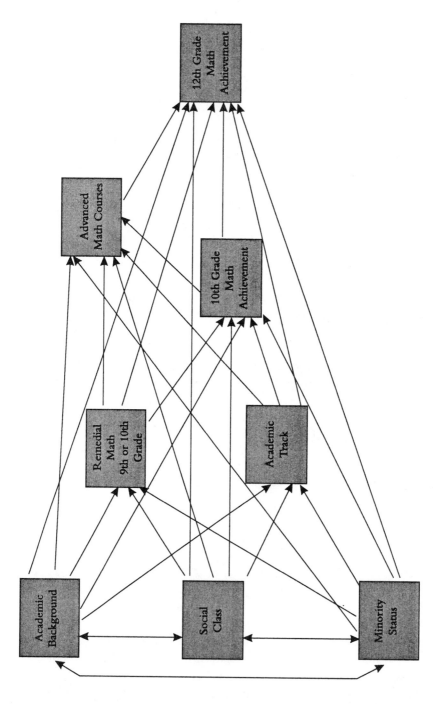

Figure 10.3 Path model examining the role of academic track placement on enrollment in mathematics courses and mathematics achievement in the sophomore and senior years (separate analyses for Catholic and public schools). Modified from Lee and Bryk (1988), p. 88.

introduced, relates to enrollment in advanced courses[5] and to the final outcome, twelfth-grade achievement. We analyze this model separately for students in Catholic schools and public schools because we are primarily interested in comparing the relative importance of each of these relationships across the two sectors.

Initial Correlations

We begin by examining the simple relationships among all the variables included in the model, computed (as correlations) separately for the two sectors (see Table 10.2). In general, these correlations are consistent with the observation that the relationship between social class and math achievement is weaker among Catholic than among public secondary students (.17 versus .34 at sophomore year; .24 versus .34 at senior year). Similarly, the correlation between minority status and math achievement is much weaker in Catholic than in public schools (−.19 versus −.33 at sophomore year; −.17 versus −.32 at senior year). The same pattern—weaker relationships between background and achievement among Catholic than among public school students—is also seen for academic background (.26 versus .35 at sophomore year, .29 and .37 at senior year).

There is also considerable evidence that student background characteristics are more strongly linked to key academic experiences in public schools than in Catholic schools. Although the relationships with remedial placement are similar in the two sectors, the correlations for academic track are different, with background characteristics again more influential in public schools. Academic track placement also has stronger links in the public sector to sophomore achievement, enrollment in advanced courses, and senior achievement. We must be cautious at this point, however, in over-interpreting these simple correlations among individual variables, because they do not take into account the full structure of relationships present in the data. In order to accomplish this, we turn to the path analysis.

Path Analysis Results

We discuss the results of the path analysis in two steps. In the first step, we identify the strong relationships in the model without regard to school sector. We use a graphical display method in which the width of the arrows is proportional to the relative size of these effects. Second, we estimate the effects separately for each sector, identifying the relationships that are

Table 10.2 Correlations between school background, academic organization, and achievement in mathematics (separate for Catholic, public sectors)

	Minority status		Academic background		Remedial math		Academic track 9th or 10th		Sophomore math achievement		Advanced math courses		Senior math achievement	
	Cath.	Pub.	Cath.	Pub.	Cath.	Pub.	Cath.	Pub.	Cath.	Pub.	Cath.	Pub.	Cath.	Pub.
Social class	-.10	-.28	.21	.30	-.13	-.13	.29	.30	.17	.34	.27	.35	.24	.34
Minority status			-.04	-.11	.05	.05	.01	-.13	-.19	-.33	-.10	-.20	-.17	-.32
Academic background					-.13	-.21	.28	.35	.26	.35	.33	.43	.29	.37
Remedial math, grade 10							-.20	-.21	-.27	-.28	-.30	-.29	-.28	-.26
Academic track									.29	.42	.41	.57	.36	.46
Sophomore math achievement											.54	.65	.77	.79
Advanced math courses													.63	.67

Source: Modified from Lee and Bryk (1988), 89.

stronger for public schools, those that are stronger for Catholic schools, and those that are relatively similar in the two sectors.

Not surprisingly, the strongest relationships in Figure 10.4 are for tenth-grade achievement as it predicts enrollment in advanced courses and twelfth-grade achievement, and the effect of course enrollment on senior achievement. There are several other important relationships in the model. Social class is linked to academic track placement, and academic track is subsequently related to both sophomore achievement and enrollment in advanced courses. In addition, students with a weaker academic background are more likely to be assigned remedial math placement, and this in turn is linked to lower achievement in tenth grade. Academic background appears to have a significant direct relationship to tenth-grade achievement that is not moderated through track or remedial placement.

The absence of any significant direct paths between student background characteristics and twelfth-grade achievement is especially noteworthy. This means that virtually all of the observed relationships between student background and twelfth-grade achievement, as estimated by the correlations in the right-hand columns of Table 10.2, are moderated through such key academic experiences as remedial and academic track placement and enrollment in advanced courses. We would expect sector differences in these moderating relationships if the nature of a school's academic structure influenced the social distribution of academic achievement.

To investigate this possibility, we have estimated this same path model separately for each sector. These results are summarized in Figure 10.5. The broad black lines indicate relationships that are stronger in the public sector; broad gray lines denote relationships that are stronger in Catholic schools. Narrow lines indicate relationships that are similar in both sectors.[6]

Most of the relationships in this path model are stronger in public than in Catholic schools. Two particular patterns merit special attention. First, the relationships among student background characteristics are stronger in public schools. In particular, race and social class are more closely linked to academic background. These results point to important differences in the types of students who attend Catholic and public schools. The poor and minority student in the Catholic schools is less likely to arrive at the school with a weak academic background. Part of the differences between the sectors in the relationships of social class and ethnicity to academic achievement thus works through the selection (or self-selection) of relatively more able students in Catholic schools, regardless of their social or racial background.

Second, and most important for our argument, there is evidence that the

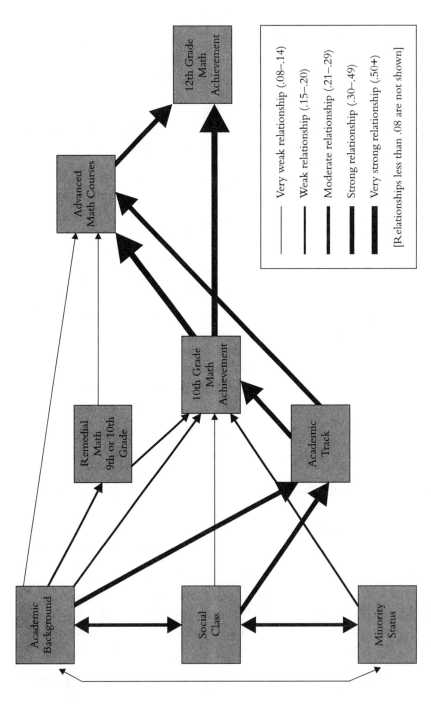

Figure 10.4 Relative strengths of relationships in path analyses predicting senior-year mathematics achievement (Catholic and public schools averaged).

Legend:

—— Very weak relationship (.08–.14)

—— Weak relationship (.15–.20)

—— Moderate relationship (.21–.29)

—— Strong relationship (.30–.49)

—— Very strong relationship (.50+)

[Relationships less than .08 are not shown]

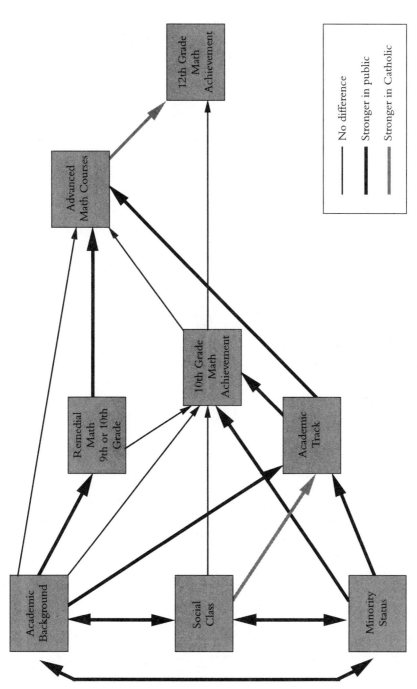

Figure 10.5 Differences in strength of relationships in path analyses predicting senior-year mathematics achievement.

social and academic background characteristics that students bring to the school are more determinative of their subsequent academic experiences in public schools. The academic background of public school students plays a stronger role in their remedial and academic track placement. Academic track placement is, in turn, a stronger predictor of both sophomore achievement and enrollment in advanced mathematics courses in public schools. Similarly, remedial placement in grades 9 and 10 is a stronger barrier to subsequent enrollment in advanced courses. The only exception to this pattern is that social class is a stronger predictor of academic track placement in Catholic schools. This finding, however, is counterbalanced by the fact that minority status is a somewhat stronger predictor of track placement in public schools.

The relationship of senior-year mathematics achievement to its major predictor—sophomore achievement—is approximately equal (and strong) in both sectors. The courses students take, however, have a somewhat stronger effect on achievement in Catholic schools. There are two possible explanations for the latter finding. The first focuses on efficiency in teaching; Catholic school students may acquire somewhat greater knowledge from each additional course. The second explanation derives from our use of generic course titles to describe the advanced courses students take. On average, there may be some differences between the sectors in actual content of courses with such labels as "Algebra II" or "Trigonometry." Without data more detailed than that available from HS&B, it is not possible to untangle these two possible explanations.

Another pattern observed in the overall model (Figure 10.4) is also true for both individual sector models: there are no residual direct relationships between academic or social background and senior-year achievement. That is, once curricular placement, course choices, and prior achievement are taken into account, social and academic background are not directly associated with twelfth-grade achievement. Rather, the path analyses indicate that it is *through* students' academic experiences that many of the observed differences in the social distribution of achievement in Catholic and public schools are created.

Thus we find that public high schools are more differentiating than their Catholic counterparts with respect to the backgrounds that students bring to the schools. That is, students' personal and academic background play a more substantial role in the public sector in determining subsequent academic experiences. Moreover, these findings are consistent with our contention that the organizational structure of Catholic high schools attenuates the effects on achievement of the initial differences that students bring to the school.

Hierarchical Model

Although we found in the path analysis that differences in students' academic experiences account for the link between social background and achievement, these results provide only indirect evidence that aspects of school organization actually create these effects. On the basis of our fieldwork, we theorized that the more constrained academic life in Catholic schools—greater academic requirements for all students, regardless of track, and a normative stance that encourages students to pursue academic work—attenuates the differentiating effects that normally accrue from personal and academic background. The hierarchical linear model analysis presented in this section provides a more direct empirical test of the proposition that school organization has powerful effects on the social distribution of achievement.

Significant analytic problems have plagued past research on how the organization of schools affects the individuals within them.[7] With the development of hierarchical linear models, however, many of these methodological difficulties have been resolved. Our research questions can be phrased in hierarchical terms: How do specific aspects of schools as organizations influence the relations occurring within them? More specifically, within each school there is a set of relations between student background and twelfth-grade academic achievement that we have termed the social distribution of achievement. The nature of this social distribution varies from school to school. Here we seek to explain this variation in terms of specific indicators of the academic organization of schools and their normative environments.

Formally, we characterize the social distribution of achievement in each school in terms of four distinct parameters or school effects:

- The average level of achievement;
- The size of the minority gap (the mean difference in achievement between white and minority students);
- The degree of social class differentiation (the extent to which social class differences among students predict subsequent achievement); and
- The degree of academic differentiation (the degree to which initial

differences in academic background predict subsequent achievement differences).

An equitable social distribution of achievement is demonstrated by a specific pattern among the four school effects. "Good" schools are characterized by a high level of average achievement, a small minority gap, and weak differentiating effects with regard to social class and academic background.

The individual variables that are hypothesized to affect these four indicators of social distribution of achievement in public and Catholic schools are described in Table 10.3.[8] These variables are organized into five categories. The first, student body composition, consists of demographic characteristics

Table 10.3   School variables influencing the social distribution of achievement

---

I. Student Body Composition
   • Average academic background (of students within the school)
   • School social class (average social class of students within the school)
   • Minority concentration (schools in which more than 40 percent of students are minority)
   • School size (total student enrollment)
   • School sector (Catholic or public)
II. Perceived Teacher Quality and Interest in Students
   • Teacher interest (average of student responses about teachers' interest in them)
   • Staff problems (principals' reports about staff absenteeism and lack of motivation)
   • Teaching quality (average of student responses about their teachers' classroom behaviors)
III. Disciplinary Climate of the School
   • Disciplinary incidence (frequency of problems in the school)
   • Feeling of safety (average of student perceptions)
   • Fair, effective discipline (average of student perceptions)
IV. Academic Climate of the School
   • Average hours homework (as reported by students)
   • Academic emphasis (average of student responses about the school's emphasis on academic work)
   • Students' academic attitude (average of student responses about how academic work is valued by students)
V. Academic Organization
   • Proportion in academic track (as reported by principals)
   • Average number of math courses taken (averaged across students in the school)
   • Diversity of math courses taken (variation among students in their courses of study)

---

of schools (social and racial composition, and the average academic preparation students brought to their high schools). In a sense this group may be viewed as control variables—aspects of schools that, though affecting the social distribution of achievement, are also distinct from internal organizational characteristics. The structural characteristics of a school—school size and whether the school is within the Catholic or the public sector—are also included in this group.

The second set of variables focuses on teachers and teaching. It includes students' perceptions of the degree to which the faculty are interested in them, students' opinions about the general quality of instruction in the school, and principals' assessments of the degree to which staff behaviors such as absenteeism and lack of motivation or commitment present problems for the school. We argued in Chapter 5 that the quality of human relations in schools can influence the engagement of both teachers and students in the work of the school. Although these variables are rather weak indicators of a caring environment, they represent the only information available in the *HS&B* core data on this dimension. (A more complete examination of this topic is taken up in the next chapter, where the smaller but richer *ATS* data set is used.)

School climate, in terms of order-discipline and academic emphasis, is considered in the next two groups. The quality of the disciplinary climate is tapped by several variables: a composite measure of the incidence of discipline problems, students' perceptions of the school as an unsafe environment, and a factor measuring students' opinions about the fairness and effectiveness of adults' exercise of discipline in the school. The academic climate is measured by factors such as the average amount of time students spend on homework, the degree to which students perceive an academic emphasis in their school, and average student attitudes toward academics. Taken together, variable sets II, III, and IV provide a diverse array of indicators of a school's normative environment.

The final set of measures focuses on aspects of the academic organization of schools. One variable measures the proportion of students in the academic curricular track. Another useful measure is the average number of advanced mathematics courses taken in each school. A third measure, the diversity of courses taken in mathematics, captures a different aspect of academic organization—the extent to which students within the same school pursue different courses of study. Each of these is an aggregate measure of information from individual students. Taken as a set, they provide an approximation of the central construct of interest here—the structure of a school's curriculum and the set of policies and practices through which students are linked to it. Again, this is the best that we can achieve given the limitations of *HS&B*.

The aim of our current inquiry is to identify a set of school characteristics that demonstrate the following pattern of statistical associations:

- A positive relationship to average achievement;
- A positive relationship with the minority gap (variables that act to reduce the differences in achievement between white and minority students in a school);
- A negative relationship with the social class differentiation effect (variables that act to weaken the relationship between individual social class and achievement); and similarly
- A negative relationship with the academic differentiation effect.

We may test the adequacy of our explanation that academic and normative aspects of schools combine to influence the social distribution of achievement in two ways. The first test is to see whether any of the school-level measures of normative environments and academic organization explains variation in the four school effects described earlier. A more restrictive test involves determining whether these variables can actually account for the "common school effect" first reported by Coleman and his colleagues. That is, after we add such characteristics to the model, do the Catholic school advantages of higher achievement and a more socially equitable distribution of that achievement still persist, or have we explained them away?

The Average Social Distribution of Achievement in U.S. High Schools

The hierarchical linear model analysis requires that we estimate a set of relations within each school and then examine how these relations vary across schools depending on specific organizational features of schools. Ideally, we would like to have data on a large number of students in each school and a relatively large number of schools in order to maximize the power of our analyses to detect the hypothesized effects. *HS&B*, however, collected data from relatively few students in each high school. (The typical sample size is about 30 students per school.) Fortunately, information was collected on two cohorts of students, those who were seniors in 1980 and a second group who were seniors in 1982. By combining the information from the two cohorts, we were able to strengthen the analysis. One additional problem, however, had to be solved. The mathematics tests employed in 1980 and 1982 were somewhat different. In order to overcome this inconsistency, the two tests were equated using a technique known as item response theory (IRT) to place them on a common scale. All results from the hierarchical linear model analysis are based on this IRT metric and expanded sample.

We began the analysis by estimating for each school the four effect sizes that characterize the social distribution of achievement.[9] The average size and variability in each of these effects across the *HS&B* school sample are reported in Table 10.4.[10] The senior-year achievement level in an average U.S. high school is 12.13 IRT scale points. There is considerable variability among schools, with average achievement levels commonly ranging from 6.14 to 18.11 points. On average, minority students achieve 2.78 points lower than their white schoolmates at the end of senior year (that is, the average minority gap is −2.78). The size of the minority gap also varies substantially across schools, with differences as large as −5.07 and as small as −0.49 not uncommon. Expressed in terms of years of learning, the average

Table 10.4 Average size of the four parameters for the social distribution of mathematics achievement in senior year

	Average school effect[b]	Range in school effects[c]	Average effect in terms of years of high school learning[d]
Average achievement	12.13★★★	(6.14, 18.11)	—
Minority gap	−2.78★★★	(−5.07, −0.49)	4.5
Social class differentiation[a]	0.97★★★	(−0.03, 2.06)	2.2
Academic differentiation	2.58★★★	(1.20, 3.96)	5.6

Source: Modified from Lee and Bryk (1989), 180.

a. For these analyses, the student social class and academic background measures were restandardized to a mean of 0 and variance of 1.0. This permits a direct comparison of the relative size of social class and academic differentiation slopes.

b. These results are in the IRT metric and not the "number of items correct" as used in Figures 10.1 and 10.2.

c. These are 95 percent confidence bands based on the hierarchical linear model estimates for the true variability in each of the four school effects (Bryk and Raudenbush 1992, 108). That is, 95 percent of all schools would fall within these ranges.

d. For social class and academic differentiation, this is the predicted difference in senior-year achievement between students at the 25th and 75th percentiles on these individual background characteristics. Results are expressed in terms of years of high school learning—the same metric used earlier in this chapter.

★$p < .05$.   ★★$p < .01$.   ★★★$p < .001$.

minority gap of 2.78 IRT scale points is equivalent to 4.5 years—a very large difference.

We also found significant social class and academic differentiation in U.S. high schools. The degree of academic differentiation is especially large. In a typical high school, the predicted achievement difference in senior year between students with strong academic backgrounds at high school entry and those with weak ones is 5.6 years of high school learning. In terms of social class difference among students, the comparable predicted difference in senior-year achievement is 2.2 years. The results presented in Table 10.4 also indicate that there is considerable variability among schools in both social class and academic differentiation. Interestingly, we can find schools in which minority performance approximates white achievement (that is, schools with minority gaps near zero) and in which social class differentiation is inconsequential (social class effects near zero). All schools, however, appear to engage in some degree of academic differentiation; effects near zero are highly implausible.

On balance, a degree of extrapolation is involved in expressing estimated effects in terms of students' years of learning, and these effects should not be interpreted too literally.[11] Our point is simply to demonstrate that the degree of differentiation in student performance by race, class, and academic background is large. Even if the years of learning conversion were incorrect by a factor of two and the results in Table 10.4 were halved, we would still judge the degree of differentiation as substantial. Moreover, unlike the simple results with which we began this chapter, each of these effects is estimated net of the others. That is, for example, the average minority gap of 2.78 points is adjusted for social class and academic background differences among students. The unadjusted effects are considerably larger.

Sector Effects Model

The sector effects model evaluates the effects of school sector on the social distribution of mathematics achievement (see Table 10.5). The results of this analysis indicate a more equitable social distribution of achievement in Catholic schools. Consistent with information previously displayed in Figures 10.1 and 10.2, average math achievement is about 2 points higher in Catholic than public schools, and the minority gap is smaller by 1.22 points. The amount of social class differentiation is also somewhat weaker. Academic differentiation, however, appears similar in the two sectors. Again, each effect is the computed net of the other variables in the model.

In order to lend these results a more substantively meaningful perspective,

Table 10.5 Sector effects on the four parameters for the social distribution of mathematics achievement in senior year

	Catholic sector effect[b]	Catholic school effect in terms of years of high school learning
Average achievement[a]	1.98***	3.2 years higher
Minority gap	1.22**	2.0 years less
Social class differentiation	−0.34	0.6 years less
Academic differentiation	0.12	0.2 years more

Source: Modified from Lee and Bryk (1989), 182.

a. Average social class, minority concentration, and average academic background were also included in the model for average achievement. This adjusts for the effects of student composition in each school on average math achievement.

b. These are the estimated mean differences between public and Catholic schools on each of the four distributive effects.

**$p < .01$.   ***$p < .001$.

we also present the Catholic sector effects on the social distribution of achievement in terms of years of high school learning (see Table 10.5). On average, senior-year achievement is 3.2 years higher in Catholic than public schools. The size of the minority gap is 2.0 years less and the degree of social class differentiation about 0.6 years less. The magnitude of these Catholic sector effects appears quite substantial when compared with the average effects previously reported in Table 10.4.

Compositional Effects Model

Before examining the effects of academic organization and normative environment, we first consider whether the effects reported in Table 10.5 may simply reflect the different types of students enrolled in these schools. A partial control for this was introduced in the sector effects model, where school social class, minority concentration, and average academic background were used to predict schools' average mathematics achievement. Such compositional characteristics, however, might also affect the size of the minority gap and the degree of social class and academic differentiation. In order to investigate this, minority concentration is included in the model predicting minority gap, school social class is included in the model for social class differentiation, and average academic background is included in the model for academic differentiation. Because these school composition effects may be different in the two sectors, sector-by-school interaction terms are also included.

In general, no compositional effects were found for either the minority gap or academic differentiation. We did find a strong effect of school social class on average achievement, and the size of this effect is different in the two sectors. Similarly, the degree of social differentiation within schools depends on school social class, and this effect also operates differently in the two sectors. Because the interactions of student and school social class and sector are difficult to describe in numerical terms, we instead offer a graphical representation (see Figures 10.6, 10.7, and 10.8). We present the relationships between student social class and achievement in three different types of Catholic and public schools: (a) schools with a social composition like that of the average Catholic high school; (b) schools with a social composition like that of the average public high school; and (c) schools serving a "disadvantaged" student population (defined as one standard deviation below the public school mean for social class composition).[12]

Not surprisingly, student achievement is higher in more advantaged schools in both the public and the Catholic sectors. Compare, for example, the predicted achievement for an average social class student in either sector from Figure 10.6 to the predicted achievement levels for comparable students in Figures 10.7 and 10.8. There is also a significant Catholic sector advantage for most students. The size of this advantage, however, depends

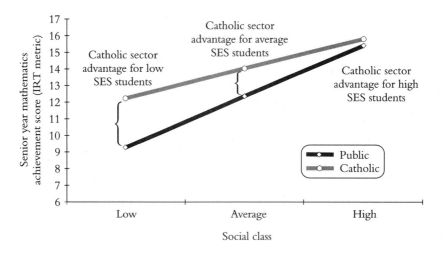

Figure 10.6 Comparison of social differentiation in Catholic and public schools whose social composition is like that of the average Catholic school.

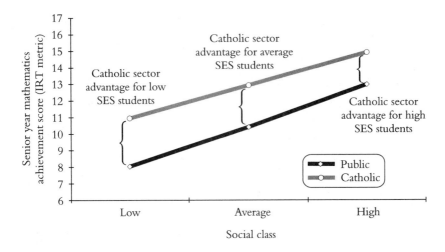

Figure 10.7 Comparison of social differentiation in Catholic and public schools whose social composition is like that of the average public school.

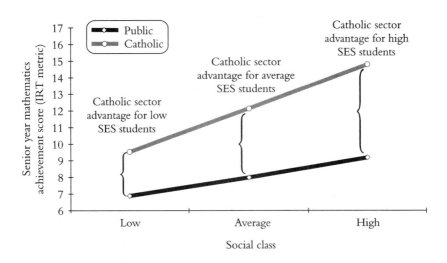

Figure 10.8 Comparison of social differentiation in Catholic and public schools serving large numbers of disadvantaged students.

on both the social class background of the student and social class composition of the school. This can be seen by comparing the size of the various braces in Figures 10.6, 10.7, and 10.8. In the typical Catholic school, the biggest advantages accrue to the most disadvantaged students (Figure 10.6). In schools with social compositions similar to that of the average public school, the Catholic school advantage is relatively constant for students of all social class levels (Figure 10.7). The comparison in schools serving large numbers of disadvantaged students is particularly interesting (Figure 10.8). Here, the student social class slope is slightly less in the public sector, which implies that achievement is distributed more equally in these schools with regard to students' social background than in comparable Catholic schools. When this effect is seen in combination with the very low average level of achievement in the public high schools, however, we find a not particularly desirable form of equity—everybody does poorly. In fact, a student of the lowest social class in a disadvantaged Catholic high school is outperforming the majority of students in a comparable public school.

The results of the model for the effects of sector on social differentiation were thus a bit misleading, in that they masked important effects of a school's social class context. When these context effects are explicitly taken into account, we find even stronger evidence that Catholic schools promote higher levels of achievement, especially for disadvantaged students. In sum, Catholic schools closely approximate the empirical criteria set out earlier as describing an equitable social distribution of achievement.

Final Explanatory Model

The final step in our analysis involves examining how the social distribution of mathematics achievement depends on specific characteristics of the academic organization and normative environment of schools as described in Table 10.3. The aim in building these models was to identify the school characteristics associated with each of the social distributional effects.[13] Table 10.6 presents the results of the final explanatory model. As mentioned earlier, a critical test of our proposition about the importance of academic organization and normative environment on the social distribution of achievement is whether or not specific measures of academic organization and normative environment can explain away the observed sector differences.

The difference in average achievement between schools in the public and Catholic sectors, reported earlier in Table 10.5, in fact disappears once we take into account differences in the number of mathematics courses

Table 10.6 Final model of the effects of academic organization and normative environments on the social distribution of achievement in senior year

	Effect estimates
Average Achievement	
School social class	1.03★★★
Minority concentration	−1.79★★★
Average no. math courses taken	0.80★★★
Average hours homework	0.40★
Staff problems	−0.44★★
Sector	0.16
Minority Gap	
Staff problems	0.21
Disciplinary incidence	−0.76★
Sector	0.07
Social Class Differentiation	
School social class	−0.04
Diversity in math courses	0.19★
Fair discipline	−0.23★
School size	0.17★
Staff problems	−0.26★★
Sector	−0.08
Sector × school social class	−0.13
Academic Differentiation	
Diversity in math courses	0.27★★
Fair discipline	−0.48★★★
School size	0.33★★★
Staff problems	−0.16
Academic attitudes	0.25★★
Sector	0.55★★★

Source: Modified from Lee and Bryk (1989), 184.

Note: All continuous school-level predictors were standardized to a mean of 0 and variance of 1. This creates a standard metric for the effect estimates which allows direct comparison of the relative importance of individual school-level factors in explaining each of the four social-distribution outcomes. The two discrete variables, sector and minority concentration, retain their original coding.

★$p < .05$.   ★★$p < .01$.   ★★★$p < .001$.

taken, the average time students spend on homework, and principals' reports about problems with staff. The average number of math courses taken has the largest organizational effect, but substantial effects also appear for the average time on homework and reported staff problems. The direction of these effects is consistent with our expectations. Mathematics achievement is higher in schools in which students take more courses in mathematics and spend more time on homework and in which there are fewer problems with staff. Thus it appears that the differences in average achievement between public and Catholic schools are directly linked to key organizational conditions that vary across the two sectors.

Similarly, differences between Catholic and public schools in the achievement of minority and white students also disappear once we take into account differences in the disciplinary climate of schools in the two sectors. Our analysis indicates that the minority gap is largest in schools in which there is a high incidence of disciplinary problems. Thus the smaller minority achievement gap in Catholic schools is linked to the fact that these school environments are more orderly and less disruptive.

The results presented in Table 10.6 also provide strong evidence that the academic organization of schools plays a central role in converting initial differences in social class and academic background into differences in academic achievement. Diversity in courses taken in mathematics and larger school size are both associated with a more stratifying distribution of achievement in schools with regard to social class and academic background. In contrast, schools where discipline is perceived by students to be fair and effective are less differentiating. Positive schoolwide attitudes toward academics, however, are associated with a more academically differentiated distribution of mathematics achievement.

We also observe that the large sector-by-school social composition interaction effects described in Figures 10.6, 10.7, and 10.8 largely disappeared (that is, neither school social class, sector, nor the interactions of sector and school social class are statistically significant predictors of social class differentiation within schools). The differential pattern of school social composition effects for public and Catholic schools displayed in these three figures appears to work largely through basic features of the organization of schools (overall size and differentiation in students' courses of study) and their normative environment (perceived fairness and effectiveness of discipline, and the level of commitment among staff).

Interestingly, although on average the level of academic differentiation is similar in Catholic and public high schools (as shown in Table 10.5), Catholic schools are actually more differentiating than we would expect, given their favorable organizational characteristics (smaller size, less differentiation in course-taking, fewer staff problems, more positive attitudes toward academics, and fairer and more effective discipline). This finding is an unanticipated one that merits closer scrutiny in subsequent research.

The pattern of effects for staff problems across the four school indicators

The Impact of Academic Organization

is also noteworthy. Schools with a high incidence of staff problems are equalizing in the distribution of academic achievement—everyone tends to do poorly in such schools. The school average achievement is reduced, the achievement of white students looks a bit more like the achievement of black students, and the achievement of socially and academically advantaged students is more like that of their disadvantaged counterparts. No one benefits when the faculty's commitment to the school begins to break down.[14]

THE RESULTS REPORTED here reinforce both statistical and field evidence presented earlier in this book that the organizational structure and normative environment within Catholic schools exert a pull toward academic pursuits for all students. As we saw in Chapter 4, notwithstanding differences in personal background, a much larger proportion of students pursue an academic program in Catholic schools, and those who do not still take more academic courses. The path analysis results in this chapter indicate that although a portion of the observed differences in track placement and enrollment in academic courses result from variations in the types of students educated in Catholic and public schools, there is also considerable evidence that organizational differences foster substantially different academic experiences for students in the two sectors.

These findings prompted the final analysis of this chapter. Is the more equitable social distribution of achievement in Catholic schools directly linked to the distinctive organizational features identified in our field studies—a highly prescriptive academic curriculum that fosters a commonality of academic experiences among students and a strong normative environment that binds teachers and students together? To investigate this question, we turned to a hierarchical linear model analysis.

Some of the strongest relationships that we found in this analysis involved course enrollment and how this is distributed among students. These results suggest that the academic organization of the school, in terms of the breadth of curricular offerings and expectations about the number of academic courses required of all students, structures differential learning opportunities. A favorable distribution of achievement—one that maintains a high average achievement level as well as being socially equitable—is more likely to arise when the average level of enrollment in academic courses is high and variations among students' programs of study are small.

How schools should respond to differences in student background and interest is a central organizational problem in education. In principle, initial differences among students can either be amplified or ameliorated as a result of subsequent school experiences. The constrained academic structure in Catholic high schools acts to minimize such differences. In contrast, the modern comprehensive public high school, with its highly differentiated academic structure, tends to amplify initial social differences among students and thus to culminate in a less equitable distribution of achievement.

In short, the academic organization of high schools has a significant impact on the social distribution of achievement within them. The effects of a larger school size (see Table 10.6) are particularly noteworthy in this regard. Although school size has no effect on average achievement, it has a strong impact on social and academic differentiation. Quite simply, it is easier to create a more internally differentiated academic structure in a larger school. The limited fiscal and human resources generally found in small schools preclude extensive organizational differentiation. Although organizational differentiation is not a necessary consequence of a larger school size, size does act as a facilitating factor. When accompanied by a prevailing educational philosophy that views individual differences in ability and interest as the organizing principle for determining the subject matter to which students are exposed, the observed results are not surprising.

Our analyses also suggest that the determinants of the social distribution of achievement may involve more than just the academic structure of the school. Normative elements in schools also appear to play a role. Although the measures of normative environment from HS&B are not particularly strong, these data do offer some support for this contention. The effects associated with staff problems, for example, suggest that the interest and commitment of teachers contribute significantly to academic achievement. Closely aligned with this finding is the fact that academic achievement, particularly for minorities, is higher in schools with orderly environments. At a purely behavioral level, minimizing disciplinary problems is a necessary condition for the routine pursuit of academic work. But there may be more to this than just an absence of disorder. Students' perception of the fairness and effectiveness of disciplinary action by adults, for example, is also linked to the social distribution of achievement.

The overall pattern of results indicates that attaining a more equitable social distribution of achievement is not a simple pursuit. No single school measure (other than sector) was associated with both high levels of achievement and low differentiation. This implies that the "common school effect" is a complex organizational phenomenon. In general, individual school factors that simultaneously produce high average achievement and contribute to internal differentiation are more common than those that are associated with both high achievement and social equity. For example, both school social class and an absence of staff problems are associated with academic excellence that is inequitably distributed.

We are drawn back to some of the ideas with which we began this book. Larger integrating forces are at work in Catholic high schools than any short list of distinctive organizational components can encompass. Although specific organizational features are clearly important, alone they do not account for the coherence in school life that we observed in these settings. These statistical findings thus redirect our attention to the nature of social life in Catholic high schools and the institutional purposes enacted here.

❖ 11 ❖

The Impact of
Communal Organization

As we noted at the beginning of this book, our study of Catholic high schools grew out of the "common school hypothesis" articulated by Coleman, Hoffer, and Kilgore in 1981. If the analyses offered by Coleman and his colleagues were correct, Catholic schools as a group were advancing greater educational equity—a major public policy objective over the last quarter century. Understanding how the organization of Catholic high schools might create these socially desirable consequences was our primary interest. Our work began within the framework of research on effective schools. We embarked on both field studies and analyses of *High School and Beyond* data with a focus on factors that had already been identified as associated with effective schools—homework, discipline and order, instructional methods, teacher expectations, school leadership, and the like. The findings presented in Chapter 10 grew out of this initial conceptualization.

These results, however, worried us a bit, in that they suggested a school policy of a core of academic coursework for all high school students—regardless of background or espoused future plans—with a correspondingly diminished role for course electives and student choice. Were the organization of secondary schooling to move in that direction, we feared that undesirable consequences might ensue. Students who were not academically oriented might be alienated by such a change, and the already high dropout rates in American schools might be further exacerbated.[1] This possibility led us to investigate what is known about dropping out in public and Catholic schools.

Recent research has shown that dropout rates are very low in Catholic high schools—only about one-fourth as high as in public schools.[2] Over

14 percent of public high school sophomores do not graduate with their cohort two years later; in Catholic schools, the figure is only 3 percent.[3] There are considerable demographic differences between students who stay in and drop out of high school (see Table 11.1). Minority students in both public and Catholic schools are more likely to drop out than whites. The dropout rates for minorities in Catholic schools, however, are considerably less than for their counterparts in the public sector. Eighteen percent of the blacks and 16 percent of the Hispanics who attend public schools drop out, compared with 7 percent and 11 percent, respectively, in the Catholic sector. Social class is related to dropping out in both sectors, with less advantaged students considerably more likely to leave school early.

Reflecting the more equitable social distribution of achievement in Catholic schools, discussed in Chapter 10, social class is not as strongly related to dropping out in Catholic as public schools. The relationships displayed in Figure 11.1 show that the slope of the line for public schools is somewhat steeper than for Catholic schools.[4] Thus, not only is the average dropout rate lower in Catholic schools, but the social background of students is also less strongly associated with the likelihood of students' leaving school before graduating. Because this topic has been pursued in more depth elsewhere,[5] it suffices here to note that the highly structured academic programs of Catholic high schools not only produce relatively high levels of academic

Table 11.1 Demographic characteristics of students who drop out of public and Catholic high schools compared with those who remain until graduation

	Public schools		Catholic schools	
	School completers	Dropouts	School completers	Dropouts
% of total	84.6	15.4	96.0	4.0
% of whites	85.2	14.8	96.9	3.1
% of blacks	82.2	17.8	93.0	7.0
% of Hispanics	83.9	16.1	88.9	11.1
% of females	86.9	13.1	97.5	2.5
Social class	0.10	−0.36	0.52	−0.08

Source: Data from *High School and Beyond.*

Note: The total sample is all those students in the *HS&B* study who were sophomores in 1980 who either stayed in the same school or dropped out of school. "School completers" are those who were enrolled as seniors in the same school in 1982. "Dropout" means those who left school altogether. Transfer students and early graduates are not considered in this grouping. The proportions reported here were computed using the *HS&B* design weights. The sample of 160 schools is the same as that in the analyses in Chapter 10.

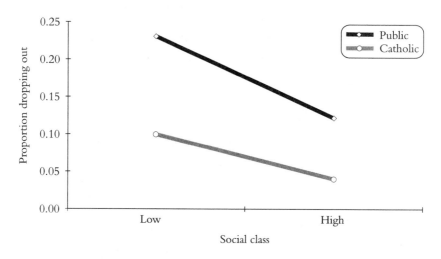

Figure 11.1 Catholic and public schools: Relationship between social class and dropping out of school.

achievement equitably distributed but also appear to be both effective and equitable in keeping students in school. Although the pattern of statistical results seems clear, the reasons behind the pattern are more elusive.

The empirical findings on drop-out rates led us to consider further the relatively high levels of teacher and student involvement that we had observed. As noted in Chapter 3, even though instruction seemed quite ordinary in Catholic high schools, students appeared very involved in what they were learning, the classroom environments were orderly, students rarely cut class, and absenteeism was low. These observations seemed particularly striking because a common explanation offered for students' lack of engagement with schooling emphasizes the uninteresting materials and unscintillating instruction found in most high schools.[6] In the Catholic schools we visited, students were engaged even though much of the teaching had these qualities.

Equally puzzling were the teachers themselves. They appeared highly committed to their work, took on a host of duties in addition to their classroom responsibilities, and worked long hours. They also seemed very satisfied with their work—all this in spite of salary levels that averaged no more than 70 percent of prevailing public school wage scales and without the security provided by tenure. At a time when merit pay proposals and higher salaries were being advocated as important policies for improving schools, the dedication of Catholic school teachers seemed virtually unaffected by their monetary compensation. We do not mean to argue that teachers, especially those in Catholic schools, don't deserve higher salaries, but it seems clear that economic incentives are not the primary considerations prompting high levels of commitment among the adults in these schools.

What was it about Catholic schools that fostered engagement in students and commitment in teachers? The extant research on effective schools was not very helpful in thinking about this matter, because it focused almost exclusively on academic outcomes. As an alternative, we returned to our field observations of life in Catholic schools, summarized in Part II. Whether sitting in an English class of twenty-five students, walking school corridors during class breaks, sitting in crowded lunchrooms while students were eating, or attending a sporting event after school hours, we were struck by the pervasive warmth and caring that characterized the thousands of routine social interactions in each school day. Coupled with this, we heard the claim "we are a community" repeated often. For adults, especially principals, the idea of building and nurturing a school community was a major concern.

As social scientists, our initial reaction to such rhetoric was skepticism. What does it really mean to talk about a school as a community? The pervasiveness of this language, however, coupled with the manifest qualities of the social relationships in these schools, eventually led us to believe that this was more than a rhetorical exercise. We sensed something special in the organization of these schools, above and beyond the constrained academic structure, that was central to their operations.

Corroborating evidence to support our suspicions came from other field studies that reported a distinctive ethos or "sense of community" in good schools.[7] But because these reports focused on the climate of good schools, it was hard to distinguish whether a "sense of community" indicated a distinctive type of school organization or was just a by-product of the operations of good schools. And if it was the result of distinctive organizational features, which features were involved?

Moreover, in the schools we visited, members said "We *are* a community," not "We have a *sense* of community." We gradually came to accept this expression quite literally, which sent us back to reconsider some older ideas about the school as a "small society."[8] The conceptual framework used in Chapter 5 to describe the social organization of Catholic high schools as communities emerged relatively late in our research, as we continued to think about possible explanations for the high levels of student engagement and teacher commitment we had observed.[9] We return to this framework here with the aim of testing empirically whether the communally organized schools are more engaging environments.

We hypothesized that schools organized as communities have direct consequences for both teachers and students. For teachers, working in communally organized schools should enhance the likelihood of attaining the intrinsic rewards so essential to the profession.[10] In such contexts, teachers should express greater satisfaction with their work, report a heightened sense of enjoyment and efficacy in their work, and their morale should generally be higher. Further, the presence of highly committed teachers is likely to be infectious. Drawing faculty together results in a social solidarity that also draws students into the mainstream of school life. The actual processes through which this occurs are probably quite complex: the personal interest of individual teachers in individual students fosters a social bonding of these students to the school and to the core activities that manifest the school's goals. When this social activity is widespread, a normative environment is created in which caring and a sense of hope and purpose come to characterize the personal experiences of both adults and students.

These arguments suggest that even though the effects of a communally organized school begin with the adults, powerful social consequences for students should also result. Negative student behaviors that demonstrate disaffection, such as cutting class and unexcused absenteeism, should be less prevalent. Moreover, because students feel as though they belong to something of value, alienation should be reduced and dropping out less common. In positive terms, such environments should foster students' interest in academics, the chief "business" of school.

Our notion of communal school organization involves a social context that significantly affects the nature of human interactions and the meanings conveyed through those interactions. The major effects of a communal school organization on teachers and students, we believe, are located most directly in the personal and social rather than in the academic domain. Nevertheless, we also maintain that the quality of the social engagement of adults with one another and with students is foundational to a school's academic mission. It provides encouragement for teachers to work hard at their uncertain profession and for students to commit energy to learning subject matter whose immediate utility may be far from obvious. As a result, we expect that a communally organized school indirectly engenders positive academic outcomes for students through the increased efforts of teachers and students.[11]

Investigating the Consequences
of Communal School Organization

Measurement of Communal School Organization

An important aspect of this investigation was developing a quantitative indicator of communal organization that captured the basic features of schools articulated in Chapter 5.[12] Our aim was to develop not a general school climate measure of teachers,' students,' or principals' *perceptions* of the school, but rather an organizational measure that tapped specific social *behaviors* and key *structural features*. Drawing on observations from the field sites and on a theoretical analysis of the construct "communal school organization," we defined three critical components:[13] (1) a set of shared values among members of the school community (administrators, teachers, students, and parents); (2) a set of shared activities, both academic and nonacademic in nature; and (3) a distinctive set of social relations among school members fostered by two key organizational features: a diffuse teacher role and faculty collegiality.[14]

Shared values. Schools organized as communities exhibit a set of common understandings among members of the organization. These include tenets about the purpose of the school, about what students should learn, about how teachers and students should behave, and—most important—about the kind of people students are and are capable of becoming. Such educational concerns in turn reflect more fundamental beliefs about the nature of the individual and society. Not any set of values will do. For a school to operate as a community, its members (especially its adult members) must share a commitment to the community. Such a commitment requires regular public expressions of concern and action toward the common good as well as a shared understanding of the nature and importance of the common good. Such public activity is a necessary counterbalance, we contend, to the individualistic pursuits that dominate contemporary American life.

Shared activities. Membership in a communal school is also characterized by a common agenda of activities. The activities, which may range from required academic courses to such schoolwide events as assemblies or football games, serve a pragmatic function. They provide school participants with face-to-face encounters in which they get to know one another. They afford a common ground that facilitates personal ties and socializes members to school norms. In addition to fostering relationships among school participants, shared activities also serve a symbolic function. They link students, families, teachers, and administrators to the school's traditions and engender meaning for those who embrace these traditions.

The academic life in schools in which students have little choice in their educational program offers a special form of ritual. The experience of each individual, through his or her course of study, shares much in common with the academic experiences of others. If the academic program changes little from year to year, students also share academic experiences with the school's alumni, which links each new student to what Bellah and his colleagues have called a "community of memory."[15] Symbolically, students' efforts are placed within a larger context that simultaneously binds them to the past and turns them toward the future.

Social relations. An "ethic of caring," described by Nel Noddings,[16] typifies the social relations in a communally organized school. Caring is reflected in the visible affiliation among teachers—who hold one another in high esteem—and in teachers' strong personal interest in the students. This type of social relations not only characterizes behavior but is also an object of explicit instruction, a "habit of the heart"[17] that schools overtly strive to foster among students.

Two features of a school's formal organization play a pivotal role here: collegial relationships among the adult members and a diffuse teacher role. Collegial interactions have both academic and social components. Academic collegial activities—in which teachers seek one another's help with classroom problems and plan activities together—nurture a cooperative work ethic. Social collegial activities foster relationships of personal value and encourage teachers to see their schools as friendly and caring places. A diffuse role for teachers means that staff members have broad responsibilities beyond their normal classroom duties. Schools in which the adults are expected to take on diffuse roles recognize that the explicit and implicit objectives of schooling extend beyond the intellectual to include students' social and personal development. Adults see students as "whole persons" to be educated rather than as distinct intellectual capacities to be advanced or particular problems to be solved.

A composite measure. We contend that none of the three critical components of a communal organization is sufficient by itself. Rather, these features, existing jointly, reinforce one another to create a school life that powerfully affects its members. Numerous shared activities promote personal contacts among students and adults. When an ethic of caring is conveyed through these interactions, the social bonding of teachers and students to one another is nurtured. Active rituals, in turn, locate the current social group within a larger heritage, which can serve as a source of profound human meaning. Most important, the underlying values of the institution—shared by its members—provide the animating force for the entire enterprise.

Using this basic conceptualization, we formed a measure of communal school organization from twenty-three individual components: six indicators of shared values about school purpose, adult beliefs about student capabilities, and beliefs about appropriate teacher and student behavior; six indicators of shared activities in both the academic and the extracurricular realms; six indicators of faculty collegiality; and five indicators of diffuse teacher roles (see Table 11.2).[18] We have validated both the reliability of the overall measure and the appropriateness of treating this as a composite through extensive psychometric analysis.[19]

Sample and Plan for Analysis

The investigations in this chapter use information from the Administrator and Teacher Survey *(ATS)*, which was administered to a subsample of the original *HS&B* high schools. The purpose of the *ATS* was to provide information about the attitudes, behaviors, and work conditions of the adults in these schools. The twenty-three indicators described in Table 11.2 rely heavily on these supplementary data, collected in 1984, as well as on information from the original *HS&B* questionnaires administered to principals and students in 1980 and 1982. A small amount of information on social interactions among students, teachers, and parents was also drawn from the Teacher Comment File collected in 1980 along with the original *HS&B* data. Our sample for these analyses includes 340 schools (303 public and 37 Catholic), 8,650 teachers, and 9,633 students.[20]

We investigate the consequences of communal school organization on several measures of teachers' commitment and students' engagement. The teacher outcomes include self-reports of teachers' efficacy and satisfaction with their work, students' reports about the degree to which their teachers enjoy their work, and school measures of staff morale and teacher absenteeism. Student engagement is measured by students' self-reports about the frequency with which they cut class and miss school without being ill, teachers' reports about the frequency of disorder in their classrooms, students' reports about their interest in academics, and the measure of ultimate student disengagement and alienation: dropping out.

Our first analyses describe basic relationships between school sector, communal school organization, and teacher and student outcomes. If our hypotheses are correct, we anticipate finding levels of both teacher commit-

Table 11.2 Indicators of communal school organization

Community index	Kind of measure
I. Shared Values	
A. Adult beliefs about school purpose	
1. Teacher agreement on school goals	Kendall's coefficient of concordance for teacher goal rankings of eight different school goals.
2. Reported teacher consensus on beliefs and values	School mean of teacher reports that the faculty agree about these matters.
B. Adult beliefs about student capabilities	
1. Teacher beliefs that students can learn	School mean of teacher reports that their students are capable of learning.
2. Teacher and administration agreement that students can learn	Similarity measure of teacher/principal reports on this issue.
C. Beliefs about behavior of students and teachers	
1. Teacher and administration agreement on standards of discipline	School mean based on a composite of three teacher questions concerning schoolwide disciplinary standards.
2. Student consensus about teachers' role	Similarity measure of student responses to ten different characteristics of good teachers.
II. Shared Activities	
A. Academic agenda	
1. Track commonality	Similarity measure of students' track placements.
2. Course-taking commonality	Similarity measure of students' courses taken.
3. Commonality of math/science course-taking	Similarity measure of specific math and science courses taken.
4. Teacher knowledge of students (class-based)	Log of odds that teachers know a given student (aggregated across students).
B. Extracurricular agenda	
1. Percentage of students involved in extracurricular activities	Log of odds of student participation.
2. Percentage of students in leadership roles	Log of odds of student involvement in leadership roles.

III. Social Relations

A. Academic collegiality

1. Percentage of teachers who obtain help from colleagues — Log of odds that teachers report using other teachers for help in solving classroom problems.

2. Teacher cooperation with colleagues — School mean based on a composite of four teacher questions about cooperation.

3. Teacher time planning with other teachers — School mean of teacher reports on amount of time spent collaborating with other teachers.

4. Staff commitment to evaluation — Principal report on staff's engagement in evaluation.

B. Social collegiality

1. Participation in faculty social events — School mean of teacher reports on amount of time spent socializing with other teachers.

2. Perception of staff support — School mean of teacher and principal reports on staff support.

C. Extended teaching roles

1. Teacher time in extended roles — School mean of teacher reports on amount of time spent in outside-of-class contact with students.

2. Percentage of teachers involved in extracurriculars — Log of odds of teacher participation.

3. Teacher knowledge of students (beyond class) — Log of odds that teachers know a given student minus those known from class (aggregated across students).

4. Teacher contact with students outside class — Log of odds that teachers have spoken to a given student outside of class (aggregated across students).

5. Student perception of teacher interest — School mean based on a composite of four student questions about teachers' interest and influence.

Note: See also notes 18 and 19 for details on construction of Community Index.

ment and student engagement to be higher in Catholic than in public schools. We also expect to find a greater level of communal organization in Catholic schools and a positive relationship between communal organization and both teacher and student outcomes. Second, we examine whether communal school organization can explain the observed differences between Catholic and public schools in teacher commitment and student engagement. We take into account, in these analyses, other characteristics of schools, teachers, and students that might also induce effects on commitment and engagement and that may partially explain these outcomes. Considering other characteristics is important: if these background factors facilitate a more communal organization of Catholic schools but are not included in the analysis, then "community" might be a spurious explanation for differences in engagement and commitment between the two school sectors.

Are Outcomes, Communal Organization, and Sector Related?

Catholic/public differences in teacher and student outcomes. If we consider the Catholic school advantage over public schools on the various teacher and student measures employed as outcomes in this chapter, we find that all effects favor Catholic schools and that most effects are very large (1 s.d. or more) (see Table 11.3). Catholic school teachers consider themselves more

Table 11.3 Mean differences in teacher commitment and student engagement between Catholic and public schools

	Unadjusted Catholic school effect (in s.d. units)
Teacher Outcomes	
Teacher efficacy	0.93
Enjoyment of work	1.14
Staff morale	1.00
Teacher absenteeism	−1.47
Student Outcomes	
Class cutting	−1.16
Incidence of classroom disorder	−1.09
Interest in academics	0.35
Student absenteeism	−1.53
Dropping out	−1.54

Source: Data from *High School and Beyond* and *Administrator and Teacher Survey.*

efficacious and are seen by their students as enjoying their work more. These teachers have higher morale and are less likely to be absent from their jobs. Catholic school students cut class much less often, and their teachers report fewer incidents of classroom disorder. Students in Catholic high schools also are somewhat more interested in academics, absent less often, and less likely to drop out. These findings are consistent with information reported in Chapters 3 and 4 from teachers and students in our field-site schools.

Catholic/public differences in communal school organization. An examination of Catholic/public differences on the indicators of communal school organization reveals large Catholic school effects—over 2 standard deviation units for the composite measure (see Table 11.4). Moreover, Catholic schools are higher on each of the twenty-three separate indicators. Large effects (over 1 s.d.) were found for individual components within each of the three major elements (shared values, shared activities, and social relations), as well as for six of the eight subcomponents. These data provide strong empirical evidence that, compared with public schools, Catholic schools are more appropriately characterized by shared beliefs about school purpose, student capabilities, and norms of behavior. They also provide more common activities—both academic and nonacademic—for students. Teachers in Catholic schools are more collegial and much more likely to exhibit extended teacher roles. It seems safe to conclude that when Catholic school personnel proclaim "We are a community," they are describing an organizational reality that does differentiate their schools from public high schools.

Relationship of teacher and student outcomes to communal school organization. To investigate the relationship of engagement behaviors to communal school organization, we examine the correlations between the community measure and the set of dependent measures of teacher commitment and student engagement (see Table 11.5). In general, the community index is strongly and positively associated with these outcomes—that is, both student engagement and teacher commitment are considerably more prevalent in communally organized schools. These relationships are somewhat stronger for teacher commitment than for student engagement. Teachers consider themselves much more efficacious, enjoy their work more, and have higher morale if they teach in schools that are organized communally. The level of teacher absenteeism is also somewhat lower. Similarly, students are less likely to cut class, be disorderly, be truant, and drop out if they attend schools that are high on the community index. Although students in communal schools are more interested in academics, this relationship is weaker

Table 11.4   Mean difference in components of school community measure between Catholic and public schools

	Unadjusted Catholic school effect (in s.d. units)
Community index (composite)	2.25
I. Shared Values	
A. Adults beliefs about school purpose	
1. Teacher agreement on school goals	0.05
2. Reported teacher consensus on beliefs and values	1.03
B. Adult beliefs about student capabilities	
1. Teacher beliefs that students can learn	1.12
2. Teacher and administration agreement that students can learn	0.07
C. Beliefs about behavior of students and teachers	
1. Teacher and administration agreement on standards of discipline	0.81
2. Student consensus about teachers' role	0.65
II. Shared Activities	
A. Academic agenda	
1. Track commonality	1.15
2. Course-taking commonality	1.21
3. Commonality in math/science course-taking	1.35
4. Teacher knowledge of students (class-based)	0.12
B. Extracurricular agenda	
1. % Students involved in extracurricular activities	1.46
2. % Students in leadership roles	0.52
III. Social Relations	
A. Academic collegiality	
1. % Teachers who obtain help from colleagues	0.46
2. Teacher cooperation with colleagues	0.80
3. Teacher time planning with other teachers	0.67
4. Staff commitment to evaluation	0.27
B. Social collegiality	
1. Participation in faculty social events	1.63
2. Perception of staff support	0.73
C. Extended teaching roles	
1. Teacher time in extended roles	0.48
2. % Teachers involved in extracurriculars	0.31
3. Teacher knowledge of students (beyond class)	0.58
4. Teacher contact with students outside class	0.24
5. Student perception of teacher interest	1.36

Source: Data from *High School and Beyond* and *Administrator and Teacher Survey.*

Table 11.5 Correlation of teacher commitment and student engagement outcomes with school community measure

	Correlation with community index
Teacher Outcomes	
Teacher efficacy	.54
Enjoyment of work	.55
Staff morale	.54
Teacher absenteeism	−.24
Student Outcomes	
Class cutting	−.36
Incidence of classroom disorder	−.43
Interest in academics	.15
Student absenteeism	−.36
Dropping out	−.36

Source: Data from *High School and Beyond* and *Administrator and Teacher Survey*.

Note: All measures are aggregated to the school level, since community index is a school measure.

($r = 0.15$) than for other engagement outcomes. Overall, as expected, we are much more likely to find highly committed teachers and engaged students in a school organized as a community.

Does Communal Organization Account for Sector Differences in Commitment and Engagement?

Before we are able to conclude that communal organization is responsible for the higher degree of engagement of Catholic school teachers and students, we must consider whether schools might have other characteristics that could also account for the observed differences. A variety of school characteristics may be related to communal organization, and each might also contribute to a more highly engaged staff and students. These characteristics include small size, a racially, ethnically, and/or socially homogeneous student population, a higher average social class, and a higher average academic background. Because we know Catholic schools are somewhat more likely to be characterized by these features, we must take them into account. In addition, for the teacher outcomes, we have introduced controls for personal characteristics of teachers such as gender, minority status, level of education (in terms of advanced degrees), and teaching experience. For the student outcomes, we have also included adjustments for students' social class, their race/ethnicity (black or Hispanic), and their academic background.

The results of our analyses are presented in Table 11.6.[21] The sector effects are again reported in the metric of standard deviation units, with a positive sign indicating a higher level of outcome in Catholic schools. The unadjusted differences, previously presented in Table 11.3, are the base on which these analyses build. The first column in Table 11.6 presents the Catholic school effect on each outcome after adjusting for the school-level and individual-level (teacher or student) characteristics described above. The second column describes the reduced or residual Catholic school effect after taking into account the greater level of communal organization in Catholic schools. The differences between columns 1 and 2 represent the extent to which the Catholic school effect on teacher commitment and student engagement is explained by the greater prevalence of communal school organization in the Catholic sector. We also present the proportional

Table 11.6 Catholic school effect on teacher commitment and student engagement outcomes, with and without adjustment for the school community measure

	(1) Adjusted Catholic school effect (in s.d. units)[c]	(2) Residual Catholic school effect, after adjusting for communal organization (in s.d. units)	(3) Percentage reduction in magnitude of Catholic school effect
Teacher Outcomes[a]			
Teacher efficacy	0.49	0.31	37%
Enjoyment of work	0.88	0.05	95
Staff morale	0.81	−0.03	100
Teacher absenteeism	−1.54	−1.60	0
Student Outcomes[b]			
Class cutting	−1.19	−0.81	33
Incidence of classroom disorder	−0.71	−0.22	69
Interest in academics	0.36	−0.11	100
Student absenteeism	−1.26	−1.11	12
Dropping out	−0.81	−0.53	35

Source: Data from *High School and Beyond* and *Administrator and Teacher Survey.*

a. Adjustments include teachers' characteristics (gender, minority status, education, experience) and school characteristics (average academic background, school average SES, minority concentration, racial and social diversity, and school size).

b. Adjustments include student characteristics (race/ethnicity, social class, academic background) and school characteristics (average academic background, school average SES, minority concentration, racial and social diversity, and school size).

c. All effects reported in column 1 are highly statistically significant, $p < .001$.

reduction in the size of the Catholic school effect in column 3. These proportions indicate how much of the Catholic school effect on each outcome may be attributed to communal school organization.

Adjusting for school, teacher, and student background differences reduces the magnitude of the Catholic school effect on several teacher and student outcomes (compare column 1 in Table 11.6 with Table 11.3): the magnitude of the Catholic school effect on teachers' sense of efficacy, enjoyment of work, student incidence of classroom disorder, and the probability of dropping out were reduced by taking school and personal factors into account. Even so, the magnitude of the Catholic school effects still remains substantial for all teacher and student outcomes—the effects in Table 11.6, column 1, are still quite large.

Once communal school organization is considered (column 2), however, several of the Catholic school effects become negligible. This is the case for teachers' enjoyment of work, staff morale, the incidence of classroom disorder, and students' interest in academics. The results in column 3 suggest that virtually all of the Catholic school effect on these outcomes works through the greater level of communal organization in Catholic schools. Communal organization also accounts for at least one-third of the Catholic school effect on teacher efficacy, students' class cutting, and dropping out. For two outcomes, however, teacher and student absenteeism, very little of the Catholic school effect is explained by communal organization.[22] The absenteeism findings notwithstanding, it is still clear that the greater prevalence of communal school organization in the Catholic sector accounts for much of the observed difference between Catholic and public schools in the commitment of their teachers and the engagement of their students.

In order to give substantive meaning to the results presented in Table 11.6, we engage in a hypothetical experiment. We employ a prediction equation technique to examine the likely improvement in teacher commitment and student engagement that would result for the average public school *if* that school were organized like the average Catholic school.[23] These analyses employ the same set of teacher, student, and school control variables that we employed in the analyses presented in Table 11.6, but use data from students and teachers in public schools only. The results represent the predicted effect on commitment and engagement if the average public school had the same degree of communal organization as the average Catholic school (see Table 11.7).

For every outcome, public school teachers and students would demonstrate higher commitment and engagement if their school were more communally organized. For three teacher outcomes—efficacy, enjoyment, and

Table 11.7 Expected amount of improvement in teacher commitment and student engagement if the average public school were communally organized like the average Catholic school

	Standardized effect size of improvement (in s.d. units)	Predicted percentile (compared with a base of 50)
Teacher Outcomes		
Teacher efficacy	1.01	84
Enjoyment of work	0.99	84
Staff morale	1.21	89
Teacher absenteeism	−0.12	45
Student Outcomes		
Class cutting	−0.52	30
Incidence of classroom disorder	−0.58	28
Interest in academics	0.42	66
Student absenteeism	−0.21	42
Dropping out	−0.32	37

Source: Data from *High School and Beyond* and *Administrator and Teacher Survey.*

staff morale—the effects are large (over 0.9 s.d.). For three student outcomes—class cutting, classroom disorder, and interest in academics—the effects are also quite substantial (approximately 0.5 s.d.).

We have computed a measure of the relative improvement that would occur in a typical public school *if* it had the same level of communal organization as the average Catholic school. The figures in the second column of Table 11.7 represent the predicted percentile that would accrue for each teacher and student outcome if a more communal organization were adopted. These predictions should be compared with the 50th percentile, which is the standing for the average public school. The effects on teachers' efficacy, enjoyment of their work, and staff morale are substantial indeed. A change toward a more communal organization would raise the typical public school from the 50th to over the 80th percentile on these three teacher outcomes. Students' interest in academics would rise to the 66th percentile. On measures of student disengagement, the average public school's percentile would drop—from the 50th to about the 30th percentile for class cutting and classroom disorder, and to the 37th percentile for the drop-out rate. Major social and personal consequences for both teachers and students are linked to teaching and learning in a communally organized school.

Reflections on Schools as Communities

As we developed these ideas about communal school organization, we worried about possible negative consequences that could be associated with this organizational form. In principle, the notion of a community requires a certain "turning within" that may be accompanied by a "spurning without."[24] The benefits of community may be gained at the price of limited tolerance for the unfamiliar and the diverse. This mistrust of the outside world is described, for example, in Alan Peshkin's account of a fundamentalist academy, a school with a very strong communal organization.[25]

Both our field observations and the statistical analyses presented in this chapter, however, affirm that it is possible to attain the benefits of community without extreme social closure. To be sure, there are conditions of membership for both teachers and students in Catholic schools, as described in Chapter 5, but such limits are neither particularly pervasive nor extensively used.[26] As a result, the communally organized Catholic school is quite diverse—socially, ethnically, and religiously. The cohering force of the Catholic school thus does not derive from any rigid restriction on school membership or other efforts to enforce likemindedness.

Rather, the ultimate grounding of the distinctive form of social life observed in Catholic schools resides in the tradition of these schools, as discussed more formally in Chapter 1 and as expressed in the words and actions of students and faculty described in Chapters 3–5. There is ample evidence that the post-Vatican II Catholic school takes seriously the ideal of advancing the common good based on a larger conception of a properly humane social order.[27] The formation of each student as a person-in-community is the central educational aim of these schools. From this perspective, schooling involves more than conveying the acquired knowledge of civilization to students and developing in them the intellectual skills they need to create new knowledge. Education also entails forming the basic disposition for citizenship in a democratic and pluralistic society. A commitment to the pursuit of truth, human compassion, and social justice is essential to society's well-being. Fostering such a commitment makes serious demands on schools. If they are to teach children how they should live in common, they must themselves be communities. The school must be a microcosm of the society—not as it is, but as it *should be*.[28] The results presented in this chapter suggest that such a social environment is highly engaging and draws out students' best efforts.

Further, an educational philosophy of person-in-community influences the way schools organize themselves as workplaces for adults. The collegial relations formed around a small work group provide a basis for meaningful human effort. The empirical results presented here suggest that such environments elicit teachers' strong commitment. In these places, teachers' labors are not adequately captured in the exchange language of dollars earned for services rendered. Teaching is more likely to be seen as cooperative activity infused with personal value. The daily work of committed adults literally grounds their being, making the words "I am a teacher" a reality.

Bureaucratization of Schooling

The conception of a school as a community contrasts sharply with the dominant image of the public sector as a large bureaucracy. Many critics now argue that much of the contemporary difficulty in American education can be seen as a cumulative consequence of a century-long effort to formalize schooling in accordance with the basic principles of a modern bureaucracy. In the search for efficiency, adult labor has been organized into specialized tasks. Teaching roles have been categorized by subject matter and type of student. In order to limit individual discretion, social interactions have become rule-governed and affectively neutral, with individual authority emanating from a formal role rather than from the person.[29]

Although the term "bureaucracy" typically has a negative connotation today, the idea of a school organized in accordance with its principles was a cornerstone of modern progressive thought. Bureaucratizing schooling was intended to redress the parochialism and inefficiency that pervaded schooling in the late nineteenth century. These efforts achieved special prominence in the 1960s as part of a larger societal embrace of the scientifically managed organization. Rapid gains were anticipated from increased technological and human resources, coupled with modern management techniques. It was also thought that a modern school bureaucracy could ensure equal educational opportunities to the poor, minorities, and other disadvantaged groups. Through specialization of teachers' work and a broadening of curricular offerings, the high school would become a universal institution.

These aims, however, have not been achieved. Recent accounts of public high schools tell us that developments over the last two decades have instead fostered student passivity and teacher alienation.[30] A reliance on specialization and centralization has promoted a breakdown in human commitment and contributed to the creation of transient relationships, a disintegration of common bonds, and a retreat from shared responsibility. The work ethic of the modern high school has become "That's not my job!"

Increased school size, greater curriculum complexity, and a dense external policy network with conflicting accountability demands have resulted in organizational environments marked by distrust, social conflict, and a lack of personal regard for parents, students, and staff. These forces appear especially disruptive in large urban districts, where everything tends to be more extreme: more programs, larger school size, greater density of conflicting political demands, and more severe resource constraints.

On balance, many of the aims for bureaucratization were noble. These ideas provided a powerful framework for an expansion of schooling that sought to efficiently deliver new educational opportunities in a nondiscriminatory fashion. But in encouraging a view of schools as a production process, this perspective has tended to undervalue the personal aspects of school life. It has also underestimated the important educative role played by normative features in the small society of the school.

During the 1980s, as more and more weaknesses in the bureaucratization of schooling were exposed, a renewed emphasis on strengthening the social ties between students and adults emerged. In the current search for "nonbureaucratic" possibilities,[31] elements of community—such as cooperative work, effective communication, and shared goals—have been identified as critical ingredients for successful organizations of all types, including schools. Yet there is something a bit troublesome about this approach. The social elements of a school community are not instruments but ends in themselves. As Dewey noted, education is a social process, and the school is a form of communal life deliberately designed to promote it: "The school must itself be a community life in all which that implies. Social perceptions and interests can be developed only in a genuinely social medium—one where there is give and take in the building up of common experience."[32] And elsewhere: "Much of present education fails because it neglects this fundamental principle of the school as a form of community life. It conceives of the school as a place where certain information is to be given, where certain lessons are to be learned, and where certain habits are to be formed."[33]

The social interactions of schooling are not simply a mechanism for accomplishing some other aim; they are education itself.[34] In this regard, the school is different from other workplaces. It is not the same as the factory or the corporation, where social relations among adults and students are regularly viewed as another factor to be manipulated in facilitating work productivity. Genuine human concern must animate the schooling enterprise.

Student Selectivity Revisited

This chapter brings our empirical analyses to a close. Critics of past research on public and private schools have posited a selectivity hypothesis as an alternate explanation for reported private school effects. They have claimed that because more advantaged students enroll in private schools, the "superior" effectiveness of these schools may be explained by their more selective clientele rather than by any differences in educational practices. This explanation is less salient, however, in comparing public and Catholic schools than it is for comparisons with non-Catholic private schools. The background of students in Catholic and public high schools is rather similar. Although the most disadvantaged students are somewhat underrepresented in Catholic high schools because the jump in tuition from Catholic elementary to secondary schools poses a barrier to access for the poorest children, Catholic high schools educate a broad cross section of American students. Even so, we suspect that some readers may still hold that selectivity represents a plausible explanation for the findings in this book.

Our own concerns about selectivity led us to include a variety of statistical controls in our analyses for both demographic differences among students and compositional differences among schools. Still, it is always possible that other unmeasured individual characteristics of students and aggregate characteristics of student groups (that is, compositional factors) contribute to explaining the differences in student outcomes between sectors. Within the Catholic sector, we identified one factor that might play such a role—the extent to which a Catholic schools' tuition represents a significant financial sacrifice to the family.[35] We showed in Chapters 7 and 8 that such sacrifice is related to the quality of Catholic schools attended by students from poor and lower middle-class families and to their achievement at sophomore and senior year. These findings are consistent with the critics' claims that there is something special about the particular disadvantaged families who choose to send their children to Catholic schools. We agree, but even in the education of these children, we find considerable evidence that Catholic schools are doing something different.

Close consideration of the pattern of relationships involving financial sacrifice provides evidence of such school effects. The analyses in Chapters 7 and 8 demonstrate that financial sacrifice and social class generally have similar effects within the Catholic sector. Unlike social class, however, financial sacrifice is not directly related to any of the key elements of student engagement (academic attitudes, school-related behaviors, and academic courses taken). These findings indicate that although affluent families directly encourage positive student engagement with schooling,[36] this is not the case for students from less advantaged families. Such families try to pick a good school and to be involved with their children's learning at home. When it comes to choosing appropriate in-school experiences for their children, however, disadvantaged families are more dependent on the guidance of the school. Our analyses thus indicate that poor families' commitment to education has effects in large part because such families choose schools that take active responsibility for engaging students in learning.[37]

The results presented in this chapter elaborate how this enhanced engagement occurs. Even after introducing extensive statistical controls for the characteristics of students, teachers, and schools, we have found substantial variation among schools in teacher commitment and student engagement that is largely explained by the communal character of schools. Our results indicate that the internal organization of schools as communities fosters, *literally creates,* the engagement of school members in its mission.

We reiterate a point made earlier. Our intent in making comparisons between Catholic and public schools is not to argue for the superior effectiveness of Catholic schools. Rather, the cross-sector comparisons in Part II have helped us to identify distinctive organizational features of Catholic schools. In Part IV, we have used these comparisons as one way to test the importance of these organizational features. Our ability in Chapters 10 and 11 to account for most of the observed differences between public and Catholic high schools in the social distribution of achievement and the levels of engagement of teachers and students constitutes a critical test of the organizational explanation developed in Part II. Even more compelling, the empirical models used in Chapters 10 and 11 explain variation among schools in *both* the Catholic and public sectors. That is, public schools that have a more equitable social distribution of achievement share organizational properties with Catholic high schools that also demonstrate these same effects.[38] Equally important, both public and Catholic high schools that engage their teachers and students have the characteristics of communities.[39] This pattern of effects both within and across the public and Catholic sectors strengthens our claim that these results tap fundamental consequences of school organization rather than some residual selectivity phenomenon.

More generally, the findings presented in this book draw attention to what we consider to be a larger and more problematic conceptual issue with the selectivity argument. This hypothesis presumes that students' lack of engagement with schooling is determined largely by neighborhood circumstances and family background. When these externalities are seen as all-powerful, schools may consider themselves to be merely hapless victims of the "inputs" they receive. Indeed, much of the alienation and lack of student interest found in urban public high schools surely reflect the destructive societal forces at work in underclass communities. But this admission does not obviate two other equally compelling observations—that large urban schools and the bureaucracies that operate them produce anomic environments and that a different organization of schools can have different effects. From our perspective, the continued reliance on the selectivity hypothesis as an explanation for Catholic school effects is part of a larger worldview in which individuals are seen as primary and the operations of institutions as simply an aggregate manifestation of individuals pursuing their self-interests. In contrast, our results indicate that teachers and administrators can organize their work in different ways, can create more engaging environments, and, as a result, can have a very different effect on students.

Family background does matter. Its influences are seen in both public and Catholic schools. Part of the higher levels of achievement in Catholic schools is linked to this factor. Similarly, some of the enhanced levels of teacher commitment and student engagement found in Catholic schools accrues from the less troublesome students who attend these schools. None of this, however, mitigates our major finding that the constrained academic structure of Catholic high schools and their communal organization also produce desirable effects. Both families and schools make independent contributions to student learning.

In addition, we suspect that there is a "third category" of effects at work here. We will argue in Chapter 12 that the Catholic high school benefits from being a *voluntary community* in which the members, both students and faculty, have made a deliberate choice to participate. Although this voluntary association is not a necessary feature of a communally organized school,[40] it does help to sustain the fragile personal relations among students, school professionals, and parents found in these settings. Such relations act as a social resource for the school; they support both the classroom work of teachers and the larger collective efforts of adults and students to maintain the school community. Although we say more about this in the next chapter, our point here is simply to clarify that the nature of the *relationships* between families and schools can have effects on students that are separate and distinct from the effects of both family background and school organization.

❖ V ❖
IMPLICATIONS

❖ 12 ❖

Catholic Lessons
for America's Schools

How do Catholic high schools manage simultaneously to achieve relatively high levels of student learning, distribute this learning more equitably with regard to race and class than in the public sector, and sustain high levels of teacher commitment and student engagement? What lessons do these schools provide for educational reform?

The Functioning of Effective Catholic High Schools

Our investigation has combined fieldwork in a small number of "good" Catholic high schools, extensive analysis of a national data base on Catholic and public high schools, and an exploration of the social and intellectual history of these institutions. We conclude that effective Catholic high schools function on the basis of four foundational characteristics: a delimited technical core, communal organization, decentralized governance, and an inspirational ideology.

A Delimited Technical Core

The central tenet of the academic organization of the Catholic high school is a core curriculum for all students, regardless of their personal background or future educational plans. This curriculum is predicated on a proactive view among faculty and administrators about what all students can and should learn. These beliefs connect to a long-standing Catholic tradition about what constitutes a proper humanistic education.

Required courses predominate in students' study plans in Catholic high schools, and electives are limited in content and number. Some students may begin the curriculum at a more advanced level and proceed in more depth, but the same basic academic goals apply for everyone. Although some tracking occurs, this programmatic differentiation does not produce the invidious consequences found in the public sector, in part because the tracking structure in Catholic schools is constrained in its scope and its number of levels. Potential negative consequences are also moderated by school policies that allocate limited fiscal and human resources so that all students make satisfactory progress. At base is an active institutional purpose, the aim of a common education of mind and spirit for all, that integrates these structures and policies.

This constrained academic organization has important consequences. As discussed in Chapters 4 and 10, it is a major contributor to the more equitable social distribution of achievement found in Catholic high schools. It also uses efficiently the limited resources characteristic of many of these schools and permits a relatively informal organizational life, with attendant personal and social consequences for both adults and students.

Communal Organization

As discussed in Chapters 5 and 11, the academic structure of Catholic high schools is embedded within a larger communal organization that is formed around three core features. First is an extensive array of school activities that provide numerous opportunities for face-to-face interactions and shared experiences among adults and students. The shared academic experiences that result from a common curriculum are a major contributor in this regard. There are also numerous school events—athletics, drama, liturgy, and retreat programs—that engender high levels of participation and that provide more informal occasions for interactions between students and adults. These school events also afford connections between current school members, those who came before, and those who may come after. Established rituals provide occasions for locating the current social group within a larger tradition.

Second are a set of distinctive structural components that enable the community to function. Chief among these is the extended scope of the role of the teacher. Teachers are not just subject-matter specialists whose job definition is limited by the classroom walls; they are mature people whom students encounter in the hallways, playing fields, the school neighborhood, and sometimes even in their homes. In the numerous personal interactions that occur between adults and students outside of classrooms, many opportunities are afforded for expressions of individual concern and interest.

Collegiality among teachers represents another important structural component in a communal school organization. Catholic school faculty spend time with one another both inside and outside of school. Social interactions serve as a resource for school problem solving and contribute to adult solidarity in the school's mission. In such contexts school decision making is less conflictual and more often characterized by mutual trust and respect.

The relatively small size of Catholic high schools also provides a significant advantage. The coordination of work in larger schools typically imposes demands for more formal modes of communication and encourages increased work specialization and a greater bureaucratization of school life. In contrast, a smaller school size facilitates personalism and social intimacy, both of which are much harder to achieve in larger organizational contexts.

Third and crucial for communal school organization is a set of shared beliefs about what students should learn, about proper norms of instruction, and about how people should relate to one another. Underpinning these specific beliefs is a set of general moral commitments. The Catholic school sees itself as a community that respects the dignity of each person, where members are free to question within a commitment to genuine dialogue, and where an ethos of caring infuses social encounters. The common ground established here orders and gives meaning to much of daily life for both faculty and students.

Decentralized Governance

The governance of Catholic high schools is decentralized, as discussed in Chapter 6. The specific governance arrangements vary from school to school, depending upon the nature of school ownership (parish, diocesan, or private). The "Catholic school system" is in reality a very loose federation. Virtually all important decisions are made at individual school sites. To the best of our knowledge, no current effort to promote decentralization in the public sector approaches this level of school-site autonomy.

Inside the school, considerable deference is accorded to the principal. In daily operations, principals' decision making tends to have a paternalistic quality, which at its best is similar to the approach of a wise and caring parent. Traditionally this mode of leadership typified the religious control of Catholic high schools, where, until very recent times, religious members have held the principalship almost exclusively. Much of the flavor of paternalistic control remains today, even as lay members increasingly take on the principalship. Whether and how this role will develop in the future is uncertain. The large number of lay faculty in Catholic schools has fired a democratizing spirit that will surely raise questions about the continued appropriateness of this hierarchical form of leadership.

It is not unusual for a new principal to be selected from a school's faculty. The motivation for assuming the principalship more often focuses on the opportunities for institutional leadership than on individual career advancement. The economic rewards to the principalship are very modest, and the individuals who take on the role are more likely to see it as a chance to help the school rather than as a means for personal gain. Although each diocese has an education office, with a superintendent and a small support staff, the Catholic school principalship is seldom viewed as a stepping stone to a "plum job downtown."

Externally, Catholic high schools, like all private schools, are subject to market forces. These market effects were quite apparent in the 1970s, when parents spurned Catholic schools that adopted innovations then popular, such as an expanded personal development curriculum. As a result, these reforms never took deep root in Catholic schools. Market influences can also be seen in Catholic school history. They were an important reason, for example, that vocationalism was never strongly pursued in the Catholic sector. Today these forces contribute to the relatively low dropout and expulsion rates. Because most Catholic schools are not overenrolled, there is an institutional interest in holding students in order to balance budgets.

Even so, the control of Catholic school operations involves considerably more than market responsiveness to clients. Many important observations about these schools cannot be reconciled in these terms. Market forces cannot explain the broadly shared institutional purpose of advancing social equity or account for the efforts of Catholic educators to maintain innercity schools (with large non–Catholic enrollments) while facing mounting fiscal woes. Likewise, market forces cannot easily explain why resources are allocated within schools in a compensatory fashion in order to provide an academic education for every student. Nor can they explain the norms of community that infuse daily life in these schools.

Complementing the market influences at work in the Catholic sector is a leavening force that both grounds institutional policy and guides the largely autonomous day-to-day behavior of individuals within the organization. This force is the set of fundamental beliefs and values that constitute the spirit of Vatican II.

An Inspirational Ideology

At the crest of Catholic school enrollment in 1965, serious questions were raised about continuing a separate Catholic school system. The Catholic ghetto had broken down. Many Catholics had successfully entered mainstream American life, and the need for a separate school system was no longer apparent. Vatican II, in proclaiming a new role for the Church in the modern world, however, created such a purpose. The charter for Catholic schools shifted from protecting the faithful from a hostile Protestant majority to pursuing peace and social justice within an ecumenical and multicultural world. Each school would seek to enact the image of a prophetic Church. Though thoroughly engaged with American culture, Catholic schools sought to offer a strong countervailing image in their aims, organization, methods, and daily life. This new conception of the Catholic school has sometimes created internal dilemmas, as the external culture often intrudes and schools fall short of the ideals that they set for themselves.[1] Nevertheless, the discourse about these aims remains vital, and efforts toward them continue to make moral claims on individual and collective action.

Two important ideas shape life in Catholic schools, making them very different from their organizational counterparts in the public sector: *Christian personalism* and *subsidiarity*. Christian personalism calls for humaneness in the myriad of mundane social interactions that make up daily life. Crucial to advancing personalism is an extended role for teachers that encourages staff to care about both the kind of people students become as well as the facts, skills, and knowledge they acquire. Moreover, personalism is a communal norm for the school—the kind of behavior modeled by teachers and held out as an ideal for students. As such, personalism is valued not only because it is an effective device to engage students in academic work but also because it signifies a moral conception of social behavior in a just community. As such, personalism makes claims on human endeavors to act, beyond individual interest, toward a greater good.

Similarly, subsidiarity means that the school rejects a purely bureaucratic conception of an organization. There are advantages to workplace specialization, and it is hard to imagine the conduct of complex work without established organizational procedures. Subsidiarity, however, claims that instrumental considerations about work efficiency and specialization must be mediated by a concern for human dignity. Decentralization of school governance is not chosen purely because it is more efficient, although it does appear to have such consequences. Nor is it primarily favored because it creates organizations that are more client sensitive, although this also appears to be true. Rather, decentralization is predicated on the view that personal dignity and human respect are advanced when work is organized in small communities where dialogue and collegiality may flourish. At root is a belief that the full potential of human beings is realized in the social solidarity that can form around these small group associations. These social commitments are particularly important in modern society because they help mediate the gulf between the intimacy of the family and the impersonalism of the state and the multinational corporation.

In a related vein, subsidiarity also makes a claim on the policymaking activities of higher-level institutions. For the Catholic Church, a commitment to subsidiarity means that dioceses and religious orders see their role as enhancing the function of local institutions where they currently exist and promoting the development of new institutions in response to new needs. Rather than regulating human activity under the homogenizing norms of a central bureaucracy, the role of external governance is to facilitate and stimulate collective local action.

Underpinning these organizational tenets is a vital Catholic social ethic. Three principles from our discussion in Chapter 1 stand out. First is a belief in the capacity of human reason to arrive at ethical truth. An immediate implication of this belief is that education must aim to develop in each person the critical consciousness that enables and motivates this pursuit. The Catholic school's emphasis on an academic curriculum for all is one direct consequence of this stance. Moreover, such an education involves nurturing both mind and spirit, with equal concern for what students know and for whether they develop the disposition to use their intellectual capacities to effect a greater measure of social justice. This is the Catholic conception of an education of value for human development and democratic citizenship.

The second principle affirms a public place for moral norms. The spirit of Vatican II has softened Catholic claims to universal truth with a call for continuing public dialogue about how we live as a people. The freedom, indeed, the obligation to engage respectfully in such discourse is the essence of a humane society. This principle implies a very different conception of religious instruction. In contrast to the pre-Vatican II emphasis on indoctrination in the "mind of the Church," contemporary religion classes now emphasize dialogue and encounter. Drawing on systematic Christian thought, teachers encourage students to discuss and reflect on their own lives in the context of classic questions about the nature of person and society. Moreover, this intellectual activity is embedded within a school life that seeks to promote the experience of a just community for both students and adults. At work here is an educational philosophy that maintains that personal formation occurs best through an interplay between individual reflection and social action. This new orientation is a major reason that Catholic schools are now more inviting places for non-Catholics.

A third principle focuses on the power of the symbolic as an integrative force in human life. It is here that Catholic religious tradition is most directly manifest. Several images are especially pertinent. The words and life of the "man called Christ" stimulates reflections about how students should live as persons-in-community. The notion of the "Kingdom of God" offers a vision toward which human effort should be pointed. Finally, the image of the "resurrection destiny" nurtures hopefulness—as Christ triumphed over death, so shall mankind. Here is the sustaining force for the day-in and day-out struggle against tyranny, poverty, and injustice. Such images evoke our humanness. They add depth to a schooling process that is otherwise dominated by a rhetoric of test scores, performance standards, and professional accountability.

This complex set of ideas does not yield easily to simple procedural knowledge about the proper conduct of school affairs. The rhythms of Catholic school life require regular reflection on the spirit of Vatican II:

> Let there be unity in what is necessary,
> freedom in what is doubtful, and
> charity in everything.

Although simple in wording, these phrases offer much wisdom. To be sure, they are not a utilitarian calculus of optimization, satisficing, and cost-benefit trade-offs. They draw us back, rather, to simpler and much older understandings about the nature of the good life.

Some may question our claim of a causal role for this inspirational ideology. There are no variables in *HS&B* that measure these key concepts directly. Furthermore, unlike the effects of academic organization or communal school structure, which can be largely captured in regression analyses and effect sizes, estimating the influence of ideology is a more complex and less certain endeavor. Ironically, these effects are harder to study and yet also more pervasive.

Even so, there is much evidence that the ideology of Catholic schools shapes the action of its members. The influence of ideology is seen in an academic organization that uses conventional instruments, such as tracking, while consciously avoiding the reproduction of inequity. It is also seen in the explicit content of the shared values that ground the Catholic communal organization—caring and social justice. It is apparent in survey opinions offered by students about their teachers and the personal ways in which their teachers engage their interest. It is also reflected in teachers' accounts of how they make sense of their work lives and why they choose to teach in a Catholic school. Similarly, the reasons principals give for assuming a leadership role and the school goal they mention as most dear—building the community of the school—demonstrate this drawing force.

To ignore the importance of ideology because it cannot be easily captured in statistical analyses or summarized with numbers would be a serious mistake. Statistical analyses can help us to see some things, but they can also blind us to the influence of factors that are beyond their current horizons. We believe that true renewal of our educational institutions will require melding insights from scientific pursuits with inspiration from our evocative traditions.

Implications for Current Educational Reform Efforts

A multitude of efforts are currently under way to improve schooling in the United States. Our research has focused on Catholic high schools, and we have particularly sought to understand how the organization of these schools creates an academically productive and socially engaging environment for a diverse cross section of students. Much of what we have learned bears directly on the broader endeavors to reform schools in the public sector. What potential lessons for public schools can Catholic schools offer?

Efforts to Increase Academic Standards

Increasing academic standards has been an important national policy concern since the early 1980s. In this regard, our findings on the consequences of the academic organization of Catholic schools represent a strong challenge to the laissez-faire philosophy of the contemporary public high school, which affords students considerable latitude in choosing their courses of study within a curriculum that is highly differentiated in terms of both subject matter and difficulty. In contrast, more academic coursework is required of all students in Catholic schools, and the emphasis is especially noticeable for students enrolled in general and vocational programs. Of particular importance, our analyses indicate that disadvantaged students benefit most from attending schools in which there is a strong normative pull toward a core of academic work for everyone.

Beyond the direct consequences of enhanced student achievement, other social-psychological and organizational consequences also accrue. A common core of academic work provides students with more authentic standards against which to judge their efforts. One invidious consequence of the vertical differentiation of curriculum in today's public high schools is that students develop unrealistic understandings about work and the adequacy of their current efforts. In contrast to some public high school norms, one rarely succeeds in life by "just showing up."

Schools built around a focused academic curriculum also create a less cumbersome work environment for students, faculty, and administrators. The complex academic organization of the "shopping mall high school" demands an extensive apparatus of scheduling, academic counseling, and curricular advertising. A simpler instructional program reduces administrative demands and provides more opportunities for informal social interaction. The constrained academic structure of Catholic high schools promotes greater commonality in student experiences. It also structures commonality in work conditions for teachers. The extensive work specialization that accompanies a highly differentiated curriculum divides both faculty and students alike. In "shopping mall high schools," departments become more salient, and teachers are likely to describe their primary organizational commitment in terms of this affiliation. The public places in such schools become "someone else's responsibility," as the teacher's domain tends to be bounded by his or her classroom walls. Further, when teachers define their roles primarily in terms of subject matter, no one in the school attends to the totality of students' experiences. The organization operates under the assumption that an educated person will somehow result from an accumulation of discrete academic experiences from some approved list.

On balance, we do not argue that achieving a high level of personal interaction is impossible in the more differentiated environment characterized by the "shopping mall high school." The formal structure of such schools, however, does constitute an imposing barrier. Even if adults are consciously committed to fostering personalism, the task is surely much harder in such places.

Promoting Human Engagement

Extensive policy initiatives have been directed at enhancing the engagement of both students and teachers in schoolwork. Typically, these efforts appeal to a form of individual interest. Some focus on intrinsic concerns. A common claim is that greater student engagement can be obtained by offering a more diverse curriculum taught in a more stimulating fashion. In a related vein, it is argued that teachers are likely to put in more effort when they teach subject matter of personal interest to them.

Other proposals focus on extrinsic interests. Plans to reward students with jobs, college tuition, sometimes even money for simply staying in school are of this sort. Sanctions, such as prohibiting drivers' licenses to those who drop out, seek the same end by denying "wayward" students something they value. Merit pay proposals constitute a complementary initiative for teachers. Some versions of accountability programs involve the use of both sanctions and incentives to promote greater teacher effort.

These initiatives all draw on basic tenets of individualism of either the expressive type, in appeals to intrinsic personal interests, or the utilitarian type, in the use of "carrots and sticks."[2] Instead, the Catholic school directs attention to the social basis for human engagement. The daily life in these schools is itself a source of considerable meaning for members. For students, the school constitutes a network of caring relations that binds them to the place, its people, and its programs. For teachers, meaning is found in the lives they touch and the larger social justice mission in which their work is embedded. The analyses presented in Chapter 11 provide strong evidence that schools organized according to these social principles have the power to engage their participants.

Strengthening Parent-School Relations

Some reform efforts focus on enhancing parents' involvement with schools and with their children's education. Although parents are important in the Catholic high school, their role is somewhat different from what one might expect given the discussion of this theme in the current school reform literature. Catholic school parents do participate in a wide range of school activities, from parent nights to fund-raising to attending student events. Positive consequences (academic, social, and personal) accrue for students when parents spend time with them around school-related matters, as documented in Chapter 8. Such parental support also eases the work of school staff by ensuring that students attend regularly, do their homework, and adhere to the school's behavioral standards.

Catholic high school parents, however, are not especially active in the day-to-day operations of schools and do not play a major role in school decision making. Although a few parents' names may appear on a school's board of directors, even here their function is limited largely to fund-raising and institutional trusteeship rather than involving daily school operations. In general, we found very low levels of democratic participation by parents in the governance of Catholic high schools.[3] Although there may be reasons to promote greater parental involvement in these matters, our research on the operation of effective Catholic high schools provides no evidence to support such recommendations.

Similarly, given the private status of Catholic high schools, there is a natural temptation to conceive of the relationship between parents and the school in market terms. To be sure, there are features of the relationship that resemble the exchange of goods and services. The "firm" (the Catholic school) has a "product" that "consumers" purchase. The firm has an interest in pleasing these consumers, and it regularly evaluates its internal operations in the light of consumer feedback. But the actual dynamics of parent-school relations are much more subtle than this caricature of a market metaphor conveys.

As described in Part II, the foundation of the relationship between parents and Catholic schools is fiducial, predicated on trust between professionals and parents. Such trust is especially apparent in schools with relatively high concentrations of disadvantaged students. As our analyses in Chapters 7 and 8 indicated, many low-income parents make a considerable financial sacrifice to send their children to a Catholic school. Often these parents may not be particularly well educated or have a clearly articulated conception of the education they desire for their children. In choosing a Catholic school, they trust that its staff will provide their sons and daughters with an education that will help them to become good people, to get a decent job eventually, and to be happy and productive adults. When it comes to what students actually *do* in school, these parents rely on the judgment and expertise of the staff, who in turn work under a moral obligation to act in the best interests of their students. The school is responsible for educating and caring about every child. These responsibilities include defining the specific content and methods of instruction. At times, this may mean counseling parents about what they must do to support their children's life chances. Moreover, a fiducial relationship is reciprocal, also making demands on parents to support the work of the school and to encourage their children's best efforts.

The parent-school relationship in the Catholic sector thus appears distinctive, mirroring neither the democratic localism envisioned in some versions of urban school reform[4] nor the contract-for-services image offered by others. The voluntary association of both parents and professionals to the Catholic school licenses a distinctive form of relationship between these two groups. These interactions are not appropriately described in the language of "client responsiveness" often used to characterize effective suburban schools or captured in the image of "satisfying the consumer" envisioned by market advocates. Neither idea adequately captures the human qualities present in these interactions and the intentionality conveyed through them.

Although *High School and Beyond* offered little information about the nature of parent-school relations, our field interviews provided considerable

evidence that these relationships were very important to all school participants—teachers, students, and parents. The participants' accounts suggest
to us that trust relationships may be more essential to schooling than has
generally been acknowledged, particularly in the context of efforts to provide greater educational opportunities for disadvantaged youth. If correct,
this observation poses a major challenge for urban education. The large
public schools and bureaucratic structures found in most cities constitute
major impediments to forming and maintaining the relationships of trust
observed in Catholic schools.

Greater School Autonomy:
Principal Leadership and Teacher Empowerment

The primary problems of schools, according to other reform proposals,
derive from the way control is exercised within them. These reform efforts
focus on the ineffectiveness of centralized school system bureaucracies in
managing the work of teachers. It is argued that more authority must
devolve to professional staff in individual schools if more responsive institutions are to be attained. Dominant in the 1980s, this issue seems likely to
persist through the 1990s as well.

This reform movement began with concerns about strengthening principal leadership as a major effort toward site-based management. A second
stream developed around activities to enhance teacher professionalism,
including new roles for teacher leaders and a greater emphasis on school-
site decision making. The experience of Catholic high schools is relevant
to both topics.

Principal leadership. We described in Chapter 6 a distinctive role for
principals in Catholic schools. In contrast with extensive central office
control in the public sector, Catholic school principals experience only
limited external regulation from dioceses and religious orders. Catholic
schools are somewhat constrained by public regulations, however. For
example, they are subject to judicial mandates on matters of due process.
They also tend to follow, even when they are not required to do so, a wide
range of public sector policies such as the hiring of certified teachers.
Nevertheless, the external regulatory shell is substantially thinner for Catholic school principals, who, as a result, enjoy considerably more autonomy
over school matters. Similarly, internal decision-making processes are simpler, with much discretion afforded to principals. Although dialogue and
collegiality among faculty and administration are valued, decision making
in these schools is not "by committee."

A purely functional analysis of the Catholic school principalship is thus consistent with reform efforts to promote greater principal authority over core school matters, including the hiring and firing of teachers. We emphasize, however, that the exercise of this authority is tempered by ideology. Principals are expected to act within the moral principles undergirding all Catholic schools. Their actions are closer to paternalistic than to autocratic control. Here again, ideas about the school as a community where people care about each other tend to moderate the functioning of a structure that otherwise appears ripe for the abuse of power.

Teacher professionalism. Although we observed some good teaching, as described in Chapter 3, instruction in the Catholic high schools we visited was generally quite ordinary. Classroom work was largely textbook-driven, and lecturing was a common mode of delivery. Catholic schools have moved away from the more extreme didactic instruction of an earlier era, but efforts to improve teachers' subject-matter knowledge and pedagogical skill are as necessary here as in the public sector. Catholic school students would also benefit from more opportunities for active learning experiences and more sustained discussion of subject matter than we typically observed in our field sites.

The limited fiscal resources available in many Catholic schools are very noticeable in this area. Inner-city Catholic schools with high proportions of children from low-income families have found it particularly difficult to attract well-educated faculty. The low salaries in these schools result in high faculty turnover, making it difficult to maintain a stable and competent teaching force.[5] Similarly, funds for staff development are scarce. Much like their counterparts in the public sector, for urban Catholic schools human resource development is a major need. Enhancing the academic capabilities of Catholic school teachers would certainly enrich their students' intellectual experiences.

Nevertheless, the nature of teaching found in Catholic schools casts an odd light on current efforts to enhance the professionalism of teachers. We have documented an extended teacher role and have seen that faculty tend to describe their work in moral terms. This transformative agency, however, remains largely unaddressed in contemporary discussions about the professional education of teachers.[6] Yet these matters are clearly salient for public school teachers even if mostly relegated to personal reflections about the conduct of their classroom affairs.[7] In focusing almost exclusively on technical knowledge and skill, current efforts at "teacher professionalism" represent a very restricted view of the term professional.

Traditionally, a moral dimension undergirded the practice of all professions.[8] Technical competence in the execution of specialized tasks was embedded within a larger sense of public obligation to enhance civic life. Lawyers were to advance justice, doctors were to care for the physical well-being of the people, and ministers were to tend to the spiritual welfare of the community. The earliest forms of commercial activity—in the creation of goods and services of value to the community—also included this moral dimension. When Catholic school teachers speak of their work as a calling, vocation, or ministry, they tap a long-standing tradition about the nature of a profession. From this perspective, it is the contemporary secular discussions about professional work that appear odd.

Regardless of how we interpret this development, the moral dimension is largely absent today from most public discussions about the teaching profession. Moreover, we suspect that any effort to reintegrate such a moral dimension would lead to considerable difficulties. The current conception of the teaching profession, based on technical expertise, fits productively within a view of the school as a bureaucracy. An important characteristic of such organizations is that appropriate behavior is defined as the affectively neutral exercise of authority, circumscribed by explicit rules. To justify these rules, public bureaucracies rely on "objective knowledge" about school operations and their effects.[9] As long as we conceive of teaching as bound largely by such knowledge, professionalism and bureaucracy coexist quite nicely. Reintroduction of a more transformative role for teaching, however, would necessitate a much wider realm of both discretion and responsibility for teachers, with judgments about the appropriate exercise of such authority depending much more on the social consent of the school community. Because the level of discretion and human judgment implied in transformative education sharply conflicts with fundamental features of a public bureaucracy, a transformative view of education and the existing organizational structures of public schooling would fit together uneasily, if at all.

A related concern arises about current efforts to expand faculty control over school-site decision making. As documented in Chapter 11, Catholic school teachers enjoy more academic and social collegiality and have more influence over school matters than do their public school counterparts. Understanding this phenomenon requires that we again pay close attention to the embedded understandings at work within Catholic schools. Although there is typically greater faculty voice in these schools, this voice, like the exercise of principals' authority, is anchored in shared beliefs and norms. Faculty participation is circumscribed by a larger institutional commitment to advance social justice. Without similar embedded understandings, public schools would not necessarily benefit from greater faculty voice. What the "voice" says and what forces give rise to the voice are of critical importance.

Educational Markets as a Basis for School Improvement

Concerns have also recently been directed to the nature of school governance. After a century and a half of strong public support for a publicly controlled and managed educational system, advocacy for greater parental choice within an expanded educational market has become widespread. We have already noted that some aspects of Catholic school operations are influenced by market concerns. We have also described how the spirit of Vatican II has catalyzed dramatic changes in Catholic schools over the past twenty years. Taken together, these two control mechanisms—ideology and markets—jointly shape the operations of Catholic schools. Vatican II ideals inspire human action, and the market acts as an empirical lever. Absent either one, the contemporary Catholic school would surely be a very different institution.

It would therefore be inappropriate to assume that a new system of education, just because it was market-driven, would produce effects similar to those described here for Catholic schools. Popular arguments for a system of market controls in education commonly employ a microeconomic explanation that bears little relation to the ideas about schools-as-communities that we have discussed. Under this microeconomic view, teachers' entrepreneurial motives would make schools into more efficient service providers. This conception of teacher thinking and behavior is quite antithetical, however, to the social foundations of a communal school organization. Although individual entrepreneurship may fuel economic development, it rings less true as a basic motivation for processes of human betterment. There is no evidence that such motives currently play a role in motivating teachers in Catholic schools. More generally, it is difficult to envision how unleashing self-interest becomes a compelling force toward human caring.

These observations are relevant in part because so much of the current rhetoric about privatization and choice can be traced to studies by Coleman and others on public and private schools and the subsequent policy debate that they engendered. A brief review of these findings is instructive. Most important, many of the positive effects found in Catholic schools are not characteristic of non-Catholic private schools. For example, the more equitable social distribution of achievement, or "common school effect," that occurs in Catholic schools does not typify other private schools. Similarly, the reduced dropout rates and unusual effectiveness of Catholic high schools for at-risk youth are not characteristic of private schools in general.[10] The special effectiveness of Catholic girls' schools also does not appear to generalize across the private sector as a whole.[11]

Advocates of choice have argued that "effective organizational practices" are more likely under a market system because these practices are currently more prevalent in private schools, which benefit from a higher degree of school autonomy. Although this public-private comparison is a valid one, it is also important to recognize that within the private sector, some of the so-called effective organizational practices are actually more prevalent among non-Catholic than Catholic private schools. However, the positive student outcomes described above do not generally occur in these non-Catholic private schools.[12]

Extant research indicates differences among private schools in both their internal organization and their outcomes. These findings raise doubts about any blanket claim that a move toward greater privatization will ensure better consequences for students. Rather, we must focus on the specific ideology at work in private schools if we are to discern their effects fully. We note, in this regard, that many of the descriptors currently used for effective schools, as places where faculty have a "sense of ownership" and adults and students share an "organizational saga," have a strong particularist bent to them. In an earlier time, the conditions that are now described as promoting organizational excellence were seen as breeding grounds for intolerance and exclusivity.

Much more attention is required to the actual content of the values operative in schools and to the consequences that derive from these values. Fundamental to Catholic schools are beliefs about the dignity of each person and a shared responsibility for advancing a just and caring society. Not surprisingly, the educational philosophy that derives from these goals is well aligned with social equity aims. When such understandings meld to a coherent organizational structure with adequate fiscal and human resources, desirable academic and social consequences can result. When this particular value system is lacking, however, a very different pattern of effects seems likely.

Some Larger Lessons

The School as a Voluntary Community

As an alternative to describing a school as a "market-responsive firm" we offer the idea of a school as a "voluntary community."[13] The latter is faithful to both our field observations in Catholic high schools and their guiding intellectual traditions. We also believe that this concept is more likely to serve current school improvement efforts, particularly for the disadvantaged.

The notion of a school as a voluntary community synthesizes three important features of Catholic high schools. First, a communal organization structures daily life within the school. The major components of this organizational form and its consequences for students and faculty have been detailed extensively throughout this book.

Second, each school possesses a relatively high degree of autonomy in managing its affairs. This autonomy is important because much of the rationale for activity within a communal organization relies on traditions and local judgments. Such schools do not meet the criteria and operating principles of centralized bureaucracies, where standardization is seen as an organizational imperative and particularisms as imperfections needing redress. As noted earlier, not everything essential to a school community can be formally justified with the objective data increasingly demanded by public bureaucracies. For example, although most educators acknowledge the importance of rituals and traditions in creating an engaging school life, a causal demonstration of these effects is exceedingly difficult to establish. In the absence of such objective knowledge, however, the legitimacy of these activities remains in some doubt. Similarly, many educators are actively involved in efforts to promote more authentic forms of classroom instruction, yet public accountability demands objective assessment of teachers' effectiveness. This demand translates, usually, into reliance on nonauthentic standardized tests to show "success," and the use of such tests in turn tends to constrain the amount of authentic instruction actually attempted.

Third, the voluntary association of both students and teachers with the school marks individual membership. Implicit here is the idea that participation in a particular school is not an inalienable right. Catholic school faculty go to great lengths to help students and work with parents, but reciprocity is also expected. Students who seriously or chronically violate the community's norms must leave. Indeed, students are more likely to exit for this reason than for poor academic performance.[14] Faculty who don't share the school's beliefs and commitments usually move on as well, mostly by their own choice. Because membership involves an ongoing exercise of free will, individuals are less likely to interpret school life as coercive and are more likely to feel a sense of identification expressed in the phrase "This is *my* school."

The notion of membership in a school community in turn licenses a different form of social relations among parents and professionals. Rather than "the contract" that formalizes marketplace interactions or "the client and interest politics" that characterize the public bureaucracy, a set of fiducial commitments is at the core of the voluntary community. The importance of these trust relationships is readily seen in school life. Effective teaching makes personal demands that leaves teachers vulnerable—literally putting themselves on the line each day. To maintain such commitments, teachers need support both from their colleagues and from parents. A considerable measure of trust is required among all participants to sustain engaging teaching.[15]

Thus Catholic schools work better not because they attract better students (which is somewhat true) or because they have more qualified faculty (which does not appear to be the case). In general, these "inputs," or what economists call "human capital," are quite ordinary. Rather, Catholic schools benefit from a network of social relations, characterized by trust, that constitute a form of "social capital."[16] In this regard, voluntary association functions as a facilitating condition. Trust accrues because school participants, both students and faculty, choose to be there. To be sure, voluntary association does not automatically create social capital, but it is harder to develop such capital in its absence.

Our investigation of Catholic schools suggests that the formation of a school as a voluntary community has important institutional and personal consequences. On the organizational side, a voluntary community enjoys a base of moral authority. Such authority depends on the consent of those influenced by it, and it is made possible by the commitment from both teachers and students to a particular school. The presence of moral authority is important because much of what happens in schools involves discretionary action. Great effort may be required within public bureaucracies to secure basic agreements on issues that are intrinsically matters of judgment. In a voluntary community, much of the effort expended on such matters can be redirected toward the actual work of schooling. Moreover, many potentially contentious issues never develop into conflicts, because communal norms define a broader realm of "what is appropriate here." The value that these communities place on social interactions that are respectful and civil also means that when disagreements do occur, participants presume the good intentions of all concerned. The suspicion, fear, and distrust that often afflict the interest politics surrounding public education create a very different atmosphere for negotiating problems.

A base of moral authority helps to guide the work of individual adults. Such influence is particularly important because autonomous action characterizes much of teaching. As policymakers of the 1960s and 1970s found, the behavior of teachers is relatively impervious to direct regulation. In part this independence reflects the relatively private nature of teaching—typically an individual adult working with a group of students behind a closed door. Also significant is that the craft of teaching involves complex and spontaneous judgments. Because such decisions draw substantially on personal experiences, beliefs, and values, the normative standards of a voluntary community help to order these judgments.[17]

For all participants, personal experiences in a voluntary community have inherent meaning above and beyond their instrumental value. Communalism is an ethical end in itself; members derive personal support from others with whom they share this commitment. Students who participate in this type of schooling derive more from their education than something that is endured for the present in order to get a good job in the future. Similarly, teachers' efforts in such environments involve more than earning an income to support out-of-work activities. School administration also takes on a distinctive character: tending to the meaning-inducing quality of school life becomes a deliberate aim, on a par with concerns about the efficient organization of instruction. In such contexts, the managerial ethic of the bureaucracy is tempered by a personalism more characteristic of the family.

For adolescents, participation in a voluntary community is especially salient. Although it is widely acknowledged that high schools should help students develop their individual identities, such development occurs best through interaction with a strong collective identity. Personal growth and self-awareness emerge not from isolated independent behavior but rather from sustained participation in a social life marked by open communication, honesty, caring, and respect. There is a clear tension here. The collective must be sufficiently strong to engage individuals, but it must also allow for individual freedom. In this regard, the voluntary community strives to be a nonalienating society,[18] seeking a dynamic balance between participation in a collective life and recognition of the individuality of each person. Acknowledging the inevitable tension between private and social identity, the voluntary community seeks to negotiate this dilemma. Ironically, a collective that over-respects the private realm leads not to personal development but to anomie—a characterization appropriate for many comprehensive public high schools today.[19]

Many desirable personal and institutional consequences derive from the organization of schools as voluntary communities. Nevertheless, we reiterate our doubts that the specific consequences described in this book for Catholic high schools would appear more broadly should a market-based system of schooling emerge in the United States. In particular, without commitment to the specific values operative in the Catholic sector, we suspect that neither the quality of internal life found in these schools nor the more equitable social distribution of achievement would result. Rather, a market system seems apt to produce a highly differentiated set of schools, in which educational opportunities would be even more inequitably distributed among individuals and communities than is already the case. We are reminded of Weber's maxim that "capitalism stripped of its religious imperative is a cloak of steel, a cage of iron." A market system of schools, absent a vital moral imperative, would likely come to resemble this image.

The High School as a Bridging Institution

We have attempted to convey the beliefs present in Catholic high schools and the ways in which they are enacted through a deliberately formed school life. Organized as voluntary communities, Catholic schools can sustain such strong norms because they have the authority to shape a particular school life and to defend it as a conscious choice to all who choose to participate in it. Our research demonstrates that disadvantaged children benefit greatly from attending such schools. The particular combination of organizational structure, social behavior, beliefs, and sentiments found in Catholic high schools constitutes a distinctive approach to the education of the disadvantaged, which we summarize in the idea of a "school as a bridging institution."

The philosophy of a bridging institution is dialogical. On the one side is an empathetic orientation toward children and their families that is grounded in an appreciation of the worth of each person without regard for outward appearance, customs, or manners.[20] The school welcomes all who choose to come, and it conveys to parents and children a sense of security, personal well-being, and engagement. On the other side is a clear recognition of the demands of contemporary middle-class American life for which the school consciously seeks to prepare its students. From this perspective, the school is of value to the disadvantaged student because it is culturally different. School staff aim to provide an education that will enable each student to develop the knowledge, skills, dispositions, and habits necessary to function effectively in a modern democratic society.

The tasks of the bridging institution involve constant tensions. While remaining sensitive to the mores of family and community, the school must also challenge behaviors and attitudes clearly at odds with the child's educational progress. Social idealism is a source of inspiration, yet the school and its students must also live in this world. The school espouses a caring community, but it also operates within a larger culture that values hard work, delayed gratification, and material success. While schools are committed to preparing students with the intellectual and social competencies required for functioning in contemporary middle-class American life, they also seek to hone a critical consciousness toward social life as it should be. Students are to be competent in modern society, but never totally at ease.

In these efforts, the Catholic school takes its cue from the Vatican II pastoral constitution *The Church in the Modern World*. It neither denies modern society, as the Neoscholastic Church once did, nor automatically affirms existing arrangements as proper and good. Rather, the school operates on a principle of critical engagement with society and seeks to form such capacities and dispositions in its students. For school leaders, charting such a course involves continuous navigation through a sea of dilemmas.[21] The religious tradition provides much guidance. It stabilizes what schools will and will not do, and affords a sense of sureness about the importance of these endeavors.

Staff members in a bridging institution seek to nourish and validate the best of family and community ties, while also providing a link to a very different world. The chasm between these two worlds, however, is often quite wide. The transitions are difficult both for the individuals who seek to cross over from one world to the other and for those institutions that seek to act as a bridge. Social mobility extracts a price as it draws individuals into the sometimes alien world of middle-class America. Schools may strive to help students balance the familiar and the unfamiliar, but success often means leaving home both physically and metaphorically.[22]

Nevertheless, neither a lapse into a romanticism that blindly reaffirms the intimacy and comfort of family and community nor an institutional silence about these matters is productive. Schools undeniably act as agents of socialization. This role, played by every school, is especially salient in the inner city, where the formation of a two-class society appears imminent. If real educational opportunities are to be afforded students who live in "underclass" neighborhoods, they must have access to schools that create an internal life similar to the one we have described in the Catholic school sector. Anything less may consign these students to a growing permanent underclass.[23]

The moral grounding of the Catholic school underlies its effectiveness in advancing social equity aims. The moral grounding provides a catalyst for activism and a surety of purpose. It undergirds the strong institutional norms that appear so essential to the education of disadvantaged youth—for they, more than anyone else, must rely on the expertise, good intentions, and efforts of societal institutions for their advancement. In contrast, a system of schools restricted to a language of markets and individual choice is likely to afford only further opportunities for the disadvantaged to fail and then to attribute that failure to themselves.

This line of analysis raises questions about whether Americans can attain moral aims such as equality of educational opportunity without an enlivened moral discourse about schooling. The absence of a contemporary public rhetoric about the proper formation of persons and the advancement of the common good is quite noticeable. Public educational policy has instead searched for instrumental levers to advance moral purposes. In the recent past, busing programs, magnet schools, and individual educational plans have served as levers. Now school improvement plans, accountability systems, and markets are offered as solutions. To be sure, different organizational arrangements can facilitate different consequences. We have argued throughout this book, for example, in favor of the constrained academic structure and communal organization of Catholic high schools. Ultimately, however, it is school values, norms, and traditions that influence the selection of "appropriate structures" and create meaning for participants within whatever structure they happen to confront. Although policy levers can tilt practice in a preferred direction, policymakers tend to accord such instruments more power than is warranted. Whatever specific reform initiative is chosen, it must eventually be enacted by individuals in schools, each of whom draws on his or her own personal beliefs and operates within a larger context in which moral conversation generally holds a very uncertain status.

Schools as Mirrors of Society

Institutional norms and enculturation. The enculturation aims of the Catholic school are deliberate and multilayered. Most visible in religion classes, these aims are also evident in school programs such as retreats, volunteer service, and liturgies. These activities are further complemented by the extensive lessons conveyed through daily social encounters. Numerous opportunities for expressions of community run through all of this. Literally every aspect of school life affords an occasion for teaching.[24]

To be sure, enculturation is not limited to denominational schools. Enculturation occurs in public schools, even though they do not have religion classes or appear as deliberate in their efforts to form a coherent social life. For example, Philip Cusick and Christopher Wheeler report that "reformed" high schools convey a distinct vision of a society in which individuals strive for personal success while pursuing their self-interest.[25]

Institutional norms are competitive, individualistic, and materialistic. Although the private visions of individual teachers may be broader and more humane, it is the institutional norms that are continually reinforced by daily school life.

Much of this enculturation is conveyed through the academic organization of the public high school, in particular through the differentiated curriculum, student tracking, and teacher assignments. Not only do such academic structures produce an inequitable social distribution of achievement, but they also socialize students to internalize the causes. Upper-track students come to attribute their success to individual ability and effort and to ascribe the plight of low-track students to an absence of such personal qualities. Similarly, lower-track students come to see themselves as "not good at school" and as personally responsible for their school failure. Subsequent affluence and poverty in adult life are therefore seen as appropriate consequences, with questions about broader societal responsibility for inequity less likely to arise.

Enculturation in public schools also occurs through routine social encounters. Such encounters are regulated by explicit codes of conduct that specify prohibited behaviors and elaborate individual rights to be ensured. These codes define the minimum standards of social order necessary for the academic work of the school to proceed. Few see them as an embodiment of the ideal of justice or any other ideal.[26] Gerald Grant's account of life at an urban comprehensive high school is particularly poignant in this regard. Adults' moral authority collapsed at Hamilton High during the 1960s and 1970s under a blizzard of regulations. In the minds of school participants, "doing the procedurally correct thing" replaced "doing the right thing." Opportunities to articulate commitments to truthfulness, tolerance, fairness, caring, and justice were forgone. As Grant describes it, students instead learned "how to manipulate the rule system to advance their self-interests."[27]

Such studies highlight education as a cultural enterprise and remind us that at the center of any culture are understandings about human nature and human relations. Public education is not value-neutral; its values mirror our larger society. The vision conveyed in the public school is one of *homo economicus:* rational men and women pursuing their self-interest, seeking material pleasures, guided toward individual success. Without deliberate thought or serious debate, this vision of the individual and of the good life has been gradually adopted as the enculturation aim of public schools over the last half century.

The Catholic school offers an alternative vision in its efforts to shape persons-in-community. This vision is predicated on a two-fold belief in the dignity of each human being and in the responsibility of each to advance peace, justice, and human welfare. The Catholic school contends that education means forming the conscience of all students toward an awareness of the stake they share in common. From this perspective, a proper education cannot be affectively neutral. The Catholic school argues that schooling demands an impassioned rationality shaped by a vision of the common good, a vision that itself is always open to challenge and clarification. Such an education is accomplished through inspiration, not coercion; through dialogue, not dogma. It involves not only classroom teaching but also participation in a communal life that exemplifies its values.

Religious and secular understandings. The traditional academic program of the Catholic high school, complemented by a symbolically rich communal life, affords opportunities for students to encounter questions about how we should live together. These schools contrast sharply with the secular high school bureaucracies described by Grant, Cusick, Wheeler, and Lightfoot, which rarely catalyze a sense of moral obligation on the part of teachers or students toward any enterprise beyond the individual self.[28] Such schools neither make demands on the human conscience nor help their members discern what commitments are worth holding.

At base here is a serious dilemma for public education. In a society that relegates to the private realm most discussions about "what is good" and about the moral grounding for such choices, how are we to enjoin a collective will to do good, to advance equity, to value truth, and so on?[29] A public discourse narrowly framed within a utilitarian calculus of individual self-interest is weak in this regard. Constrained by this rhetoric, much of what Americans value appears to be without reason.[30] In terms of schooling, why should students develop a sense of craft in their work if most of it goes unseen? Why should teachers work hard educating disadvantaged children when it is easier to derive personal satisfaction (or when the school actually rewards) teaching more academically talented students? Why should the disadvantaged in our society be of personal concern when it is the government's responsibility to ensure that every person has equal opportunity?

Every school enacts some philosophy of education. Even the narrowest and most secular philosophy presumes certain propositions about individuals and society. These philosophies convey both a preferred ordering for society and an ethic for how individuals should live within it. Formally, this combination of an order and an ethic constitutes a religious understanding.[31] Although the idea of any connection between religion and public education probably seems antithetical to most Americans today, the ties here are historically quite deep.

It is widely acknowledged that democracy depends on a broadly shared prudence about the nature of our individual and group interests and a civic conscience that makes moral claims on citizens to act in accord with such knowledge.[32] From this perspective, education for democratic citizenship requires sustained encounters that pose questions for students about the nature of person and society and about appropriate and worthy personal and social aims. Regardless of whether or not we actually refer to these ideas as religious understandings or whether we describe related schools' efforts as either character formation or personal development, it seems clear that education for democratic citizenship must direct students' attention to these concerns. Thus although we can easily recognize the difference between public buildings and houses of worship or between legislatures and episcopal synods, when we speak about the content of education the divide between "secular" and "religious" is necessarily ambiguous. We might properly call a purely secular experience "training" but hardly "education." A democratic education demands a melding of the technical knowledge and skill to negotiate a complex secular world, a moral vision toward which that skill should be pointed, and a voice of conscience that encourages students to pursue it.

The aims of education. Contemporary Catholic educational philosophy actually shares much common ground with postmodern social thought. Although postmoderns acknowledge the power of technical rationality (for example, scientific inquiry and policy analysis) to improve the human condition, they criticize the desiccated quality of life engendered by the technical-legal language that now dominates public affairs and increasingly encroaches on the most intimate aspects of personal life.[33] Such developments have extended human control over a vast array of material phenomena, but it is equally true that much of daily life is inherently uncertain and ambiguous. At its best, technical rationality is silent on such matters. At its worst, it is highly misleading, conveying a false sense of control where little really exists.[34]

In educating for postmodern life, schools must simultaneously help students develop the necessary technical competencies to function in the twenty-first century while also encouraging a sense of hopefulness in confronting the unknown and a sense of belonging in a large, complex, and highly specialized society. In balancing these diverse concerns, school communities should be structured so that students can experience the ways in which symbols, rituals, and traditions bring meaning to life as well as gain the knowledge they need to exert control over their material affairs. The language of schooling must both tap the evocative and expressive powers found in the humanities and capture the instrumental capabilities afforded by precise, technical representation found in mathematics and science.[35] It must help children to envision possibilities and then equip them with the necessary knowledge and skill to pursue them.

The issues raised here have direct implications for current discussions about educational goals. Much concern has been voiced of late about America's declining competitiveness in the world. We frequently hear that education must be restructured to allow the nation to regain its once preeminent position. Central to these arguments are calls for more systematic assessments of what students know and can do. Academic knowledge and skill is important, but education also concerns shaping the human will to display a sense of craft in one's work, a commitment to caring in personal relations with others, and a shared sense of responsibility for social welfare. In our view, these personal dispositions of citizens are as important to a productive economy and a convivial public life as the content knowledge and academic skill that the schools seek to teach. We must value not just what students know and can do but also their dispositions to use these capabilities productively and prudently in pursuit of human betterment.

More generally, greater attention must be paid to the language we employ about the purposes of schooling and the structure of its institutions, processes, and methods. The concepts of contemporary secular discourse shape patterns of meaning and also afford or preclude possibilities for transcending those meanings. What deeper understandings are conveyed, for example, by our common rhetoric of schools as efficient service providers to clients? Or of teachers as subject-matter specialists? Or of accountability and incentive systems designed for greater productivity? Does such rhetoric fire the hearts and minds of students and teachers? Viewing contemporary public education through a Catholic school lens raises questions about the secularization of schooling that has gradually occurred over the last half century. Although this secularization has forcefully redressed the intolerance of an earlier age, it has also brought new social ills no less threatening than the problems it was meant to remedy. Mirroring the spiritual vacuum at the heart of contemporary American society, schools now enculturate this emptiness in our children. This development is important to all of us, because life in a free society presumes broadly shared commitments to basic principles of truth, justice, and human compassion. So much of the livability and vitality of a free society depends on the "right living" of its people. In its absence, we are less secure and less free.

In this regard, the special role played by scientific inquiry in educational policymaking demands closer scrutiny. That enculturation is a complex process, slow to show its effects, means that these effects remain rather elusive in the face of the typical methods used by social scientists to establish causation. Although there is power in the means–ends paradigm of science, much of education will not readily yield to its probings. To the extent that we recognize this limitation, scientific inquiry can advance practice. The imminent danger, however, is in affording a greater influence to scientific evidence and its underlying concepts than they merit.

Because many important educational aims are not easily studied, less empirical evidence accumulates about them. Over time the topics that are extensively studied gradually take on a greater salience in public discourse than those that are not. This dominance, however, does not necessarily reflect an assessment that these particular ideas are intrinsically more valuable; it often indicates only that they are empirically more accessible. Thus to the extent that the results of scientific inquiry exert hegemony over subsequent public conversations, conceptions about the purposes and methods of education are gradually reframed in a truncated rhetoric that is more likely to injure future practice than to enhance it. It is the modernist's "fool's gold," where the scientistic literally drives out the evocative.

The Nature of Systemic Change

During the past three decades, when considerable governmental effort has been directed toward advancing the equality of educational opportunity, Catholic schools have undergone substantial reorganization toward the same end. Given the rather closed, doctrinaire, and austere character of Catholic schools in the 1950s, the transformation to the contemporary scene has been quite remarkable. Although we did not set out to study this process of social change, we were increasingly drawn to this subject as we proceeded in our attempts to understand how and why Catholic schools work as they do. Although our comments on this topic are more speculative, we include them here because they are germane to current initiatives to restructure American education. We intend these reflections as a counterpoint to current endeavors.

At the core of the institutional change in Catholic schools since 1960 is the intellectual and social renewal of Catholicism constituted at Vatican II. In reality, this renewal affirmed and liberated forces that had been at work in the Church over several decades. With a long-awaited official sanction, however, an explosion of individual human effort and collective activity ensued. The immediate aftermath of Vatican II was a period of great intensity and excitement, but also much concern and doubt. Many traditional practices, beliefs, and customs were suddenly called into question. Members of religious orders became disenchanted and left in large numbers. From the inside, this upheaval bore little resemblance to any textbook lesson about strategic planning or systematic social change. The process was not without direction, however—the ideas of Vatican II illuminated a path. Ultimately, through extensive public conversations about these ideas and through critical personal reflection, individual consciences were reshaped. Catholics began to see their place in the world differently, and they gradually reordered their feelings and actions in accord with these new understandings.

Some structural features provided an assist. The period following Vatican II was a time of substantial institutional retrenchment in the American Catholic Church. The precipitous drop in religious order membership, the rapidly rising demands on extant resources, and a heightened awareness of fiscal constraints forced a reexamination of the fundamental aims of Catholic education. Any complacency about traditional methods was likely to be challenged. As schools closed and others were threatened, core purposes were debated. Many teachers (especially religious members) left, creating serious fiscal and staffing problems in many schools. Yet this dissolution also held the seeds for renewal, forged by the new faculty, largely made up of young and energetic laypersons. Reared in a post-Vatican II Church, they brought its questioning spirit and openness into the schools.

The institutional Church catalyzed the process of change by orchestrating extended public conversations and periodically issuing statements to animate this activity. The prophetic Church was also working, however, through the diverse and varied activities of individual lay and religious members. Institutional change was externally supported but not externally imposed. Rather than relying exclusively on a system of sanctions and incentives to coerce human action, the Church encouraged a process of dialogue and reflection. Its aim was to engender personal commitment—one individual at a time—to the message of Vatican II.

It has been noted frequently that schooling has at best a modest technology. The core of operations involves many personal interactions, the character of which involves people changing people. Effectiveness rests largely on the good efforts of teachers and students and on their mutual trust. Stated somewhat differently, schools are places where personal meaning and human intentionality matter. The latter forms the basic context for school operations and their effects. Educational policy may reach to the school district, to the school building, even into the classroom, but ultimately it must touch the hearts and minds of teachers and students if significant structural change is to occur.[36] Such change requires an appeal to reason, as for example, in demonstrations through research that some new educational innovation is superior to current practice. But it also requires an appeal to human will—to stir a sense of concern, on some occasions outrage, about current conditions and to make a moral claim on the individual conscience to react.

In this regard, we view the transformation of Catholic schools over the last quarter century as an example of the power of an inspirational ideology to catalyze change. As individuals in schools discussed new ideas and reflected on their personal actions in the light of these ideas, an enhanced social awareness led both to modifications of subsequent action and to more nuanced understandings of the guiding principles themselves. On balance, we note that ideology, like tradition, can blind as well as inspire. If one is captivated by a sense of purpose, it is easy to ignore accumulating evidence about a lack of real progress. For effective renewal, ideological inspiration must remain yoked with practical reflection. For Catholic schools in the 1970s and 1980s, economic forces helped to maintain this connection; each school regularly had to explain its actions to a larger public whose support the school needed for its continued existence.

Finally, the renewal of Catholic schools over the last three decades illustrates the value of sustaining a prophetic force within a large institution. It was the individual lay and religious members, both activists and scholars at work in the nineteenth and twentieth centuries, who eventually helped move the Catholic Church toward Vatican II. Although the institutional Church periodically acted to restrain or suppress this prophetic activity, the Church was ultimately transformed by it. A similar approach can be applied to public schools.

Systemic control is an organizational imperative, particularly in urban districts administered by large bureaucracies. Those charged with exercising this control tend to drive out the "prophets" from within their midst. Over the longer term, however, the continued vitality of public education depends on the renewal force engaged through such prophetic activity. In this regard, urban Catholic schools can function as a public resource. These schools offer a distinctive vision and unique organizational practices whose effectiveness is now well documented. That these schools exist, whether one ultimately affirms or rejects their specific ideas and practices, helps to sustain a dialogue about the purposes, methods, and effects of education in America. Such conversation is essential to democratic life.

THE PURPOSES SERVED by public education are currently under intense scrutiny and criticism. Many maintain that the existing system has lost its position as an agent of the common good. The old arguments about "common schools" seem hollow when viewed against the reality of a system that affords unparalleled opportunities for some individuals while simultaneously undereducating large segments of society and denying basic human dignity to the most disadvantaged. Although we agree with such claims, we do not intend to demean the good efforts of many individual public school teachers, principals, and administrators. Rather, we have used a comparative framework in this book—public versus Catholic—to illumine the difficult organizational conditions under which these public educators work. They are among the few in our society who confront, day in and day out, the social and personal problems that many citizens are reluctant even to acknowledge, much less address directly. We are convinced that the work of these educators can be both more effective and more personally rewarding if conducted in environments similar to those described in this book.

The reflections offered in this chapter have raised questions about the wisdom of current attempts to promote school change. Efforts at redistributing power, whether through decentralization of authority to principals, enhanced parent control, increased teacher professionalism, the introduction of new accountability systems, or even market forces are all technical solutions in search of some golden end. Each involves an application of instrumental authority rooted in coercive power. In our view, the problems of contemporary schooling are broader than the ineffective use of instrumental authority. At base is an absence of moral authority. As long as moral inspiration remains largely absent from public education, the social resources required for broad-based change will remain uncatalyzed. The current need is a matter not only of restructuring but of renewal.

Our research began as a search for the key organizational elements that produce the desired outcomes observed in Catholic high schools. As this work proceeded we gradually added a second focus on the "public theology" at work in these schools—on the nature of their institutional vision and the sources of hopefulness that ground these communities' vitality and inspire human effort. We are convinced that if we are to have a renewed public philosophy for education in America—one that is capable of ennobling the work of faculty and staff and awakening the hearts and minds of young people—it must involve more serious dialogue between the instrumental and evocative realms that we have pursued in our research.

In offering these reflections, we have specifically avoided constructing them as policy recommendations, because we believe such an approach to be more prescriptive than we intend or is appropriate. We see our work, rather, as extracting from the study of Catholic schools "lessons" that anyone who is interested in school improvement might fruitfully ponder.

The Catholic schools we have studied are relatively simple organizations with modest resources. Nonetheless, they manage to educate a broad cross section of Americans. We contend that large numbers of children currently educated in public schools would benefit from attending schools organized around the strong normative principles found in the Catholic sector. We are reminded in this regard of the two central characters, Lafeyette and Pharaoh, in Alex Kotlowitz's *There Are No Children Here.* In our field visits to Catholic schools, we were told about students whose home environment and community context were similar to Lafeyette's and Pharaoh's—chaotic, precarious, and often beyond their parents' control. We are convinced that children like these can learn in an educational environment that combines a strong emphasis on academic work with a caring ethos that demands personal responsibility and the good efforts of all participants.

It is not clear to us that public schools can better serve disadvantaged children who want to learn and can also encourage larger proportions of the students to share these aims unless many more schools are transformed in accord with principles like those found in Catholic schools. To be sure, not all students would benefit from such an educational experience. Some do well in comprehensive high schools as currently operated. Others may require something more akin to a total institution, such as a boarding school, to alter their life chances significantly. We see the ideas offered in this book as of most value in the context of current school decentralization efforts. Increasingly the public sector is spoken of as a "system of publicly supported schools" rather than as a centrally controlled bureaucracy. From this perspective, there is no reason why schools organized like Catholic schools could not (and should not) be major components in such a system. That religious orders founded Catholic schools and that these schools continue to benefit from a religious tradition offers no particular barrier to the creation of "secular schools" espousing a similar set of humanistic beliefs and social principles and maintaining a similar organizational order.

To be sure, were such a movement to develop, it would raise nettlesome questions about the highly visible role played by moral beliefs and values in the functioning of schools. Americans would be required to confront a whole new domain of concerns: where must there be unity (that is, what should be properly required of all schools), and where should freedom prevail? We do not pretend to answer such questions, nor do we believe that we should try. This is the proper domain of a renewed public discourse about what it means to be an educated citizen in a postmodern democratic society.

Epilogue: The Future of Catholic High Schools

In the mid-1980s, Catholic high schools were emerging from a very tumultuous fifteen-year period of organizational change. Although not completely stabilized, the institutional hemorrhaging that had characterized the 1970s—school closings, declining enrollments, and rapidly diminishing numbers of religious faculty—had been substantially reduced. With the research of Coleman and others bringing positive attention to Catholic schools, much psychic support was offered both to those who had lived through the changes and to those who had more recently joined in the mission. It was a welcome respite from what had been most difficult times.

An Update on the Seven Schools

It is appropriate to revisit the seven field-site schools with which we began our inquiry.

St. Edward's has continued to grow and prosper under the stable leadership of Brother Plodzik. The school completed two successful capital campaigns in the 1980s, raising $2 million for new facilities for computer education, religious education, and a business program, and another $4.1 million for an arts and athletic center. The enrollment from public elementary schools in the Louisville area has increased to 20 percent (it was 5 percent at the time of our field visits), and the number of non-Catholics has doubled, to 10 percent. The school has made a major commitment to a financial aid program, and about a quarter of all students receive some assistance. The annual aid budget is almost $400,000. St. Edward's current fiscal priorities include building an endowment to stabilize tuition costs (which have jumped 150 percent in nine years) and extending the resources for financial aid that currently limit the number of disadvantaged families who have access to the school.

None of this surprised us. St. Edward's had by far the strongest institutional base of all the schools we visited in terms of teaching faculty, physical plant, and the human and fiscal resources in its parent and local community. A seasoned and active board of directors continues to provide considerable managerial expertise for the school. A long-term planning process, which we heard about during our visits, now focuses on defining the school for the year 2010. St. Edward's is committed to providing a strong liberal arts education within a Catholic tradition for its boys without regard to race, religion, or financial resources. The school also espouses some of the contemporary rhetoric of school improvement, emphasizing, for example, more opportunities for cooperative learning among students and individual demonstrations of proficiency in core subjects.

The future looks bright for St. Edward's, and it is a future that is very much under the school's control. Yet St. Edward's is experiencing some problems that even the strongest of Catholic schools cannot avoid. The proportion of religious faculty, which now stands at 9 percent, continues to decline. The religious community knows that its days in the school are numbered. Keeping the religious tradition alive, when the sponsoring order is gone, is a major challenge ahead.

For *St. Richard's,* the 1980s was a time of institutional growth. Favorably located in the suburban Boston ring, St. Richard's has become a more selective institution over the last decade. The school, which now attracts students from over fifty different cities and towns, had 700 applicants in 1991 for the 250 slots in ninth grade. The college attendance rate for graduates of St. Richard's has jumped to 90 percent, and student diversity has also increased. About 15 percent of the students are now either black or Hispanic, compared with a virtually all-white enrollment in the early 1980s. Concerns about finances persist, because the school remains heavily dependent on tuition. As with St. Edward's, tuition at St. Richard's has also increased by 150 percent over the last nine years. To ameliorate these jumps in tuition somewhat, a student assistance program awarded $100,000 in financial aid last year.

St. Richard's appears stronger now than during our visits. The school has made efforts to improve its programs in computer education and fine arts and to expand its library. St. Richard's actively markets itself as a safe, caring school environment with a mission of "taking kids from wherever they are academically and seeking to add something of value." Given the high level of fiscal and human resources in its surrounding communities and its generally positive reputation, St. Richard's appears poised to move along the same path as St. Edward's. Much development of both the academic programs and financial base, however, is still needed. Unless this occurs, the future is not assured.

According to the principal, *Bishop O'Boyle* "is doing about as well as can be expected for a small private school. We continue to hold our own." Enrollment remains low but steady at 130 students. Only a single religious faculty member remains at the school, but faculty membership has otherwise been stable. At $4,000 per year, the current tuition is still the highest of the seven schools we studied. Relative to other independent schools in the Baltimore area, however, Bishop O'Boyle is reasonably inexpensive. A small financial aid program has been initiated, and the school hopes to expand it in the future. Grants from several foundations have helped the school in several respects: improving its computer offerings and library, starting a development office, and marketing itself. Like St. Richard's, Bishop O'Boyle's favorable location in an affluent suburban community has helped to keep it alive. Although the size of the facility limits enrollment, a future expansion is being considered.

Recent reports from our urban field sites prompt greater concern. Father O'Leary is still at the helm at *St. Cornelius'*. When asked, "How are you doing?" he replied, "Well, we're still paying the bills!" Finding new ways to pay the bills has been a major concern for the past nine years, and progress has occurred. The school recently hired a development director, finally freeing O'Leary of responsibility for fund-raising. St. Cornelius' now receives about $50,000 in Ohio state funds for "mandated educational services." Donations from corporations, foundations, alumni, and individual donors are aggressively sought. A diocesan inner-city school fund provides some aid, and a recently initiated weekly Bingo program adds another source of support. Several Sisters of Notre Dame have joined the faculty, helping to keep costs down because of their reduced salaries. Nonetheless, tuition has doubled since our initial visits and now stands at slightly more than $2,000 per year. In 1990–91, the school distributed over $130,000 in scholarship aid, and it is seeking additional funds to expand access to the school for disadvantaged students.

A major concern is St. Cornelius' drop in enrollment from 950 to 575 students since our initial visits. Recruitment efforts to stabilize enrollment have become increasingly important, and the school is also trying to upgrade instructional facilities in computing and science and to modernize an aging physical plant. For the moment, at least, the future looks guardedly positive.

School staff believe that finances and enrollment will stabilize soon. Given the school's good reputation and the serious problems of the local public schools, St. Cornelius' continues to represent an attractive alternative for those Cleveland families who can afford it.

To our dismay, *St. Madeline's* health is poorer than we had expected. The neighborhood surrounding the school has become heavily Hispanic, with most residents very poor recent immigrants who are unable to afford the school's tuition. As a result, enrollment has fallen precipitously from 660 girls to 350. Although the principal considers this a good size for the school in educational terms, St. Madeline's financial condition has become precarious. A further decline in enrollment could easily force the school to close its doors.

Responding to these financial and enrollment concerns takes a substantial amount of the school administration's time. Several new initiatives address these needs. As at St. Cornelius', a Bingo program has been introduced, and a development office now pursues foundation grants. The school currently recruits students from thirty different feeder elementary schools, both public and private. St. Madeline's has also started a work program, through which both students and parents may partially defray tuition by assisting at the school. A financial aid program now distributes over $100,000 annually to one-third of the students. Although only four teachers are religious members, another eight sisters aid the school in some capacity. This *increase* in religious staffing since 1983 attests to the strong personal and institutional support for St. Madeline's within the Catholic religious community.

Sister Nancy, the current principal, was on the faculty during our field visits. She acknowledges that the school's survival "will take a lot of work." Nevertheless, she remains very committed to St. Madeline's because it serves an important social mission in the Los Angeles community. The school provides a safe haven for girls in a troubled part of the city and affords productive life chances to some who otherwise might not have them. The school's graduates continue to do well. Both the salutatorian and valedictorian from the Class of 1990, for example, received scholarships from Stanford. St. Madeline's stands as a very important institutional presence to the girls it educates and to the larger neighborhood.

Of the schools that we visited in the mid-1980s, *St. Peter's* seemed in the worst straits. We were thus gratified to find the school still in operation, although "it is a continuous struggle," according to the principal. The school is now officially designated as diocesan, rather than the inter-parish status it carried during our field research. St. Peter's receives no financial support from the bishop, however. It has been sustained over the last decade by grants of almost half a million dollars from local foundations. These funds have allowed the school to address basic physical plant needs noted during our visits—a new roof, an overhaul of boilers, and painting.

Like St. Madeline's, St. Peter's had been adversely affected by changing community demographics, which have made it more difficult to attract tuition-paying students from nearby neighborhoods. Ironically, the school has benefited from the closing of several other Catholic schools in San Antonio. These school closings have created opportunities for St. Peter's to expand geographically its recruitment of students and to attract several highly regarded faculty members to strengthen its teaching programs. As at St. Madeline's, several religious order members have offered their services to the school at reduced salaries. Tuition has nevertheless more than doubled. Overall, St. Peter's is not a particularly healthy school. Only the personal commitments of a dedicated faculty, coupled with some well-placed support in the San Antonio community, have kept this school alive.

Unfortunately, the 1980s were not so kind to *St. Frances'*. Like so many other inner-city Catholic schools over the last two decades, the school was unable to cope with escalating costs and changing urban community demographics. Having accumulated some $750,000 in debt, the school was forced to close in 1988, and its building was sold.

Lingering Issues

As we have seen, a substantial transformation has occurred in Catholic schools over the last three decades. We were impressed by what we observed in our field visits to seven schools, and our statistical analyses have both validated and generalized these observations. A renewed sense of mission coupled with a social vitality are now common characteristics of Catholic high schools. They have come a long way from the parochial "ghetto schools" of the first half of this century. Yet a quarter century after Vatican II, many issues remain unsettled, primarily in the areas of governance and finance. If left unattended, these issues could unravel the good work that has been accomplished.

Governance

Much of the current governance concerns are external to schools and reflect evolving efforts since Vatican II to work out appropriate relationships between Church officials in Rome, local bishops, and American Catholic (and typically lay) institutions. Decisions in the past few years to close inner-city schools in several major metropolitan areas—Washington, D.C., in 1989, Detroit in 1990, Boston in 1991, and Philadelphia in 1992—have provoked considerable controversy. The broad lay participation and sense of collegiality that had grown since Vatican II were seemingly set aside in favor of centralized decision making. Such incidents mark a continuing disquiet with the American Catholic Church. Although the clerical hierarchy still has the power to exercise forms of control characteristic of the old "Roman Church," it must also confront a confident, well-educated, and committed lay population pressing for institutions more consonant with American democratic principles.

Of broad current concern are efforts directed from Rome to develop a Universal Catechism as a basis for religious instruction in all Catholic institutions. Following Vatican II, considerable discretion was afforded schools to modify their religious programs in accord with the teaching promulgated by the council. As we have recounted, substantial changes have occurred. In the process Catholic schools have become much more engaged with, albeit still critical toward, contemporary culture. Although the content and pedagogy of the Universal Catechism are still under development, there is great concern in the United States that Roman Church officials will seek to impose on American institutions their conception of a postmodern Church, which many lay and religious Catholics view as more compatible with the nineteenth rather than the twenty-first century. To them, a cold wind is again blowing in the church, one that threatens to subvert the important purposes now served by Catholic schools.

On balance, preserving the Catholic character of schools as they become lay institutions is a broadly shared concern. It would be imprudent to underestimate the powerful homogenizing forces that mass media and marketing have had on Catholic schools. In addition, Catholic schools today have connections to many professional educational organizations that bring a wide range of secular ideas into them. The gradually increasing numbers of non-Catholic faculty represent another potent secularizing force. Although these individuals bring subject-matter expertise that is much needed, they also express somewhat different motives for teaching in Catholic schools and may introduce different conceptions of a "good school" into conversations about future directions. In such circumstances, Catholic educators must struggle to discern the valuable contributions of this larger, secular culture while maintaining fidelity to the religious ideals that have vitalized Catholic schools since Vatican II. Such openness with roots inevitably creates organizational tensions and dilemmas, of which the current move toward a Universal Catechism and the concerned reactions to it are but one manifestation.

At a more fundamental level lies a continuing unease about the proper purpose of Catholic schools. From a traditional point of view, Catholic schools ought to be a primary educational arm of the institutional Church. The Church has a set of rules that make demands on its members, and it may act in a coercive fashion, commanding obedience at the potential price of expulsion. From this perspective, Catholic schools are private institutions that should aggressively teach the basic tenets of Catholic faith to anyone who is or might become a Church member. Catholic schooling should properly be directed toward the formation and maintenance of a sectarian membership.

An alternative conception—one that we have stressed here—envisions Catholic schools as a realization of the prophetic Church that critically engages contemporary culture. Anything that even remotely smacks of "indoctrination in the mind of the Church" can seriously undermine this more public function. Rather, the major value of Catholic schools is embodied in the tradition of thought, rituals, mores, and organizational practices that form these schools. From this perspective, Catholic education represents an invitation to students both to reflect on a systematic body of thought and to immerse themselves in a communal life that seeks to live out its basic principles. The aim of this type of schooling is to nurture in students the feelings, experiences, and reflections that can help them apprehend their relations to all that is around them—both the material world and the social world, both those who have come before and those who will come after. According to many of the dedicated religious and laypeople that we met in the course of our research, this is what Catholic schools should represent. To be sure, the schools provide a religious education—but one broadly defined for life in society and not just in the sect.

Significant internal governance issues, primarily those that concern the appropriate role of the growing number of lay faculty, also need to be addressed. We were impressed by the dedication of these individuals to their students and schools. Their commitment of time and energy affirms their belief in the ideals of these institutions. We have argued that these broadly shared commitments play a critical role in the successful functioning of Catholic schools. Anything that threatens the trust on which these personal commitments rest—such as "top-down" decisions to close schools—could undermine the quality of communal life and its positive social consequences. Such an unfortunate breakdown could be prompted by an edict from Rome or a local bishop's seat that fails to recognize the important responsibilities assumed by lay individuals in advancing the work of Catholic schools.

Breakdowns might also emerge within schools. Despite the overwhelming numbers of lay faculty, religious members still dominate the principal-ships and boards of directors. Control over individual schools rests largely with these religious members, who tend to function in a paternalistic (or maternalistic) mode. Although the exercise of this control may be quite caring and benign, it is oddly anachronistic for a modern American lay institution. More participation in school decision making by lay faculty seems inevitable if their dedication, commitment, and good will is to be sustained. The risks here are considerable and the probability of a successful transition modest.

Catholic schools must develop their own distinctive forms of faculty participation and school leadership compatible with the institutions' com-munal character. Neither conventional ideas about bureaucratic control through rule writing nor simple democratic procedures such as rotating departmental chairs and instituting school management committees are likely to be adequate in this context. A suitable alternative will require balancing several important considerations. First, the efficient management of day-to-day school affairs must be maintained. Whatever its merits as an inclusive strategy, "decision making by committee" comes up very short on this account. Second, teachers must have a broad sense of influence over key institutional policies. The exercise of such influence, however, will increase the demands on everyone's time, a commodity already highly taxed in Catholic schools. Third, room must be afforded for vision and leader-ship. The centrality of Catholic tradition—forging unity on what is essen-tial—must be preserved in order to ensure the continued vitality of these schools.

In a sense, adapting to lay leadership is just one more dilemma posed for the Catholic schools as a culturally engaged institution. How does an institution appropriate the best of contemporary culture (such as principles of effective organizational management and budgeting) while at the same time maintaining its distinctive roots? A productive course will demand some blending of the diverse concerns we have identified above. The end result is likely to be a form of school governance in which the Catholic tradition affords a context of common purposes to be advanced by the school and authority is collectively delegated by faculty to a principal or a leadership team who work in a consultative mode with all other school members.

Finances

The fiscal pressures that we observed during our field visits continue despite the considerable efforts by schools to alleviate them. In each of the field-site schools still operating, tuition has at least doubled. Notwithstanding the positive research reports that lent Catholic schools considerable public esteem in the 1980s, continuing fiscal pressures have caused a further decline in the number of Catholic schools. In 1991 there were 10 percent fewer schools than in 1983, when we began our study. Because these numbers include the recent opening of new Catholic schools in suburban areas (to which middle-class Catholics migrated in large numbers in the 1960s and 1970s), the actual loss of institutions in urban neighborhoods is even more severe. Despite often heroic efforts by individual Catholic religious and laypeople, inner-city Catholic schools are closing at an alarming rate. This trend, first noticed in the late 1960s, shows no sign of abating.[1]

Such fiscal problems pose a double bind for many Catholic schools. Even as they raise tuition annually and search for additional sources of revenues to meet the escalating costs demanded just to keep the school doors open, administrators continue to worry about the conflicting pressures of keeping tuition-paying enrollment up and remaining accessible to families from a broad range of social and economic backgrounds. In the face of diminished (or in many cases nonexistent) external Church subsidies, constant pressure to raise faculty salaries to a "living wage," the substantial costs of previously deferred maintenance, and, as in public schools, a new need to upgrade programs and develop faculty to educate students for a postindustrial age, the financial needs seem endless. Some schools, such as St. Edward's, are able to do it all, or almost all. Others, such as St. Peter's, squeak by, addressing only the most essential maintenance, accepting high faculty turnover (as a consequence of low salaries), and deferring major initiatives for instructional improvement.

Diocesan and religious order leaders who are in a position to offer financial support receive requests for assistance that are overwhelming in number and scope. Catholic schools now compete with numerous other social ministries for funding, and Church officials must regularly make wrenching choices among ministries that all appear to involve essential goods. Most troublesome, perhaps, is the manner in which arguments about resource allocation are increasingly phrased. A major rationale for the school closings in both Boston and Washington, D.C., for example, was that only a small number of students would be affected. Decision makers also noted that the substantial resources deployed in these schools could be reallocated to other religious education programs that would reach more students. Such cost-benefit arguments of a modern bureaucracy, however, rarely address the genuine human concerns of individual school communities.

Viewing urban schools as prophetic institutions brings a different perspective to these deliberations and raises a different set of questions. What value, for example, should be accorded the continued presence of a school in a neighborhood that has already been stripped of so many other institutions? How does one quantify the sense of opportunity, hope, and human caring that the presence of such an institution visibly conveys? Close personal attachments typically mark the lives of the students, parents, and teachers who are members of these schools. Such relations contrast sharply with the complex, impersonal interactions of the public bureaucracies to which many urban residents must often turn for their most basic human needs—housing, food, social welfare, and safety. This alternate view of urban Catholic schools directs attention to the moral qualities conveyed by our institutions and the ways in which these moral qualities should shape the decisions we make about them. Such concerns do not easily enter the instrumental calculus of a public administration focused on bottom-line values such as minimizing costs and maximizing tangible benefits.

Would the Continued Demise of Catholic Schools Advance the Common Good?

In exploring the organization and operation of Catholic high schools we have sought to identify features that typify "good" schools wherever they exist. Organizational characteristics such as small school size, a constrained and academically oriented curriculum, a communal school organization, and a focus on character as well as academic development have broad applicability for both public and private schools. Similarly, the basic value system of Catholic schools, expressed through a philosophy of person-in-community, is compatible with core American democratic ideals. As such, these values are also broadly generalizable. We thus contend that the Catholic high school—particularly the inner-city Catholic high school—offers a model for what many public schools could and perhaps should become.

The continuing financial challenges confronting Catholic schools are deeply disturbing. Quite simply, despite the best efforts of many individuals and organizations, inner-city Catholic schools are on their way to becoming an endangered species. Yet any policy discussion about public support for these schools leads quickly to statements about the importance of preserving the iron wall of separation between church and state. Public funding is seen as coming dangerously close to violating this separation. When we began our work, we too shared this position. As we have probed more deeply into the operations of Catholic schools, however, and reflected on their practices in the light of contemporary public concerns, our automatic endorsement of this prohibition no longer looks as simple as it once did.

The original intent of the "establishment clause" in the U.S. Constitution, which has been used as a basis for denying public funds to religious schools, was to ensure a government separate from the control of any single religious institution. Set in the context of the European conflicts of the eighteenth and nineteenth centuries, when the Catholic Church sought to establish an integrated religious state, these concerns were justified. It was not the intent of the founding fathers, however, to remove religious understandings from public life. The democracy that they sought to create rested on fundamental religious beliefs about the dignity of individuals and the proper forms of human association. The broad imparting of these moral ideas was viewed as central to the preservation of democracy.[2] The concern was that no *single* religion should be established as the state religion in the United States, lest the contentious church-state conflicts of Europe be transplanted to the New World. The authors of the Constitution maintained that freedom should abound in the area of religion and that public policy should act to sustain pluralism.

From the vantage point of the overwhelmingly secular character of contemporary society, the fear of establishing a church-state in America is anachronistic.[3] Further, with Vatican II's *Declaration of Religious Freedom* and closely related statements by the World Council of Churches in 1961, any lingering institutional aspirations were officially closed several decades ago. As late as 1960, public concern was raised about this matter during the presidential campaign of John Fitzgerald Kennedy, a Catholic. More recently, however, the fear of "Romanism" has apparently been put to rest. Although there may be other reasons to oppose public support for Catholic schools, such support would surely not institutionalize a church-state in the United States.

Two of the nonreligious arguments also raised in opposition to public support for Catholic schools are, first, that such schools are socially divisive and, second, that they are elitist. Catholic schools were seen during the late nineteenth and early twentieth centuries as a threat to the nation. There was public fear that the separate education of Catholic immigrants would eventually undermine American democracy. History, however, did not bear out these fears. Catholic schools have afforded significant social and educational opportunities for diverse immigrant populations who, as a group, have achieved remarkable social mobility and incorporation into American society.[4]

Critics also charge that, regardless of their past history, Catholic schools are elitist—seeking out students who are easier to educate and leaving the remainder to the public sector. The evidence presented in this book, however, contradicts this claim. Although it is true that many of the nation's poorest citizens increasingly cannot afford to attend Catholic schools and that others would not choose to even if they could, a broad cross section of Americans in terms of race, social class, and even religion now attend these schools. In addition, all available evidence suggests that if greater levels of support were available for the education of the disadvantaged, Catholic schools would welcome the opportunity to educate more of these students. Although the discretionary resources of religious orders and dioceses have dwindled over the last several decades, both continue to allocate a disproportionate share toward keeping inner-city schools open and accessible to the disadvantaged. (The relatively large numbers of religious members currently associated with both St. Peter's and St. Madeline's is noteworthy in this regard.) This commitment to urban Catholic schools is matched with extensive in-kind contributions from individual lay teachers who, by accepting very modest salaries, forgo considerable personal benefits in choosing to work in these schools.

On the other side of the ledger, much can be made of the public purposes served by Catholic schools. From a fiscal perspective, these schools are efficient, accomplishing a great deal on very modest resources. From the most instrumental vantage point, an obvious reason that the public should be concerned with the continued survival of Catholic schools centers on the pressures on the public purse that would arise if the more than 600,000 students currently enrolled in 1,300 Catholic high schools were to enter the public sector. This influx would further strain public school system budgets that are already struggling, particularly in urban contexts.

On the academic side, students in Catholic high schools demonstrate a relatively high level of achievement, and this achievement is distributed more equitably than in the public sector with regard to characteristics such as race and social class. Individual Catholic schools are also significant institutional resources in many urban communities that over the last two decades have been ravaged by the loss of numerous organizations that support communal life.

Although we have emphasized the education of disadvantaged students, we note that Catholic schools also advance an important agenda in the education of their more advantaged counterparts. In schools with large proportions of low-income students, the social justice mission of Vatican II is tangibly manifested in the daily work of faculty and staff—caring for and educating some of the least advantaged in the society. The concern for social justice, however, is also manifest in the schooling of the advantaged. Catholic schools deliberately strive to inculcate an understanding of and commitment to social justice in all their students. Many of these students are likely to move into powerful positions in society as adults and, as a result, will have disproportionate influence in the shaping of American culture. How such students think, feel, and behave is central to the kind of society the United States is likely to become. The Catholic school emphasizes to its students the value of leadership for social justice and hopes this message will become internalized in adulthood.

Traditional arguments against public support for Catholic schools—the fear of religious establishment, social divisiveness, and elitism—thus seem ungrounded. We discern nothing fundamentally undemocratic about Catholic schools' educational philosophy of person-in-community and their ethical stance of shaping the human conscience toward personal responsibility and social engagement. To the contrary, these religious understandings order daily life and its outcomes in very appealing ways. This is not a narrow, divisive, or sectarian education but, rather, an education for democratic life in a postmodern society. From our vantage point, it is difficult to envision a much stronger claim to the title of "common school."

More generally, these observations direct our attention to the role of religious understandings in public education. Past discussions about this topic have tended to focus on highly visible events such as Bible reading, school prayer, and crèches at Christmas. For several decades now, vigorous efforts have been under way to banish all such symbols from schools, and counterefforts have arisen in their defense. In our view the central issue is not the presence or absence of these activities in schools. For some, these symbols have meaning; for many others, they do not. Much more important is the quality of the interior life that schools foster in their students, the voices of conscience they nurture or fail to nurture. In this sense, *all* education conveys religious understandings, that is, a set of beliefs, values, and sentiments that order social life and create purpose for human activity.[5] These may be comprehensive ideals that ennoble the person and reach out broadly to others, or they may narrowly focus only on advancing material self-interest.

In the public sector, parents are increasingly free to choose among mathematics and science academies; among schools that focus on fine arts, drama, modern languages; and among a diverse array of pedagogical alternatives such as open classrooms and Montessori. In the realm of moral vision, however, freedom is constrained. The choice offered by the Catholic school is apparently not appropriate. Yet the important social purposes served by this continuing prohibition are not obvious to us. Are there good reasons why freedom should not prevail in this domain too? Perhaps. But to us, the contemporary Catholic high school looks more like a renewing force in our society than something to fear.

This issue is particularly striking when viewed from the perspective of contemporary urban schools. The problems of education in large cities have never been greater. The sweeping economic and social changes over the last two decades have left the poor heavily concentrated in cities, creating a new class of truly disadvantaged. At a time when the link between quality education and economic advancement, both individual and societal, appears stronger than ever, urban institutions appear overwhelmed, unable to cope with the enormity of the demands and the accumulated constraints under which they work.

Earlier in this century, Catholic schools played a major role in the education of urban immigrants. Catholic school systems in archdioceses such as Boston, New York, and Chicago once rivaled the corresponding public school systems in size. Social gospel Protestants were also a vital force in the cities. With their own sets of religious understandings, they too brought personal concern and a willingness to commit effort on the behalf of others. These individuals and institutions had drawbacks, but they were an active humanitarian force. Such a force is in very short supply today. At a time when the problems are more pervasive and the needs more expansive, there are fewer societal resources to draw upon. We therefore ask: What public purpose would be served by the continued demise of Catholic schools? Will the educational opportunities available to urban poor improve as a result? Will urban neighborhoods grow stronger as these institutions disappear? Would large public school bureaucracies suddenly become more responsive if these schools didn't exist? Although positive answers to each of these queries are possible, they do not appear very likely.[6]

The system of education in the United States is extremely secular in nature. Most Western democracies, during the course of their modern development, worked out accommodations for religious schools and in most cases provided them with financial support paralleling that of government schools.[7] The rationales for this financial support include the preservation of disappearing educational options in Australia, a concern about equity in the United Kingdom, and a desire for greater responsiveness to parental choice in Canada and the Netherlands. In most of these countries, the private educational sector is composed largely of religious schools. For example, 93 percent of French private schools are Catholic. In England, Scotland, Canada, Germany, Belgium, the Netherlands, and elsewhere, the system of "government" schools includes religious schools. Many of these arrangements are holdovers from the mid-nineteenth century, but these policies have actually been extended over the last two decades in Belgium, Canada, and England.[8]

The situation in Australia is especially relevant, because the Australian constitution contains an "establishment clause" for church-state separation identical to that in the U.S. Constitution. The Australians, however, have chosen to interpret the provision differently. Although government schools in Australia were historically decreed to be "free, compulsory, and secular," governmental support for private schools was initiated in the 1950s in response to a financial crisis in the private sector. This support has gradually increased, and currently the government aids all private schools, both religious and secular, based on expenditure levels in government elementary and secondary schools.[9]

Most modern democracies have affected a greater accommodation between the secular and the religious school, and between the moral and instrumental realms in their society, than has the United States. As America looks to expand the resources that care for its children, these comparative experiences cause us to question whether the rigid exclusion of religious schools from public support advances the common good. Increasingly, we look abroad for guidance as we grow uneasy about falling behind at home. The experiences of Catholic schools both here and elsewhere provide many lessons we need to ponder.

Notes

1. The Tradition of Catholic Schools

1. The seminal work on the assimilation of Catholic ethnics into mainstream America has been conducted by Greeley and colleagues. See, for example, Greeley and Rossin (1966). Interestingly, historians of education have begun to focus some attention on the role of Catholic schools in educating immigrants. See, for example, Fass (1989).

2. For information on the base year and the first follow-up of *High School and Beyond,* see NCES (1982). For information on the *Administrator and Teacher Survey (ATS)* supplement, see Moles (1988). The *ATS* data, though collected in 1984, were unavailable until 1988.

3. Supplemental information from the National Catholic Educational Association (NCEA) has also been cited throughout this book.

4. We use the term "institutional analysis" in the sense defined by Bellah et al. (1991, 288ff.). Our development of this book was driven by an effort to understand the operations of Catholic schools. As this work proceeded, we became increasingly aware of the limitations of existing social science frameworks for explaining the phenomena under study. (See, for example, Bryk, 1988.) During the final text revisions, we came across *The Good Society* (Bellah et al., 1991), where we found a more formal expression for the mode of inquiry we had gradually cobbled together. Our research is both analytic and normative. It focuses on concerns about institutional effectiveness, but also recognizes that this institutional effectiveness is morally premised. Further, we agree with Robert Bellah and his colleagues that rather than simply accepting normative understandings as given, they must be scrutinized, compared, and critiqued. They note, "If the central traditions and vitality of a society and its major institutions are moral, then they depend on argument and debate for their ongoing vitality" (p. 289). We believe that a study of the moral premises of the Catholic school can constructively contribute to a debate about the kinds of schools we seek for all our children.

5. The basic historical division presented here is taken from Hennesey (1981). Similar organizations can also be found in the writings of Gleason (1987) and Buetow (1970). In more detailed accounts, the middle period of growth and expansion is often further

subdivided around critical events such as the third Baltimore Council, concluded in 1884 and considered a major milestone in the development of Catholic schools, and the period following World War I, in which controversial issues were raised and the system consolidated in response.

6. This idea is developed by Neuhaus (1987). It is also noted in Bellah et al. (1985).

7. Good books that bear on the social and intellectual history of Catholic schools include Hennesey (1981); Coleman (1982); Dolan (1985); and Gleason (1987). For a single-city account of these developments, see Sanders (1977). We have relied heavily on these sources. We have also drawn on several Catholic "classics": Burns (1912); Burns and Kohlbrenner (1937); and Buetow (1970, 1988).

8. Dolan (1985), 249.

9. The sectarian equivalent of this is the modern undergraduate-graduate school, in which undergraduate education often subsidizes graduate training and graduate students provide relatively inexpensive labor for the colleges.

10. Buetow (1988), 30.

11. Burns and Kohlbrenner (1937).

12. Ibid., 15.

13. Cunningham (1940) and Depuis (1967).

14. Adler (1982). Adler advocates a classic curriculum as a common general education for all high school students. A related program in higher education is specified by Robert Maynard Hutchins (1954).

15. Burns and Kohlbrenner (1937), 210.

16. Dolan (1985), chap. 4.

17. Ibid., 254.

18. Ibid., 263.

19. For example, Burns and Kohlbrenner (1937), 41, note that the program of study for these academies followed the *Rules of the Ursuline Religious* first printed in Paris in 1705.

20. Dolan (1985), 250.

21. Buetow (1970), 60.

22. These ideas are further developed in Dolan (1985), chap. 4, and Coleman (1982), chap. 7.

23. The New York situation is detailed in Ravitch (1974).

24. See Dolan (1985), 266, for a further discussion of this history.

25. For a discussion of these arrangements, see Cremin (1988).

26. See Dolan (1985), 275.

27. See Cremin (1957) for a discussion of Horace Mann, his views about education, and his efforts to institutionalize common schools in Massachusetts during the first half of the nineteenth century.

28. See Cremin (1988), 127.

29. This response was coined by Chesterton in response to the question "What is America?" Quoted in Mead (1974).

30. For an account of these experiences in the context of urban minorities in Chicago, see Sanders (1977).

31. Dolan (1985), 319.

32. For a further discussion, see Veverka (1984), 28.

33. Ryan (1963), 37.

34. Greeley and Rossi (1966).

35. Quoted by Veverka (1984), 58, from the editorial policy statement of the *Crusader,* n.d.

36. Quoted by Veverka (1984), 58, from Franklin Ford, editor of the *American Standard.*

37. Quoted by Veverka (1984), 80.

38. The motto "For God and country" was first introduced as a theme for the 1918 meeting of the National Catholic Educational Association.

39. A critical source of information on this debate is Miller (1952).

40. Miller (1952) cites as an example of this point a speech at the sixth annual meeting of the organization in 1905 by the Reverend Hugh Henry, rector of the Roman Catholic High School in Philadelphia.

41. It was not until 1928 that secondary schools became a separate department in the NCEA, distinct from the colleges and universities.

42. Miller (1952), 21. Rev. M. P. Dowling, S.G., asserted this view in "The Catholic College as the Preparation for a Business Career," presented at the First Annual Conference of the Association of Catholic Colleges, 1899.

43. McClusky (1964), 89.

44. National Center for Education Statistics (1987), 54.

45. See Caterall (1988) and Ryan (1963).

46. NCEA (1990a).

47. Ibid.

48. In 1987–88, religious men and women in Catholic high schools were paid an average of about $15,000, about the same salary as a new lay teacher without advanced degrees. This rose from about $11,000 in 1984. See NCEA (1988), 11–12, and NCEA (1985), 202.

49. These data are from NCEA (1970), NCEA (1980), and NCEA (1988). For a more extensive discussion of the financial problems confronting Catholic schools, see Bryk and Holland (1985).

50. McBrien (1980), 643.

51. For the Church's encounter with European intellectualism in the latter half of the nineteenth century, see Aubert (1978), chap. 7.

52. There is considerable irony in all of this. As postmodern scholarship has increasingly turned its attention to the excesses of Enlightenment thought, it has brought renewed attention to Aristotelian ideas. See, for example, MacIntyre (1981).

53. Here too Neoscholastic thought taps postmodern reflections about the relationship between scientific knowledge and symbolic understandings, and man's need for both. See, for example, Levine (1985).

54. For a modern Neoscholastic account of these concepts, see Maritain (1946). Neoscholasticism went to great lengths to distinguish between the concepts of the "individual" (Enlightenment man) and the "person." Although Neoscholasticism affirmed the dignity of the person-in-community, it took sharp issue with the concept of "individual" over "society" as a central organizing premise of liberal thought. It is to this scholarship that the concept of person-in-community affirmed by the bishops in the aftermath of Vatican II, is linked.

55. These ideas are developed by Maritain (1946) and are also treated in Maritain (1958).

56. Maritain (1943), 47.

57. Maritain's principal writings on education appear in *Education at the Crossroads* (1943), which was first delivered as the Terry Lectures at Yale, and in a series of other essays, later collected in a volume entitled *The Education of Man* (1962).

58. For a more recent criticism of Dewey's writings on this point, see Bowers (1987).

59. Maritain (1943), 47.

60. Maritain's comments on this point were prescient. Renewed concerns about this issue have appeared in a variety of places, including Janowitz (1983); Butts (1988), 162–194; and Gutmann (1987).

61. Maritain (1962), 65.

62. Closely related arguments on this account can be found in Bellah et al. (1985), who describe a modern crisis of commitment resulting from the disappearance of religious understandings from public discourse about our social life.

63. Maritain (1962), 69. Emphasis added.

64. An active scholarship has emerged in the last twenty years on the relationship of religion to public life. As our inability to solve the excesses of modernity have become increasingly apparent, there has been a revival of interest in the supportive role that religious understandings may play. A key notion is that for these understandings to enter public life, they must be broadly accessible, in order that the public might engage them at least partially on some basis other than faith. The resort to reason is one obvious option. Examples of this new scholarship include Richey and Jones (1974); Lovin (1986); and Marty (1987).

65. In the post-Vatican II period, the Catholic theological basis for social action has been approached from a variety of perspectives. For a discussion of some of these approaches, see Curran (1975), chap. 1.

66. For a sympathetic discussion by an "outsider" of the strengths of Catholicism as it confronts modern American life, see Gilkey (1975).

67. For a poignant account of this loss of community, see Bellah et al. (1985). On the need to reconstruct a public discourse on matters of social and political ethics, see Diggins (1984); Lovin (1986); and Wolfe (1989). For a discussion of this in the context of a need for a revitalized educational philosophy, see Bowers (1987).

68. For a further discussion of these ideas, see Dulles (1982), 23–24.

69. For a discussion of the emergence of social Catholicism in Europe in the nineteenth century, see Aubert (1978), chap. 8.

70. Coleman (1982), 159.

71. Aubert (1978), 146.

72. For an extensive account of social Catholicism in America interpreted through a post-Vatican II perspective, see Dolan (1985), chaps. 12–14.

73. Quoted in Dolan (1985), 345.

74. For a discussion of this broader movement, see Cremin (1988), part 1.

75. Coleman (1982), 171.

76. See Dolan (1985), chap. 14, for a discussion of this developing lay social movement.

77. Furfey (1936). Furfey's contribution to a radical Catholic social ethics is discussed extensively in Curran (1975), chap. 3.

78. For a good account of Christian personalism "lived," see Coles (1987), chap. 5.

79. Coleman (1982), 161.

80. This is the major theme in Kung (1988).

81. Abbott (1966), 199.

82. Abbott (1966), 7.

83. Abbott (1966) states that of the council statements, constitutions carry the most weight, followed in order by declarations and decrees. The documents generally carry two names: one in Latin, which is typically symbolic and highly evocative (e.g., *Gaudium et Spes*); and a second in English, which is more descriptive of the document's contents.

84. The Catholic theological scholar Avery Dulles summarized the current state of understandings about the council: "While leaving open many questions, the council did present a solid core of unequivocal teachings." He organizes these points of consensus around ten basic principles. The formulation presented in this section draws from this assessment. See Dulles (1982), chap. 2.

85. Interpretation of this notion that dogma must develop remains quite controversial. See Dulles (1982), 190ff.

86. Quoted in Dulles (1988), from Decree on the Apostolate of the Laity and *Gaudium et Spes*.

87. Dolan (1985), 426.

88. "The Church in the Modern World," Vatican II decree, cited in Abbott (1966), 92.

89. Gilkey (1975).

90. See Hunt (1980), 203–210. This moral dilemma in Boston, and its resolution, is also described in Lukas (1985).

91. For a secular parallel analysis, see Bowers (1987). Bowers argues that a new educational philosophy is needed to redress the imbalance caused by radical individualism. His arguments share much in common with Catholic scholarship on this point.

92. NCCB (1972). Note the choice of the key word, person, and not individual, an important distinction in Neoscholastic writings.

93. Sacred Congregation for Christian Education (1977).

2. Research Past and Present

1. Sara Lawrence Lightfoot (1983) develops the idea of institutional goodness as the basis for a broader conceptualization for effective schools. We find this idea quite compatible with our own, although our choice of research methods is somewhat different.

2. In developing this chapter we have benefited greatly from several published volumes that provide extensive statistical description of Catholic secondary schools. These include Coleman, Hoffer, and Kilgore (1981); Greeley (1982); NCEA (1985); and Benson and Guerra (1985). Prior to this work, there was very little known about these schools. We have relied heavily on these sources in addition to our own analyses of *High School and Beyond,* as well as our prior published work in this area: Bryk et al. (1984). As a matter of convention in reporting descriptive statistics in this chapter, the reader may assume that all data are from our own analyses of *HS&B* unless a specific alternative citation is provided.

3. Numerous critiques and reanalyses followed the publication of *Equality of Educational Opportunity*. Three of the major contributions to this debate were Moynihan and Mosteller (1972); Jencks et al. (1972); and Averch et al. (1971).

4. Rather than summarize individual studies, we rely here on two comprehensive and competent reviews: Purkey and Smith (1983) and Rosenholtz (1985). Especially influential individual studies include Edmonds (1979) and Rutter et al. (1979). Two other widely cited studies are Brookover et al. (1979) and Weber (1973).

5. The body of research on both effective schools and Catholic schools that we review here includes major studies we considered at the outset of our work. The considerable body of school effects research that appeared subsequently is reviewed as appropriate throughout the book.

6. See Cibulka, O'Brien, and Zewe (1982).

7. Greeley (1982); Coleman, Hoffer, and Kilgore (1981, 1982).

8. *Harvard Educational Review,* 51(4) 1981; *Sociology of Education,* 55(2/3) 1982; *Sociology of Education,* 58(2) 1985.

9. See *Sociology of Education,* 58(2) 1985, for a series of studies on *HS&B* longitudinal data. These were data collected two years later, when 1980 sophomores were 1982 seniors.

10. The best examples of this can be seen in the titles of relevant articles; see, for example, Alexander and Pallas (1985).

11. Jencks (1985).

12. Recent developments in statistical methodology for the analysis of hierarchical data permit an investigation of a broadened conceptualization of school effects that focuses direct attention on the social distribution of school effects rather than just average differences. For example, Raudenbush and Bryk (1986) illustrate how these methods can be employed to examine simultaneously the effects of school-level variables on both the average level of achievement and the degree to which social class influences achievement. These analyses suggests a reconceptualization of the "effective school" as one with both high average levels of achievement and a relatively weak relationship of achievement to entry characteristics, such as social class and ethnicity. We employ these methods in analyses presented in Chapters 10 and 11.

13. Hoffer, Greeley, and Coleman (1985).

14. The research propositions and summary themes are described in Holland and Bryk (1985).

15. For more information on the *HS&B* design, see Coleman, Hoffer, and Kilgore (1982). See also Lee and Bryk (1988, 1989).

16. For a report on these, see Heyns and Hilton (1982).

17. Moles (1988).

18. All of the data used in these school descriptions were collected during the 1982–83 school year. In the interest of improving the readability of the text, however, we have deliberately used the present tense.

19. As already noted, most of the data presented in this chapter were collected in the early to mid-1980s. As such, they represent a precise description of the schools in that period. To the extent that we have evidence that the schools have materially changed in the interim, this is noted in the Epilogue.

20. NCEA (1985), 16; NCEA (1990a), 18–19.

21. NCEA (1985), 142–149.

22. Coleman, Hoffer, and Kilgore (1981), p. 68.

23. NCEA (1986).

24. NCEA (1985).

25. NCEA (1990a).

26. Approximately 90 percent of elementary schools are run by parishes and substantially subsidized by them. In contrast, over 70 percent of Catholic secondary schools are sponsored by either dioceses and religious orders. Although a small number of these, particularly those with high concentrations of low-income students, receive some subsidy, by and large secondary schools are much more tuition dependent than Catholic elementary schools.

27. Powell, Farrar, and Cohen (1985), 172ff.

28. Coleman, Hoffer, and Kilgore (1981), 19.

29. NCEA (1985).

30. Coleman, Hoffer, and Kilgore (1981), 60–64.

31. The 1982–83 *Statistical Report* (NCEA 1983) documents declining student/teacher ratios in Catholic secondary schools between 1969 and 1983. No comparable data exist for earlier years, but it is clear from aggregate demographics on pupil enrollments and staffing that typical class size was considerably larger in the 1950s and early 1960s.

32. The arguments about economies of scale and formalized social interaction that relate to school size are summarized along with the related research in Bryk, Lee, and Smith (1990).

33. See Bryk and Driscoll (1988), which contains a full exposition of arguments, theory, and empirical evidence to support this statement.

34. The positive effect of small size on teacher satisfaction is also reported in Lee, Dedrick, and Smith (1991). The effect on teachers is likely to foster such positive attitudes in students.

35. Goodlad (1984) suggested that secondary schools should enroll between 500 and 600 students. Interestingly, the school size distribution for the Catholic sector is centered directly on this norm.

3. Classroom Life

1. The rectangular row and column seating arrangement appears to be a universal characteristic of secondary education. Other researchers, such as Goodlad (1984) and Sizer (1984), have found similar arrangements in the field sites they visited.

2. For Catholic high schools, see NCEA (1986), 141–142. For public high schools, see Goodlad (1984), 107.

3. The teachers in NCEA (1986) report that about 10 percent of their class time is devoted to tests and quizzes. These results are reasonably consistent with our data if we factor in a full-period test every three weeks, in addition to the 2.1 minutes of quiz time we observed.

4. These engagement rates appear to be higher than those reported in field studies of public high school classrooms. See, for example, the descriptive accounts in Sizer (1984). See also Powell, Farrar, and Cohen (1985).

5. NCEA (1986), 140.

6. Ibid., 142. The *ATS* survey of teachers in *HS&B* schools (described more fully in Chapter 11) supports these findings, in particular the finding of job satisfaction that is

considerably higher in Catholic than in public schools. See also Lee, Dedrick, and Smith (1991).

7. In a recent national survey of Catholic high school teachers, "a view of teaching as ministry" was the third most important reason cited for teaching in Catholic high schools. The first two reasons given were "a desire to teach in this kind of educational environment" and "a love of teaching." See Benson and Guerra (1985), 17.

8. NCEA (1986), 143.

9. The importance of intrinsic or psychic rewards to teachers has been well documented in the seminal work of Lortie (1975). As in our research, Lortie found that the main rewards in teaching derived from the positive feelings associated with success in working with individual students. External rewards such as income were less influential.

4. Curriculum and Academic Organization

1. For an extended account of these developments see Powell, Farrar, and Cohen (1985), chap. 5. See also Lazerson (1985), chap. 2; Cusick (1983).

2. An interesting description of this can be found in Philip Jackson's (1981) case study account of a comprehensive suburban high school. Ekstrom and her colleagues (1987, table 18, p. 50) report that the proportion of high schools offering advanced placement courses grew from 15 percent in 1972 to 36 percent in 1982.

3. The proportion of students in the nonacademic tracks grew from 54 percent in 1972 to 62 percent in 1982, according to Ekstrom et al. (1987), table 22, p. 58.

4. Several reasons were offered in our field visits for this. First, logistical problems and constrained school resources limited the ability of Catholic schools to move aggressively in making such innovations. Second, market forces played a role. Parents expressed increasing concerns about lowered academic standards, and some schools reported a "softening" in student enrollment. Finally, there was the "pull of tradition" back to an educational philosophy with a strong classical humanist bent. For further discussion, see Bryk et al. (1984).

5. The distribution of core academic courses required in Catholic schools we visited is quite compatible with recommendations from a number of reports calling for reform of public secondary education. Goodlad (1984), for example, recommends an increase in the number of required academic courses and a decrease in the number of electives, especially in vocational education. Boyer (1983) and the National Commission on Excellence in Education (1983) are quite similar.

6. The National Commission on Excellence in Education (1983) recommended that high school students "lay the foundations in the Five New Basics" by taking 4 years of English, 3 years of mathematics, 3 years of science, 3 years of social studies, and a half year of computer science. A National Center for Education Statistics bulletin (1984) summarized the analysis of 12,000 transcripts from 1982 high school graduates and found that Catholic school students averaged over 3.2 more years of course work than public school students in the five "new basics" areas. The *Bulletin* does not compare Catholic and public school students in each subject area.

7. These results on students' course enrollments by academic and nonacademic tracks were previously reported in Lee and Bryk (1988). Similar results were also reported by Hoffer, Greeley, and Coleman (1985).

8. This section draws on data from classroom observations in the ninth and eleventh grades, consisting of both clinical and structured observations in 162 classrooms. We also conducted structured interviews with department heads in English, mathematics, and religion, and with the teachers whose classes we observed. Curriculum guides, both current and from past years, were also collected and analyzed.

9. This expectation stands in sharp contrast to recent descriptions of the highly varied expectations that can be found across different ability levels within the comprehensive high school. See the discussion in Powell, Farrar, and Cohen (1985, chap. 2) on classroom teaching. Similar accounts can be found in Cusick (1983); Goodlad (1984); and Oakes (1985).

10. Buetow (1988), 245.

11. NCEA (1985), 208.

12. This change is attributable in part to an increased interest in religious education by lay Catholics. It also reflects confused feelings among the aging religious staffs, who received theological training prior to Vatican II.

13. Conversations with Father O'Leary at St. Cornelius' and with religion teachers at St. Edward's and St. Richard's.

14. Choice and Conscience Committee (1980).

15. See Healy (1981).

16. See, for example, Shafer and Olexa (1971); Rosenbaum (1976); Bowles and Gintis (1976); and Oakes (1985).

17. Our field observation runs counter to results from Rosenbaum's (1976) in-depth study of social stratification within a single public high school. In the Rosenbaum field site, the transitions occur in only one direction—down—into less competitive nonacademic programs. Our observations here, too, run counter to recent descriptions of public high schools. See, for example, the Powell, Farrar, and Cohen (1985) discussion of the academic specialty shops in *The Shopping Mall High School*.

18. Variations on this argument can be found in Braddock (1981); Goldberger and Cain (1982); and Alexander and Pallas (1983, 1984, 1985).

19. Rosenbaum (1976) reported that many of the students in his sample who were in nonacademic tracks still labored under the illusion of the possibility of college attendance. This was true despite the fact that those students not in the college-prep track were highly unlikely to attend college. In his sample, less than 5 percent of such students were in four-year colleges the year after high school graduation.

20. It is important to recall that these data are only from students who are still enrolled in high school in the spring of their senior year. Dropouts have been excluded. Because drop-out rates are higher in the public sector (see Chapter 11), the results would be even more pronounced if these students had been included.

21. The sample includes all *HS&B* students who fit our standard criteria (nontransfers, nondropouts) and who have transferred from a Catholic elementary school to a public high school. The sample size for this subgroup is 769 students.

22. The method of calculating the predicted proportion of C→P students who would be in the academic track if they had gone to Catholic high schools involves multiplying the unstandardized regression coefficients for Catholic school students for each background variable by the mean on that variable for the C→P group, summing these effects, and adding them to the regression constant. Results are as follows.

Background variable	Regression coefficient for Catholic schools (unstandardized)	Mean for C→P students	Increment to proportion
Home ownership	−.024	.862	−.021
Repeated elem. grade	−.090	.083	−.007
Religiousness	.019	.072	+.001
Female	−.026	.504	−.013
Hispanic	.064	.067	+.004
College plans, gr. 8	.234	.505	+.118
Black	.060	.041	+.002
Family size	−.014	6.720	−.100
Single-parent family	−.045	.818	−.037
Non-Catholic	−.000	.087	−.000
Social class	.161	−.207	−.003
Regression constant	.658		
Proportion of C→P group predicted in academic track if they were in Catholic high school	.602		
Proportion of C→P group actually in academic track in public high school	.406		
Catholic school academic track advantage	.196		

23. See Lee (1985), 227, for details of the significance testing method employed here. Our estimates of the "Catholic school track advantage" based on the C→P analysis are quite similar to those reported by Kilgore (1984) in a school-level analysis using a combined Catholic-public sample on base-year *HS&B* data.

One obvious criticism of this analysis is that the students who leave the Catholic sector after grade 8 might be deliberately choosing public secondary schooling in order to pursue a nonacademic track that is unavailable in the local Catholic high school. Although there is some merit to this objection, our analyses suggest that this is unlikely to explain away the rather large observed effects for two reasons. First, we know that although 50.5 percent of the C→P reported college plans in the eighth grade, only 40.6 percent are enrolled in an academic program at grade 10. This subgroup thus also displays the same aspirations/track incongruity characteristic of public secondary schools. Second, in other analyses, we found that the C→P group was not overrepresented in nonacademic public school programs once their background characteristics were taken into account. If some unmeasured selection factor were operative, we would have expected to find such overrepresentation.

24. We ran school-level regressions predicting the number of courses offered in each subject-matter area as a function of size, the square of size, sector, and school SES. The school SES variable represents a proxy for school fiscal resources. We found statistically significant sector effects for offering foreign language, personal development, and business courses. Catholic schools offer significantly more foreign language courses, but they offer

significantly fewer personal development and business courses. In general, school SES is positively related to the number of courses offered, with statistically significant results occurring for mathematics and foreign language courses. The estimated coefficient for school size is positive for all of the outcomes and statistically significant in all cases except personal development courses. Statistically significant negative curvature was encountered for mathematics, science, and foreign language offerings. That is, the relationship between size and course offerings in these areas leveled off for large schools.

25. See Heyns and Hilton (1982). These researchers found the reliability of the math test to be higher than for the *HS&B* tests in other areas.

26. To justify the combined sample, we evaluated interaction effects between school sector and other predictor variables. Only in the vocational track was the set of interaction terms marginally statistically significant, and we therefore proceeded with combined sector analysis.

5. Communal Organization

1. See, for example, Rutter et al. (1979); Lightfoot (1983); Sizer (1984); and Grant (1985). Hallinger and Murphy (1986) also include a sense of community in their conceptual framework for effective schools.

2. The idea of boundaries is a central feature in sociological discussions of geographic communities. Lightfoot (1983) uses this idea in describing the psychological hold that the schools she studied created on their students. Our field experiences are consistent with her observations.

3. Healy (1981), 166.

4. This is supported by general findings about Catholic schools. NCEA (1985), 71ff.

5. NCEA (1985), 212.

6. Ibid.

7. Ibid.

8. Ibid., 71ff.

9. Ibid., 88.

10. See Chubb and Moe (1988).

11. See Chubb and Moe (1987).

12. See ibid., 31.

13. This phenomenon is demonstrated in *HS&B* data from both principals and teachers. First, principals were queried about rewards they offer for good teaching. Although 22 percent of public school principals responded that "assigning teachers to teach better students" was one such reward, only 10 percent of Catholic school principals offered such a response. Second, we examined the relationship between teachers' years of experience in their schools and the ability level of the students they taught relative to the school's average. In public school teachers there is a significant linear relationship ($F = 10.3$, $p < .001$), with more experienced teachers teaching students they consider more able. For Catholic high school teachers, however, no such relationship exists ($F = 1.0$, n.s.).

14. Similar reports can be found in the NCEA (1986) report on low-income Catholic high schools. Both their school descriptions in chapter 2 and responses in chapters 10 and 11 corroborate our field observations.

15. NCEA (1985), 75–76.

16. NCEA (1986), 51–53.

17. Ibid., 62.

18. NCEA (1985), 73ff.

19. See, for example, Grant (1988). See also Cusick and Wheeler (1988).

20. This changing perspective is conveyed, for example, in Tyack and Hansot (1982). Some accounts of public high schools, such as Cusick (1983), Sizer (1984), and Grant (1988), emphasize the absence of an explicit moral vision in the schools.

21. This is a central thesis in the ethno-historical account of Hamilton High School by Grant (1988).

22. In the *HS&B* survey, only 42 percent of the public school seniors reported that the strictness of discipline at their school was "excellent" or "good." Only 36 percent offered a similar rating when asked about the fairness of discipline. The comparable figures for Catholic schools were 72 percent and 47 percent, respectively.

23. Green (1985) captures this moral aim of schooling in the concept of a "conscience of craft." Such a conscience requires expert knowledge, but it also involves a personal disposition toward one's work. An emotional commitment must be forged. Green writes, "To possess a conscience of craft is to have acquired the capacity for self-congratulation or deep self-satisfaction at something well done, shame at slovenly work, and even embarrassment at carelessness" (p. 5). It is interesting that in developing this idea of a "conscience of craft," Green cites the writings of Thomas Aquinas. This is another instance in which long-standing philosophical beliefs ground Catholic school practice.

24. See, for example, Grant (1985); NCEA (1986); and Lesko (1988).

25. Benson and Guerra (1985).

26. NCEA (1986), 52.

27. This finding was reported by Barker and Gump (1964). They detail the pervasive effects of school size on the nature of social interactions within schools. In general, as schools grow in size, the opportunities for personal, face-to-face interactions decrease. Even though efforts are made to afford more opportunities for student involvement, these increases are not commensurate with the larger size. Further, even with a more extensive array of extracurricular opportunities, social fragmentation remains common.

28. See Bryk and Frank (1991) and Bidwell and Quiroz (1991).

29. Recall from Chapter 3 that students from schools in the two sectors assess their teachers very differently. For example, 55 percent of Catholic school students believe most of their teachers enjoy their work; the comparable figure for students in public schools is 37 percent. Sector differences concerning teachers' respectfulness and patience are also evident (see Figure 3.3).

30. This idea of the public functions of particular classics of art and religion is developed in Tracy (1986). In arguing against a narrow instrumental definition of rationality, Tracy emphasizes the disclosive and transformative potential of such classics. They invite interpretation from all who are willing to truly engage with them. As such, Tracy argues, they are public. Further, there exists at least in principle the possibility of a communal consensus on some interpretative truth.

31. Lesko (1988) provides a more in-depth description of a high school Mass celebration, and students' reactions to it, in her ethnography of St. Anne's.

32. NCEA (1985), 68.

33. Ibid., 118.

34. Chubb and Moe (1988), 1078, table 6.

35. Ibid.

36. Ibid., 1083, Table 8.

37. We know of no national data on the prevalence of school chaplains in Catholic high schools. It is possible, however, to develop a crude estimate from related information in NCEA (1985), 64–65. Based on the percentage of religion department faculty who are priests and the incidence of liturgical services on campus, we estimate that between 25 and 50 percent of the schools had the services of a chaplain in 1984. Because of the declining numbers of ordained priests in the United States, some Catholic high schools have found it increasingly difficult to attract a chaplain. Working with adolescents requires some special skill and interest, and many older priests prefer parish work or social service. Of the seven schools we visited in 1983, five had a chaplain on their staff. We suspect that the prevalence of chaplains has declined further in the interim and that pastoral ministers are becoming increasingly common substitutes for priest-chaplains.

38. Also relevant here are the case study profiles from the field research reported in NCEA (1986), 24–25.

39. The conception of work as a "calling" can have profound implications on the psychic rewards that one derives from these efforts. MacIntyre (1981) argues that this characterization of practical activity makes a person's work morally inseparable from his or her life. The individual is drawn into a community of practice whose activity has intrinsic meaning and value that transcends the obvious external rewards of production and financial remuneration (chap. 10). Similar ideas are developed by Bellah et al. (1985), chap. 3.

40. NCEA (1986), 130.

41. Benson and Guerra (1985), 13–14.

42. See, for example, Lortie (1975).

43. Such selectivity may be more difficult in the future if fiscal pressures on Catholic schools continue to grow or if the predicted general shortage of teachers materializes. Given the relatively low salaries they offer, Catholic high schools might encounter difficulty in attracting and maintaining strong lay staffs. In such an environment, academic credentials could be given more credence than normative considerations. There is some current evidence for this in the areas of mathematics and science, where a teacher shortage is apparent. In these two subject areas, the proportion of non-Catholics among Catholic school faculties is higher than in any other department. See NCEA (1986), 126. Data on motivations for teaching in low-income Catholic schools are particularly noteworthy. For non-Catholics teaching in such schools, such practical considerations as "the only teaching position available to me" or "a means of gaining experience" are more likely to be mentioned than the educational and religious reasons that are generally characteristic responses for teachers in Catholic schools. See NCEA (1986), 130. Thus in the curricular areas where fewer qualified candidates exist, some compromises have occurred in terms of social commitments.

44. See, for example, Peshkin's (1986) account of life in a fundamentalist academy.

45. See Powell, Farrar, and Cohen (1985), 58–66 and chap. 4 on the "unspecial."

46. This characterization of the comprehensive public high school has been developed in a number of places. See, for example, Cusick (1983) and Powell, Farrar, and Cohen (1985).

47. Grant (1988).

48. *Daedalus* 110 (4) 1981; also Lightfoot (1983). Our remarks here should not be interpreted as implying that moral school communities are totally absent from the public sector or limited to homogeneous rural communities. For example, another portrait by

Lightfoot (1983) provides a very vivid account of such a community within a large urban magnet school. The recent research on high schools suggests, however, that such public schools may be rather rare.

49. For a further and more detailed elaboration of the basic principles contained in this philosophy statement, see "Profile of the Graduate of a Jesuit High School at Graduation," Jesuit Secondary Education Association, Commission on Research and Development, photocopy, no date.

6. Governance

1. Forty percent of all Catholic high schools are private, 34 percent are diocesan, and 26 percent are parish or inter-parish schools. NCEA (1988).

2. In two reviews of the effective schools literature, which together summarize hundreds of studies, leadership on the part of the principal was singled out as a key element characterizing schools that are academically effective for disadvantaged students. See Purkey and Smith (1983), 427–454, and Rosenholtz (1985), 352–388. Effective principals are the interpreters of the school's instructional goals. They "convey certainty that teachers can improve student performance and that students themselves are capable of learning . . . They set explicit operational goals regarding students' performance, which are clearly communicated to their staff members . . . Effective principals press for greater commitment on the part of teachers, hold teachers accountable for their actions, and communicate high expectations about the progress teachers are capable of making" (Rosenholtz, 1985, 361).

3. Although we did not observe this arrangement in any of the schools we visited, larger, better-funded schools may have both a headmaster (a president) and a principal. In such schools, leadership responsibilities are divided between the president, typically responsible for external matters (for example, the school board and fund-raising), and the principal, who focuses on internal concerns (for example, academic programs and student welfare).

4. Our discussion of the Catholic school principalship draws heavily on the dissertation research of Holland (1985). For a review of the extant literature on this topic through 1985, see Holland (1985), chap. 3.

5. This depiction of Father O'Leary's typical day is based on a number of data sources. For each of the principals in our seven field-site schools we collected logs of workday activities on a sample of four different occasions over the fall of 1983. These logs provide detailed summaries of how each principal spent each 15-minute segment of the workday. Additional information came from two interviews with each principal, a principal questionnaire, and transient observations of the principals during our two visits to the school. These data were at least partially cross-validated with information from interviews with a sample of school teachers, parents, board members, and the superintendent of schools for the diocese. This typical-day description of Father O'Leary shares many common features with the workdays of the other principals we observed. For more details, see Holland (1985).

6. Gorton and McIntyre (1978); Abramowitz and Stockhouse (1980).

7. Time logs completed by principals in our field sites confirm results from other research that the principal's role is one of high involvement in interpersonal relationships. See Wolcott (1973); Gorton and McIntyre (1978); and Morris et al. (1984).

8. This interplay of faith, doubt, and action can also be found in the case study descriptions of principals in low-income Catholic schools in NCEA (1986).

9. The literature on public school administration tends to emphasize the managerial aspects of this job and is relatively silent on the question of spiritual or moral leadership. The emphasis is on academic excellence and positive morale. In this regard, Catholic school principals more closely approximate heads in other private schools in their general orientation to their work.

10. According to NCEA (1985, 41), 28 percent of the staff in private (religious order) schools in 1984 were religious, whereas in diocesan and parish schools religious constituted about 20 percent of the staff. In 1988 the general pattern was the same, although the numbers were lower; see NCEA (1988). Although there are no national data, our fieldwork suggests that diocesan and parish schools are also more likely to have religious staff from several different orders. Such schools benefit from the individual services provided, but they are less likely to receive the institutional supports that accrue when a single religious order provides a strong sponsorship. The latter is much more likely to occur in private schools.

11. NCEA (1988), 23.

12. NCEA (1985), 88. Sixty percent of the principals report that their boards are exercising more influence now than five years ago.

13. A recent study indicates that such control is extremely important to fostering the self-efficacy and satisfaction of teachers. See Lee, Dedrick, and Smith (1991).

14. Benson and Guerra (1985), 138.

15. In questionnaire data from our field sites, only 7 percent of teachers reported that they had much say in financial management and planning occurring within the school.

16. NCEA (1986), 281.

17. Ibid., 275–276.

18. NCEA (1985), 125.

19. Over 95 percent of the Catholic school principals surveyed in *HS&B* responded that confrontations among teachers "occur either rarely or never." When principals were asked about confrontations between administrators and teachers, again over 95 percent reported "rarely or never." The comparable figures for public school principals are 85 percent and 81 percent, respectively.

20. For an early treatment of this topic, see Cohen (1982).

21. Teacher demographics support this prediction. In the NCEA (1986) study sample, for example, over 80 percent of the lay teachers were under 45 years of age, while less than half of the religious were in this age group. NCEA (1986), 245.

22. For a further discussion of the idea of beliefs and values as a control mechanism in education, see Weiss (1990). In brief, she argues that, although this mechanism is hard to manipulate and takes considerable time to work its course, the ultimate effect is likely to be persuasive and deep.

23. Novak (1974).

7. The Transition to High School

1. NCEA (1985) reports a small percentage of Catholic secondary schools that contain students in grades 1 to 12 (4 percent), and others who enroll students in Grades 7 or 8 to 12 (10 percent). Eighty-five percent are grade 9–12 institutions.

2. In 1980–81, the average tuition and fees paid by parents of students in Catholic elementary schools was $259 (NCEA 1982). Tuition income covers approximately 40 percent of the total cost, and the remainder is derived largely from parish and religious-order subsidies. The comparable figure for Catholic secondary schools for that year, from *HS&B* data, is $850. At the secondary level, tuition represents about 65 percent of total school costs (NCEA, 1985, 102).

3. Caterall (1988).

4. A limitation of this investigation should be noted. In these analyses, we have ignored those students who might transfer from sector to sector more than once. We have investigated the numbers of multiple between-sector transfer students, as explained in the note to Table 7.1. Of the sample of students who end up in public high school, less than 1 percent have transferred more than twice. For their counterparts in Catholic high schools, the percentages are slightly higher. 1.6 percent transferred more than twice. For both sectors, these percentages of students are relatively low, which is why we have ignored multiple transfers as a separate group. Small sample sizes limit separate analysis of this multiple-transfer group.

A further note about the statistics reported in this chapter is in order. The data base consists of students enrolled in public and Catholic high schools who have stayed in school through the end of the twelfth grade. The transition estimates are based on retrospective reports of their educational histories. As a result, the transition probabilities may differ from those that we might estimate if we had a true random sample of children followed longitudinally. Most notably, the educational histories of school dropouts are not included here. For the descriptive purposes of this chapter, however, we do not believe that the biases introduced, if any, are likely to affect materially the basic conclusions.

5. Our original analytic sample included all Catholic school students fitting the criteria described in Chapter 2, and an 11 percent sample of public schools fitting the same criteria. In order to estimate transition probabilities generalizable to the high school population of Catholic and public school students in the United States, a different weighting factor was used for the two school sectors, when combined into a single sample. For the Catholic schools students, the panel weight supplied by *HS&B* in the first follow-up data was used. For the public school sample, the weighting factor was calculated in several steps:

- a. Percentage of total public school sample (25,875) that was in the same school two years later (22,436) is 86.71 percent;
- b. Public school sample with full test data (21,279) that was also in the same school: $21,279 \times .8671 = 18,451$;
- c. Proportion of this total that was in our public school sample of 1,883: $1,883/18,451 = 0.102054$. We can consider 0.102054 our sampling probability for public school students.
- d. Weighting factor for public school sample = panel weight/0.102054.

6. Recall that these students from non-Catholic private schools are excluded from consideration in these analyses. At no grade level does the excluded group exceed 5 percent of the in-school elementary or secondary population.

7. Our sample for these analyses, drawn from *HS&B*, includes only those students who were in the same high schools in both their sophomore and their senior years.

Students who transfer or drop out of high school after sophomore year are not included in this sample.

8. The discriminant analysis was run to answer the question: Which background characteristics of those students whose entire elementary school experience was in the Catholic sector are associated with the choice of high school sector, Catholic or public? Only a single significant discriminant function emerged.

Variable	Loadings on function
Parental education	−.49
Parental occupation	−.27
Non-Catholic	.31
Family size	.34
Home ownership	−.29
College plans, gr. 8	−.45
Repeated elem. grade	−.25
Family discretionary income	−.47

(Variables in analysis that did not enter for function: single-parent family, female, black, Hispanic, religiousness.)

	How function loaded on grouping variable
Public high school choice	.57
Catholic high school choice	−.33

9. The variable for discretionary income is constructed as follows. Based on 1980 poverty statistics, family income is rescaled in two steps: (1) a subsistence level is first subtracted ($3,400); then (2) the total number of family members (parents plus children) is multiplied (by $1,100) and subtracted. The mean discretionary income variable for Catholic families in this sample is $16,259, which is about half of the gross family income figure.

10. From *HS&B*, the average family income for students in public high schools in 1982 (the same year for which the figures in Table 7.4 are computed) was $27,851.

11. This discriminant analysis was meant to answer the question: Which types of students select which types of Catholic high schools? The characterization of the five types of schools has been described above and in Table 7.5. Two significant discriminant functions emerged from the analysis.

Variable	Loadings on function 1	Loadings on function 2
Social class	.73	−.11
Black	.19	−.34
Religiousness	.28	.45
Catholic elem. experience	−.36	.22
Public elem. experience	.40	−.31
Parent engagement (student)	−.15	.20
Parent involvement (school)	.20	.25

Variable	Loadings on function 1	Loadings on function 2
Single-parent family	.03	−.44
Family size	.02	.35
Home ownership	.25	.33

(Variables in analysis that did not enter for either function: academic background, financial sacrifice, Hispanic, and non-Catholic.)

	How functions loaded on grouping variable	
	Function 1	Function 2
Type of School		
Boys' religious order	.34	−.40
Boys' diocesan	.14	−.26
Girls' religious order	.10	−.05
Girls' diocesan	−.89	−.24
Coeducational	.01	.17

12. These analyses use logistic regression methods, where the school-level outcome variable is divided into thirds and merged with student-level predictors. The analysis estimates the probability of being in the top versus the bottom third of the distribution for each student background characteristic, controlling for all other background characteristics included in the analysis.

8. Variations in Internal Operations

1. For a discussion of the two-stage model of how school resources can affect student achievement, see Murnane (1981). We also acknowledge helpful discussions with Richard Murnane on the conceptualization of this argument.

2. In this chapter, we present the final results from a large number of regression analyses. The basic process model and reporting format was developed from many smaller analyses, where we worked with a few variables and clusters at a time. These data explorations involved literally hundreds, perhaps more than a thousand, computer runs. Although formally this is a hierarchical linear modeling problem (that is, with predictors at both the student and the school level), it was not feasible at the time this work was done (in the mid-1980s) to use these techniques. Usable software was not yet available, and the necessary data analytic experience had yet to accumulate. Presently these methods and software are well established; see, for example, Bryk and Raudenbush 1992.

Given the nature of the models investigated here, which combine an extensive list of student- and school-level predictors, and the exploratory purposes of this chapter, we believe that the use of multiple regression is justified. The most likely analytic problem is that the reported standard errors are too small and the significance tests too liberal. Because we are not formally testing any hypotheses in this chapter and focus principally on identifying sturdy statistical relations in the data, these problems are not especially important in this instance. In Chapters 10 and 11, however, where we do test the central claims of this book about the effects of academic structure and communal organization, we employ the more appropriate hierarchical techniques.

3. Some student outcomes (for example, achievement test scores) are well measured in quantitative studies such as *HS&B;* others (for example, attitudes toward students who get good grades, or self-concept) are less well measured by survey methods. The relative reliability of variables, unfortunately, confounds aspects of precision of measurement with substantive interpretation of comparative strengths of relationships. These unavoidable statistical difficulties complicate any such study and are especially complicating when examining multiple outcomes.

4. In this instance, data on a larger set of schools and a hierarchical linear model analysis would provide a better basis for addressing these concerns.

5. That students who participate in sports simultaneously evidence lower achievement but higher aspirations is probably related to the attraction of college sports and possibly its attendant scholarship support.

6. The women's role measure is a composite factor based on the degree of students' agreement with the following statements: (a) working mothers of preschool children can still be good mothers (reverse coded); (b) men should work while women care for the home and family; and (c) women are happiest making a home and caring for children. Each item was rated on a 4-point scale assessing the degree of respondents' agreement with each statement. The variable is a sum across the three items, with higher values indicating more stereotyping attitudes.

7. Rodriguez (1982) spells out this phenomenon more generally, but also in relation to his own experiences in Catholic elementary and secondary schools. For a recent ethnographic account of the personal dilemmas experienced by disadvantaged youth in middle-class Catholic schools, see O'Keefe (1991).

8. Bryk et al. (1984), 69–70.

9. See Bryk, Lee, and Smith (1990). The research on size suggests that the positive benefits of larger size on economies of scale are more than offset by the more bureaucratic and formal social interactions that ensue. In addition, larger public high schools are more socially stratifying in terms of student academic pursuits and outcomes.

9. Single-Sex versus Coeducational Schools

1. For a further discussion of this point, see Tyack and Hansot (1988).

2. Pius XI, "Christian Education of Youth," 26–27. Cited in Buetow (1970), 261.

3. Fison (1959). Cited in Buetow (1970), 262.

4. These data are taken from NCEA (1985). The data were collected in 1983 from the principals of all of the nation's Catholic high schools.

5. Personal communication with Fred Brigham, based on an internal NCEA tabulation, July 28, 1988.

6. Bryk et al. (1984), 46. Also cited in NCEA (1985), 154–155.

7. This change has been best documented at the level of higher education, but the phenomenon has taken place within Catholic and independent secondary schools as well. See Hyde (1971); Astin (1977a, 1975b); Block (1984); and NCEA (1985), 152.

8. Astin (1977a).

9. Graham (1970, 1974); Tidball and Kistiakowsky (1976); Oates and Williamson (1978); Block (1984).

10. Graham (1974), 5.

11. Dale's three-volume work (1969, 1971, 1974) investigates pupil-teacher relationships, social aspects, and attainment and attitudes within single-sex and coeducational schools in the United Kingdom. Feather (1974) studied schools in Australia, and Finn (1980) compared U.S. and British schools of 1970. Jones, Shallcross, and Dennis (1972) compared schools in New Zealand. Schneider and Coutts (1982) investigated this issue in Canadian Catholic schools.

12. Dale (1969, 1971); Jones, Shallcross, and Dennis (1972); Feather (1974); Schneider and Coutts (1982).

13. Jones, Shallcross, and Dennis (1972) and Trickett et al. (1982) support the more academic environment of girls' schools. Dale (1969, 1971) and Feather (1974), however, found no relationship between single-six schooling and academic orientation.

14. Coleman, Hoffer, and Kilgore (1982) stress this point.

15. See Winchel, Fenner, and Shaver (1974); Lockheed (1976) and Trickett et al. (1982).

16. Two older British studies (Dale, 1971, 1974) offered mixed results. Since the initiation of our research, several more recent reports on this topic have appeared. Two studies in developing countries have shown results that favor single-sex education for girls and coeducation for boys (Jiminez and Lockheed, 1989; Lee and Lockheed, 1990). For recent U.S. domestic research, see Riordan (1990). Riordan (1990), along with Lee and Bryk (1986) and Lee and Marks (1991), constitute the major evidence on the effects of single-sex schooling in the United States. For a critique of this evidence, see Marsh (1989) and a rejoinder by Lee and Bryk (1989).

17. We have excluded from the analysis 8 of the 83 Catholic high schools on the *HS& B* file—those which enroll more than 25 percent vocational track students. Of the excluded group, 5 are girls' schools, 3 are coeducational schools, and no boys' schools are excluded. Of the schools which remain in the sample, the average vocational enrollment is 6 percent.

18. For a discussion of the statistical details of this problem, see Anderson et al. (1980).

19. Specifically, we regressed each outcome variable against a model consisting of a dummy variable for single-sex versus coed schools, the list of personal, family and academic and background variables from Table 9.1, two dummy variables for academic and general track membership, and three measures of school social context (average social class, percentage of black students, and percentage of Hispanic students). For the change analyses, we introduced sophomore status as another covariate in addition to the background, track, and school composition measures.

The use of controls for school social context is based on findings from previous research using *HS&B*, which has shown that school social context is an important predictor of academic achievement above and beyond the effects of student-level social demographic characteristics. In research on private school effects, the inclusion of social context variables has resulted in substantially different effect estimates. See Hoffer, Greeley, and Coleman (1985) and Willms (1985).

20. There is a third standard, frequently used in interpreting effective sizes, that is based on the normal probability distribution. By this standard, an effect size of 0.20 means that the probability of the score of a randomly chosen student from a single-sex school exceeding the score of a randomly chosen counterpart from a coed school is approximately 0.54. From this point of view, the statistically significant results reported here might appear small.

The use of this standard for research on high schools can be very misleading, however, for reasons detailed by Jencks (1985). In brief, a great deal of learning has occurred by sophomore year in high school. As a result, student performance is extraordinarily variable and comparing an estimated school effect against this standard will produce an artifactually small estimate.

21. Hoffer, Greeley, and Coleman (1985) show that a standardized effect size of 0.10 on the gain from sophomore to senior year on one of the *HS&B* academic achievement measures is equivalent to the amount of learning demonstrated by the average public school student during one full year of secondary school instruction.

22. The typical procedures for estimating variance components in nested models produce biased estimates when the data are unbalanced, as in the *HS&B* sample employed in this investigation. As an alternative, we used a procedure known as restricted maximum likelihood estimation, which allows us to compute the between-school variance component in the presence of unbalanced nested data. The latter provides a consistent estimate of the variance between schools under the assumption that the outcome variables are normally distributed. Our analytic model treated schools as a random factor and adjusted for the same set of student-level covariates (specified as fixed factors) that were employed in estimating the effects in Tables 9.2–9.4. This is an example of a random intercept model in a hierarchical linear model analysis. For further discussion, see Bryk and Raudenbush (1992).

Here we estimated the between-school variance for each outcome. We then computed new effect size estimates for each dependent measure, where the standard deviation between schools rather than between students is used as the denominator in the effect size calculation.

23. Single-sex schools are much more likely to be sponsored by religious orders. For girls' schools, it is impossible to separate a single-sex organization effect from a religious order governance effect, because these two variables are almost totally confounded in that instance. The data on boys' schools, however, is sufficient to sustain further analysis. In particular, we recomputed the boys' school effects reported in Tables 9.2–9.4 under an analytic model that adjusted for that factor. That is, we added a control variable that distinguished boys' schools operated by religious orders from those run by other organizations, such as parishes and dioceses. The boys' school effects remained virtually unchanged. Although we cannot totally discount the possibility of a governance effect, we have no evidence that particularly favors this alternative explanation.

24. Using the same analytic sample, the average of student ratings of their schools is presented for the three types of schools:

	Boys' schools	Coed schools	Girls' schools
Perceived quality of teaching	0.73	−0.13	0.53
General school rating	0.29	−0.12	0.14

The "perceived quality of teaching" variable is an aggregate of two student-level factors: (1) student perceptions of the quality of instruction; and (2) the students' reports about the proportion of their instructors who have certain desirable characteristics (e.g., are patient, present materials clearly, treat students fairly, return graded work promptly.) Variables are standardized (mean = 0, s.d. = 1) around the Catholic school mean. The "general school rating" variable is an aggregate of a student-level factor created from students' ratings of various aspects of their schools (e.g., condition of buildings, library facilities, the school's reputation in the community, fairness and effectiveness of discipline, faculty interest in students).

25. See Lee and Bryk (1986) for a more extended discussion of possible alternative school-level explanations for the effects shown in this chapter.

26. Lee and Marks (1990) used *HS&B* data to follow these same students beyond high school. In particular, they examined the effects of attending a single-sex high school (again, separately for males and females) on attitudes and behaviors in college. Because 85 percent of the sample attended college, the decision to go to college was not considered as an outcome. Less than 20 percent of the sample attended Catholic colleges, and very few (about 9 percent for women, 2 percent for men) attended single-sex colleges. Students who attended single-sex high schools were neither more nor less likely to select a single-sex college.

27. The decision that some schools have made to change from single-sex to coeducational organization was not made simply to improve the social environment. Such decisions are always multifaceted, usually involving questions of enrollment, scale, and cost. The assumption that today's adolescents are somehow more content in the presence of the opposite sex and that they will therefore desire to attend coeducational schools is quite prevalent among school personnel. The issue we address here is that decisions favoring coeducation may be made at some cost, and the cost may be in the important area of academics. Academic considerations (and costs) should be a factor in this important decision that educators face more and more frequently.

10. The Impact of Academic Organization

1. Murnane (1975) describes the stronger influence of school than home on math learning. Heyns and Hilton (1982) have computed the reliabilities for all 1980 *HS&B* achievement tests, and find those in math to be the highest. On the basis of our field studies, we believe that the results reported here generalize to other subject matter areas. Unfortunately, the *HS&B* data are not adequate to investigate such phenomena.

2. For the purposes of this comparison, lower middle class is defined as −1 s.d. (one standard deviation below the mean) on the student social class measure. Upper middle class is defined as +1 s.d.

3. For these analyses, the construct of academic background has been operationalized as the sum of two *HS&B* variables: (1) whether the student had ambitions to attend college when he or she was in the eighth grade (0 = no; 1 = yes); and (2) whether or not the student repeated an elementary grade (0 = yes; 1 = no). Both of these variables were previously found to be strongly related to both social class and achievement.

4. For use in regression, the categorical "track" variable must be dummy coded, even though students are distributed in three curriculum tracks. We have created only a single dummy variable—academic versus nonacademic track—because the comparatively small proportion of Catholic students (10 percent) in the vocational track argues against specific examination of general versus vocational track effects.

5. We have included in our variable definition only those courses beyond Algebra I, which is most frequently taken in the freshman year.

6. See Lee and Bryk (1988), 78–94, for a more detailed explanation of the path analyses presented here.

7. For a general review of the methodological problems associated with multilevel analysis, see Burstein (1978; 1980). Raudenbush and Bryk (1988) provide a general review of recent developments in hierarchical linear models and discuss how these techniques largely resolve the problems of multilevel analysis. For a general text on using these methods in organizational research, see Bryk and Raudenbush (1992).

8. Additional details about variables used in this analysis are provided below. See also Lee and Bryk (1989).

Student-Level Dependent Variable

Math achievement	Senior-year IRT math score, measured in either 1980 or 1982. Unweighted mean = 12.221, standard deviation = 6.976.

Student-Level Predictors

Academic background	A factor composite of *HS&B* variables that indicate if the respondent has taken remedial math and/or English (BB011A or BB011B), expected to attend college in eighth grade (BB068A), has been read to before starting school (BB095), and has ever repeated a grade (FY59).
Minority	A dummy variable (1 = black or Hispanic; 0 = others).
Social class	The *HS&B* standardized composite.

School-Level Predictors

I. The Social and Academic Composition of Schools

Sector	An effects-coded dichotomous variable, coded 1 for Catholic schools, −1 for public schools.
Average academic background	School average of the student-level variable.
School SES	Average SES of students within the school.
Minority concentration	An effects-coded dichotomous variable, coded 1 if enrollment in excess of 40% minority (black and/or Hispanic), −1 otherwise.
School size	Total enrollment of the school, reported by the principal (SB002A).

II. Perceived Teacher Quality and Interest in Students

Teacher interest in students	School average of students' rating of their teachers interest in them (FY69J).
Staff problems	A composite of two principals' reports about staff absenteeism and lack of commitment and motivation (SB056E, SB056F).
Perceived quality of teaching	A factor composite of student report about the percentage of teachers who enjoy their work, make clear presentations, work students hard, treat students with respect, are witty and humorous, don't talk over students' heads, are patient and understanding, return work properly, and are interested in students outside of class (school average of FY68 series).

III. Discipline Climate of School

Disciplinary incidence	A composite index based on: (i) a factor score from students' reports about the incidence of students talking back to teachers,

refusal to obey instructions, attacks on teachers and fights with each other (school level averages from the YB019 series); and (ii) the school average of student reports about their own discipline problems in school, suspension, probation, and cutting class (school average of variables from the BB059 series).

Feeling of safety	Percentage of students who feel safe in the school environment (school average of dummy coded BB059F).
Fair and effective discipline	Students' ratings of the fairness and effectiveness of discipline within the school (FY67F and FY67H, averaged to the school level).

IV. Academic Climate of the School

Average homework	Hours per week students spend on homework (school average of BB015, recoded to hours/week).
Academic emphasis	Students' reports about lack of academic emphasis in the school (school average EB035A).
Academic attitudes	Factor composite based on student attitudes toward getting good grades (YB052AA and YB052AB) and interest in academics (BB008 series), averaged to the school level.

V. Academic Organization

Proportion in academic track	Percentage of students in the academic program (from BB002).
Average math courses	Average number of advanced mathematics courses taken by students (a school measure of the emphasis on academic coursework, from FY5A–FY5E).
Diversity in math courses	Standard deviation in the number of advanced mathematics courses taken by students (a school measure of differentiation in academic coursework from the FY5A–E series).

9. Twenty-two schools contain no information about the minority gap, because there is no variation within these schools in students' race/ethnicity. Although this poses a problem for ordinary regression analyses conducted separately within each school, it does not create a problem for the HLM analysis. The HLM methodology uses whatever information is available in each school to estimate its effects (Bryk and Raudenbush 1992).

10. All hierarchical linear model analyses were weighted at the school level using the *HS&B* school weight. Because students in *HS&B* were selected with equal probability within each school, no student-level weights were needed. The results reported here generalize to U.S. public and Catholic high schools.

11. As noted earlier, the "years of learning" metric was introduced by Hoffer, Greeley, and Coleman (1985) to lend substantive interpretability to estimated raw effect sizes in the *HS&B* data. Its ease of interpretation makes it highly attractive for descriptive purposes, as is the case. We caution, however, against a strict literal interpretation of these results, particularly as we consider more extreme cases. The predicted learning from a year of high school, 0.625 points, is rather small in part because it is based on observed gains between sophomore year and senior year, when a significant number of public school students have stopped taking math courses. Although some math learning can

occur through other courses, such as science, the amount is certainly reduced compared with earlier years in high school.

12. The equations used to develop the line graphs in Figure 10.6–10.8 are based on the hierarchical linear model results from the compositional effects model described in this section. The predicted intercepts are based on the level-2 model for "average achievement," and the predicted slopes are based on the level-2 model for "social class differentiation" (that is, the slope of math achievement on SES within schools). Specifically, the predicted intercepts use the HLM estimates for school social class, sector, and the school social class by sector interaction effects in the model for average achievement. The predicted slopes are based on the comparable estimates for the SES slope model. Values of (1 and −1) were substituted for sector (Catholic and public respectively). Values of (0, −0.34, and −0.68) were substituted for school social class (the Catholic sector average, the public sector average, and "disadvantaged schools" respectively). All other variables were assumed to take on constant predictor values of zero for purposes of generating these comparisons.

13. To build the explanatory model, we began with the reduced context effects model described in the previous section. Each of the four remaining categories of variables was considered separately in predicting each social distribution parameter. Effects with *t*-statistics less than 1.5 were dropped, and a composite model was estimated, based on the remaining variables from each category.

14. The possibility of a selection artifact confounding these HLM results is discussed in some detail in Lee and Bryk (1989). In brief, it would be difficult to account for the observed findings for several reasons. First, the mechanism required to introduce confounding into the model for mean achievement differences is different from the factors that bias estimation of the slope model. Thus the mechanism by which the selectivity hypothesis might work in this case would have to be rather complex. Second, the final model includes several specific school organization variables, even though a number of aggregate student composition variables were considered for inclusion but failed to achieve significance. If student selectivity were the main explanation, we would have expected stronger compositional effects. Third, somewhat different factors are at work in the choice process between public and Catholic schools and in the choice process among schools within the two sectors. A model tapping selection artifacts to explain between-sector difference is unlikely to account equally well for variability among schools within each sector. Yet the final model does. We therefore conclude that the overall pattern of results from these analyses, taken in conjunction with the path analysis results, tilts in the direction of a school organization explanation.

11. The Impact of Communal Organization

1. This argument is reviewed in McDill, Natriello, and Pallas (1986).

2. Coleman and Hoffer (1987).

3. These figures do not include students who transferred to different schools within or between sectors. According to Coleman and Hoffer (1987, 106), although approximately equal numbers of students transfer sector between sophomore and senior year (about 18,000 students), the transfer *rates* of students moving from Catholic to public schools during this period are higher (8.1 percent) than the reverse (0.5 percent of public school students transfer to Catholic schools). It is possible that such transfers could be viewed

as a type of dropping out (of sector, not of high school). We have some research evidence that Catholic school students who transfer to public school after tenth grade share some of the "at risk" characteristics of public school students who drop out. It is possible that the availability of the option of a Catholic-public transfer at this point actually allows at-risk students to stay in school. Such a hypothesis leads to a conclusion that the Catholic school drop-out rate reported by Coleman and Hoffer was somewhat too small. For an expansion of the argument, see Lee and Burkam (1992).

4. The "low" and "high" social class designations include the lower and upper thirds of the social class distribution for the entire population, and are defined identically for both sectors.

5. Additional and more elaborate analyses of the social distribution of dropping out in Catholic and public schools are reported in Bryk and Thum (1989). Their results confirm and extend the basic patterns reported by Coleman and Hoffer (1987) that Catholic schools are also effective in retaining disadvantaged students in school.

6. For descriptions of the generally "flat" teaching in public high school classrooms, see Boyer (1983); Goodlad (1984); and Powell, Farrar, and Cohen (1985).

7. See, for example, Rutter et al. (1979) or Lightfoot (1983). Grant (1988) also alludes to this notion.

8. The conceptualization of the school as a small society was first laid out by Waller (1932) and is reviewed by Bidwell (1965).

9. Although many of the observations included in Chapter 5 were dispersed through-out Bryk et al. (1984), there was no section entitled "communal organization." In earlier drafts of this book, Chapter 5 was called the "Culture of Catholic High Schools." Only toward the end of our research did we come to believe that we were actually describing a distinct organizational form with its own norms and structure.

10. Dan Lortie (1975) has argued that it is intrinsic rather than extrinsic rewards (for example, salaries) that motivate teachers, a finding that is strongly supported by Rosen-holtz (1989).

11. For empirical evidence supporting this conclusion, see Bryk and Driscoll (1988) and Driscoll (1989).

12. One limitation of the measure developed in this chapter is that it does not include any information about the presence and importance of rituals in school life. As discussed in Chapter 5, a great deal of attention is paid to religious services and retreat programs in Catholic schools. Rituals are not limited by any means, however, to private schools. Experiences such as an Outward Bound program can serve a similar cohering function for schools. Ethnic activities in individual schools, such as a black history month, can be equally salient. Unfortunately, the *ATS* data base provides no information on school rituals, and thus we had no choice but to exclude this component from the index.

13. An extensive amount of background research and analytic work underpins the formal definition of a communal school organization adopted in this chapter and initially detailed in Bryk and Driscoll (1988) and extended in Driscoll (1989). In brief, the construct evolved out of three interrelated lines of work. First, a close reading of field accounts of schools with a "sense of community" led to a search for organizational features common to these institutions. Second, we examined the work of public philosophers such as Hannah Arendt, Alisdair MacIntyre, Hans-Georg Gadamer, Michael Sandel, William Sullivan, Richard Rorty, and especially Richard Bernstein about the role of communities in the creation of human meaning. Also significant were the writings of John Dewey

on the social dimensions of schooling—particularly the roles played by adult values, organizational structure, and the social routines of daily life—in addition to pedagogy and curriculum. Third, we reviewed the sociological literature on communities, especially work by Tonnies (1955) and Weber (1973), and on the context of schooling by Waller (1932) and Bidwell (1965).

14. Given the rather loose entry and exit controls over students and faculty in Catholic schools, we have not included these boundary-setting conditions as a core element in the communal organization construct. Moreover, we wanted an explicit definition of communal organization that might be equally valid in not only private but also public schools, where such controls are typically weaker. To check on possible selectivity biases, however, we introduced specific statistical controls for student and teacher characteristics in the analyses presented in this chapter.

15. Bellah et al. (1985).

16. Noddings (1988).

17. Bellah et al. (1985).

18. The Community Index consisted of twenty-three separate measures of various facets of communal school organization. In order to combine logically the twenty-three measures into a single composite measure, various statistical manipulations were required. First, each indicator was scaled so that a positive score was theoretically consistent with a communally organized school. In several cases this required reversing the natural metric. For example, all of the similarity measures used in COMINDEX were originally constructed as diversity measures, sample variances computed separately for each school based on individual responses from within the school. Because we hypothesize that low diversity is characteristic of communal organization, we transformed the final scores into similarity measures by multiplying by (-1). In this transformed metric, a high score reflects communal organization.

Second, because the community indicators involved different kinds of statistics (for example, school variances, proportions, and correlations), these measures were subject to normalizing and standardizing transformations in order to place them on a common metric. For school percentages and proportions, the normalizing transformation is the log odds ratio. Correlation measures were subject to a Fisher Z transformation, and the natural log was taken for school variance measures. Finally, each indicator was then standardized to a mean of zero and a variance of 1 to place them on a common scale. Extreme standardized values, in excess of $+/-3.0$, were trimmed to $+/-3.0$, respectively, in order to ensure that an outlier response on one measure did not exert undue influence on the overall index.

The final composite measure, COMINDEX, is the school average across the twenty-three separate indicators of communal organization. If data were missing on an indicator for a particular school, that indicator was ignored in the averaging that produced a COMINDEX score for that school. Details of each individual indicator are summarized below.

> IA1. *Teacher agreement on school goals. ATS* items T07A–H, in which teachers were asked to rank order eight school goals. The measure is a Kendall's coefficient of concordance computed separately for all teacher responses within a school. The normalizing transformation applied was a Fisher Z.
>
> IA2. *Reported teacher consensus on beliefs and values. ATS* items TI9E, TI9M,

in which teachers reported on colleagues' shared beliefs and clarity of school goals. The measure is the mean of the two items aggregated across teachers to the school level.

IB1. *Teacher beliefs that students can learn.* ATS item TI9L. School mean of teachers' responses to a single item, "Many of the students I teach are not capable of learning the material I am supposed to teach them." The response scale was reversed on this item so that positive values imply a more communal organization.

IB2. *Teacher/administration agreement that students can learn.* The squared difference between measure IB1 and the principals' response to the identical question (*ATS* item P35U). The scale on P35U was reversed for consistency and the natural log applied to the squared difference as a normalizing transformation.

IC1. *Teachers and administration agree on standards of discipline.* A factor composite of three teacher items for *ATS* (TI9aa, TI9bb, and T30), aggregated to the school level. These items ask about the uniformity in schoolwide standards of behavior and discipline and whether teachers and administrators were in close agreement on such matters.

IC2. *Student consensus about teachers' role.* A measure of consensus among students within each school about their definition of a good teacher. It is based on *HS&B* items FY68A–J, which ask students to note the importance of such characteristics as clear presentations, making students work hard, being patient, and treating students with respect. A sum of squared deviations was computed for each item for each school, and then aggregated across items to create a lack of consensus measure for each school. A natural log transformation was applied to the sum of squares and the sign reversed in order to create a consensus measure.

IIA1. *Track commonality.* Based on student reports in *HS&B* of their track placement in senior year (FY2). The proportion of students in the academic (p1), vocational (p2), and general tracks (p3) were computed for each school. A diversity measure was calculated for each school based on $p1(1-p1) + p2(1-p2) + p3(1-p3)$. This was normalized through a natural log transformation and the sign reversed to create a commonality measure.

IIA2. *Course-taking commonality.* From *HS&B* items FY4A–L, we computed the number of courses taken by each student in language, business, English, history, math, and science. A sum of squared deviates was computed for each subject-matter area for each school, and then aggregated across subject-matter areas to create a course-taking diversity measure for each school. A natural log transformation was applied and the sign reversed to convert to a commonality measure.

IIA3. *Commonality in math/science course-taking.* From *HS&B* items FY5A–H, a count of advanced math and science courses taken (by title, e.g., Physics, Chemistry, Trigonometry, and Calculus) was computed for each student. Based on this, a commonality measure was computed as in IIA2.

IIA4. *Teacher knowledge of students (class-based).* Based on the Teacher Comment File question 3 in *HS&B*, which reports on the proportion of teachers responding that have had a particular student in their class. A log odds ratio was computed for each student and averaged across students to create a school measure.

IIB1. *Percentage of students involved in extracurricular activities.* Based on *HS&B* items FY38A–K, which asked students about their participation in a wide range of possible after-school activities. A school percentage for participation was computed and a log odds transformation applied to normalize the measure. Note, for all proportion-based measures, as in IIA4 and IIB1, the proportion was constrained to the range of $.03 \leq p \leq .97$ to minimize the creation of extreme values on any single indicator.

IIB2. *Percentage of students in leadership roles.* Also used *HS&B* items FY38A–K, but focused only on students responding "3" ("have participated in a leadership role") to these items. The measure was created using the same procedure as described in IIB1.

IIIA1. *Percentage of teachers who obtain help from colleagues.* Based on *ATS* item T03D, which asked teachers about the extent to which their colleagues help them with instructional problems. The proportion of teachers in each school offering a positive response was computed and a log odds transformation applied.

IIIA2. *Teacher cooperation with colleagues.* A factor composite based on *ATS* items T19DD, TI9KK, TI9V, TI9C, which asked teachers about the level of cooperation, respect, coordination, and collegiality within the faculty. The measure is a school mean.

IIIA3. *Teacher time planning with other teachers.* A school mean based on *ATS* item T13, which asked teachers about the amount of time spent meeting with other teachers on a range of instructional concerns.

IIIA4. *Staff commitment to evaluation.* A school measure based on a principal's report, *ATS* item P35B, about the focusing of staff efforts to evaluate programs and activities.

IIIB1. *Participation in faculty social events.* A school mean based on *ATS* item T12, which asked teachers how often they participated with colleagues in school socials such as pot-luck lunches, parties, and group events.

IIIB2. *Perception of staff support.* A composite of teachers' and principals' perspectives based on *ATS* teacher item TI9GG (this school seems like a big family) and principal item P35L (staff members support and encourage one another). A school mean was computed for TI9GG and this in turn was averaged with P35L.

IIIC1. *Teacher time in extended roles.* Based on *ATS* items T21A, F, G, H, I, and J, which asked teachers about the amount of time spent in such activities as conducting make-up work for students, counseling, coaching, and participation with students in outside-of-class events. The measure consists of the school mean for the total amount of teacher time spent on these activities.

IIIC2. *Percentage of teachers involved in extracurriculars.* Based on *ATS* items T21H and I, in which teachers reported their responsibilities, if any, for coaching sports and directing extracurricular activities. The measure is based on the percentage of teachers indicating a positive response to the items, converted into a log odds ratio.

IIIC3. *Teacher knowledge of students (beyond class).* Based on questions 1 and 3 in

the Teacher Comment File of *HS&B*. Question 1 reports on the proportion of teachers who know a student and question 3 on the proportion
of teachers who have had a target student in their class. A separate measure was constructed for questions 1 and 3 using the procedure outlined
in IIA4. The indicator is based on differences between the question 1
and 3 measures.

IIIC4. *Teacher contact with students outside of class.* Based on Teacher Comment
File question 7 in *HS&B*, which provided information about the proportion of teachers that have talked with a particular student outside of
class. The measure was created using the procedure outlined in IIA4.

IIIC5. *Student perception of teacher interest.* A factor composite based on *HS&B*
student items FY62D, FY67E, FY69H, and FY69J, which asked stu-
dents about their teachers' influence with regard to post–high school
plans, their teachers' interest in them, and personal motives for teaching.
The measure is a school mean of the individual student factor scores.

For further technical details and psychometric properties of each measure, as well as the
overall index, see Driscoll (1989).

19. Complete details of construction of the variable COMINDEX are provided
by Bryk and Driscoll (1988). Correlations between the individual components and
COMINDEX range between .22 and .63, with an average correlation of .45. The
coefficient of generalizability for the variable, which is a measure of reliability, is .81.
Thus the overall measure is quite reliable. Analyses reported by Driscoll (1989) affirm
the hypothesized structure of the three major components (shared values, shared activities,
and social relations) and provide further empirical support for forming the aggregate
measure.

20. See Moles (1988), for a full description of the *ATS* study. The sample employed
here is identical to the sample used for the analyses in the Bryk and Driscoll (1988) paper,
except that 17 non-Catholic private schools were dropped. Criteria for including or
dropping schools, also detailed there, meant that *ATS*-sample schools with a high degree
of faculty turnover, and with a large amount of change in the disciplinary and educational
climate between 1982 and 1984, or schools with very small numbers of teachers in the
sample, were not included.

21. As in the final analyses in Chapter 10, which investigated the social distribution
of achievement, we employ hierarchical linear modeling in this multivariate analyses.
However, unlike the HLM analyses in Chapter 10, we have restricted our investigations
here to adjusted mean differences between schools in the various measures of commitment
and engagement. The relatively small within-school sample sizes in the *ATS* (approximately 25 teachers per school) means that these data are not especially powerful for
modeling random slopes in an HLM. Similarly, the student data used in this chapter are
from the sophomore cohort only, with typical school sample sizes of about 30. In contrast,
to increase the power of the analyses conducted in Chapter 10, we combined the
sophomore and senior student cohorts to obtain within-school samples of approximately
60 students.

22. The reason for this may be policy related. In the case of teacher absenteeism,
school policies in Catholic and public schools differ considerably. A paid substitute usually
takes the classes of the absent public school teacher, but substitutes are less common in

Catholic schools. Other faculty usually pitch in to cover for the absent teacher. Because of the burden placed on their co-workers, teachers may think twice before taking a day away from school. Catholic and public schools also differ in the way they handle student absences. When Catholic school students are absent, their parents are typically contacted quite early in the day, if the reason for the absence has not been communicated to school beforehand. Public schools are not nearly so prompt in contacting parents when students do not appear at school on time. A similar argument might be made in terms of cutting class. Unoccupied students are considerably more noticeable in a small Catholic school, where students have very few free periods. In a large public school students have more unscheduled time, which means that groups of students are commonly seen in hallways and lounges. Thus differences in teacher and student absenteeism are more likely to be explained by variation in policy between the sectors rather than by variation in organizational properties.

23. The method used to compute these effects is as follows:

  a. Compute the unstandardized difference on the community index for Catholic and public schools.
  b. Multiply (a) by the HLM coefficient for the community index for each teacher and student outcome, but now based only on the public school data. This product represents how much the public school average on each outcome would change if it had the same score on the community index as the average Catholic school.
  c. Divide (b) by the standard deviation of each outcome pooled within public schools. This transforms the gains computed in (c) to an effect size in standard deviation units.
  d. Convert (c) to a percentile score, using a standard normal table.
  e. Add or subtract (d) from the average percentile score, 50.

24. Coleman (1987) mentions this possibility in his description of value communities.
25. See Peshkin (1986).
26. In addition to the analyses presented here, Driscoll (1989) provides further corroboration on this point. Her analyses introduce additional controls for student selectivity (that is, the degree to which a school can control its student membership); degree of administrative control by the school principal over faculty hirings and dismissals, and degree of parental conflicts with staff. The same basic pattern and magnitude of effects appear as in Table 11.6. Further, they occur for both public and Catholic schools. Her analyses also corroborate our findings that social and ethnic diversity are unrelated to community school formation.
27. This statement is a logical inference on our part rather than a strict statistical inference. That is, we have no direct measure of educational philosophy to relate to teacher and student outcomes. In making this inference, we rely on the intellectual history and field observations detailed in Parts I and II. Driscoll (1989) also lends support to the conclusion. She reports that communal school organization is more prevalent in the Catholic sector even after adjusting for size, social class, student selectivity, administrative control over faculty, parental cooperation, and social and ethnic mix. These results further support our claim that the intentionality of the adults, associated with the distinctive traditions of the schools, deliberately work to create a communal organization that broadly affects both students and faculty.

28. This idea of the school as a microcosm of society is a major theme in the writings of Durkheim (1961, 1956) and Dewey (1966, 1981). Both argue that the society to be modeled should be of some ideal form that would foster a disposition in children to act toward creating such a society. Although much of their writing has been very influential in educational theory, their views about the social character of schooling and the common good have not held sway against the forces of liberal individualism that dominate educational practice in the public sector.

29. Bidwell (1965).

30. Sedlak et al. (1986).

31. Hawley (1976).

32. Dewey (1966).

33. Dewey (1981), p. 238.

34. Gutmann (1987) and Bryk (1988).

35. We note that as tuitions rise, financial aid programs are increasingly common in Catholic high schools. In a 1990 survey (NCEA, 1990b), 87 percent of the schools reported having such a program. On average, 17 percent of the students in these schools receive assistance, and a typical grant covers about 40 percent of tuition costs. In terms of the financial sacrifice variable used in the *HS&B* analyses of Chapters 7 and 8, we do not know how much tuition was actually paid by each family. Rather, the financial sacrifice variable was constructed from information on family income and school tuition. This does not, however, detract from our findings; if anything, it strengthens our interpretations. The financial sacrifice variable indicates the extent to which attending a Catholic high school is highly valued by a student and his or her family. This valuation is easily attached to both winning a scholarship and having to pay the full tuition.

36. We are referring to the positive effects of social class on student attitudes, behavior, and course-taking demonstrated in Chapter 8.

37. As an additional empirical test of this proposition, Lee (1985) reestimated the separate Catholic and public path models presented in Chapter 10, with the addition of the financial sacrifice measure in the Catholic school model. Lee noted that selectivity also exists within the public sector, for example, through residential housing patterns and magnet schools, but is harder to quantify with *HS&B* data. This comparison of effects in these two path analyses thus tilts in the direction of explaining away the Catholic sector effects as a function of family selectivity (that is, financial sacrifice) while acknowledging no selectivity effects whatsoever within the public sector. Even in this more conservative comparison, the same pattern of results as that reported in Chapter 10 was found. Catholic schools encourage a greater intensity of academic work from similar students.

38. For further evidence on this point, see Lee and Bryk (1989), who demonstrate that the model estimated in Chapter 10 explains differences in the social distribution of achievement among schools equally well in both the Catholic and the public sectors.

39. Evidence on this point consists of the reanalyses undertaken for Table 11.7. The effects of communal organization reported here are based on models computed only within the public sector. These results demonstrate that communal organization distinguishes among public schools in terms of the engaging quality of their environments. Corroborating evidence on the effects of communal organization in the public sector can also be found in Driscoll (1989).

40. In defining communal school organization in this chapter, we deliberately excluded entry and exit controls over student and faculty membership as a key element in

this concept. Although, as discussed in Chapter 5, the idea of membership is central to a community and entry and exit controls are related to this, we believe that these controls are better viewed as facilitating conditions for the development and maintenance of a communal school organization than as a necessary component. Several aspects of our analyses support this position. We found among Catholic schools, for example, that although these entry/exit controls were present, they were not used extensively, and were not strong instruments enforcing a likemindedness among students and faculty. We also found in the *HS&B* data examples of ordinary public schools organized as communities with the attendant consequences described in this chapter. For a further discussion of this, see Driscoll (1989).

12. Catholic Lessons for America's Schools

1. The tension between a Catholic emphasis on community and the cultural emphasis on competition and individualism is well described in Lesko (1988). On the difficulties encountered with the education of blacks and Hispanics, see O'Keefe (1991).

2. These two strands of individualism are widespread in American life. For a further discussion of both see Bellah et al. (1985).

3. We emphasize that this account only applies to Catholic high schools. Because the vast majority of Catholic elementary schools are operated by parishes, which in the post-Vatican II period have added some democratic structures such as local school boards and parish councils, a different set of findings might obtain. Even here, however, the substantial discretion afforded pastors can undermine sustained parental participation.

4. The principal example of this is the decentralization of the Chicago public schools through the creation of parent-dominated local school councils with authority to hire and fire the principal and to approve the school budget and school improvement plans. (For further discussion, see Moore, 1990.) Earlier versions of this include community control of the New York public schools, begun in the late 1960s (Levin, 1970). For a more general historical account of democratic localism see Katz (1987).

5. For example, Bryk et al. (1984) reported, on the basis of *HS&B* data, higher annual faculty turnover rates in Catholic (12.4 percent) than in public (7.2 percent) high schools. Moreover, the proportion of public high school teachers on staff for more than ten years (38.3 percent) was more than double that in Catholic high schools (18.4 percent).

6. One exception in this regard is Noddings (1988). More generally, the transformative view of teaching is taken up at length in Jackson (1986). It is also an important theme in the edited volume by Goodlad, Soder, and Sirotnik (1990).

7. For an ethnographic-journalistic account of the "voices of conscience" in one teacher's work see Kidder (1989). More academic treatments of this topic can be found in Hansen (1991) and Bookstrum (1991).

8. Contrasting the traditional and modern concepts of a profession is an important theme in Bellah et al. (1985). MacIntyre (1981) offers a foundational treatment of this topic.

9. By the term objective knowledge we mean those generalizations based on rigorous social scientific research. We are indebted here to ideas expressed in Lindblom and Cohen (1979) and Lindblom (1990) that challenge the authoritative quality of such information and its role in public decision making.

10. Coleman and Hoffer (1987).

11. In addition to the research reported in Chapter 9, Riordan (1985), using NLS72 data, also found positive effects on achievement for Catholic girls' schools. A report on recent field research in progress (Lee and Marks, 1991), however, suggests that this pattern may not be generally characteristic of other non-Catholic schools. Should these findings be sustained by further analyses, they would confirm other evidence that private schools are very diverse, with few generalizations appropriate for the entire set.

12. We are referring here to arguments offered by Chubb and Moe (1990).

13. Since Tocqueville in 1832, many have argued that voluntary association plays a central role in the functioning of American democracy. For purposes large and small, mundane and noble, Americans voluntarily associated to advance shared interests. Such associations are marked by both common sentiments and cooperative activity (Tocqueville, 1969). In choosing the term "voluntary community," we seek to capture both the cooperative ethic characteristic of free association and the deeper and more intimate form of social engagement characteristic of the communal life. This form of social engagement contrasts with the more delimited associative relationships characteristic of the formal organization.

We also deliberately distinguish ourselves from the concept of a functional community articulated by Coleman and Hoffer (1987). In an argument also offered to explain the particular effectiveness of Catholic high schools, they hypothesize that Catholic high schools form functional communities organized around individual parishes that bring parents and students together. Such functional communities promote face-to-face interactions across the generations and produce a form of social capital that facilitates the work of the school. Although this idea has much appeal, Coleman and Hoffer provide no direct empirical evidence that such social relations among schools and families actually characterize modern Catholic high schools. Our field observations do not support their claim. The basic argument, furthermore, is predicated on a false premise—that most Catholic high schools are organized around individual parishes. Although most Catholic elementary schools are parochial schools, this is true of less than 20 percent of all Catholic high schools. The vast majority are either private or diocesan and draw students from highly diverse geographic areas. This geographic separation actually argues against the intergenerational closure speculated by Coleman and Hoffer.

14. See NCEA (1985), 212–213. Although academic difficulties and change of residence are the major reasons for students' voluntary withdrawal from a Catholic high school, student misbehavior is described as the major grounds for expulsion or suspension in their schools.

15. This theme is extensively developed in an essay by Cohen (1988).

16. Coleman (1987) introduced the idea of social capital in the context of describing Catholic high schools as functional communities. His explanation, however, was located outside the school, in the structure of relationships among parents and their children. We agree with Coleman that Catholic high schools benefit from a form of social capital, but we locate that capital in the relations among school professionals and with their parent communities.

17. The role of teachers' beliefs and tacit understandings has become an important theme in research on teaching. See, for example, the review paper by Clark and Peterson (1986).

18. For closely related ideas in the context of intentional communities, see Shenker (1986).

19. Durkheim (1956, 1961) provides the theoretical grounding for the relationship between individuation, collective membership, and anomie. In the context of adolescent development, a foundational analysis is offered by Newmann (1981).

20. For an account of this empathetic understanding as infused with Catholic values, see Coles's (1987) account of Dorothy Day's life in the Catholic Worker movement.

21. The work of the bridging institution is inherently uncertain as staff seek a proper balance amidst competing aims. Not surprisingly, close scrutiny of school practices will raise legitimate questions even from sympathetic critics. See, for example, the study of minority student experiences in two Jesuit high schools by O'Keefe (1991).

22. For a moving autobiographical account in the context of Catholic schooling, see Rodriguez (1982).

23. The idea of an underclass has been developed by Wilson (1987) and subjected to considerable debate and scrutiny in an edited volume by Jencks and Peterson (1991). In brief, Wilson argues that economic and demographic forces reshaped many of our urban centers during the 1970s and created a distinct separate underclass. We are now witnessing a secondary consequence of this phenomenon, as the children of the underclass are increasingly entering the public school system. What was an economic and demographic problem (involving, for example, the movement of jobs and institutions to the suburbs) may now beginning to manifest itself as a cultural issue.

24. Formally this is described as a *permeation* theory of schooling. For further discussion of this in the context of Catholic education, see Martheler (1978).

25. See Cusick and Wheeler (1988).

26. Pincoffs (1986) elaborates the distinction between the minimums required for the maintenance of order in order to sustain the academic programs of the school and the larger set of moral ideals that properly form character education aims.

27. Quotation from Grant (1985), 141. More generally, see Grant (1985, 1988).

28. See, for example, the account of life at Highland Park High School, an affluent suburb of Chicago, in Lightfoot (1983).

29. On the dilemma of modern liberalism and a call to re-engage in a civic discourse about moral aims and a social process of values evaluation, see Lovin (1988). On forming the voices of social conscience, see Green (1985).

30. This is a central theme in the critique of middle-class American life offered by Bellah and his colleagues (1985). In particular, they note that with the gradual disappearance from public discourse of our "second language" (the biblical and republican traditions of America that Bellah in earlier work termed *civil religion*), we are left without a rhetoric with which to account for the personal and social commitments we hold dear. As a result, parents are often unable to convey these beliefs and sentiments to their own children.

31. This definition of religious understanding is developed by Booth (1985), who argues that much secular discussion grapples with issues that were traditionally thought of as religious problems. The arguments employed in these modern discussions cover ground similar to that of traditional religious rhetorics but are somewhat truncated. They are devoid of humility and lack a source of hopefulness, according to Booth. As a result, they tend to have little personal engaging force. Further, "systematic wonder" represents a basic disposition toward learning. As such, no serious effort to educate can be advanced without encountering these issues. In this sense all educational encounters (as distinct from training) involve a religious experience.

32. The arguments on this point are summarized in Bellah et al. (1985). See also Bellah's earlier work on this topic (including 1970, 1974, 1975). On the primacy of developing prudence through moral education, see Green (1988). On the role of public schools in promoting value articulation, see Lovin (1988), and in promoting a civic conscience, see Butts (1988).

33. Much of this appears under the label of rational choice theory, of which a good example is Becker (1981). For the growing influence of this conception, see Coleman (1990). For a forceful economic critique of rational choice theory, see Etzioni (1988) and Wolfe (1989). For a more philosophical treatment, see MacIntyre (1981), Sullivan (1986), and Bowers (1985, 1987).

34. For a sociological account of this, see Levine (1985).

35. See, for example, Tracy (1986).

36. The historical inability of educational policy to make a substantial impact on what teachers actually *do* is well documented by Pauly (1991).

Epilogue: The Future of Catholic High Schools

1. Vitullo-Martin's (1981) analysis showed that inner-city Catholic schools closed at a rate of two to five times higher than did other Catholic schools during the period from 1967 to 1973.

2. An extensive scholarship has developed over the past two decades on the constructive role of religious understandings in American public life. This topic is sometimes referred to as civil religion. See, for example, the collection of essays in Richey and Jones (1974); or Bellah et al. (1985). Another collection is Lovin (1986). The essay by Franklin I. Gamwell, "Religion and Reason in American Politics," directly addresses the founding fathers' purposes for the establishment clause. On this topic, which has provoked heated debate, Gamwell strives to articulate a middle ground between extreme secularist and religionist positions.

3. Draheman argues for an expansion of the interpretation of the Constitution's establishment clause on similar grounds: "The Supreme Court's enforcement of the establishment clause's structure seems ironically unpatriotic because it threatens the religious underpinnings of our national self-esteem . . . Religious and governmental authorities continue to compete to provide order and meaning in Americans' life" (Draheman, 1991, 112).

4. See Greeley (1985).

5. This conception of religious understanding is based on Paul Tillich's claim that religion is the ultimate concern that informs all other activity in one's life. See Tillich (1957). This idea is elaborated by Gamwell (1986) with the notion that religious understanding is a comprehensive ideal for human life. A similar concept is used by Booth (1985) in his analysis of the truncated rhetoric employed in modern science.

6. See Peterson (1990). Peterson argues that large city school bureaucracies act like monopolies that have no need to be responsive to their clients. From this perspective, even if the students now attending urban Catholic schools returned to the public system, their additional "voices" would not be heard. More likely, many of these families would flee to the suburbs, further weakening the political base for urban development.

7. There is an extensive literature on this topic. For example, see Sherman (1983); Boyd (1989); Glenn (1989); and Walford (1989).

8. The form of funding varies by country. In the most liberal option (the Netherlands), the government allows any "responsible authority" (for example, local governments, religious organizations, or other groups espousing a particular worldview) to establish schools, and governing boards are reimbursed for operating costs on a per-pupil basis. In some countries (Belgium, Scotland) the government directly finances all schools, denominational or not. In Canada, policies vary by province, from direct grants to independent schools (Quebec, British Columbia) to a fully dual system including Catholic schools (Ontario). French and English private schools may choose their level of support, which increases according to the degree of control relinquished to the state over such matters as curriculum, testing, and teachers' salaries. English private schools (including the elite "public" schools) may also receive governmental scholarship support for less affluent students who otherwise qualify for admission. German denominational schools receive support from both the central and local governments. See Walford (1989).

9. This aid is now based on the Schools Recurrent Resource Index, which allocates aid according to a ratio of the school's private resources (tuition, fees, contributions) to the total resources it requires to operate at the standard of government schools. Government support began with tax deductions (1952), then moved to providing grants for science buildings and equipment (1963). The support subsequently jumped to contributions to cover school operating costs, and at present the financial contribution to private schools is considerable (Boyd, 1989; Sherman, 1983).

References

Abbott, W. M., general editor. 1966. *The documents of Vatican II*. J. Gallagher, translation editor. New York: Guild Press.

Abramowitz, S., and E. A. Stockhouse. 1980. *The private high school today*. Washington, D.C.: National Institute of Education.

Adler, M. G. 1982. *The paideia proposal: An educational manifesto*. New York: Macmillan.

Administrator and Teacher Survey (ATS). See Moles 1988.

Alexander, K. L., and M. A. Cook. 1982. Curricula and coursework: A surprise ending to a familiar story. *American Sociological Review*, 47(5): 626–640.

Alexander, K. L., M. A. Cook, and E. L. McDill. 1978. Curriculum tracking and educational stratification. *American Sociological Review*, 43: 222–237.

Alexander, K. L., and A. M. Pallas. 1983. Private schools and public policy: New evidence on cognitive achievement in public and private schools. *Sociology of Education*, 56: 170–182.

——— 1984. In defense of "Private schools and public policy": Reply to Kilgore. *Sociology of Education*, 57: 56–58.

——— 1985. School sector and cognitive performance: When is a little a little? *Sociology of Education*, 58: 115–126.

Anderson, A., A. Auquier, W. W. Hauck, D. Oakes, W. Vandaele, and H. I. Weisberg. 1980. *Statistical methods for comparative studies: Techniques for bias reduction*. New York: Wiley.

Arendt, H. 1979. *The recovery of the public world*. New York: St. Martin's Press.

Astin, A. W. 1977a. *Four critical years: Effects of college on beliefs, attitudes, and knowledge*. San Francisco: Jossey-Bass.

——— 1977b. On the failure of educational policy. *Change*, 9: 40–45.

Aubert, R. 1978. *The Church in a secularized society*. New York: Paulist Press.

Averch, H. A., S. J. Caroll, T. S. Donaldson, H. J. Kiesling, and J. Pincas. 1971. *How effective is schooling? A critical review and synthesis of research findings*. Santa Monica, Calif.: Rand.

Barker, R., and P. Gump. 1964. *Big school, small school: High school size and student behavior*. Stanford, Calif.: Stanford University Press.

Becker, G. 1981. *Treatise on the family.* Cambridge, Mass.: Harvard University Press.

Bellah, R. N. 1970. *Beyond belief.* New York: Harper & Row.

——— 1974. Civil religion in America. In R. E. Richey and D. F. Jones, eds., *American civil religion.* New York: Harper & Row.

——— 1975. *The broken covenant.* New York: Seabury Press.

Bellah, R. N., R. Madsen, W. M. Sullivan, A. Swidler, and S. M. Tipton, eds. 1987. *Individualism and commitment in American life.* New York: Harper & Row.

Bellah, R. N., S. M. Tipton, A. Swidler, and W. M. Sullivan. 1985. *Habits of the heart: Individualism and commitment in American life.* New York: Basic Books.

——— 1991. *The Good Society.* New York: Knopf.

Benson, P. L., and M. J. Guerra. 1985. *Sharing the faith: The beliefs and values of Catholic high school teachers.* Washington, D.C.: National Catholic Educational Association.

Bernstein, R. J. 1983. *Beyond objectivism and relativism: Science, hermeneutics, and praxis.* Philadelphia: University of Pennsylvania Press.

——— 1987. The varieties of pluralism. *American Journal of Education,* 95: 509–525.

Bidwell, C. E. 1965. The school as a formal organization. In J. G. March, ed., *Handbook of organizations.* Chicago: Rand McNally.

Bidwell, C. E., and P. A. Quiroz. 1991. Organizational control in the high school workplace: A theoretical argument. *Journal of Research on Adolescence,* 3: 211–229.

Block, J. H. 1984. *Sex role identity and ego development.* San Francisco: Jossey-Bass.

Bookstrum, R. 1991. The moral meaning of a class rule. Paper presented at the annual meeting of the American Educational Research Association, Chicago.

Booth, W. C. 1985. Systematic wonder: The rhetoric of secular religions. *Journal of the American Academy of Religion,* 53: 677–702.

Bowers, C. A. 1985. Culture against itself: Nihilism as one element in educational thought. *American Journal of Education,* 93: 465–490.

——— 1987. *Elements of a post-liberal theory of education.* New York: Teachers College Press.

Bowles, S. S., and H. Gintis. 1976. *Schooling in capitalist America.* New York: Basic Books.

Boyd, W. L. 1989. Balancing public and private schools: The Australian experience and American implications. In W. L. Boyd and J. G. Cibulka, eds., *Private schools and public policy: International perspectives,* 149–170. Philadelphia: Falmer Press.

Boyer, E. L. 1983. *High school: A report on secondary education in America.* New York: Harper & Row.

——— 1987. *College.* New York: Harper & Row.

Braddock, J. H. 1981. The issue is still equality of educational opportunity. *Harvard Educational Review,* 51(4): 490–496.

Brookover, W., C. Beady, P. Flood, J. Schweitzer, and J. Wisenbaker. 1979. *School social systems and student achievement: Schools can make a difference.* New York: Praeger.

Bryk, A. S. 1988. Musings on the moral life of schools. *American Journal of Education,* 96(2): 256–290.

Bryk, A. S., and M. E. Driscoll. 1988. *The school as community: Theoretical foundation, contextual influences, and consequences for students and teachers.* Madison, Wis.: National Center for Effective Secondary Schools, University of Wisconsin.

Bryk, A. S., and K. A. Frank. 1991. The specialization of teachers' work: An initial exploration. In S. W. Raudenbush and J. D. Willms, eds., *Schools, classrooms, and pupils: International studies from a multilevel perspective,* 185–202. San Diego, Calif.: Academic Press.

Bryk, A. S., and P. B. Holland. 1985. *A report on Catholic school finance.* Washington, D.C.: National Catholic Educational Association.

Bryk, A. S., P. B. Holland, V. E. Lee, and R. A. Carriedo. 1984. *Effective Catholic schools: An exploration.* Washington, D.C.: National Catholic Educational Association.

Bryk, A. S., V. E. Lee, and J. B. Smith. 1990. High school organization and its effects on teachers and students: An interpretive summary of the research. In W. T. Clune and J. F. Witte, eds., *Choice and control in American education,* vol. 1, 135–226. Philadelphia: Falmer Press.

Bryk, A. S., and S. W. Raudenbush. 1992. *Hierarchical linear models: Applications and data analyses methods.* Newbury, Calif.: Sage Publications.

Bryk, A.S. and Y. H. Thum. 1989. The effects of high school organization on dropping out: An explanatory investigation. *American Educational Research Journal,* 26(3): 353–384.

Buetow, H. A. 1970. *Of singular benefit: The story of Catholic education in the United States.* New York: Macmillan.

———— 1988. *The Catholic school: Its roots, identity, and future.* New York: Crossroad.

Burns, J. A. 1912. *The growth and development of the Catholic school system in the United States.* New York: Benziger Brothers.

Burns, J. A., and B. J. Kohlbrenner. 1937. *A history of Catholic education in the United States.* New York: Benziger Brothers.

Burstein, L. 1978. Assessing differences between grouped and individual-level regression coefficients: Alternate approaches. *Sociological Methods and Research,* 7(1): 5–28.

———— 1980. The analysis of multi-level data in educational research and evaluation. *Review of Research in Education,* 8: 158–233.

Butts, R. F. 1988. The moral imperative for American schools: '. . . inflame the civic temper . . .' *American Journal of Education,* 96(2): 162–194.

Carriedo, R. A. 1985. A study of Catholic high school teachers. Ed.D., dissertation, School of Education, Harvard University.

Caterall, J. S. 1988. Private school participation and public school policy. In T. James and H. M. Levin, eds., *Comparing public and private schools,* Vol. 1: *Institutions and organizations,* 46–66. Philadelphia: Falmer Press.

Catholic University of America. 1967. *The new Catholic encyclopedia.* New York: McGraw-Hill.

Choice and Conscience Committee. 1980. *Choice and conscience in perspective.* Los Angeles: Archdiocese of Los Angeles.

Chubb, J. E., and T. M. Moe. 1987. No school is an island: Politics, markets, and education. In *Politics of Education Association Yearbook,* 131–141. Washington, D.C.: Politics of Education Association.

———— 1988. Politics, markets, and the organization of schools. *American Political Science Review,* 88(4): 1065–87.

———— 1990. *Politics, markets, and America's schools.* Washington, D.C.: Brookings Institution.

Cibulka, J., T. O'Brien, and D. Zewe. 1982. *Inner city private elementary schools: A study.* Milwaukee, Wis.: Marquette University Press.

Clark, C. N., and P. L. Peterson. 1986. Teachers' thought processes. In M. C. Whitrock, ed., *Handbook of research on teaching,* 3d ed. 255–296. New York: Macmillan.

Clune, W. T., and J. F. Witte, eds. 1990. *Choice and control in American education,* 2 vols. Philadelphia: Falmer Press.

Cohen, D. K. 1982. Policy and organization: The impact of state and federal educational policy on school governance. *Harvard Educational Review*, 52, 474–499.

——— 1988. Knowledge of teaching: Plus que ça change . . . In P. W. Jackson, ed., *Contributing to educational change*, 27–84. Berkeley, Calif.: McCutcheon.

Coleman, J. A. 1982. *An American strategic theology*. New York: Paulist Press.

Coleman, J. S. 1987. The relations between school and social structure. In M. T. Hallinan, ed., *The social organization of schools: New conceptualizations of the learning process*. New York: Plenum.

——— 1990. *Foundations of social theory*. Cambridge, Mass.: Harvard University Press.

Coleman, J. S., E. Campbell, C. Hobson, J. McPartland, A. Mood, F. Weinfeld, and R. York. 1966. *Equality of educational opportunity report*. Washington, D.C.: U.S. Government Printing Office.

Coleman, J. S., and T. Hoffer. 1987. *Public and private high schools: The impact of communities*. New York: Basic Books.

Coleman, J. S., T. Hoffer, and S. B. Kilgore. 1982. *High school achievement: Public, Catholic, and private schools compared*. New York: Basic Books.

Coles, R. 1987. *Dorothy Day: A radical devotion*. Reading, Mass.: Addison Wesley.

Cremin, L. A., ed. 1957. The *Republic and the School: Horace Mann on the Education of Free Men*. New York: Teachers College Press.

Cremin, L. A. 1988. *American education: The metropolitan experience, 1876–1980*. New York: Harper & Row.

Cunningham, W. F. 1940. *The pivotal problems of education*. New York: Macmillan.

Curran, C. E. 1975. *New perspectives on moral theology*. South Bend, Ind.: University of Notre Dame Press.

Cusick, P. A. 1983. *The egalitarian ideal and the American high school*. New York: Longman.

Cusick, P. A., and C. W. Wheeler. 1988. Educational morality and organization reform. *American Journal of Education*, 96(2): 231–255.

Daedalus. 1981. *America's schools: Portraits and perspectives*, 110(4). Proceedings of the American Academy of Arts and Sciences.

Dale, R. R. 1969. *Mixed or single-sex school?* Vol. 1: *A Research study about pupil-teacher relationships*. London: Routledge & Kegan Paul.

——— 1971. *Mixed or single-sex school?* Vol. 2: *Some social aspects*. London: Routledge & Kegan Paul.

——— 1974. *Mixed or single-sex school?* Vol. 3: *Attainment, attitudes, and overview*. London: Routledge & Kegan Paul.

Depuis, A. M. 1967. History of education: Renaissance and humanism. In Catholic University of America, *The new Catholic encyclopedia*, vol. 5, 119–123. New York: McGraw-Hill.

Dewey, J. 1934. *A common faith*. New Haven, Conn.: Yale University Press.

——— 1966. *Democracy and education*. New York: Macmillan.

——— 1981. My pedagogic creed. In J. McDermott, ed., *The philosophy of John Dewey*. Chicago: University of Chicago Press.

Diggins, J. P. 1984. *The lost soul of American politics: Virtue, self-interest, and the foundations of liberalism*. New York: Basic Books.

Dixon, W. J., M. B. Brown, L. Engleman, J. W. Frare, M. A. Hill, R. I. Jennrich, and J. D. Toporeck, eds., 1983. *BMDP statistical software*. Los Angeles: University of California Press.

Dolan, J. P. 1985. *The American Catholic experience: A history from colonial times to the present.* Garden City, N.Y.: Doubleday.

Draheman, D. L. 1991. *Church-state constitutional issues: Making sense of the establishment clause.* New York: Greenwood Press.

Driscoll, M. E. 1989. The school as community. Ph.D. dissertation, Department of Education, University of Chicago.

Dulles, A. R. 1982. *The survival of dogma: Faith, authority, and dogma in a changing world.* New York: Crossroads.

———— 1988. *The reshaping of Catholicism.* San Francisco: Harper & Row.

Durkheim, E. 1956. *Education and sociology.* Glencoe, Ill.: Free Press.

———— 1961. *Moral education: A study in the theory and application of the sociology of education.* Glencoe, Ill.: Free Press.

———— 1973. *On morality and society.* Edited by R. N. Bellah. Chicago: University of Chicago Press.

Edmonds, R. 1979. Effective schools for the urban poor. *Educational Leadership,* 37: 15–24.

Ekstrom, R. B., M. E. Goertz, J. M. Pollack, and D. A. Rock. 1987. Who drops out of high school and why: Findings from a national study. In G. Natriello, ed., *School dropouts: Patterns and policies.* New York: Teachers College Press.

Ekstrom, R. B., D. A. Rock, and M. E. Goertz. 1988. *Education and American youth: The impact of the high school experience.* Philadelphia: Falmer Press.

Etzioni, A. 1988. *The moral dimension: Toward a new economics.* New York: Free Press.

Fass, P. S. 1989. *Outside in.* New York: Oxford University Press.

Feather, N. T. 1974. Coeducation, values, and satisfaction with school. *Journal of Educational Psychology,* 66: 9–15.

Finn, J. D. 1980. Sex differences in educational outcomes: A cross-national study. *Sex roles,* 6: 9–25.

Fison, B., C.M.F. 1970. Coeducation in Catholic schools: A commentary on the institution of coeducation. In H. A. Buetow, ed., *Of singular benefit.* New York: Macmillan.

Fliegel, S. 1990. Creative non-compliance. In W. T. Clune, and J. F. Witte, eds., *Choice and control in American education,* vol. 2, 195–216. Philadelphia: Falmer Press.

Furfey, P. H. 1936. *Fire on the earth.* New York: Macmillan.

Furniss, W. T., and P. A. Graham, eds. 1974. *Women in higher education.* Washington, D.C.: American Council on Education.

Gamwell, I. 1986. Religion and reason in American politics. In R. Lovin, ed., *Religion and American public life.* Mahwah, N.J.: Paulist Press.

Gilkey, L. 1975. *Catholicism confronts modernity.* New York: Seabury Press.

Gleason, P. 1987. *Keeping the faith: American Catholicism, past and present.* Notre Dame, Ind.: University of Notre Dame Press.

Glenn, C. L. 1989. *Choice of schools in six nations.* Washington, D.C.: U.S. Department of Education.

Goldberger, A. S., and G. G. Cain. 1982. The causal analysis of cognitive outcomes in the Coleman, Hoffer, and Kilgore report. *Sociology of Education,* 55(2/3): 103–122.

Goodlad, F. 1984. *A place called school: Prospects for the future.* New York: McGraw-Hill.

Goodlad, F., R. Soder, and K. A. Sirotnik, eds. 1990. *The moral dimension of teaching.* San Francisco: Jossey-Bass.

Gorton, R., and K. McIntyre. 1978. *The senior high school principalship*. Vol. 2: *The effective principal*. Reston, Va.: National Association of Secondary School Principals.

Graham, P. A. 1970. Women in academe. *Science,* 69: 1284–1290.

———— 1974. *Women in higher education: A biographical inquiry*. ERIC Document no. ED 095 742. New York: Barnard College, Columbia University.

———— 1984. Schools: Cacophony about practice, silence about purpose. *Daedalus,* 113(4): 29–57.

Grant, G. 1985. Schools that make an imprint: Creating a strong positive ethos. In J. H. Bunzel, ed., *Challenge to American schools*. New York: Oxford University Press.

———— 1988. *The world we created at Hamilton High*. Cambridge, Mass.: Harvard University Press.

Greeley, A. M. 1982. *Catholic high schools and minority students*. New Brunswick, N.J.: Transaction Books.

———— 1985. The Catholic school. In *American Catholics since the council: An unauthorized report*. Chicago: Thom Mac.

Greeley, A. M., and P. H. Rossi. 1966. *The education of Catholic Americans*. Chicago: Aldine.

Green, T. F. 1985. The formation of conscience in an age of technology. *American Journal of Education,* 94: 1–32.

———— 1988. The economy of virtue and the primacy of prudence. *American Journal of Education,* 96: 127–142.

Gutmann, A. 1987. *Democratic education*. Princeton, N.J.: Princeton University Press.

Hallinger, P., and J. F. Murphy. 1986. The social context of effective schools. *American Journal of Education,* 94: 328–355.

Hansen, D. T. 1991. The emergence of shared morality in a classroom. Paper presented at the annual meeting of the American Educational Research Association, Chicago.

Hawley, W. D. 1976. The possibility of nonbureaucratic organizations. In W. D. Hawley and R. D. Rogers, eds., *Improving urban management*. Beverly Hills, Calif.: Sage Publications.

Healy, T. 1981. Belief and teaching. *Daedalus,* 110(4): 163–175.

Hennesey, J. 1981. *American Catholics: A history of the Roman Catholic community in the United States*. New York: Oxford University Press.

Heyns, B. L. 1974. Social selection and stratification within schools. *American Journal of Sociology,* 79: 1934–1951.

Heyns, B. L., and T. L. Hilton. 1982. The cognitive tests for High School and Beyond: An assessment. *Sociology of Education,* 55: 89–102.

High School and Beyond (HS&B). See NCES 1982.

Hill, P. T., G. E. Foster, and T. Gendler. 1990. *High schools with character*. Santa Monica, Calif.: Rand.

Hoffer, T. 1986. Educational outcomes in public and private schools. Ph.D. dissertation, Department of Sociology, University of Chicago.

Hoffer, T., A. M. Greeley, and J. S. Coleman. 1985. Achievement growth in public and Catholic schools. *Sociology of Education,* 58: 74–97.

Holland, P. 1985. The Catholic high school principal: A qualitative study. Ed.D. dissertation, Graduate School of Education, Harvard University.

Holland, P., and A. Bryk. 1985. *Field research methodology: Technical report*. Washington, D.C.: National Catholic Educational Association.

Hunt, T. C. 1980. Catholic schools today: Redirection and redefinitions. *Living Light*, 17(3): 203–210.

Hutchins, R. M. 1954. *Great books: The foundation of a liberal education*. New York: Simon and Schuster.

Hyde, S. 1971. The case for coeducation. *Independent School Bulletin*, 31: 20–24.

Jackson, P. W. 1981. Secondary schooling for children of the poor. *Daedalus*, 110(4): 39–57.

———— 1986. *The practice of teaching*. New York: Teachers College Press.

————, ed. 1988. *Contributing to educational change*. Berkeley, Calif.: McCutcheon.

———— 1991. The enactment of the moral in what teachers do. Paper presented at the annual meeting of the American Educational Research Association, Chicago.

James, T., and H. M. Levin. 1983. *Public dollars for private schools: The case of tuition tax credits*. Philadelphia: Temple University Press.

————, eds. 1988. *Comparing public and private schools*. Vol. 1: *Institutions and organizations*. Philadelphia: Falmer Press.

Janowitz, M. 1983. *The reconstruction of patriotism and education for civic consciousness*. Chicago: University of Chicago Press.

Jencks, C. 1985. How much do high school students learn? *Sociology of Education*, 58(2): 128–135.

Jencks, C., and P. Peterson, eds. 1991. *Urban underclass*. Washington, D.C.: Brookings Institution.

Jencks, C., M. Smith, M. J. Bane, D. Cohen, H. Gintis, B. Heyns, and S. Michelson. 1972. *Inequality: A reassessment of the effects of family and schooling in America*. New York: Basic Books.

Jiminez, E., and M. E. Lockheed. 1989. Enhancing girls' learning through single-sex education: Evidence and a policy conundrum. *Educational Evaluation and Policy Analysis*, 11(2): 117–142.

Jones, J. C., J. Shallcross, and C. L. Dennis. 1972. Coeducation and adolescent values. *Journal of Educational Psychology*, 63: 334–341.

Katz, M. B. 1987. *Reconstructing American education*. Cambridge: Harvard University Press.

Kidder, T. 1989. *Among schoolchildren*. Boston: Houghton-Mifflin.

Kilgore, S. B. 1983. Statistical evidence, selection effects, and program placement. A reply to Alexander and Pallas. *Sociology of Education*, 56: 182–186.

———— 1984. Schooling effects: Reply to Alexander and Pallas. *Sociology of Education*, 57: 59–61.

Kohlbrenner, B. J. 1937. *A history of Catholic education in the United States*. New York: Benziger Brothers.

Kotlowitz, A. 1991. *There are no children here*. New York: Doubleday.

Kung, H. 1988. *Theology for the third millennium: An ecumenical view*. New York: Doubleday.

Lazerson, M. 1985. *An education of value: The purposes and practices of schools*. New York: Cambridge University Press.

Lee, V. E. 1985. Investigating the relationship between social class and academic achievement in public and Catholic schools: The role of the academic organization of the school. Ed.D. dissertation, Graduate School of Education, Harvard University.

Lee, V. E., and A. S. Bryk. 1986. The effects of single-sex secondary schools on student achievement and attitudes. *Journal of Educational Psychology*, 78(5): 381–396.

———— 1988. Curriculum tracking as mediating the social distribution of high school achievement. *Sociology of Education*, 61(2): 78–94.

———— 1989. A multilevel model of the social distribution of high school achievement. *Sociology of Education*, 62(3): 172–192.

Lee, V. E., and D. T. Burkam. 1992. Transferring high school: An alternative to dropping out? *American Journal of Education*, 100(4).

Lee, V. E., R. F. Dedrick, and J. B. Smith. 1991. The effect of the social organization of schools on teacher satisfaction. *Sociology of Education*, 64(3): 190–208.

Lee, V. E., and M. E. Lockheed. 1990. The effects of single-sex schooling on student achievement and attitudes in Nigeria. *Comparative Educational Review*, 43(2): 209–231.

Lee, V. E., and H. M. Marks. 1990. Sustained effects of the single-sex secondary school experience on attitudes, behaviors, and values in college. *Journal of Educational Psychology*, 82(3): 578–592.

———— 1991. Which works best? The relative effectiveness of single-sex and coeducational secondary schools. Paper presented at the annual meeting of the American Educational Research Association, Chicago.

Lee, V. E., and J. B. Smith. 1990. Gender equity in teachers' salary: A multilevel approach. *Educational Evaluation and Policy Analysis*, 12(1): 57–81.

Lesko, N. 1988. *Symbolizing society: Stories, rites, and structure in a Catholic high school.* Philadelphia: Falmer Press.

Levin, H. M., ed. 1970. *Community control of schools.* Washington, D.C.: Brookings Institution.

Levine, D. N. 1985. *The flight from ambiguity: Essays in social and cultural theory.* Chicago: University of Chicago Press.

Lightfoot, S. L. 1983. *The good high school: Portraits of character and culture.* New York: Basic Books.

Lindblom, C. E. 1990. *Inquiry and change.* New Haven, Conn.: Yale University Press.

Lindblom, C. E., and D. K. Cohen. 1979. *Usable knowledge.* New Haven, Conn.: Yale University Press.

Lockheed, M. E. 1976. *The modification of female leadership behavior in the presence of males.* Princeton, N.J.: Educational Testing Service.

Lortie, D. C. 1975. *Schoolteacher.* Chicago: University of Chicago Press.

Lovin, R. W., ed. 1986. *Religion and American public life.* Mahwah, N.J.: Paulist Press.

———— 1987. The public purposes of liberal education. *Perspectives*, 17: 6–12.

———— 1988. The school and the articulation of values. *American Journal of Education*, 96(2): 143–161.

Lukas, J. A. 1985. *Common ground: A turbulent decade in the lives of three American families.* New York: Knopf.

MacIntyre, A. C. 1981. *After virtue: A study in moral theory.* South Bend, Ind.: University of Notre Dame Press.

March, J. G., ed. 1965. *Handbook of organizations.* Chicago: Rand McNally.

Maritain, J. 1943. *Education at the crossroads.* New Haven, Conn.: Yale University Press.

———— 1946. *The person and the common good.* Translated by J. J. Fitzgerald. London: Geoggrey Bles.

———— 1958. *The rights of man and natural law.* Translated by D. C. Ansom. London: Geoggrey Bles.

———— 1962. *The education of man.* Garden City, N.Y.: Doubleday.

Marsh, H. W. 1989. Effects of attending single-sex and coeducational high schools on achievement, attitudes, behaviors, and sex differences. *Journal of Educational Psychology,* 81: 70–85.

Martheler, B. L. 1978. Socialization as a model for catechetics. In P. O'Hara, ed., *Foundations of religious education,* 64–92. New York: Paulist Press.

Marty, M. E. 1987. *Religion and republic.* Boston: Beacon Press.

McBrien, R. P. 1980. *Catholicism.* Vol. 2. Minneapolis: Winston.

McClusky, N., ed. 1964. *Catholic education in America: A documentary history.* New York: Teachers' College, Columbia University.

McDill, E. L., G. Natriello, and A. M. Pallas. 1987. A population at risk: Potential consequences of tougher school standards for student dropouts. In G. Natriello, ed., *School dropouts: Patterns and policies,* 106–147. New York: Teachers College Press.

Mead, S. E. 1974. The nation with the soul of a church. In R. E. Richey and D. G. Jones, eds., *American civil religion,* 45–75. New York: Harper & Row.

Miller, M. J. 1952. *General education in the American Catholic secondary school.* Washington, D.C.: Catholic University of America Press.

Moles, O. C. 1987. Who wants parent involvement? Interest, skills, and opportunities among parents and educators. *Education and Urban Society,* 19: 137–145.

——— 1988. *High school and beyond: Administrative and teacher survey (1985). Data file users' manual.* Washington, D.C.: Office of Educational Research.

Moore, D. R. 1990. Voice and choice in Chicago. In W. T. Clune and J. F. Witte, eds., *Choice and control in American education,* vol. 2, 153–198. Philadelphia: Falmer Press.

Morris, V., R. Crowson, C. Porter-Gehrie, and E. Hurwitz. 1984. *Principals in action.* Columbus, Ohio: Charles E. Merrill.

Moynihan, P., and F. Mosteller. 1972. *On equality of educational opportunity.* New York: Random House.

Murnane, R. 1975. *The impact of school resources on the learning of inner city children.* Cambridge, Mass.: Ballinger.

——— 1981. Interpreting the evidence on school effectiveness. *Teachers' College Record,* 83(1): 19–35.

Murphy, J. 1980. *Getting the facts.* Santa Monica, Calif.: Goodyear.

National Assessment for Educational Progress. 1984. *Reading report cards: Trends in reading over four national assessments, 1971–1984.* Princeton, N.J.: Educational Testing Service.

National Catholic Educational Association (NCEA). 1970. *A statistical report on Catholic elementary and secondary schools for the years 1967–68 to 1969–70.* Washington, D.C.: National Catholic Educational Association.

——— 1980. *Catholic high schools and their finances.* Washington, D.C.: National Catholic Educational Association.

——— 1982. *U.S. Catholic elementary and secondary schools, 1981–82.* Washington, D.C.: National Catholic Educational Association.

——— 1983. *Statistical report, 1982–83.* Washington, D.C.: National Catholic Educational Association.

——— 1985. *The Catholic high school: A national portrait.* Washington, D.C.: National Catholic Educational Association.

——— 1986. *Catholic high schools: Their impact on low-income students.* Washington, D.C.: National Catholic Educational Association.

——— 1988. *Catholic high schools and their finances, 1980 and 1988.* Washington, D.C.:

National Catholic Educational Association.

——— 1989. *Catholic high schools and their finances, 1989.* Washington, D.C.: National Catholic Educational Association.

——— 1990a. *United States Catholic elementary and secondary schools, 1989–90: Annual statistical report on schools, enrollment, and staffing.* Washington, D.C.: National Catholic Educational Association.

——— 1990b. *Catholic high schools and their finances.* Washington, D.C.: National Catholic Educational Association.

National Center for Education Statistics. 1982. *High school and beyond 1980 sophomore cohort first follow-up (1982): Data file user's manual.* Washington, D.C.: National Center for Education Statistics.

——— 1987. *Digest of educational statistics.* Washington, D.C.: Government Printing Office.

——— 1984. *Bulletin.* February.

National Commission on Excellence in Education. 1983. *A nation at risk: The imperative for educational reform.* Washington, D.C.: U.S. Government Printing Office.

National Conference of Catholic Bishops (NCCB). 1972. *To teach as Jesus did: A pastoral message on Catholic education.* Washington, D.C.: U.S. Catholic Conference.

——— 1979. *Brothers and sisters to us: U.S. bishops' pastoral letter on racism in our day, Nov. 14, 1979.* Washington, D.C.: U.S. Catholic Conference.

Natriello, G., ed. 1987. *School dropouts: Patterns and policies.* New York: Teachers College Press.

NCCB. *See* National Council of Catholic Bishops.

NCEA. *See* National Catholic Educational Association.

NCES. See National Center for Educational Statistics.

Neuhaus, R. J. 1987. *The Catholic moment: The paradox of the Church in the post-modern world.* San Francisco: Harper & Row.

Newmann, F. M. 1981. Reducing student alienation in high schools: Implications of theory. *Harvard Educational Review,* 51: 546–564.

Noddings, N. 1988. An ethic of caring and its implications for instructional arrangements. *American Journal of Education,* 96: 215–230.

Novak, M. 1974. The social world of individuals. *Hasting Center Studies,* 2, 3, 43.

Oakes, J. 1985. *Keeping track: How high schools structure inequality.* New Haven, Conn.: Yale University Press.

Oates, M. J., and S. Williamson. 1978. Women's colleges and women achievers. *Journal of Women in Culture and Society,* 3: 795–806.

O'Keefe, J. M. 1991. Higher achievement scholars: A study of the experiences of minority and low-income students. Ed.D. dissertation, Graduate School of Education, Harvard University.

Pauly, E. 1991. *The classroom crucible: What really works, what doesn't, and why.* New York: Basic Books.

Peshkin, A. 1986. *God's choice: The total world of a fundamentalist Christian school.* Chicago: University of Chicago Press.

Peterson, P. 1990. Monopoly and capitalism in American education. In W. T. Clune and F. Witte, eds., *Choice and control in American education,* vol. 1: 47–78. Philadelphia: Falmer Press.

Pincoffs, E. 1986. *Quandaries and virtues: Against reductivism in ethics.* Lawrence, Kans.: University Press of Kansas.

Powell, A. G., E. Farrar, and D. K. Cohen. 1985. *The shopping mall high school: Winners and losers in the educational marketplace*. Boston: Houghton-Mifflin.

Purkey, S. C., and M. S. Smith. 1983. Effective schools: A review. *The Elementary School Journal*, 83(4): 427–454.

Raudenbush, S. W., and A. S. Bryk. 1986. A hierarchical model for studying school effects. *Sociology of Education*, 59: 1–17.

———— 1988. Methodological advances in analyzing the effects of schools and classrooms on student learning. In E. Z. Rothkopf, ed., *Review of Research in Education*, vol. 15: 423–476. Washington, D.C.: American Educational Research Association.

Ravitch, D. 1974. *The great school wars*. New York: Basic Books.

Richey, R. E., and D. E. Jones, eds. 1974. *American civil religion*. New York: Harper & Row.

Riordan, C. 1985. Public and Catholic schooling: The effects of gender context policy. *American Journal of Education*, 5: 518–540.

———— 1990. *Girls and boys in school: Together or separate?* New York: Teachers College Press.

Rock, D. A., R. B. Ekstrom, M. C. Goertz, T. L. Hilton, and J. Pollack. 1985. *Excellence in high school education: Cross-sectional study, 1972–1980*. First report. Princeton, N.J.: Educational Testing Service.

Rodriguez, R. 1982. *Hunger of memory*. Boston: Godine.

Rorty, R. 1989. *Contingency, irony, and solidarity*. Cambridge: Cambridge University Press.

Rosenbaum, J. E. 1976. *Inequality: The hidden curriculum of high school tracking*. New York: Wiley.

Rosenholtz, S. J. 1985. Effective schools: Interpreting the evidence. *American Journal of Education*, 93: 359–388.

———— 1989. *Teachers' workplace*. New York: Longman.

Rutter, M., B. Maughan, P. Mortimore, J. Outson, and A. Smith. 1979. *Fifteen thousand hours: Secondary schools and their effects on children*. Cambridge, Mass.: Harvard University Press.

Ryan, M. P. 1963. *Are parochial schools the answer?* New York: Holt, Rinehart & Winston.

Sandel, M. J. 1982. *Liberalism and the limits of justice*. Cambridge: Cambridge University Press.

Sanders, J. W. 1977. *The education of an urban minority*. New York: Oxford University Press.

Schneider, F. W., and L. M. Coutts. 1982. The high school environment: A comparison of coeducational and single-sex schools. *Journal of Educational Psychology*, 74: 898–906.

Sedlak, M. W., C. W. Wheeler, D. C. Pullin, and P. A. Cusick. 1986. *Selling students short*. New York: Teachers College Press.

Shafer, W. E., and C. Olexa. 1971. *Tracking and opportunity: The locking out process and beyond*. Scranton, Pa.: Chandler Publishing.

Shea, W. M. 1989. Qualitative wholes: Aesthetic and religious experience in the work of John Dewey. *American Journal of Education*, 98: 32–50.

Shenker, B. 1986. *Intentional communities*. London: Routledge & Kegan Paul.

Sherman, J. D. 1983. Public finance of private schools: Observations from abroad. In T. James and H. M. Levin, eds., *Public dollars for private schools: The case of tuition tax credits*. Philadelphia: Temple University Press.

Sizer, T. R. 1984. *Horace's compromise: The dilemma of the American high school.* Boston: Houghton-Mifflin.

Sullivan, W. 1986. *Reconstructing public philosophy.* Berkeley, Calif.: University of California Press.

Tidball, M. E., and V. Kistiakowsky. 1976. Baccalaureate origins of American scientists and scholars. *Science,* 193: 646–652.

Tillich, P. 1957. *Dynamics of faith.* New York: Harper & Row.

Tonnies, F. 1955. *Community and association* (Geminschaft und gesellschaft). Translated by L. P. Loomis. London: Routledge & Paul.

Tocqueville, A. de. 1969. *Discovery in America.* Translated by G. Lawrence and edited by J. P. Mayer. New York: Doubleday Anchor.

Tracy, D. 1986. Particular classics, public religion, and the American tradition. In R. Lovin, ed., *Religion and American public life,* 115–131. Mahwah, N.J.: Paulist Press.

Trickett, E. J., J. J. Castro, P. K. Trickett, and P. Shaffner. 1982. The independent school experience: Aspects of the normative environment of single-sex and coed secondary schools. *Journal of Educational Psychology,* 74: 374–381.

Tyack, D., and E. Hansot. 1982. *Managers of virtue: Public school leadership in America, 1820–1980.* New York: Basic Books.

——— 1988. Silence and policy talk: Historical puzzles about gender and education. *Educational Researcher,* 17(3): 33–41.

United States Catholic Conference. 1977. Sacred congregation for Christian education. *The Catholic school.* Washington, D.C.

Veverka, F. B. 1984. For God and country: Catholic schooling in the 1920s. Ph.D. dissertation, Teachers' College, Columbia University.

Vitullo-Martin, T. 1981. How federal policies discourage the racial and economic integration of private schools. In E. M. Gaffney, ed., *Private schools and the public good.* Notre Dame, Ind.: University of Notre Dame Press.

Walford, G., ed. 1989. *Private schools in ten countries: Policy and practice.* London: Routledge & Kegan Paul.

Waller, W. 1932. *The sociology of teaching.* New York: Russell & Russell.

Weber, G. 1973. Inner city children can be taught to read: Four successful schools. *Council for Basic Education.* Occasional papers, 18.

Wehlage, G. G., R. A. Rutter, G. A. Smith, N. Lesko, and R. R. Fernandez. 1989. *Reducing the risk: Schools as communities of support.* Philadelphia: Falmer.

Weiss, J. 1990. Control in school organizations: Theoretical perspectives. In W. T. Clune and J. F. Witte, eds., *Choice and control in American education,* vol. 1: 91–134. Philadelphia: Falmer Press.

Willms, J. D. April, 1985. Catholic school effects on academic achievement: New evidence from High School and Beyond follow-up study. *Sociology of Education,* 58: 98–114.

Wilson, J. T. 1987. *The truly disadvantaged.* Chicago: University of Chicago Press.

Winchel, R., D. Fenner, and P. Shaver. 1974. Impact of coeducation on 'fear of success' imagery expressed by male and female high school students. *Journal of Educational Psychology,* 66: 726–730.

Wolcott, H. 1973. *The man in the principal's office: An ethnography.* New York: Holt, Rinehart & Winston.

Wolfe, A. 1989. *Whose keeper? Social Science and moral obligation.* Berkeley: University of California Press.

Index